]
WORKING CLASS

D0347457

For
Mary-Rose

Industrialization and the Working Class:

The English Experience, 1750–1900

JOHN BELCHEM

Scolar Press

First published in paperback in 1991 by
Scolar Press
Gower Publishing Company Limited
Gower House
Croft Road
Aldershot
Hants GU11 3HR
England

Gower Publishing Company
Old Post Road
Brookfield
Vermont 05036
USA

British Library Cataloguing in Publication Data
Belchem, John
    Industrialization and the working class: the English
    experience, 1750-1900.
    1. England. Industrialisation. Social aspects,
    history
    I. Title
    303.4′83′0942

Phototypeset by Input Typesetting Ltd, London

ISBN 0 85967 891 1

Reprinted 1996

Printed and bound in Great Britain by
the Ipswich Book Company, Suffolk

Contents

PART TWO: 1850–1875

PART THREE: 1875–1900

Acknowledgements

This study does not claim to be a conspectus of recent writing in modern English social and labour history, a state-of-the-art survey of the history of the working class. It is impossible to keep pace with the volume of writing, specialized and general, covering this deservedly popular subject. What is offered here is a stock-taking exercise of a personal kind, an attempt to assess the significance of some of the most important recent historiography. I hope that readers will be encouraged to follow up references in the notes, where I try to acknowledge my vast burden of debts – with apologies for errors and omissions.

Maurice Temple Smith has offered friendly advice from the beginning, as have colleagues at Liverpool: my thanks in particular to Peter Hennock and Simon Dentith. Once again, my wife has provided the intellectual stimulus – and proletarian labour – without which this book could not have been written.

Abbreviations

ACLL	Anti-Corn Law League
ASE	Amalgamated Society of Engineers
ASRS	Amalgamated Society of Railway Servants
BPU	Birmingham Political Union
BSSLH	*Bulletin of the Society for the Study of Labour History*
CIU	Club and Institute Union
COS	Charity Organization Society
CSU	Complete Suffrage Union
EcHR	*Economic History Review*
EEF	Engineering Employers' Federation
GNCTU	Grand National Consolidated Trades' Union
GNU	Great Northern Union
HO	Home Office Papers: Public Record Office
ILP	Independent Labour Party
IRSH	*International Review of Social History*
LCS	London Corresponding Society
LDA	London Democratic Association
LTC	London Trades Council
LWMA	London Working Men's Association
MFGB	Miners Federation of Great Britain
NAOT	National Association of Organized Trades
NAPL	National Association for the Protection of Labour
NAUT	National Association of United Trades
NCA	National Charter Association
NCL	National Charter League
NMA	National Miners' Association
NUWC	National Union of the Working Classes
OBU	Operative Builders' Union
SDF	Social Democratic Federation
SL	Socialist League
TUC	Trades Union Congress
WSPU	Women's Social and Political Union
WTUL	Women's Trade Union League

Introduction

This study is an attempt to broaden the debate about the industrial revolution and the making of the English working class, to cast aside the chronological constraints, teleological assumptions and idealist criteria which have confused discussion. Economic growth in the 'long' eighteenth century was slow-moving, broad-based and multi-dimensional, a secular process of combined and uneven development: there was no sudden and dramatic industrial revolution, no irresistible technological thrust to factory-based 'machinofacture'.[1] Similarly with class, there was no linear development towards, or away from, an ideal form of consciousness. Located in contemporary discourse, class-consciousness was *historically* determined, altering with shifts – linguistic and otherwise – in the structure of feeling, the cultural experience of the time.[2]

A diverse range of manufacturing structures coexisted across and within industries as proto-industrialization led to industrial growth in some regions and to deindustrialization in others.[3] The emergence of the factory system was the exception, largely restricted to the Lancashire cotton industry. Elsewhere, modest growth was achieved without major technological innovation, through commercial and mercantile reorganization, and changes in the organization of the production process – by more effective division of labour, and the intensification and greater exploitation of the labour force. Market relations were set free, leaving workers and consumers unprotected against competition, an abnegation of paternalism which later industrializing nations, most notably Germany and Japan, were careful to avoid.[4]

Small in relation to industrial output as a whole, textiles and iron, the most dynamic manufacturing sectors, dominated the export trade – no other European country was to have its exports so heavily in manufactures at so early a stage of development and at such a low income level. Heavy investment in railway building rectified the dangerous imbalance between the narrow industrial–manufacturing sector and the rest of the economy, but Britain failed to achieve comprehensive comparative advantage across the manufacturing spectrum. Nevertheless, mid-Victorian Britain – the workshop, not the factory, of the world – enjoyed a quasi-monopoly position as other countries sought to industrialize by importing capital goods on an unprecedented scale. Various constraints – cultural, institutional and

1

economic – hindered the further progress of industrialism. Wealth, prestige and political power remained in aristocratic and financial hands, the continuing preserve of 'Old Corruption' and the City.[5] Financial wealth stood proudly aloof from industrial capitalism, a geographical and cultural divide which gentrified industrialists, and their meritocratic managers, failed to traverse. Powerful and prestigious, the financial institutions of the City protected the rentier interests of the establishment through an externally-oriented commercial capitalism, a 'gentlemanly capitalism' in which domestic industry was of little account.[6] Within a decade or two the economy reached its climacteric, unable to compete with the productivity levels of industrial latecomers.

This study is divided into three chronological periods – 1750–1850, 1850–75 and 1875–1900 – to facilitate an overarching analysis of industrialization extending from the industrial revolution through the mid-Victorian boom to the 'Great Depression', the late Victorian climacteric. Applied to class, this extended chronology, divided into three unequal parts, highlights the complex and changing forms of class-consciousness, following the working class, not uncritically, from its heroic 'making' in the early nineteenth century, through its 'unmaking' within mid-Victorian reformism and factory paternalism, to its eventual 'remaking' in modern and unheroic form amid the self-enclosed late Victorian world of flat caps, classic slums and Saturday half-holidays.[7]

Class is used here in a loose, historical way, staying close to the origins of the language in early nineteenth-century discourse.[8] In its most common, and technically incorrect, usage, class serves as a term of social stratification, a convenient means of classifying groups according to objective, measurable criteria – income, housing, diet, education, etc. To deny the terminology of class to these 'social strata' would be unduly pedantic and linguistically inelegant. However, terms should not be confused.[9] It is misleading and unnecessary to adopt the plural form, the working classes, simply to acknowledge strata of workers differentiated by income, occupation, region or some other *internal* variable.

Class is more problematic when applied diachronically, to the historical process of class formation. What interested Marx was not simply class 'in itself', an economic category determined by power and property relations in the productive process, but class 'for itself', the organizational and ideological formation of those conscious of their economic situation, of their common interests with others similarly placed, and their common hostility to those with opposing economic interests. Class-consciousness was something beyond mere class perception, the coming together of various social or occupational groups to protect and further their own position: the class-conscious proletariat would fulfill its historic revolutionary mission, the total dissolution of class society.[10]

This idealist standard should not be applied as an historical criterion. Class-consciousness is none the less real for taking a different, non-revolutionary form: what falls short of the ideal should not necessarily be dismissed as labourist or reformist, some lower and self-interested expression of class perception. As with the distinction between stratum and class, over-stringent theory must not be allowed to obscure practice and experience, to deny validity to actual historical forms of class-consciousness.[11] Throughout this book, the language of class is used without obeisance to idealist criteria or absolute standards, the kind of abstractions seized upon by anti-Marxist historians. A true class, they maintain, must obviously possess total unity of experience, values and revolutionary purpose, a straw argument promptly demolished by the merest empirical detail.[12] This study recognizes the diversity of class experience and the changing forms of class-consciousness, historical processes which make some sense of the otherwise meaningless morass of facts.

Social scientists have distinguished four aspects of class-consciousness: class identity – the definition of oneself as working class; class opposition – the perception of employers and their agents as enduring class opponents; class totality – making both identity and opposition the central defining feature of one's total situation; and class alternative – the conception of an alternative form of social organization.[13] Consciousness thus extends from the unmediated product of daily experience – workers and their families were forcefully reminded of their class identity in everyday contact with employers, landlords, creditors, charity and Poor Law officials – to the project of the 'militant minority', the committed few who endeavoured to weld workmates and neighbours into a self-aware and purposeful working class.[14]

Class identity was remarkably strong in nineteenth-century England, reinforced through networks of collective mutuality and associational culture. Collective self-help agencies offered not the kind of 'privatized' provision advocated by right-wing radicals today, but a range of benefits and services – medical, educational and recreational – organized and enjoyed in democratic and participatory manner. Inclusive Chartist-style recruitment was, however, an actuarial problem until the rise in real wages in the late nineteenth century.[15] In marked contrast with Germany where the establishment of the Social Democratic Party preceded and controlled the development of industrial, social and cultural associations, the labour movement was unable to establish a comprehensive labour alliance, to subsume the various forms of autonomous working-class mutuality within a counter-cultural party framework.[16] The spirit of convivial mutuality extended down to the street, where the unorganized poor upheld their own defensive form of class pride in pubs, cornershops and the occasional night out at the music-hall.[17] Militant class-consciousness was little in evidence, but loyalty and pride were fundamental facts of class life, the essential mores of a segregated society.[18] Not the agency of revolutionary social change, class-consciousness was the means by which workers came to terms with the permanence of industrial capitalism.

Class, unfortunately, is not the only term which defies simple definition. 'Skill' was a crucial concept for male workers, a property right they struggled to defend through collective organization: in England, as in continental Europe, the labour movement was born in the craft workshop, not in the dark satanic mill.[19] The retention of skilled status, an ideal to which all workers aspired, depended on the interplay between 'genuine skill' – the necessary exercise of dexterity, judgement and knowledge – and 'socially constructed skill' – the specious status upheld by organizational prowess.[20] Lacking technical expertise and an ideology of management, employers were often forced to concede considerable autonomy to 'skilled' workers, although they generally derived some benefit from the arrangement. By allowing spinners to appoint their own piecers, employers were relieved of direct responsibility for labour recruitment and discipline, self-enforced on the shopfloor through traditional gender and family roles. Apprenticeship rules operated in a similar manner, providing employers with skilled workers trained at workers' expense. The ratio of apprentices to journeymen and the terms of their employment, however, provoked recurrent and bitter workplace conflict.[21]

Work itself is defined rather narrowly in conformity with the contemporary convention that took no account of unpaid housework. Domesticity was probably the least unhappy option for working-class married women, but for many it was a cruelly illusive ideal.[22] Where the male 'family wage' was not forthcoming, there was no release from the double burden of unpaid housework and ill-paid waged-work. Unable not to work, they were driven lower and lower into unskilled and sweated sectors by the force of social convention which condemned but continued to exploit their labour. Although restricted to the workplace, the sections dealing with work thus take account of increasing sexual segregation.[23] Their main purpose, however, is to examine workplace culture and changes in the labour process, crucial areas of working-class experience excluded from the institutional agenda of traditional labour history.[24] Struggles for control over the speed, intensity and rhythm of work were often conducted

– with considerable success – outside a formal trade union framework, within the secret language of the workshop.[25] But the workplace was not always an arena of conflict. In mid-Victorian Lancashire, paternalist initiatives established a factory culture within which employment relations were reciprocal or even consensual in character. At the very least, account must be taken of the sociability of work.[26]

In large towns and cities, social life came to depend less on the workplace and more on the 'community', another problematic term.[27] Given the absence of pronounced residential segregation in most industrial cities, community cannot be defined in simple territorial terms. The working-class community, historical geographers insist, was a creative mixture of social and spatial factors, of locally-based pubs, chapels, co-ops and clubs, serving the needs of relatively independent, self-sufficient urban villages, demarcated districts within which workers moved and married. Upward mobility was an attractive prospect for families enjoying relative prosperity, but many decided against the risk of moving, of losing contact with the community support services on which they depended at less favourable times. Hence, there is little evidence of residential segregation *within* the working class, no simple correlation between housing quality and occupational status. Uniform housing stock, back-to-back or terraced, accommodated working-class households of widely different status and income. Household income and the life-cycle were the crucial variables, factors too often ignored in the standard-of-living debate.[28]

Occupational and regional differentials must be assessed in the evolving context of the family cycle, a levelling influence on working-class living standards. Not restricted to lowly and specific groups in the labour force, poverty was a regular feature of almost *all* families at some time in their development, especially in old age or before children started earning.[29] Age was a particularly important factor. There was no sudden shift into retirement, but incomes were markedly reduced often from as early as age 45 – skilled workers were usually forced down the job and wages hierarchy when considered past their prime. Social convention aside, married women had far less opportunity than their present-day counterparts to resume paid work once free of their childcare responsibilities. The pattern of childbearing began to change after 1870, but it was not until the mid-twentieth century that the modern life-cycle emerged, with a marked clustering of children into the early years of marriage. Well into the nineteenth century, the median age of women at the birth of their last child was about 39 and many went on having children into their early forties – those marrying after the Second World War, however, aided by a fall in the age of marriage, completed their childbearing

significantly earlier, on average by about 28. Family earnings fluctuated violently in the old life-cycle, at the mercy of sickness, death
and other adversities. Confronted by the unpredictable, the working
class displayed a reluctance to plan: chance and luck were considered
the source of worldly success.[30]

The crucial family and generational variables of the old life-cycle
defy statistical representation in real wage indices. Leaving clio-
metrics aside, this study concentrates on the social history of the
household economy: the changing composition of earnings – the
introduction of exclusively monetary forms of payment and the ideal
of the male 'family wage';[31] and the patterns of expenditure, credit
and 'thrift in reverse' by which working-class families made ends
meet, despite the censorious criticism of middle-class observers.[32]

Divided chronologically, each part of the book begins with an
examination of economic performance, followed by sections on
working-class living standards, housing, work, popular culture and
collective political behaviour, with a brief concluding section on middle-class views of the working class during the period. Limited as it
is, this last section takes some account of the need to locate the
working class within the complex framework of class relationships:
it focuses on socially concerned members of the middle and upper
classes, the commentators and critics who set the terms of the contemporary debate about the working class and the 'Condition of England'.

One final point requires explanation: the prominence accorded to
popular radicalism. Without such extended treatment, it would not
be possible to engage critically with the linguistic structuralism by
which working-class ideology is judged and found wanting.[33] Traditional and populist in content, radical political discourse acquired
remarkable oppositional force when articulated on the mass platform,
a context of class which should not be ignored.[34] Popular politics
must not be dismissed or left behind in the forward march of labour
history, the broad advance of the social history of the working class.

PART ONE:
1750–1850

1 The Industrial Revolution

Reduced to myth by the latest generation of economic historians, the 'first industrial revolution' no longer serves as the paradigm of modernization, the historical guide to economic development. Industrialization in Britain was unique and atypical, a secular process of combined and uneven development markedly different from nineteenth-century European and recent Third World experience.[1] In the absence of a sudden and dramatic take-off, the transition to 'machinofacture', to highly mechanized, factory-based mass-production industry was cautious and protracted, far from complete by the 1840s when over 75 per cent of manufacturing remained in unmodernized industries, small in scale, little affected by the use of steam power and characterized neither by high productivity nor comparative advantage.[2]

But the industrial revolution is not a complete misnomer. By the 1840s, Britain exhibited a number of features characteristic of a 'developed' rather than a pre-industrial economy, structural changes accomplished in pioneer manner, without any sudden or significant increase in income level or overall economic growth. Most notable was the low proportion of the labour force employed in agriculture, well below the European norm. Already achieved before parliamentary enclosure, high levels of agricultural productivity enabled the release of labour at an unusually early stage in the development process. The triumph of the industrial revolution, Crafts observes, lay in getting a lot of workers into industry rather than obtaining high productivity from them once there.[3]

Growth in real output did not reach three per cent a year until the 1830s, but the slow-moving, broad-based economic growth of the 'long eighteenth century' was sufficient to break through the homeostatic mechanism of the pre-industrial demographic system, allowing population to continue rising without severe detriment to living standards.[4] Well below recent Third World levels, this moderate but sustained population growth produced an expanding, dependable home market, the consumer base that justified and permitted capital accumulation in the 'age of manufactures'.[5] Much of the output of the most dynamic manufacturing sectors, however, was sent overseas. Small in relation to industrial output as a whole, textiles and iron dominated the export trade, another peculiarity of British development. No other European country had its exports so heavily in manufactures at such an early stage and at such a low income level. Boosted by the colonies, the largest free trade area in the eighteenth century, Britain was well placed to exploit its comparative advantage in a narrow range of manufactured exports: cotton textiles and other goods intensive in the use of coal and low-grade mechanized labour, factor endowments which carried Britain to dominance as 'the workshop of the world'.[6]

Despite this accolade, Britain never enjoyed a comprehensive, broad-based comparative advantage across the manufacturing spectrum: its high share of world trade was based overwhelmingly on dominance of textiles, in particular 'King Cotton'. The economic pacesetter, cotton was the innovative force promoting the 'factory system', although various constraints – financial, 'psycho-social' and technological – limited its growth and efficiency. The investment boom of the 1820s added momentum to economic concentration and vertical integration,[7] but small to middling firms remained preponderant. Horner's study of the Lancashire textile industry in 1841 revealed a broad base of nearly 400 firms, most of which were in single-process production, using no more than 20 horsepower, and employing a labour force of less than 100. At the base of the pyramid, they supported a narrowing pinnacle culminating in a few dozen 'giant' firms of 100 horsepower and over, mostly in combined spinning and weaving. The median size firm in this largest sector process, however, still employed only between 200 and 300 hands. In subsidiary processes, small firms and traditional technologies flourished in symbiotic relationship with the needs of large primary concerns, a characteristic feature of growth industries.[8]

Specialist in coarse yarn for the export market, Fielden Brothers was probably the largest textile concern at this time with a working capital in excess of £500,000, a staggering figure by early Victorian standards. At Waterside, an enormous combined spinning and weaving complex employing 1000 workers, the Fieldens indulged their every technological whim – in 1825 the mill housed one per cent of all the powerlooms in Great Britain – but much of the labour remained unmechanized. Handloom weavers were still on the Waterside payroll in 1861. Dual technologies existed side by side, within and without the mills: as well as Waterside and ten other mills in the valleys around Todmorden, Fielden Brothers provided employment in the mid-1830s for 1000 domestic weavers. Waterside itself was not particularly efficient – there was no necessary relationship between size and labour-saving. When nine workers per 1000 spindles was the norm in cotton spinning, Waterside had over fifteen.[9]

In other textile industries, the pace of mechanization was considerably slower: midway through the nineteenth century, well after the classic period of the industrial revolution, silk, linen and many branches of West Riding woollens still depended on the handloom.[10] Several trades were divided between machinery and handicraft sectors, as at Kidderminster where worsted-spinning was highly mechanized while carpet-weaving relied on traditional methods and processes.[11] Across the economy as a whole, steampower made little impact before 1850. Applied to preparatory process of manufacture, the effects were secondary, leaving the main body of work to human toil and craft skill.

No longer obsessed with technological determinism, economic historians now stress the importance of what Maxine Berg has called 'the other Industrial Revolution':

> an 'Industrial Revolution' which included domestic industry and artisan workshops much more than it did the factory system; an Industrial Revolution which relied on tools, small machines and skilled labour much more than it did on steam engines and automatic processes; an Industrial Revolution which was created by women and children at least as much as it was by male artisans and factory workers.[12]

Limited in themselves, steam and factories were often the multipliers of outwork employment – cotton handloom weavers, at least a quarter of a million strong by the 1820s, had not existed as a body before the 1770s, when technological breakthrough in the new spinning factories made strong warp possible.[13] Throughout the economy, the abundant supply of labour – a crucial point of contrast with the American experience – encouraged capitalists to engage in capital-saving rather than labour-saving investment, to perpetuate low-intensity technologies and rely on workers' skills even when, in principle at least, machinery was ready to replace them. Several other factors accounted for the slow progress of mechanization. Within traditional hand technology, increased output and improved productivity were achieved at relatively little cost by better tools and by intensifying and exploiting the workforce, through the increased division of labour and the extension of 'sweating'. Expensive and still unreliable, machines failed to perform the 'self-acting' miracles promised in the patents. Best suited to large-scale production and preparatory processes, mechanization was seldom applied in workshop trades where standards of finishing were high and production runs were short, prone to seasonal and other fluctuations in fashion and demand.[14]

The threat of mechanization, however, was a constant worry for workers no longer protected against competitive pressures and unregulated change at the workplace. During the eighteenth century, workers were left to the mercy of the market, set free by the law and the abnegation of paternalism, another 'freak' feature of British industrialization – in Germany, Japan and elsewhere, paternalism was the agency of control which promoted successful industrial development.[15] Denied the legal protection of the past, workers suffered most from the fluctuations of the trade cycle, aggravated by the free-trade system. When profits fell, manufacturers tried to reduce production costs by spreading expensive fixed capital overheads – including recent boom-time investment in new plant and steampower – over a larger volume of output. This policy, of course, exacerbated the problem of over-production, but employers blamed the depression on foreign competition, on the declining prices facilitated by low wage levels on the continent. As recession deepened and trade organization weakened, they introduced a number of economies in labour costs, reducing wages and substituting skilled men by female, child and unskilled labour, preparatory, it was feared, to eventual mechanization.[16]

The mechanics of these cyclical fluctuations preoccupied an earlier generation of economic historians, interwar scholars who looked back to the industrial revolution to understand the contemporary depredations of the trade cycle. Earlier still, the standard-of-living debate was initiated by critics of the cost and suffering of cyclical depression. The origins of the debate can be traced back to the 'Condition of England' question, the stirring of middle-class social consciousness during the severe depression of the late 1830s and early 1840s.[17] What exercised the consciences of these early Victorian critics, the forerunners of the pessimist school, was not simply the disturbing scale of the depression but also the shocking existence of so much blameless poverty – clearly not attributable to individual moral feck-lessness – in the midst of such unparalleled abundance. Previous times of distress, the consequence of adverse military and meteorological factors, war, harvest failure and the like, had led to short-term distress through dearth and the shortage of physical produce, poverty in the midst of scarcity. Cyclical distress was altogether different: socially divisive, the new type of economic depression widened the gap between rich and poor with the cruel juxtaposition of endemic poverty and glutted overstocked markets.[18] Once trade recovered, however, and the industrial base expanded, heartfelt agonizing over want in the midst of plenty was forgotten amid the joyous celebration and Great Exhibition of the economic progress of the first industrial nation.

2 Living Standards

Wages and earnings

For all the statistical sophistication, new economic history has failed to resolve the debate between pessimists and optimists. Both sides are endorsed in near equal part by the latest calculations which divide the industrial revolution into two sharply contrasting wage periods, deterioration followed by advance. While M. W. Flinn spoke only of stagnation, the latest indices demonstrate a secular decline in real wages starting around the middle of the eighteenth century, deepening during the French and Napoleonic Wars, and persisting through the price peak of 1812–13 and the distress of the postwar years.[1] In London, as Schwarz's work shows, the downward trend was not reversed until the 1820s, although it was not until the 1840s that the levels of the 1740s were regained and exceeded.[2] The 'best-guess' national index compiled by Lindert and Williamson also situates the upturn in the 1820s, but their figures are far more optimistic, suggesting that real wages nearly doubled between 1820 and 1850.[3] At their simplest, the figures support a pessimist position on real wages until the 1820s and an optimist assessment thereafter.

Statistics, however, obscure much of the diversity and harshness of working-class experience. Limited to the classic period of the industrial revolution, the indices fail to take adequate account of the remarkable change in wages geography during the eighteenth century. In the 1760s most high-wage counties were in the south-east and the greatest concentration of low-wage counties was in the north: by the 1790s eight of the eleven highest-wage counties were in the north and midlands and only three were in the south-east. Protected by this reversal in regional differentials, workers – and migrants – located close to the industrial revolution, in and around the growth pole of industrial development, probably escaped the falling real wages of the late eighteenth century. In 1767–70 farm wages were 20 per cent higher in Buckinghamshire than in Lancashire, but by 1794–5 Lancashire wages stood more than a third above the level in Buckinghamshire, a differential which continued until the end of the nineteenth century.[4] Real wages in north Staffordshire rose across the board in the second half of the eighteenth century, with potters and miners – occupations transformed in size and practice – gaining substantially more than general labourers and building craftsmen. Undramatic as it was, the industrial revolution clearly had a favourable influence on labour markets in the north and much of the midlands.[5]

Rigorously restricted to the impact of industrialization, the statistical evidence deliberately excludes short-term distortions, a convenience denied the workers of the time forced to endure the violent price fluctuations of harvest crises, wartime inflationary finance and other extraneous catastrophes. Academic and unreal, statistical calculation of the standard of living contributes little to the requisite social history of earnings and expenditure. Wage payments must be assessed in the context of family income and the disproportionately high cost of living for the working class, a hardship aggravated by the family poverty cycle and the devastating impact of recurrent short-term crises.

By concentrating on money-payment and adult males, the standard-of-living statistics conceal important structural changes in the composition of working-class family income during the industrial revolution. The assumptions upon which the figures are based – the dominance of the money-wage and of the male breadwinner – lack validity until the middle of the nineteenth century, by which time workers had been deprived of traditional perquisites and rights, and the working-class family had been forced to redefine gender roles and functions. It is these changes, obscured by the statistics, which mattered most to workers when they assessed their own standard of living.

The imposition of an exclusively monetary form of wage payment marked a fundamental change in employers' attitudes to property and labour. As capitalism spread, they could no longer allow workers to appropriate any part of the materials or product of their labour, no matter how small, and this applied in all forms of industrial organization from the vastly expanded putting-out system, where competitively-minded merchants were determined to eradicate embezzlement, to the largest 'pre-factory' industrial unit, the dockyards, scene of long-running disputes over the shipwrights' chips. Whether financially compensated or not, workers bitterly resented the enforcement of this new money-wage discipline which denied them their traditional rights and perquisites, their bugging, cabbage, sweepings, blue-pigeon flying, wastages, fints, thrums, chippings, and the like.[6] For agricultural labourers, too, the old practices and customs were much valued for the margin of independence and security which they afforded. Previously self-reliant, landless wage labourers in southern and eastern counties were reduced to a demoralized and indigent state, no longer able to keep livestock of their own or gather free fuel for the cold winter months, customary rights withdrawn in the age of enclosure.[7] In the west, the 'free miners' of the Forest of Dean managed to retain grazing rights on the waste together with their encroached land, cottages and gardens, but by the 1830s they had lost customary rights to the timber and coal resources of the forest. The Crown, acting in alliance with 'foreigners' – non-resident coal merchants with capital to invest in deeper and more extensive workings – reasserted its authority, substituting contractual relations for those of right and custom.[8]

However, this 'custom to crime transition' must be placed in perspective.[9] Workshop appropriation or 'theft' was by no means eradicated – the 'Turkey trade' remained a lucrative underworld business in nineteenth-century Macclesfield where stolen raw and thrown silk continued to find its way into illicit warehouses operated by Fagin-like masterminds.[10] Employers were not always the victims of such practices: in the metal trades, the taking of a man's half-finished work, subsequently finished and sold by another as his own, was a common offence.[11] Legal processes were by no means an employer prerogative: the courts were used and endorsed by workers themselves, as in Staffordshire where miners were prepared to prosecute if workmates stole from each other.[12] In the arable eastern counties, gleaning continued to provide some labouring families with a tenth of their annual income. The power of the courts, dramatically illustrated in a famous judgment of 1788, proved ineffective against the force of local customary law, scriptural and humanitarian arguments, and the collective self-regulation exercised by the female gleaners – those who failed to obey local gleaning times and practices as determined by the 'Queen' were subjected to harsh collective sanctions. Where the law failed, farmers relied on vestry control of local relief and settlement policies to impose their authority, hoping to restrict gleaning to the resident deserving poor.[13] Up in the industrial districts, some of the less fortunate new arrivals depended upon the evasion of property and game laws to secure a miserable livelihood. In the cotton districts around Oldham, the 'low Irish' eked out their cellar existence by making and hawking besom brooms, using furze or 'ling' cut from the grouse covers on the surrounding hills. 'Oh begorra! It was hard on the poor, the gentry was,' one unfortunate immigrant bemoaned after his friend, a fellow Sligoman, was sentenced to a month's imprisonment for ling-cutting.[14]

Within this 'custom to crime transition', the imposition of the exclusive money wage was a lengthy, hard-fought and uneven process. What was at stake for workers was not simply a traditional source of 'extra' income, but the maintenance of some independence at the workplace, some control over the product and the labour process. Conflict shifted from perquisites to 'prices', the symbolic term for the piece-rate payment at which the worker, still insisting on his independence, 'sold' the results of his labour to the employer by the piece or by the day. The inflationary 1790s apart, these piece-rates or day quota rates were generally remarkably stable, in accordance with such hallowed conventions and customary expectations as the twofold differential between skilled and ordinary labourers.[15] In trades which depended on overseas markets, however, piece-rates fluctuated violently. Bythell's study of the muslin weaving rate at Bolton between 1795 and 1820 shows how 'prices' rose appreciably when markets were buoyant and raw materials scarce as in 1813–14, but slumped catastrophically when markets collapsed and raw materials were easily obtainable as in 1806–7 and 1815–17.[16] Fluctuations like these make trends in earnings difficult to assess, but even when piece-rates remained nominally stable it is not easy to extrapolate the level of actual earnings – employers were able to increase the quantum in subtle ways, and output varied from worker to worker and from season to season.

Age was probably the most important factor in determining output and earnings. Younger and stronger men in Staffordshire coal-mining were able to hew more than a 'stint' in the daily shift, and thus benefited most from a piece-rate system which allowed them to decide how hard they worked and which shifts they could afford to miss.[17] An Assistant Commissioner investigating the handloom weavers in the 1830s calculated that the youngest and fittest in the 'dandyloom' shops could earn '25 per cent more wages, in the same time, working at a wide loom, than a weaker person could earn with the same material, on a pattern no less difficult, at a narrow loom'.[18] Throughout the trades, the elderly, or rather the prematurely old, were often forced to give up the better-paid tasks, their experience and seniority notwithstanding, as they fell victim to failing eyesight, 'craft palsy', pneumoconiosis, 'shoddy fever', or some other occupational disability, which in the tragic case of the Sheffield fork-grinders killed off no less than a quarter of the workforce every five years.[19] 'Old age coming on men in my way is a very great affliction,' Henry Mayhew was informed by a 79-year-old bespectacled journeyman carpenter whose earnings had been reduced from 30s a week to a few shillings jobbing:

> We try to hide our want of great strength and good sight as long as we can. I did it for two or three years, but it was found out at last, and I had to go . . . In most shops the moment a man puts his glasses on it's over with him. It wasn't so when I first knew London. Masters then said, 'Let me have an old man, one who knows something.' Now it's, 'Let me have a young man, I must have a strong fellow, an old one won't do.'[20]

But in some trades there were strong countervailing traditions of protective mutuality. Shipwrights in the Portsmouth dockyards believed in 'shoaling', deliberately mixing productive with less productive workers in their 'day gangs', thereby maintaining decent wages for the elderly and less physically able.[21] The compositors' union would not allow any of its members to be paid for more than 60 hours work, much to the annoyance of an industrious young entrant to the trade who put in 82 hours in his first week but received only £2, the agreed rate for 60 hours, together with an 'on-the-shelf' allowance of 22 hours off his next week's workload.[22] Despite the macho-culture of the 'big hewer', miners tried to distribute work fairly and equalize earnings by 'cavilling', drawing lots for places on the easiest seams, a quarterly practice on the north-east coalfield where there were also 'voluntary' rules 'not to send up to bank more than a given quantity of coals per man'.[23]

Differences in output and earnings were kept to a minimum where group solidarity and trade societies were strong, but these forms of mutual protection did not apply in the so-called 'dishonourable' trades or in the over-stocked outwork industries. Here, in the absence of day rates or 'legal', union-backed piece-prices, opportunistic middlemen and commercially-minded masters were able to exploit cheap unskilled labour through the piece-rate system. After the collapse of apprenticeship and other safeguards, workers in the 'dishonourable' trades – the unfortunate 'refractories', 'dungs', 'blacks', 'snobs' and 'scabs' – were forced into fierce competition with each other, caught in a downward-spiralling poverty cycle with little chance of escape no matter how hard they worked. Low wages, Mayhew sadly observed, made for overwork, which in turn led to less work all round.[24] Much the same applied in the outwork industries where over-stocking led to under-selling, as surplus workers sought employment – their only source of income – at any price. The Yorkshire woollen area apart, the great expansion of the putting-out system undermined the traditional pattern of dual occupations and double earning capacity, the combination of manufacture (or mining) with smallhold-husbandry.[25]

Even in 'honourable' trades, few workers were fortunate enough to enjoy full-time work throughout the year – except in the depths of cyclical depressions, factory workers were probably best placed in this regard since employers preferred to keep expensive capital at work throughout temporary and seasonal crises.[26] Not more than one in ten 'honourable' coopers, Mayhew calculated, were employed for more than nine months a year, and the earnings of this privileged few oscillated between 30s a week during the 'brisk' summer season and a mere 10s during the 'slack' winter season.[27] Throughout the economy winter slackness was the norm, although there were exceptions such as the coal and fuel trades, and industries like paper-making and pig-iron which depended on the winter water supply until the advent of new technology. The weather was responsible for the deep seasonal trough which ran from November to February in outdoor occupations in the building trades and at the docks where employment was always at the mercy of the elements.[28] In other trades it was fashion and social convention which determined the seasonal rhythm, with the long-awaited spring flush boosting earnings after the bleak winter months. Hatters, milliners, shoemakers, dress-makers, tailors and others who supplied the 'quality' enjoyed a brisk spring and early summer but were left impoverished in high summer or 'cucumber time', when the *beau monde* and their entourage retired to their country estates. There was a brief upsurge in the autumn as a result of Christmas orders, but this soon passed and earnings declined until the spring 'flush' came round again.[29] Silk-weavers were particularly vulnerable to changes in fashion and were often left to go 'play' with no work to do. 'Mayhap the master would give an order for a certain pattern,' a Macclesfield weaver explained to the *Morning Chronicle*: 'Well, all at once the taste would pass away, and the silks would be upon the shelves. Soom'mut new was always coming up and that made the changes from the busy times to the slack times.'[30]

The possibilities of dovetailing seasonal employment opportunities were rather limited, although those who faced a slack summer could always find some other form of work: Black Country coalminers, for example, took up nailing, and London chimney-sweeps tried their hand at costermongering. Others were more mobile in search of work, brickmaking in the midlands in summer, gas-stoking in London in winter, or alternating between labouring in the country, brewing in the town and fishing at the nearest port according to season.[31] Many of the urban poor, still antipathetic to wage discipline, took advantage of summer employment in the countryside. Enamellers, fur-pullers and other 'dangerous' trades quit their wretched working conditions for a recuperative and lucrative tramp through the fields. Other fairweather travellers took to the road, following well-established harvest itineraries – the most famous circuit kept people on the road from April to November, a trail of hay and corn harvests which began in London and ran up to Yorkshire and Northumberland, across the Pennines, down through Cheshire, across the midlands and back to the Home Counties – while women and nimble-fingered girls worked the fruit and hop-picking route. In winter, the flow was reversed back into the towns: itinerant sawyers returned to urban workshops; travelling showmen sought indoor premises; navvies entered the gas works; migratory thieves from summer race-grounds and fairs reverted to nocturnal safe-breaking; and indigent travellers crowded into soup kitchens and night refuges in search of warmth and shelter.[32] Dependent on seasonal migration and the unruly 'secondary economy' of the streets, vast numbers of the casual and labouring poor lie outside the statistical confines of the standard of living debate.

The available wage statistics present other problems. Workers were responsible for a number of capital costs themselves so that weekly wages were subject to a number of out-payments and enforced deductions. Admittedly, there were some instances where the reverse was the case, where workers still received non-monetary benefits which must be added to the money-wage figures – the miners' coal allowance, free brandy on the hour for labourers who emptied cesspits, the beer consumed by thirsty coopers and others who toiled in hot conditions.[33] There is an important regional factor here too: in the north-east, the bond and bondager system of hiring persisted on farms and in the lead-mining dales, based on legally binding contracts, low cash payments and substantial allowances in kind. In Northumberland, the bondager system included the hire of a female helper for the 'hind' who received a free cottage and garden and various other allowances – out of £32 10s a year value of reward, only about £4 was in cash payment.[34] But money-wages were the new norm in most trades and regions, although the extent of deductions and out-payments varied considerably. For skilled workers, such out-goings were the necessary price of independence; for those less favourably placed, they were a register of subordination and exploitation.

The possession of personal tools – small but vital means of production – symbolized the skill, status and residual independence of the artisan, his ability to work anywhere at his trade.[35] These precious implements, always the last items to be pawned, had to be kept in prime condition, an expensive consideration. 'Grindery' cost a West-End boot-closer at the top end of the boot and shoe trade 1s 6d a week out of total earnings of 27s. Coopers who possessed tools worth £12 or more calculated the cost of wear and tear at 1s a week.[36] Hewers on the north-east coalfield generally possessed at least half a dozen picks which cost 1s 8d each and required sharpening every day, for which they paid 2d a fortnight to the colliery blacksmith, a small charge compared with the cost of gunpowder and candles, amounting to about 2s 6d a fortnight in the 1840s.[37] Control of the recruitment and payment of assistants was another costly indication of skilled status: since it provided employers with a convenient means of labour recruitment and discipline the tradition was carried over from the workshops into the new factories. Manchester cotton spinners earned £2 3s 4d a week in 1818 for spinning 20 lb at 160 hanks to the pound, but £1 2s 7d was paid to their piecers, leaving a balance of just 18s 4d after account was also taken of the average weekly cost of candles, sick benefit contributions and other expenses.[38] Given such factors, the earnings differential between skilled and ordinary workers was less than the wages figures suggest: the ratio, John Rule calculates, was not 2:1 but 3:2 or 5:3.[39] For those under threat from unskilled competition and/or mechanization, outgoings reduced earnings to unskilled levels. The plight of skilled weavers in the Bolton fancy trade, 'reduced to a level, if not below, the plain weaver', was blamed on 'the extra expense which the fancy weaver is unavoidably put to, in consequence of gaiting and draw-boys' – in 1822, earnings were down to 22s out of which 4s had to be deducted for these expenses.[40] Kidderminster carpet weavers underwent a similar decline in fortunes as prices fell by 17 per cent in 1816 and by another 17 per cent after the unsuccessful strike in 1828, leaving them with an average weekly wage of 19s 9d in the 1830s, out of which 5s 10d had to be deducted for draw-boys and shop expenses.[41]

For many workers, deductions and out-payments were a demeaning symbol of subordination and exploitation. In the putting-out sector, where direct supervision was impossible, merchants and middlemen relied upon fines and deductions to discipline the workforce and make good any losses through 'bad work', embezzlement or 'slinging'. The cause of much anger and dispute, stoppages tended to increase at times of bad trade when workers complained of 'cases of real hardship in the system – cases in which shabby and screwing agents sought, by extreme ingenuity in finding or fancying flaws, to bate down the fair price for work'. Edward Curran, the Lancashire weavers' leader, was a staunch critic of these 'unjust abatements': 'Many of us overmake our work on purpose to avoid the possibility of abatements, giving, in fact, our labour for nothing.'[42]

Other deductions were a regular charge whatever the circumstances. Whether in work or not, framework-knitters in the east midlands hosiery trade were liable for frame-rent, a much-resented charge inflated by middlemen putters-out. On top of the shilling frame rent, an unmarried journeyman knitter, unable to benefit from the family economy, had to pay a further 3s in deductions from his weekly wage of 13s 3¼d in 1811: a frame standing charge of 3d for the use of a corner of the master knitter's workplace, and a 1s fee to the master for acting as his agent in taking in work; a charge of 1s 1d for seaming the stockings, a task normally undertaken by the wife at home; and the cost of needles, oils, candles and coals.[43] Out-work weavers in the textile industries faced a similar burden of charges for loom-rent and other essentials – around Manchester, it was generally agreed that these out-goings accounted for 3d in every shilling of the handloom weaver's wages.[44] Transfer to factories did not necessarily lessen the costs – a fixed sum for overheads was held back from the earnings of Macclesfield silk-weavers employed in Brocklehursts' mill.[45] Costs increased during the cold and dark winter months, hence the celebratory 'slecking out' suppers in weaving communities when 'lighting' could be given up in the spring, but the cost of candles was a constant charge for some workers, made all the more burdensome for the Cornish tin-miners by the mineowners' monopoly of supply.[46]

In the factories the work rhythm was set by a system of rigorously enforced financial penalties, hence the popular refrain in the mills: 'A bobbin too few, or a bobbin too many / Is certain to cost the poor devil a penny.' Arbitrary fines, similar to the abatements in the outwork sector, were also imposed for 'bad work'.[47] Bitterly resented, these fines and deductions precluded amicable industrial relations, although in Coventry the cost of Christmas beef distributed to workers in the ribbon-weaving factories was 'defrayed by the accumulated fines of the year'.[48] Disputes over fines were just as frequent in the mines where hewers complained bitterly about the heavy penalties for 'a trifling under-weight or a trifling mixture of "foul" coal'. In some instances, hewers lost the value of the whole tub on account of accidental spillage ('set-out') or impurities ('laid-out'), but the government inspector calculated that the average loss by fines was not more than ½d a day a man.[49]

A further complicating factor in the assessment of actual earnings was the shortage of specie, a considerable embarrassment to the proponents of the new money-wage discipline. Without the necessary coinage, employers either resorted to part-payment in 'truck' or relied on the good offices of the public house where ready money or 'blunt' always seemed to be available. Many large employers in the early nineteenth century paid their workforce 'in the lump', depending upon local publicans to provide the coinage for individual wages.[50] A temporary expedient, Saturday night payment in the pub became the accepted practice in some districts. When Charles Shaw started work as a mould-runner in the Potteries at the end of the 1830s, he found that it was still the custom for wages to be 'fastened up in one lump until loosened at some public house':

> Men and women and children had to go there for their wages. The publican took good care to be in no hurry in changing the money given him. Each one – man, woman and child – was expected to have a hot roll and cheese, to be paid for out of the wage to be received, however small the pittance . . . Not until he was assured of a fair return for his 'change', or until he saw his adult customers were settled for a night's booze, did he bring out the change.[51]

Some workers were not only paid but were also hired in the pub, a ruinous arrangement which widened still further the gap between wages and actual take-home pay. Until a protective Act in 1843, Thames coal-whippers could only gain employment through an 'undertaker', a local publican who would only take on men who regularly consumed up to 50 per cent of their wages on the premises.[52]

Family income

Despite the attention accorded to the adult male 'breadwinner' in the standard of living debate, earnings at the time were assessed in family not individual terms, with the family often functioning as a unit of production, a pooling of resources which pushed up piece-rate earnings while keeping costs and outgoings to a minimum. In these respects, the family economy functioned best during the 'proto-industrial' phase of economic growth when the employment of women (and children) came close to a notional maximum. As the industrial revolution continued, the prospects for women – and hence family earnings – deteriorated considerably. The first victims of technological or structural unemployment, women encountered a new prejudice and sexual division of labour, the harsh economic cost of the new male breadwinner ideal. Working-class families were able to hold their own in early Victorian England only by a shift in their earnings which served to reinforce the authority of the patriarchal male.[53]

The expansion of the putting-out system undermined the old social controls by encouraging earlier marriage and higher fertility. Unrestricted by institutional or financial barriers, young couples set themselves up in unregulated trades like handloom-weaving and nail-making in the outlying villages that rapidly encircled the major manufacturing and commercial centres of the midlands and the north. Once the 'dependency hump' was traversed, the labour input of the wife and children contributed substantially to the family's earnings and purchasing power.[54] The man of the house was responsible to the putter-out – the 'fogger', 'bagman' or other middleman-agent of the central merchant capitalist – for the finished product, paid by the piece for what the family produced together as a working unit. Accordingly, he directed and organized the work of the household members, generally reserving for himself the most productive frame, loom or other device. The woman was often relegated to unskilled or preparatory tasks – picking and hand-fulling wool for combing, for example – since much of her time had to be accorded to unpaid labour, to household chores and childcare.[55]

These manufacturing families gave a powerful boost to home demand, maintaining the momentum of economic growth in the second half of the eighteenth century, at a time when male real wages were probably falling. Keen to purchase the 'decencies' offered by the new consumer market, they were prepared to work long and hard, a form of self-exploitation which cannot be explained in the subsistence terms and peasant norms of proto-industrialization theory – it was emulative expenditure which led them to relinquish the proverbial 'leisure preference', the traditional withdrawal of labour once customary expectations had been achieved.[56] But as the trade became over-stocked, an inevitable consequence of the ease of entry, no amount of labour discipline or self-exploitation could prevent a drastic fall in earnings. In such circumstances, the retention of the family as a domestic production unit made little economic sense, but many families struggled on in these adverse conditions rather than submit to workshop or factory 'imprisonment'.

The traditional gender roles of the old domestic system were reinforced in drastic fashion in the new forms of work organization, protecting the interests of men but often at the expense of total family income. Sexual segregation was rigorously enforced in the textile mills where women were denied access to the best-paid skilled jobs. Skill was a male preserve in the modern factory, protected by trade union organization and internal subcontracting systems which gave mule spinners and their like a supervisory role for which women were deemed ineligible. Building upon their traditional domestic role as work supervisors, male factory workers were able to reconstruct craft status in the new work environment, establishing a hierarchical division of labour which suited their employers' needs for a stable, disciplined labour force.[57] Textile mills apart, mechanization and the factory system brought few new opportunities for women – female employment was derisory in iron and steel, railways, chemicals and other expanding heavy industries. Legislation in 1842 restricted female work in the mines, although some Lancashire colliers, keen to maintain their family earnings, smuggled their wives and daughters underground until the mineowners called in the police. Women continued to work on the surface, particularly in the Wigan area, but these 'pit-brow lasses', notorious for their trousered attire, came under increasing criticism from male colleagues and the labour movement, staunch advocates of domestic respectability.[58] Up in the north-east, women were banished from the mines without demur: the reformulation of their role as model housewives was uncontested, a contrast to the fierce struggle over new work practices and alterations in the Bond which redefined the 'true-born' pitman as mere labourer.[59]

By no means restricted to the factory districts, sexual segregation occurred wherever men were confronted with changes in the location or process of work. Male workers in the Gloucestershire fine woollen trade managed to preserve much of their pay and status in this 'de-industrializing' region by appropriating the most efficient equipment, confining women to menial and manual tasks.[60] The flexible allocation of work tasks, a feature of the family-based putting-out industries, was replaced by rigid occupational segregation as workplace and home were separated by new labour processes. Men only were employed on the new wide frames in centralized knitting workshops in the Leicester hosiery trade. Paid individuals, not members of a household work unit, women were left at home to undertake the lowest-paid, least-skilled tasks, seaming and stitching the stockings.[61] In the eastern cereal counties women were steadily excluded from all the major tasks, although they continued to participate fully in livestock and dairy farming in the west. The family income undoubtedly suffered as a consequence – labourers had traditionally married early to maximize joint earning power – but the new sexual specialization was welcomed by men on their own economic grounds. Increasingly vulnerable to seasonal unemployment with the expansion of grain production, they were determined to restrict cheap female competition. By the beginning of the nineteenth century, ploughing, dung-spreading, threshing and harvesting had all become male preserves, with female participation limited to haymaking and weeding the corn. Since spinning and other domestic cloth trades were well on the decline in these parts, no alternative employment was available until the introduction of straw-plaiting, one of the new labour-intensive cottage industries which spread across the southern and eastern counties, sweating the cheap labour of women made redundant by the sexual specialization of agriculture and the de-industrialization of the traditional domestic manufactures of the region.[62]

Throughout the artisan trades the collapse of the traditional apprenticeship system and the consequent reduction in age at marriage led to an over-stocked labour market from which male artisans, confronted by unemployment and the debasement of craft skills, wished to exclude female competition.[63] Only in bookbinding were women able to retain their numbers and 'honourable' status, but their earning power declined dramatically. Denied membership of the trade society, they received no more than one-third to one-half of their male colleagues wages, and they were pushed increasingly into the least skilled work. In most 'honourable' trades, female employment was kept to the very minimum, an exclusionist policy rigorously pursued by the compositors who prevented any '*miss*-printing' and were particularly successful in retaining skill, status and wage levels.[64] Denied upward mobility into small master status by the capitalization of the trades, these well-paid, highly regarded 'society' men were the first to endorse the new male breadwinner ideal, symbol of the independence and respectability which all workers wished to achieve.[65]

The ideal, which implied female confinement to hearth and home, was to prove unattainable and detrimental, aggravating the hardship of the many families that lacked the requisite male 'family wage'. In these cases, the wife's contribution to the family income remained indispensable, but the force of the new convention against working women confined their employment to the lowest-paid 'dishonourable' and sweated sectors. Here their cheap labour was exploited in such a way as to reinforce still further the male hostility towards 'unfair' competition. To patriarchal artisans, the London tailoring trade became an object lesson in the evils of 'feminization' as the ever-expanding pool of cheap female labour allowed the new 'slop' employers and 'show-shop' owners to undercut male wages, skills and organization, finally forcing men out of work and into 'unnatural' dependence on their wives. Relations between the sexes were at crisis point by the early 1830s when the Owenite socialists, advocates of sexual equality and marriage reform, championed the rights of working women and called upon the London tailors union to adopt a policy of 'equalization' to unite all the workforce from the respectable 'Flints' and dishonourable 'Dungs' to the worst paid tailoresses. The union, however, decided in favour of militant rearguard action to defend sectional and patriarchal interests, but the strike was a disastrous failure. Those in control of the business promptly changed the system of payment from day-rate to piece-rate, after which sweating and feminization swept through the trade. New subcontracting systems transformed the journeyman into a 'garret master', a sweater or middleman trading upon the labour of others, ruthlessly exploiting cheap female and family labour in a desperate effort to undersell the competition.[66] This degeneration of the old family economy – the transmogrification of home into sweat-shop – occurred not just in tailoring but also in cabinet-making and other 'slop' trades where 'cheap, cheap, cheap means cheat, cheat, cheat', a maxim which poor Bezer first encountered when 'snobbing' for his cousin, a 'chamber-master' in the ladies shoe trade.[67]

Domesticity was probably the best in a narrow range of unhappy options for working-class married women, but for those employed in the sweated sector it was a cruelly illusive ideal. Until their children were old enough to contribute to the family income, there was no release from the double burden of unpaid housework and ill-paid waged-work. Unable not to work, married women were driven lower and lower into the sweated sector – or prostitution – by the force of social convention which condemned but continued to exploit their labour. Up in the industrial districts, critics of the factory system deplored the 'unnatural' behaviour of young working mothers: 'unsexed' at the mill, they left their children to be drugged to stupefaction with 'Godfrey's Cordial', 'Infant Quietness' or some other concoction of sweetened laudanum administered by wretched and incompetent hireling child-minders.[68] However, recent research has shown that not more than 25 per cent of female mill-workers were married, and of this number those with children took the utmost care to ensure they were properly looked after during the long working day by a close relative, friendly lodger or obliging neighbour – less than 2 per cent of all infant children in industrial Lancashire were left to the none too tender mercies of professional child-minders.[69] But the greatest hardship inflicted by the new discrimination against women's work was endured outside the ordinary family, by deserted wives and widows forced to work to support young children. Single women without dependants were better placed: they had the option of domestic service, which duly expanded to become the largest single occupational category in the Victorian economy, a form of 'disguised underemployment'.[70]

To return to wages geography, working-class family earnings seem to have declined most where the intensification of market competition was unaccompanied by new industrial activity. In the arable east and the de-industrializing south, the removal of traditional controls in agriculture and the trades led painfully and inexorably to discrimination against women and inadequate remuneration of men. Up in the north, higher wages prevailed: new employment opportunities in hand-domestic and mechanized sectors developed alongside the survival of traditional institutional frameworks and hiring practices in farm service and apprenticed trades.[71] Optimists in the standard of living debate assume a high level of 'mobility-induced wage drift', of movement upward and outward from low-paid to high-paid employment, from low-wage to high-wage regions.[72] But there were familial and institutional restraints on such mobility.

Upward occupational mobility was particularly hard to achieve. Working-class children generally remained tied to their father's occupation – in one-parent families they followed the trade of some other relative, much to the gratitude of the deserted wife or widow. In the skilled trades, the inheritance was highly valued – fathers placed their sons in the trade via apprenticeship, a system beyond the means of most outsiders, of parents in low-paid trades who could not afford the premium or the drop in family income while the son served his time. There were exceptions: Thomas Wood's parents, poor Yorkshire handloom weavers, endured much financial hardship to enable their son to complete an apprenticeship as a powerloom-maker – in the 1840s Wood finally settled at Oldham where he earned 32s a week working at Platt's, one of the biggest textile machine-makers, but he never forgot the years of parental sacrifice which enabled him 'to be a mechanic and have my heart's desire'.[73] In most handloom weaving villages children were caught in a poverty trap, compelled to continue in the family trade as 'there was "naught" else for them to do'.[74] Away in the large towns, there were plenty of casual jobs as pot-boys, vanboys, labourers and the like, but without parental support and influence there was little likelihood of gaining the type of employment which would ensure economic independence as an adult. With so little chance of upward mobility, most young workers settled for what they had, continuing with the family trade in the hope of some security, however poor the prospects.

Some children were resentful and rebellious, a 'teenage problem' accentuated by the decline in traditional service and apprenticeship, living-in arrangements which had removed troublesome adolescents from the home and placed them under the paternal guidance of their master-employer. Confined to wretched cottages, the teenage offspring of agricultural labourers were drawn irresistibly to the bright lights of the town, only to return bitter and resentful to the parental settlement, having failed to secure worthwhile alternative employment.[75] Comparatively well-paid, teenagers in the factory districts were far from content, particularly the young males: with little prospect of skilled adult work, they faced the unenviable choice of moving to lower-paid areas of factory work or entering the outside labour market with no apprenticeship or skill to help them.[76] In mining communities, by contrast, there was a clear and unchallenged career progression. All boys followed fathers into the pits, starting as poorly-paid 'trappers', where they conquered their fear of the terrifying pitch black as they opened and closed the underground trap doors to allow 'putters' and their tubs to pass. After a while, they became drivers and putters themselves when they contributed substantially to the family income. But it was not until they became hewers that the pitmen of the north-east set up house on their own, invariably choosing a wife from within the community.[77]

While the influence of the family probably hindered occupational mobility, it was the kinship network which best facilitated regional migration. Geographical mobility was high throughout the workforce, from the skilled 'Dons', first-rate hands who travelled or 'tramped' to improve their craft skills, down to the itinerant navvies, labourers and vagrants who spent much of their lives on the road. For skilled workers, the 'tramping' network offered protection as well as education. Whenever times were bad, accredited 'society' men went on the 'tramp', assured of employment or relief as they moved from one house of call to the next, visiting every branch of their trade society if necessary, a grand tour of some 2800 miles in the compositors' case.[78] Outside these institutional networks, the majority of the working class were able to move from one region to another with some assurance of work or support as kith and kin acted as employment and relief agency. The Irish immigrants were probably the most efficient in using the kinship network in this way, but much internal migration depended upon family and similar links. As Michael Anderson's work on the cotton districts has shown, in-migrants moved along networks of relatives and friends, often at their instigation, to temporary homes provided by them and to jobs obtained with their assistance. Sometimes it was just the teenagers who were sent north, but families generally moved together, even though the adult male was unlikely to obtain well-paid factory work and faced the undignified prospect of unemployment or housework.[79]

What hindered migration was not the family but changes in settlement and poor relief policy which forced workers back to the 'security' of their parents' villages of settlement. Young labourers in the low-wage southern and eastern counties found it increasingly difficult to establish their own right of settlement elsewhere as traditional practices which conferred such entitlement – living-in apprenticeships and yearly hiring – went into decline. The new dependence on 'parental settlement' was compounded by the operation of the new Poor Law which cut back drastically on non-resident relief, a cheap and effective means of holding labour in the parish during the winter ready for the short arable season. Immobile and demoralized, labouring families remained together, but inter-generational relationships deteriorated when parishes withdrew their financial support for the elderly, leaving families with more burdens but less income.[80]

Expenditure

The cost of living was disproportionately high for working-class families: limited purchasing power and expensive credit resources denied them the economies enjoyed by the middle and upper classes. Food was by far the most important item, accounting for up to three-quarters of the wage packet. Compelled to buy 'dear', to purchase poor quality food in small quantities for immediate consumption, the working class rarely received value for money. Often dependent upon credit, they had to pay the higher prices of the obliging small shopkeeper. Manchester mill operatives, Angus Reach reported, purchased their goods on weekly credit in small chandlers' shops, where tea was sold at 6s rather than 4s a lb as at regular dealers. 'Thus the poor mill operatives pay higher by 33 per cent for their tea than their masters.'[81]

Provisions were dearer still for victims of the truck system, captive

Leeds Trinity University
Tel: 0113 283 7244
libraryenquiries@leedstrinity.ac.uk

Borrowed Items 12/12/2015 20:24
GWENDOLEN MERLE CLARKE

Item Title	Due Date
* Industrialization and the	09/01/2016
* The Industrial Revolution	09/01/2016
* A short history of the Br	09/01/2016

* Indicates items borrowed today

Thank you for using this Unit. See you next time!

PLEASE REMEMBER TO SWIPE YOUR DVDs THROUGH THE DETACHER AT THE ENTRANCE TO THE LIBRARY

Service and opening hours details at http://intranet.leedstrinity.ac.uk/CampusServices/helpdesk

customers of the 'tommy shops' where the likes of Messrs Diggs of *Sybil* fame supplied poor quality, adulterated, under-weight food at grossly inflated prices.[82] Despite stringent legislation, the 'accursed truck system' remained common practice in early Victorian south Staffordshire where the law was openly flouted by the subcontracting butties in the coal industry and the middlemen foggers in the nail and chain-making trades.[83] Large employers too, made use of the system: 'the very worst "Tommy-shops" in this district,' Reach reported, 'are kept not by the ignorant butties, but by great iron-masters – vast capitalists who employ men by the hundred – and regularly mulct them out of five, six, ten or even more per cent of their wages by paying these wages in goods . . . charged at least five per cent above the market price.'[84] Rural East Anglia was another blackspot: the gangmasters – middlemen who supplied farmers with subcontract labour at the cheapest daily rates – were notorious truck-traders whose nefarious practices could not be challenged by the poor labourers who depended upon them for work.[85]

Beyond what was available on tick or truck, poor quality cheap food could be obtained from Saturday night markets where unscrupulous dealers disposed of their otherwise unsaleable produce. By the time working-class shoppers arrived in the evening, as soon as they received their wages, the food on offer – 'the refuse of the morning's supply', Gaskell observed – was hardly fit for human consumption. 'The workers get what is too bad for the property-holding class', Engels fulminated. Quality apart, the Saturday night market was the high point of the week for many working people, an occasion of boisterous conviviality, 'noisy vociferation' which offended the sensibilities of middle-class observers nearly as much as the putrefying odours.[86] The London Road market in Manchester was particularly lively on a Saturday night, 'one swarming buzzing mass of people':

> Itinerant bands bang and blow their loudest; organ boys grind monot-
> onously; ballad singers or flying stationers make roaring proclamations of
> their wares. . . . Boys and girls shout and laugh and disappear into the
> taverns together. Careful housewives – often attended by their husbands,
> dutifully carrying the baby – bargain hard with the butchers for a halfpenny
> off the pound. . . . The pawnbroker is busy, for pledges are being rapidly
> redeemed, and flat-irons, dirty pairs of stays, candlesticks, Sunday trou-
> sers, tools, blankets and so forth are being fast removed from the
> shelves. . . . From byeways and alleyways and back-streets, fresh crowds
> every moment emerge. Stalls, shops, cellars are clustered round with critics
> and purchasers; cabmen drive slowly through the throng, shouting and
> swearing to the people to get out of the horse's way; and occasionally
> perhaps the melodious burst of a roaring chorus, surging out of the open
> windows of the Apollo, resounds loudly above the whole conglomeration
> of street noises.[87]

As with food, so with housing: those at the bottom end of the market received scant value for money. Wretched as it was, the accommodation inhabited by the poor accounted for anything up to a quarter or even a third of a labourer's wages, while for no more than one-sixth of their income the middle class were able to enjoy comfort, luxury and the 'pure breath of heaven' in the suburbs.[88] With economic circumstance conspiring against them, the working class were often forced to forgo the luxury of separate accommodation: the nuclear household, sacred cow of English social history, was too expensive for many families. Few couples outside the late marrying middle class could afford to live on their own immediately after marriage. As at Preston, most lived with kin or in lodgings for the first few years, an arrangement which reduced the rent burden and allowed earnings to be maximized: the young wife could continue working in the mill, leaving housework and baby-minding to the older woman of the house. In John Foster's comparative study, the proportion of families who economized on housing costs by living with relatives ranged from a third in Northampton, to a half in Oldham, and over two-thirds in South Shields, where seamen husbands were often absent for prolonged periods. Where the burden could not be shared with the family, the best alternative was to take in paying lodgers, an essential source of income for many widows. In Preston, where lodgers were present in 23 per cent of all households in 1851, landladies often served as absent kin, helping lodgers adjust to urban-industrial life. An effective means of reducing exposure to primary poverty, co-residence or 'huddling' tended to increase at times of economic depression and at critical stages in the family cycle – housing space was grossly overcrowded at such times and comparatively under-utilized at others.[89]

Variations of the truck system applied to the housing market, inflating costs for those dependent on their employer. Engels and Gaskell roundly condemned the 'cottage system' which prevailed in the show-piece country mills where rents were deducted from wages 'regardless of any market rate'. The overcharged occupants were expected to patronize the company shops and taverns, while the threat of eviction kept them submissive at work.[90] In the declining out-work sector, many handloom-weavers fell victim to the 'house-trucking' system, the economics of which were explained by a poor Leeds weaver who was given work by his landlord 'just to enable him to pay the rent [which was 3s weekly], and thus to make a good return for the money invested in the house; otherwise it would be cheaper for the master to get the stuff woven by power'.[91] Factory workers were sometimes 'clogged' in similar manner: irrespective of need, spinners at Bolton were compelled to rent a house from the millowner, in line with the rule that 'a key goes to each set of mules' – Reach discovered one enterprising young spinner who sublet his home for 6d a week to 'an individual who keeps pigs in it'.[92]

Housing costs (and standards) varied considerably between and within regions and occupations. Miners in the north-east were housed rent-free in dismal pit-rows, low-quality but stratified accommodation allocated in strict accordance with the economic interests of the coalowner, hence the mass evictions during the great pitmen's strikes of 1832 and 1844.[93] Coalminers in south Staffordshire paid high rents to small landlords for housing of a lower standard still, wretched cottages built 'amidst the rubbish waste'.[94] But nearby in the Potteries, the best-paid workers aspired to owner-occupancy, pooling their resources through building clubs, following the example of Birmingham where the local artisan elite were able to enjoy the security of their own two-up, two-down houses.[95] Unduly maligned, Feargus O'Connor's Land Plan was an ill-fated attempt to extend such collective self-help provision to the lower ranks of the working class by dispensing with the elitist 'first pay first served' priority system, relying instead on small weekly subscriptions and ballots to select the lucky occupants of the first homesteads.[96]

For working-class teenagers, clothes and accessories were the first call on funds after they had paid their contribution to the family income. Imitation coral necklaces and colourful bandannas were *de rigeur* in Oldham and Ashton-under-Lyne, conspicuous symbols of the brief independence enjoyed by mill girls before drab and subordinate dependence in the husband's home.[97] For the less fashion-conscious, cheap ready made items were available on credit from travelling representatives of large Scottish firms, but many poor families had to rely on cast-off, second-hand or stolen garments. Clothes were easily fenced or pawned, hence the many recorded cases of petty theft – in Manchester there were on average 210 reports a year of washing stolen from hedges and lines.[98] There was a lucrative trade in stolen clothing, particularly in the cities where debauched old women like 'Good Mrs Brown' practised the art of 'child stripping' – luring well-dressed young innocents to their dens where they were promptly divested of boots, clothes and anything else of saleable value. One notorious dealer in Macclesfield made a profitable business of cozening grammar school boys out of their spare garments.[99]

Unable to afford much on clothing in the normal course of events, working-class families spent heavily on dress whenever prospects and earnings improved – extra harvest earnings, for example, were often expended in this way. Good clothes were a tangible asset of considerable pledgeable value at the local pawnshop, the banking and credit system which enabled many working-class families to make ends meet each week. Pledged at the pawnbrokers first thing on Monday morning, the Sunday 'best' were redeemed as soon as wages were paid the following Saturday, a standard weekly cycle for 'steady respectable' families. Credit from the pawnbroker was not cheap: no matter how small the loan or how short a time the article was in pledge, the minimum rate – ½d a month on each 2s 6d – still applied. At the illegal 'dolly shops', patronized by the 'wives and daughters of the poorest labouring people', rates were even higher, around 2d a week for a loan of a shilling. Services were costly, but pawnbrokers were trusted in the community in a way that savings banks and other external organizations were not. Thus it was common practice for poor families to deposit their savings at the pledge shop, pawning notes for a few shillings cash. Inmates of low lodging houses frequently left their personal belongings at the local pawnbrokers to avoid the high risk of theft. During the 'brisk' season, most working-class families bought decent clothing and other 'luxury' items, strategic purchases which were later 'pawned off one by one, in Winter, to help tide over bad times'. Along with good coats, jewellery and watches were highly favoured in this regard. 'It's a garjian hainjel to a feller, is a good votch, ven you're hard up', a cockney compositor attested in the 1820s, having 'popped' his £5 'ticker' more than twenty times, raising over £40 in loans. Rather than standing idle in a savings account, money invested in material goods, Melanie Tebbutt notes, provided immediate enjoyment while being easily realizable.[100]

The stigma of pauperism, of dependence upon parish or philanthropy, was far more shameful to the respectable poor than the connotations of pledging. Like the Saturday night market, the pledge shop was the people's own, displaying a vibrant and resilient popular culture. Status-conscious city clerks and poorer professional people tried to conceal their dependence on the trade, but working-class women made the most of the friendly and supportive camaraderie during the weekly trips to the pledge shop where the manager or whoever took in the goods could generally be relied upon to play to the gallery. The pledge shop together with the corner shop, it has recently been suggested, were female counterparts to the 'masculine republic' of the pub.[101]

'Uncle's cards', as pledge tickets were euphemistically called, provided a simple if expensive means of coping with the weekly budget and lessening the impact of seasonal troughs. However, at times of general economic depression, credit from the pawnshop was soon exhausted. Pawnbrokers were the first to complain at the onset of depression which decimated their profitable regular weekly trade and undermined the second-hand market, making the disposal of forfeits, never an easy task, much more difficult.[102] For working-class families, faced at the best of times with high costs of living and borrowing, depression was a disastrous experience, reducing many to dire distress.

Poverty and distress

Not restricted to lowly and specific groups in the labour force, poverty was a regular feature of the life of almost *all* working families at some stages in their development, especially in old age or before young children started earning. Investigating conditions in the more favourable economic climate at the end of the nineteenth century, Rowntree was the first to identify this cycle of poverty and distress occurring at critical stages in life: as a child dependent on parents; as the parent of children too young to work; and finally and irretrievably when too old to earn a decent living. There were only two periods of brief and relative prosperity: as a wage-earning adolescent living at home, and later when one's own children became wage-earners themselves.[103]

Parents and relatives offered as much assistance as they could, particularly in the difficult years just after marriage. When couples were able to move out and set up in a house of their own, they generally stayed in the neighbourhood, relying on the support of nearby kin to provide the services – cooking, house managing and child-minding – which allowed them to maximize joint earnings. For those without relatives at hand, other primary networks offered support and assistance through life's difficult patches. In-migrants born in the same place tended to cluster together in industrial towns, helping each other out as they adjusted to urban-industrial living. When there were no 'co-villagers' or adjacent kin, neighbours often stepped in with short-term help and assistance.[104] Support could also be obtained through the barter economy, by the exchange of services and resources within the local community. The odd jobs undertaken by the widowed, the disabled and the elderly were well patronized, particularly in the close-knit pit villages of the north-east.[105]

This internal redistribution of resources impressed Mrs Gaskell, but middle-class political economists questioned the economic rationality of the thriftless altruism which prevailed among the poor in Mary Barton's Manchester. An exchange between equals, working-class mutual aid differed in form and function from middle-class charity: those who gave expected to become recipients themselves when the wheel of fortune – or the family cycle – took another turn.[106] Functional and effective, these primary welfare networks enabled those in difficulties to maintain their independence from middle-class philanthropy and the Poor Law, but resources were soon exhausted at times of general distress or cyclical depression.

Until the 1820s when the trade cycle asserted its rhythm of over-production and depression, distress was usually caused by high prices or high taxes, short-term consequences of harvest failure, wartime emergency finance or some other crisis exogenous to the standard of living debate. For the working class, living standards were under constant pressure during the lengthy war against Revolutionary and Napoleonic France. Government spending, financed by borrowing and sharply regressive indirect taxation, widened the gap between rich and poor and led to the 'stagflation syndrome': prices rose while industrial output slowed down.[107] The 'Luddite' years of 1811–12 were probably the worst: the collapse of the investment 'boomlet' of 1809–10, including such incautious speculation in untried overseas markets as the consignment of ice skates to Rio de Janeiro, was aggravated first by a poor harvest and then by the sudden closure of the American market.[108] Matters had barely begun to improve after prices peaked in 1813 before war gave way to peace without plenty. Military demobilization, the cessation of government orders and other transitional problems were compounded by the malevolence of the elements – the spring and summer of 1816 were the worst in recorded history.[109] For most agricultural labourers matters never improved. After the lengthy investment boom of 1793–1813, they were the victims of postwar over-capacity in agriculture. Reduced to day labourers, their earnings remained well below wartime levels when Caird drew his famous wages line in 1851.[110]

Once the immediate postwar crisis passed, other workers began to benefit from low prices and general deflation. But the advance in real wages was not steadily upwards: the trade cycle asserted its rhythm in the 1820s. After the investment boom burst in 1825 and financial panic spread through the banking system, 1826 was a year of short-time working, unemployment and distress. Relief funds were organized in many towns, and funds were sent north by the London Committee for the Relief of the Manufacturing Poor, a display of traditional charitable largesse which helped to preserve public order in Stockport, at least.[111] Elsewhere, substantial military reinforcements and large-scale arrests were required to quell riotous machine-breakers who directed their anger against the new powerlooms installed in the preceding boom years.[112] As the economy picked up, spinners and others resumed full-time working in the mills, but for the handloom weavers 1826 marked a turning-point from which they never recovered. Wages were driven steadily lower as the powerloom, formerly restricted to plain goods, became more widespread in producing an ever-widening range of quality cloths.[113]

The impact of cyclical depression on working-class incomes could be catastrophic. A survey of the 'fancy trade' around Huddersfield, undertaken in the depth of the depression of 1829, revealed that

13,226 people had to subsist on 2½d per day per head.[114] Trade remained indifferent until 1833 when a properly scrutinized survey of 8362 families (49,294 persons in all) in 35 handloom-weaving and other textile communities, 33 in Lancashire and two in Yorkshire, produced similar results. Out of a workforce of 23,947, some 2287 were unemployed, but the main reason for the pervasive distress was the low earnings of those still at work, the weekly average being a mere 3s 8⅝d. When parish relief was added and expenses for rent, fuel and lighting deducted, there was no more than 2¼d per head per day for food and clothing.[115]

The slump of 1841–2, following three or four years of deepening depression, was probably the most severe. In Bolton, distress spread from the mills, where 60 per cent were out of work, to all trades in the town – no less than 87 per cent of local bricklayers were unemployed. Of the workforce at Accrington, another cotton town, 1389 were fully employed at an average wage of 8s 8d per week; 1622 were partly employed at 4s 10d each, and 727 were totally unemployed and destitute. Block-printers' wages were 11s less than before the depression, a case highlighted by Alexander Somerville: 'Need you be told that with 17s there would be loaf-bread and butcher-meat and cheese and butter used, while with 6s there can be little more than oatmeal gruel, potatoes and salt.' In the course of his survey of the manufacturing districts, Somerville collected a large number of budgets from families, each consisting of the parents and four children, and these were then averaged to represent weekly incomes of 5s 6d, 10s, 15s 6d, and 25s 6d. Only in the two higher categories was anything available for meat or butter, cheese or beer: tea was also squeezed out in the lower budgets where the redeeming feature was the considerable expenditure on milk, long before its nutritional properties were known scientifically.[116] Things were little better in Liverpool despite its different economic structure: half the tailors and shoemakers were unemployed, as were 25 per cent of the skilled smiths and engineers in the Vauxhall district where total earnings – and the consumption of meat – fell to half the level of 1835.[117] The next downturn, in 1847–8, was less severe. Workers in the booming railway construction industry were not affected, but a trade union survey of 200,000 artisans and mechanics in London reported that only one-third were in full-time employment and their wages were inadequate; another one-third were 'half-employed' and in considerable distress; the remaining one-third were unemployed and suffering terribly.[118]

Different workers suffered in different ways at times of distress or depression, but the experience of additional hardship was common to all as the downward multiplier spread through the community.

Normally protected from seasonal fluctuations and minor setbacks, factory workers were put on short time or laid off altogether. For casual labourers, spells between work lengthened, while outworkers worked harder but still could not maintain their normal standards.[119] Those who were already struggling to make ends meet probably suffered worst of all. The elderly, widowed, sick and disabled figured prominently in the survey of the poor and unemployed in Bristol undertaken at the depth of the postwar depression in 1816. Some elderly workers still managed to survive without the parish, such as the redoubtable John Bussicott, an 85-year-old shoemaker who earned 4s 6d a week at his trade; others like John Lee, a 78-year-old tailor, were less fortunate – his earnings, his landlady reported, 'do not give him natural food'. As trade declined and lodgings were given up, an important source of income was withdrawn: John Daniel, a blind ex-labourer, 'used to pay his Rent by Lodgers but is now quite distressed'; many widows were similarly impoverished – one assured the overseer that she was 'glad to wash or do any thing but can get nothing to do.' Depression also brought an end to the casual earnings upon which many families depended: John Phillips, a 31-year-old labourer, out of work for 15 months on account of illness, was forced to approach the parish when his wife could no longer find enough work to scrape together a few shillings a week to keep themselves and their young child.[120]

Statistics suggest that property crime increased at hard times – from the period of postwar distress, when crime figures rose sharply, the peak of committals coincided with economic depression. Among those committed in the Black Country in the worst years of the 1830s and 1840s, there was a marked increase in the number of adults in their late twenties and thirties, workers who turned to illegal activity – 'survival crime' – when money and jobs were in short supply.[121] These were times of social and political fear, an anxiety which probably distorted the statistics as people were far more inclined to report offences and prosecute offenders. But it seems likely that theft and violence declined significantly in the second half of the nineteenth century when economic depression proved less dire – periods of severe unemployment no longer coincided with serious subsistence problems.[122]

3 Housing

By the end of the eighteenth century, one-third of the population was already urban. London, the administrative, commercial and cultural capital, was by far the largest city with 896,000 inhabitants. Not a centre of advanced technology or large-scale manufacturing, 'artisan' London concentrated on the finishing end of the production process, importing materials from the more industrialized parts of the country. Liverpool, the next largest city with 82,000 inhabitants, was primarily a seaport with a large casual dock labour force and some small-scale manufacturing. Then there were a number of fast-growing towns serving a variety of specialized manufacturing and other economic functions: seven towns had 50,000–82,000 inhabitants, 12 between 20,000 and 50,000, and 34 between 10,000 and 15,000. Over the next few years, urban growth continued at a relentless pace, producing the great cities of the industrial north and midlands. Bradford grew from 13,000 in 1801 to 104,000 in 1851, Sheffield from 46,000 to 135,000, Leeds from 53,000 to 172,000, Birmingham from 71,000 to 233,000, Manchester from 75,000 to 303,000, and Liverpool, preserving its provincial primacy, from 82,000 to 376,000. By 1851, when 54 per cent of the population was classified as urban, roughly a quarter of the people lived in great towns of over 100,000 inhabitants, and it is these major urban centres, industrial and otherwise, which have attracted most attention in the standard of living debate.

Within these large towns and cities market forces were allowed free and unregulated rein in the provision of working-class housing: there was none of the planning, regulation and intervention which ensured the exclusive elegance of other fast-growing urban developments, the salubrious spa, resort and residential towns. Speculative 'jerry building' produced a 'cellular and promiscuous' residential style of inward-looking, dead-end alleys, courts and blindbacks, a 'perfect wilderness of foulness'.[1] Offended by the stench, the urban middle class hastened to vacate central areas in pursuit of the 'pure breath of heaven' in the suburbs, leaving their once desirable residences to be hastily converted – made-down was the apt expression used – into innumerable sub-divisions for working-class occupancy. Out in the suburbs, aristocratic landlords were more likely to welcome 'respectable' tenants wanting large houses with big gardens who paid relatively low rents than working-class or industrial residents who would pay more rent but look less decorative.[2]

Profit and social snobbery thus produced a pattern of residential segregation – the slum and the suburb – which aroused the anxiety of middle-class critics of the 'Condition of England'. By fleeing the city, they had left the working class dangerously unsupervised and undisciplined. 'Disorganic' Manchester was the shock city of the time, with a pattern of spatial segregation which kept the classes completely apart. Engels had 'never seen so systematic a shutting out of the working-class from the thoroughfares, so tender a concealment of everything which might affront the eye and nerves of the bourgeoisie.'[3] But segregation of this order was far from typical. In Leeds and Liverpool, the poor lived in courts and cellars only a few yards from front-houses occupied by tradesmen and merchants. Small-town employers lived among their employees: even if they moved out to suburban mansions they were never far away – nowhere was beyond walking distance in early Victorian Bolton, Oldham or Huddersfield.[4] Freemen land-rights and other restrictions often hindered outward expansion from the older towns, leading to intense in-filling and overcrowding of the central area: in Nottingham, for example, some 4200 people were crammed into an area of a mere 220 square yards.[5] In this regard, Birmingham, a development of the early modern period, enjoyed a substantial advantage over nearby Coventry: there was no shortage of land for in-filling in and around the central area.[6] For the most part, early nineteenth-century development was too small-scale and too dependent on in-filling to produce a rigid, segregated pattern. However, the rich employed a variety of strategies, consciously or unconsciously, to avoid social interaction. Until stirred by the Condition of England question, contact with the poor, close as they were, was minimal.[7]

While middle-class social critics anxiously explored conditions in the slums, urban workers seem not to have protested at the way they were housed. Not much is known about working-class attitudes – the history of housing has still to be written 'from below' – but the absence of overt protest can be explained in a number of ways.[8] For a start, urban housing, particularly the new back-to-backs, compared favourably with wretched rural accommodation. More important, stepwise progression up the urban hierarchy, the standard pattern of migration, prepared workers for city conditions, an acculturation process often assisted by kinship and other networks.

Rural housing was very poor, particularly in the 'open' villages, refuge of those displaced by 'improving' and parsimonious landlords: eviction, clearance and enclosure tidied up estates and reduced the poor rate burden in 'closed' parishes by denying settlement rights to under-employed labourers. A fortunate few were rehoused in model villages designed by paternalist squires. Workers on the gang system and other day labourers were forced into 'open' parishes, rural shanty towns like Disraeli's Marney, 'a metropolis of agricultural labour'. Here sanitary arrangements were primitive or non-existent; overcrowding was as high as in common lodging-houses; and the construction materials – earth floors and unceilinged thatched roofs – were markedly inferior to urban brick and stone.[9]

Parish-assisted migrants apart, it was rare for labourers and their families to move directly from the countryside to the big city. The general pattern of migration was one of short distance moves, of stepwise progression up the urban hierarchy which extended from the small rural town to the great metropolis. Preston had a large immigrant population in 1851, most of whom came from industrial villages and small towns within a 30-mile radius, and many of whom were destined to move on again to be replaced by others.[10] Each move up the hierarchy helped workers to adjust: there was no 'culture shock' for those who finally settled in large towns and cities. Aided by tramping networks and their knowledge of employment opportunities, skilled workers moved the furthest with the least difficulty – skilled glassworkers, for example, converged on booming St Helens from the north-east, Scotland and the west midlands. Irrespective of specific job opportunities, unskilled workers tended to move straight to the nearest large labour market, within which they often displayed considerable local mobility.[11]

For in-migrants who arrived without adequate means or contacts, temporary accommodation of the lowest standard was available in common lodging-houses. These wretched establishments, 'temporary asylums of want and depravity', catered mainly for travelling folk, hawkers, navvies and wayfarers with enough cash in their pockets to afford up to 3d a night for a bed or 'shake-down' shared with others – impecunious fellow travellers slept rough on brickfields or in 'Dry Arch' hotels under bridges and viaducts, and spent cold winter nights in charitable refuges, or in the dreaded casual ward of the workhouse where hard labour and forcible detention prevailed.[12] In 1832, there were over 300 common lodging houses in Manchester alone, many of them congregated in the incongruously-named 'Angel-meadow' district, the 'lowest, most filthy, most unhealthy, and most wicked locality'. Reach's investigations revealed that in a typical room about 14 feet by 12, 'more than a score of vagrants often pigged together, dressed and undressed, sick and well, sober and drunk'.[13] At Macclesfield the first inquiry by the Local Board of Health in 1852 uncovered 244 lodging-houses, many of them dens of filthiness and disease: one house had three bedrooms, the first containing 16 people sleeping on the floor, the second 12, and the third used as a privy, 'the boarded floor being literally covered with human ordure'.[14] Newly-arrived migrant families moved out as soon as they could, but all too often lodging houses became permanent homes for the near-destitute and near-criminal. Grossly overcrowded and notoriously promiscuous, common lodging-houses were the first category of working-class accommodation to come under legislative control.

Lodging-houses offered temporary shelter: back-to-backs provided a cheap and quick long-term solution, enabling the rapidly growing industrial towns of the midlands and north to keep pace with the contagion of numbers.[15] Hastily constructed in uniform rows, these one-up, one-down houses allowed no cross- or through-ventilation as there was access to air and light on one side only. The 'back' house faced on to a narrow court (facing another double row of houses), where privies and pumps were located, accessible from narrow passages between blocks of front houses. Condemned by sanitary reformers, the layout proved popular with working-class occupants since each family had its own front door and 'defensible space', separate accommodation at an affordable rent. The charge varied from 2s 6d–4s weekly according to size and region, while 'through' terraced houses cost from 5s to 7s 6d a week, beyond the means of all but the aristocracy of labour.[16] Cheap and easy to build, the rapid provision of back-to-backs reduced the persons:house ratio despite the continuing flood of migrants into the towns: during the 1820s the figure in Stockport fell from 6.4 to 5.1, but here the new houses were often no more than 12 x 15 feet.[17] The economic advantages of back-to-back construction were apparent not only to speculative builders but also to artisan building societies whose members aspired to individual owner-occupancy – the first back-to-backs in Leeds, where the style was to enjoy remarkable longevity, were built by artisans' terminating building societies.[18]

Outside the industrial towns, back-to-backs were less common and/or less beneficial. Overcrowding and mortality rates remained dangerously high amid the rookeries and cellars of the largest cities and seaports. Liverpool exhibited the worst form of back-to-back development, built on all four sides round undrained, unsewered and unventilated courts which served as 'open cesspools, dunghills, or "middens" . . . places of deposit for refuse from all the houses'. The only point in their favour was the persons:house ratio – 5.20 for the court house areas in 1841 when the overall city figure was 6.95. Rents were high in Liverpool, putting back-to-backs beyond the reach of many new immigrants and casual labourers. To cater for the bottom of the market, speculative builders offered the cheap alternative of the purpose-built cellar. Unlike conversions elsewhere, Liverpool's cellars were specifically (and unashamedly) built for residential use: by 1841, just before the belated introduction of restrictive regulations, there were no less than 7307 separate dwellings of this type. Unavoidably damp and unhealthy, these subterranean cellars, no more than ten or twelve feet square, were the lowest form of accommodation.[19] In London, where the back-to-back was almost unknown, jerry-built tenement houses and made-down mansions were subdivided into drastically overcrowded 'rookeries', 'the abodes of the improvident, the vagrant, the vicious and the unfortunate'. Here rooms were the norm of working-class housing, two rooms – the irreducible minimum of respectability – costing between 2s 6d and 4s a week. The persons: house ratio stood at 7.03 in 1801 (when the national average was 5.6) and rose ineluctably to 7.72 in 1851 by which time the population of the capital had risen to 2,363,000.[20]

The quality of working-class housing varied across the country. Standards were probably highest in manufacturing towns with large numbers of well-paid artisans. The typical artisan's cottage in Sheffield was brick-built, slate-roofed, with a cellar, living room, first-floor bedroom and second attic bedroom.[21] Birmingham had a number of so-called 'three-quarters' houses: built in pairs, each house had a ground floor parlour and kitchen, two bedrooms to the first floor and two more on the second, and an individual privy and brewhouse at the rear, all for 7s a week.[22] Within each town, accommodation ranged in quality and cost. Top of the market in Stockport at a vote-bearing rental of £10 per annum were houses with cellars and workshops attached; two-up, two-down cottages were available with privies at £8 per annum and without privies at £6–7; one-up, one-down back-to-backs rented at £5–6; cellars – 11.3 per cent of dwellings in 1831 – cost £2–4 a year; and a bed in a common lodging house cost 1d a night, or the equivalent of about £1 10s a year.[23] Graduated standards were the rule in employer-provided housing: even the dreary pit villages of the north-east boasted a 'Quality Row' reserved for deputies, overmen and the principal waggon-drivers.[24]

Although standards of accommodation varied, the correlation between housing quality and occupational status was generally weak, mediated by household income and the family cycle. The crucial factor was household income not male breadwinner status: this income depended on the number of wage-earners, which in turn depended upon a household's stage in the life-cycle.[25] These variables applied not only to rented accommodation but also to some employer-provided housing, particularly in the north-east pit villages:

A young married couple go, after their union, into one of the back or lean-to houses. Here they remain until they have a young family around them. Then they are probably transferred to one of the second class dwellings, of one room with an attic, and by the time the boys begin to work in the pit the father can claim a first-class or double house. If the family consists wholly or principally of girls, they must make shift in the second-rate house. Parents with growing boys have always the preference in obtaining work in a coal-pit, and houses in a pit-village: indeed married men without families are sometimes turned out of their own into inferior homes to make room.[26]

In large towns and cities, family and household factors precluded residential segregation by occupation or status: similar houses contained 'the whole spectrum of social classes'.[27] Upward residential mobility was not always attractive given the ever-present threat of unemployment and distress. At times of relative comfort, families preferred not to run the risk of taking on more expensive accommodation or of moving away from primary welfare networks. When there was money to spare, it was used not for housing itself, but to purchase realizable assets – 'respectable' furniture and ornaments.

During the industrial revolution, before the emergence of the 'classic' working-class neighbourhood, the sense of community was strongest in areas neglected in the historical debate, the out-townships which encircled large manufacturing and commercial centres. Here occupational solidarity reinforced communal loyalty, a combination which pushed these 'localities' to the forefront of national working-class campaigns.[28] Alongside old superstitions and customs, new religious and radical doctrines flourished[29] – Ashton, a typical factory out-township, was renowned for its Southcottianism, Mormonism and militant radicalism.[30] Much was lost when these culturally distinct communities were integrated into urban connurbations.

4 Work

Not a linear progression to large-scale factory production, industrialization in Britain did not necessarily entail the deskilling of labour. Reduced to wage-earning proletarians without rights to the materials and product of their labour, skilled workers fought hard to retain residual control over the 'labour process', over the speed, intensity and rhythm of work. Through a variety of strategies – cultural and linguistic as well as organizational and economic – they managed to 'de-commodify' labour, to defend much of their workplace autonomy against the new time and labour discipline favoured by political economists, preachers and employers.[1] Even in new forms of work organization, they often succeeded in recomposing skill and safeguarding their status, despite 'deskilling' technology and the increased division of labour. But in defending or reconstructing skilled status, their actions were divisive: not just a line drawn against employers, 'property' in skill was a frontier to be held against unfair or unskilled competition in the labour market. Skill as a property became skill as patriarchy, an appropriation which left women defenceless against the degradation of labour. Lacking the ideological and technological apparatus to assert managerial authority, employers welcomed these reformulations of skill and gender, hierarchical constructions which solved the problem of labour discipline. Compulsion, the inefficient and much-resented management of the early factory system, was abandoned in favour of benevolent paternalism, a strategy designed to elicit deferential consent at the workplace.[2]

The experience of work varied dramatically amid the combined and uneven development of the industrial revolution. Some occupations (engineering is the best studied example) were transformed and expanded by new technology and industrial change. At the other extreme were the poor handloom-weavers, victims first of over-stocking then of technological redundancy. Luxury trades and personal services continued largely unaltered, a condition which also applied in most of the food trades until the retail revolution in the late nineteenth century. Other trades supplying the basic demands of the domestic population enjoyed no such continuity. Workers in shoemaking, tailoring, furniture-making and similar trades were less vulnerable to technological displacement than handloom-weavers, but they were put under considerable pressure by changes in trade organization, work practices and the division of labour. Sexual relations reached crisis point as men struggled to retain 'honourable' status by all sorts of exclusionist means. Even so, increasing numbers fell into the sweated sector, a cruel inversion of the traditional artisan progression to independent production. Compelled to undercut traditional prices and practices in a desperate effort to survive in a fiercely competitive market, 'independent' garret-masters sweated themselves, their wives and their families.[3]

Across the honourable trades, capitalization prevented journeymen from setting up as small masters, but in the workshops – where handicraft skill was still at a premium – they were usually able to uphold the independence of 'aristocratic' status. For this purpose, the rhetoric of custom – the invention of 'tradition' to sanction and legitimize current practice – offered the best defence against unwanted changes from above. In a language dismissed by the Webbs and other pioneers of 'institutional' labour history, workers deliberately mystified the workplace, excluding employers and their market calculations from the opaque world of custom, tradition, craft mystery and skill, a separate culture upheld by secrecy, theatrical ceremony and when necessary, ritualized violence.[4] With or without formal organization, skilled workers in the trades defended their position at the 'frontier of control', but they could not always limit the employers' jurisdiction. At times of general crisis in the social relations of production, employers turned to the state and the law to enforce their control of the production process, at which point workshop struggles, previously small-scale local affairs, assumed national political importance with inter-trade cooperation and substantial trade involvement in radical protest. This was to be a recurrent phenomenon in English labour history as economic growth proceeded through a series of 'long waves' each of which involved a decisive shift in the extent of workshop subordination, when employers finally implemented their plans for the intensification of labour, the dilution of skilled labour and the introduction of new machinery.[5] Following the collapse of general unionism in the 1830s, the worst consequences were probably experienced in the building trades where 'general contractors' acquired the power to order and organize the work and labour force almost as they pleased, paying no heed to the union or to customary notions of wages, hours and output.[6] Real wages may have risen at this time of structural transformation but it would seem to have been at the cost of harder work and worsening conditions, the deleterious effects of which need to be assessed in the standard of living debate.

Most of the debate about labour discipline itself has concentrated on areas where manual modes were superseded by mechanization and the modern factory system. Before the introduction of machinery, early factories such as Wedgwood's Etruria works enabled employers to achieve greater quality control and efficiency through the synchronization of labour within a supervised chain of production: the actual pace of work, however, was still determined by the workers. In the new textile mills, power-driven machinery dictated a new and merciless rhythm, the first victims of which were the infant pauper apprentices, the 'white-slaves' sent from urban workhouses to remote water-driven mills. Away from public scrutiny and magistrates' supervision in these 'dismal solitudes of torture and of many a murder', the poor foundlings suffered every kind of punishment to keep them working from five in the morning till ten or eleven at night when they were unceremoniously 'huddled together in the "prentice house" like as many sheep waiting to be shorn'.[7] The development of steam power brought this system to an end as employers were able to relocate in the towns where the local labour force, accustomed to traditional and irregular work patterns, had to be instructed in the new discipline previously beaten into the defenceless pauper apprentices. Here the mill-owners favoured coercion rather than reward, relying upon compulsion to keep workers at work for long hours at low pay, an 'extensive' system of labour utilization which made full if inefficient use of costly investment in plant and machinery.[8]

The system of compulsion began with stringent fines for late arrival. Once on the factory floor, workers had no right to leave without a written certificate from the 'cotton *satrap* or overlooker', a form of 'imprisonment' exposed by the *Poor Man's Advocate* while investigating 'The Beauties of a Cotton Factory':

> Here are, at least, 1,000 human beings confined in an atmosphere heated to a degree of seldom less than 78 of Fahrenheit's thermometer, during 12 hours of the 24, and being sometimes as high as from 80 to 90 degrees, not one of whom can get so much as a drink of water without the consent of some ignorant and insolent 'Jack in office' . . . for *an hour after* commencing work, and for *an hour before* leaving it off, no such certificate can be obtained under any circumstances.

None of the convivial culture of the workshop was allowed to interrupt the pace of factory work, a point of much regret to leaders of the short-time movement – 'We have exchanged "footings", and other occasions of innocent enjoyment and recreation for one continued round of gloomy, unceasing, and ill-requited toil.'[9] The proscription of old customs and traditions extended into areas outside the factory, a comprehensive strategy of employer interventionism in accordance with Andrew Ure's dictum that it was 'excessively the interest of every mill-owner to organize his moral machinery on equal sound principles with his mechanical, for otherwise he will never command the steady hands, watchful eyes, and prompt cooperation, essential to excellence of product.'[10]

Relentless toil led to serious accidents, bodily deformities and physical disabilities, the details of which were gruesomely described by critics of the factory system, but it was the moral consequences of factory labour – the 'premature indulgence of sexual appetite' – that caused them the greatest concern. Factories, the surgeon Gaskell rued, were 'a prolific source of moral delinquency. The stimulus of a heated atmosphere, the contact of opposite sexes, the example of license upon the animal passions – all have conspired to produce a very early development of sexual appetencies.'[11] 'In the manufacturing districts', Reach regretted, 'everything moved quicker than in other parts of the world. The child toils sooner, attains physical development sooner, marries sooner, has children in his turn sooner, and, in the present sanitary state of matters, dies sooner.'[12]

According to the critics, the moral evils of factory employment were aggravated by the absence of proper family life, a point much discussed in subsequent historical debate. In an influential exercise in sociological history, N. J. Smelser argued that technological changes in work organization in the cotton industry in the 1820s caused a crisis within the family which was not resolved until its traditional roles and functions became more specialized and differentiated. The introduction of larger mules brought an end to the 'transitional system' of the family in the factory: henceforth spinners required so many piecers that they were forced to recruit from outside the family. At the same time, the family economy of handloom-weaving was destroyed by powerloom factories which provided employment only for young women, whose child assistants, the dressers, were hired directly by factory masters.[13] Smelser's argument, however, overlooks some important demographic factors. Even before the introduction of larger mules, few spinners would have had enough children of sufficient age to piece for them: spinning was a skilled occupation for fit young men whose working life in the job was relatively short. On the weaving side, few of the new factory workers came from traditional 'undifferentiated' families: there was no sudden and catastrophic shift from the family handloom to the factory floor. Most of the young workers attracted to the cotton towns and factories came from agricultural labour, service and other occupations in which the family did not work together as a productive unit. In the case of the Parish Assisted Migrants, labourers despatched north by rural poor law authorities, employment in the mills brought previously scattered families together again.[14]

Although Smelser misrepresented the problem, social relations in the factory were in crisis until the new-found symmetry of the 1840s between family and work. At this late stage, men entered the weaving factories in large numbers, recruiting and paying their own assistants. The family economy was duly restabilized and male authority reasserted, a necessary precondition for the success of the new employer initiatives analysed by Patrick Joyce. Abandoning the inefficient coercion of the past, new model employers displayed a benevolent paternalism which transformed the culture and conditions of the workplace. Mediated through the male authority structure of the factory, employer paternalism elicited the deferential consent of the workers.[15]

Before this shift in employer strategy, work in the factories was unremitting and unrewarding. It was the absence of any alternative that kept the workers in the factories, not some intrinsic satisfaction with their work. Marxist historians have been taken to task for over-emphasizing compulsion and ignoring voluntary submission to the wage bargain, but there is little evidence to suggest that the early factory workers entered the mills in happy anticipation of deriving pleasure from the work or from the sociability of labour – there was 'little if any talking, and little disposition to talk,' Reach observed in the Manchester mills. It was not at the workplace but in the freedom of the streets that mill-workers enjoyed conviviality and good cheer, chatting and laughing together around 'peripatetic establishments of hot coffee and cocoa vendors' until summoned to labour by the dreaded factory bell.[17]

In other work environments, where workers enjoyed greater independence, the workplace was the site for a range of informal social and cultural activities, from horseplay and practical jokes to prayer meetings and political discussion groups. Social identities were sometimes constructed around work culture, often in rhetorical and mythologized form: Lancashire handloom-weavers and the pitmen and keelmen of the north-east were among the most celebrated figures in local dialect literature.[18] But work was seldom the defining characteristic of working-class autobiographies: a necessary means to an end, work was accorded less significance than childhood, education, family and interpersonal relations, and popular leisure activities.[19]

5   Popular Culture

Throughout the standard of living debate, pessimists have condemned the destruction of traditional customs and merrie pastimes: the new time and work discipline separated work and leisure, leaving a cultural vacuum in the new industrial towns until the none too welcome advent of commercialized mass leisure at the end of the nineteenth century. While certainly under attack, popular culture proved remarkably resilient, adaptable and innovative. The patronage and protection of certain wealthy groups ensured the survival of old sports and pastimes despite prohibitionist pressure from evangelicals and other moral interventionists. When rich patrons withdrew as social segregation progressed, publicans and other small-scale capitalists stepped forward to promote hedonistic delights, old and new, on a profitable, commercial basis. What they offered was in no sense a filtered-down version of some 'higher' culture, a vulgarized form of bourgeois spa town culture. Through cheap beer, lurid sensationalism and vicarious violence, they catered for an audience beyond the reach of middle-class social control, an audience that refused to be deferential, serious or rational – the pompous and puritan, indeed, were the main targets for popular mirth and mockery. Innovators not emulators, publican-entrepreneurs allowed popular culture to adapt, adjust and develop new forms – music halls, melodramas, pantomimes, circuses, travelling menageries – which soon proved so popular that they attracted a large middle-class audience. As middle-class schemes of 'rational recreation' failed to elicit popular interest, the cultural flow was upward not downward.[1]

The prominent role of the publican is hardly surprising given the central significance of drink in working customs and leisure patterns. Workplace drinking was an occupational necessity for those who were subjected to dust and dehydration, to intense heat and physical exertion. In such cases, beer was the obvious refreshment: safer than water, cheaper than hot beverages, beer was prized for its wholesomeness, particularly as a generous girth was considered a sign of strength and health, and there was no fashionable discrimination against the rotund.[2] Besides refreshment, drink served as the symbol of comradeship at work, the means by which newcomers were accepted and initiated in the protective workshop culture. Prohibited in the new cotton factories, 'footings' were standard practice in the trades, with every new arrival expected to 'fork out the tin' for a pot of 'half and half' or whatever tipple was the custom on such occasions.[3] Before gaining final admission to the exclusive craft circle, apprentices were expected to treat their instructors: plumbers extracted drink-money when the apprentice cast his first sheet of lead, the blockcutters when he cut his first printing block.[4] For those who sought entry to an 'honourable' trade by a less orthodox route, the charges were considerably higher. William Lovett, the former Cornish rope-maker, was forced to subsidize the drinking habits of his new London workmates to the sum of 7s or 8s a week until they finally admitted him into the ranks of the honourable cabinetmakers.[5]

Similar rites of passage applied in the mining areas: in the Cornish tin mines, for example, a treat was expected when a boy first took on a man's work, and promotion to sump-man, pit-man or captain carried a similar alcoholic obligation.[6] Drinking was no less common in the industrial districts, where the calendar of drinking customs and rituals helped to relieve the monotony of work. Heavy drinking was a feature of the 'wake' suppers when lighting began in the autumn and of the 'slecking-out' suppers in March when there was no further need for candles and lamps. Any break in routine was an occasion for convivial inebriation – in the woollen districts there was always plenty of drinking at the changing from one loom to another. But given the systems of work organization in these parts, drinking customs tended to be community- rather than workshop-based. Drinking 'fines' were demanded from those unfortunate enough to be spotted at a time of some personal embarrassment or self-consciousness, such as wearing a new suit of clothes or out courting for the first time when the 'bull shilling' had to be paid.[7]

Within the culture of work, the pub served many functions as pay station, labour exchange, port of call for those on tramp, venue for initiation rites and promotion celebrations, but it was also where most men chose to spend their leisure time, drinking with their workmates. This was particularly the case on 'St Monday', that much prized assertion of independence in the face of the new time and labour discipline. Most workers who could afford to uphold the custom spent the day drinking and gambling, leaving the women to get on with the weekly washing and cleaning, although self-taught botanists and entomologists took to the countryside, and Spitalfields silk-weavers repaired to their allotments until hard times forced them to forgo the pleasures of pigeon-flying and tulip growing.[8] Down at the ale-house, all the traditional bar sports and wagers were on offer – brasses, quoits, skittles, pitch and toss, puff and dart, dominoes and "'shuvving the penny,'' "marrowing each other's coins," or "odd-man-ing"'.[9] Publicans also arranged some more exciting attractions for their large Monday clientele, most notably prize-fights and animal fights, bloody contests which remained extremely popular despite the gradual withdrawal of gentry patronage and the hostility of evangelical and humanitarian reformers. There were dog- and cock-fights nearly every Monday afternoon in the pubs in and around Birmingham where 'St Monday' displayed a remarkable longevity into the second half of the nineteenth century.[10] Until these sports were forced underground by effective legislation, the publican stood forward to champion his customers' rights against the meddlesome interference and class prejudice of those who opposed the dog- and cock-fights of the poor but ignored the foxhunting and game-shooting of the rich.[11]

The class divide was less clear-cut where pugilism was concerned. Here the new humanitarian and evangelical fervour did not deter those with means from following 'the fancy'. Protected by powerful social groups, prize-fighting was organized on a highly commercial basis with full-time professional fighters, specialized newspapers and a souvenir industry to celebrate the triumphs of the great regional and national heroes, Tom Crib, Tom Spring, Dutch Sam and the like, stars who had served their apprenticeship in local pub fights, the bedrock of the sport. Through well-established networks of pubs – many of which were owned by ex-pugilists who had survived the rigours and dangers of the profession without making it to the top – the bets and other arrangements were made for the great contests, secretly organized on the borders of counties where the circumscribed authorities had the greatest difficulty in dispersing the assembled thousands. With the advent of more efficient policing in the mid-Victorian period the great prize-fights came to an end, but pugilism in one form or another continued in many pubs.[12] In like manner, wrestling, a favourite Cornish sport, survived both the withdrawal of gentry patronage and the wrath of the local Methodists, thanks to the weekly matches promoted by publicans on 'Mazed Monday' as it was known in these parts.[13]

Weekly pleasures continued, timed to conform to the urban routine of a structured weekend – a working Saturday, a 'domestic' Sunday and an 'outdoor' Monday, the day deliberately selected for crowd occasions, sporting, recreational and political.[14] Annual festivities – the saturnalian calendar of fairs, feasts, wakes and revels – attracted greater censure from the proselytes of the new morality, discipline and order. Carnival, an important safety-valve for the release of pent-up tensions in traditional hierarchical societies, was an offensive anachronism for those whose system of social control relied upon popular education and 'rational recreation', upon the inculcation of those virtues of morality and political economy which would facilitate progress and 'improvement'.[15]

As some social critics acknowledged, there was often a respectable family side to traditional festivities. In Samuel Bamford's Middleton, new year was a time for domestic hospitality, family sharing and neighbourly fraternization, preceded by a commendably thorough cleaning of house and loom shop before the ale was tapped and the currant loaf sliced out.[16] Elsewhere in the north, 'mumming' festivities were still held at new year, a reversal ritual in which men and women exchanged clothes and visited each other's houses, demanding drink and money from the rich *en route*, a tradition practised in Bradford down to the 1860s.[17] Pancakes were enjoyed with neighbours on Shrove Tuesday, the next celebration in the Middleton calendar, but *mardi gras* was best known for the notorious annual game of street football in Derby where anything up to 1000 people joined in the rough-and-tumble as the play surged through the streets, down alleyways, across gardens, in and out of the river, leaving a trail of physical injuries, petty vandalism and much heavy drinking. After several unsuccessful attempts at suppression, the local authorities finally brought an end to the custom in the mid-1840s when they called in a troop of cavalry.[18] Simnel cake and mulled ale were the specialities of the day on 'Cymbalin Sunday' or mid-Lent Sunday, after which came Easter, a boisterous and saturnalian affair in Middleton with 'peace-egging' – demands for money or ale by young men dressed in female clothes – and the mock election of a lord mayor, a suitably paralytic lord of misrule. Festivities concluded on Easter Wednesday with White Apron Fair, when women in their finery were conducted to the ale-house, 'where they generally finished by a dance, and their inamoratos by a bottle or two, and their consequences, bruised hides and torn clothes'. May-Day, or 'Mischief-neet' as it was known locally, was set aside for the ritual settling of grudges. At Whitsun there were dances, trips to the races, and 'ale-house fuddles', although some still observed the practice of 'Whitsun ales', clubbing together with neighbours and friends 'to purchase malt which was brewed by one selected from the party, and drunk at one of the houses'. This was small beer, however, by comparison with rural areas like Oxfordshire where the erection of the maypole marked the beginning of the 'Whit-Ales', a carnival of drinking, dancing, fighting and sexual licence lasting at least a week if not a fortnight.[19]

Middleton's main carnival of the year was the August 'wakes', the summer 'rush-bearing'. The Lancashire wakes provide perhaps the best example of the survival and adaptation of popular customs during the industrial revolution. They originated in the procession of rush-carts to the parish church to mark its annual dedication when the floor would be strewn with rushes in preparation for the cold, wet winter months. Long after it had lost its purpose, the procession continued as an annual event, with morris dancers and the Queen of the Wake leading the convoy of elaborate rush-carts, the cost of which was generally defrayed by donations from the local gentry and employers. When such patronage was removed, publicans subsidized the construction and decoration of the carts, a shrewd investment in tradition.[20] By Victorian times, bull-baiting and other brutal blood sports associated with the wakes had come to an end – by this time too the moral reformers, backed by RSPCA inspectors, a troop of dragoons and reinforcements from the Metropolitan Police, had finally managed to suppress the most notorious and tumultuous bull-run of all, the annual Stamford run.[21] But there were plenty of other attractions at the northern wakes: pedestrianism or race-running, inter-communal violence with pitched battles between the crews of rival rush-carts, and the special entertainments laid on by publicans at what was their busiest and most profitable time of the year. Their grounds provided the venue for such festive sports and wagers as climbing the greasy pole, chasing the greasy pig, smock racing and eating scalding porridge. To attract families and their visitors away from the home-brew they offered singing rooms, dancing saloons and other forms of convivial entertainment.

The wakes were a time when town and city workers travelled out to the out-townships and industrial villages, reversing the Whitsuntide flow when 'country cousins' ventured into the big city – Whit Sunday in Bolton was known as 'Gaping Sunday' on account of the number of awestruck villagers who came to see the sights and enjoy the fair.[22] New steamboats transported the Liverpool working class in their thousands across the Mersey, transforming the village wakes at Tranmere and Hale into great proletarian festivals. Later to carry whole communities to the seaside for the wakes holiday, the new railways brought in larger crowds of relatives and friends to enjoy the hospitality, the publican's special entertainments and all the fun of the fair.

Crowds of all ages delighted in the treats and freaks, thrills and spills and other pleasures of the fairground, a 'kind of love market' for local teenagers.[23] Away from the travelling circuit of wakes and northern 'tides', some fairs – long since shorn of religious significance – fell victim to prohibitionist pressure. After a lengthy campaign of attrition, the Methodists on the Common Council succeeded in bringing London's greatest fair, 'old Bartlemy', to a close after they had put up the rent, limited its duration and moved the site.[24] Thereafter, the more astute showmen turned their attention to the provision of entertainment in permanent specialist locations, capitalizing on the need for amusements in the large urban areas while dissociating the business from the connotations of annual excess. The circus was one such development, achieving such success that there were permanent amphitheatres in most large provincial towns by the 1820s, by which time this new form of popular entertainment was attracting large middle-class audiences and royal patronage. There was also a travelling circuit through which links with the fairs were maintained. No less popular than the circuses were the travelling menageries, highly commercial operations, the most successful of which, run by the showman Wombwell, made a number of royal command performances.[25]

The showmen also played an important entrepreneurial role in the great expansion of popular theatre. Banished from the towns, popular theatre had been kept alive throughout the eighteenth century in tents and booths at fairs and race meetings, from which testing-ground the licensed 'legitimate' theatres, metropolitan and provincial, often recruited their best acting talent – Edmund Kean electrified Drury Lane in 1814 with a style learnt in the hard round of fairground and barnstorm acting. As well as new talent, the fairs introduced new dramatic forms: the pantomime and the melodrama, the repertoire of nineteenth-century theatre, first acquired popularity in the showmen's booths and tents. There was more than a hint of saturnalia in pantomime – the humbling of the mighty and the elevation of the clown – an entertainment for high days and holidays. In melodrama, old moral battles merged with new class conflicts – the Gothic villain in 'Black Ey'd Susan', the melodrama which introduced the convention of the miraculous last-minute reprieve from the gallows, was not merely a religious hypocrite but also a capitalist landlord. If not a fully-fledged working-class cultural form, the popular theatre of melodrama and pantomime, which soon attracted large middle-class audiences, gave vent to grievances against landowners and landlords, employers and the wealthy, the pompous and the puritan.[26]

The theatre riots of the early nineteenth century signified the arrival of an audience at odds with the refinement of the licensed theatres whose monopoly was finally removed in 1843. When the radical leader 'Orator' Hunt was physically ejected from the Theatre Royal, Manchester by a group of socialites and army officers, the management decided to keep the doors firmly closed, much to the annoyance of the 'Lancashire lads' who assembled in specially selected gangs the following evening in the hope of flexing their muscles, clogs and cudgels against the offending dandies.[27] The worst violence occurred at Covent Garden when the theatre reopened after fire in 1809 with higher prices and more private boxes: order was not restored until professional pugilists, specially hired by the management, employed assault and battery tactics in the pit.[28] Across the river, there were better arrangements for the popular audience: at the 'Victory', the Royal Victoria later the Old Vic, the pleasures of melodrama, farce and burlesque could be enjoyed for half-price admission after 8.30 p.m., hence the popular refrain 'Ven he's sitting in his glory/Half-price at the Victory'.[29] Up in the north, popular theatre proved a great commercial success, particularly for Billy Purvis, a travelling showman and stage 'Geordie' turned impresario and manager with a string of permanent theatres at Newcastle, Whitehaven, Carlisle and Greenock.[30]

Even more successful than the new popular theatre was the Victorian music hall which developed out of the pub via the 'free and easy' and the 'Cock and Bull' social gathering. These early singing saloons were designed quite simply to generate more custom and increase the bar takings, to which end publicans had always provided a useful public service letting their rooms, often free of charge, to all sorts of groups and gatherings, even temperance societies who were of course charged for the privilege. At the famous Manchester 'Apollo', tumblers of ale were passed from hand to hand along tables which ran from the door to the tiny orchestra pit with its two or three fiddles and a pianoforte. 'Just as I entered', Reach reported, 'nearly two hundred voices male and female were entreating Susanna not to cry for the minstrel who was "going to Alabama, with his banjo on his knee".'[31] 'Nigger' songs were very popular in these parts as were 'girls dancing on the stage with *such* short petticoats'. Tastes varied, however, from region to region. Londoners favoured character songs like 'The Literary Dustman' from Pierce Egan's *Life in London*, flighty songs by ladies in the briefest of muslin dresses (a speciality of the 'Royal Harmonic Saloon'), drinking choruses and sentimental ditties.[32] Up in the north-east, the pub-cum-singing rooms celebrated the dialect, humour and patriotism of Bob Cranky the 'Geordie', the collier lad who 'knaas how to wark, an' he knaas how to shork/An' he knaas how to sup good beor', a self-celebration that bordered on mockery.[33] As well as regional variations there were status differences in working-class cultural taste. Having enjoyed the good cheer of the 'Apollo', where family groups and the rest of the audience joined in every chorus '*con amore*', Reach was disappointed by what was on offer at an adjacent concert-room frequented by the 'better-class' mechanics of the Atlas ironworks together with their respectable womenfolk: 'There was a piano and some wretched sentimental singing, during which the habitués grimly smoked and drank their spirits and water. I soon beat a retreat from such dull quarters.'[34]

Entertainment was a secondary consideration in the free-and-easies, but they marked an important development in popular leisure, a move away from the male-dominated drinking culture of the traditional alehouse. It was not uncommon, indeed, for skittle alleys, billiard rooms and fighting yards to be taken over and converted into singing saloons to meet the popular demand.[35] With these early music halls, the circuses, theatres and other commercial entertainments, there was plenty of provision for leisure and amusement, supplemented by a vibrant 'street theatre' of Punch and Judy men, buskers, ballad hawkers, patent medicine salesmen, street preachers and stump orators, until the police – 'the plague of blue locusts'[36] – curbed much of the fun in this urban playground.

To counter the vulgar hedonism of commercial, drink-related amusements, middle-class reformers mounted a three-pronged offensive, offering a range of approved 'recreation' – the word itself was significant – to civilize, domesticate and edify the working man. Disturbed by the segregation of rich and poor, these middle-class reformers, the new urban gentry, hoped to reconcile the classes by a resumption of paternal patronage of leisure activities. Paternalism was rigorously reasserted on the sports field, in the concert halls and at Christmas, a typical mid-Victorian amalgam of rediscovered and invented custom which idealized the harmonious hierarchy of the past.[37] At the same time, they elevated the home as the place of family affection, quiet pleasures and domestic leisure.[38] 'Rational recreation', the third and most important thrust of the counter-offensive, proved less successful. Parsimonious local authorities were reluctant to make funds available for the provision of public parks, museums and libraries – the erosion of public rights, the privatization of property and culture continued unchecked. Where middle-class reformers provided the facilities themselves, they failed to attract the desired working-class audience. Mechanics' institutes, for example, proved popular with clerks and other white-collar aspirants of the lower middle-class, but not with the skilled working class for whose instruction in science and political economy they were intended. In their next venture, the lyceums, the rational recreationalists made more concessions to popular taste with social evenings, sporting events and excursions as well as formal lectures. But they still failed to entice the working class away from commercial pursuits or their own class-exclusive, radical and autonomous forms of collective self-improvement.[39]

The strength of commercialism was particularly apparent in popular literature where the 'useful knowledge' publications of the rational recreationalists and the radical offerings of the 'unstamped' press were squeezed out of the market by 'Salisbury Square' fiction. Cheap paper and mechanical printing were exploited to the full: popular taste, once satisfied with ill-printed ballads, broadsheets and chapbooks, was now offered the serialized delights of the penny dreadful, the feuilleton and the cheap periodical. Serialized penny novels – 'instalments of trash' – constituted the main business of Abel Heywood, leading northern distributor of cheap periodicals. A radical veteran of the 'war of the unstamped', Heywood continued to stock the full range of alternative literature, radical, infidel, socialist and the like, but his commercial success depended on the sale and distribution of the penny dreadfuls published by Edward Lloyd and his Salisbury Square associates. The first to sense the potential of the mass market, Lloyd quickly progressed from reprinting old stories to publishing specially commissioned new material, titles such as *Ella the Outcast*, *Almira's Curse* and *Lady Hamilton*, each of which had a weekly sale of over 6000 copies in Heywood's Manchester shop in 1849.[40]

Always adorned with lurid woodcuts, popular fiction was highly stylized. The Gothic novel, a sensational examination of the exotic, the grotesque and the macabre, reached its apogee in the work of G. W. M. Reynolds, Chartist, Sunday newspaper proprietor and novelist, whose voyeur's guide to *The Mysteries of the Court of London* contained 4½ million words, the equivalent of nearly 50 modern novels. Here there was ample scope for the pornography of sexuality and violence, following the tradition established in Pierce Egan's *Life in London* (1821), in which the capital contained only two classes – decadent aristocrats and outcast criminals. The criminal heroes of Ainsworth's Newgate novels – an exciting genre of crime, imprisonment, escape, recapture and hanging – achieved an unsurpassed national eminence. At Wolverhampton, the Children's Employment Commissioner questioned a number of children who 'had never heard the name of the Queen nor other names such as Nelson, Wellington, Bonaparte; but it was noteworthy that those who had never heard even of St Paul, Moses or Solomon, were very well instructed as to the life, deeds and character of Dick Turpin, the street-robber, and especially of Jack Sheppard, the thief and gaol-breaker.'[41]

Radicals and rational recreationalists were soon forced to adapt to the successful commercial formula. By the 1840s John Cleave, veteran of the unstamped and signatory of the Charter, had moved into popular fiction and Sunday newspaper-style journalism: crime, sport and salacious sensationalism replaced the radical message. *The Penny Magazine*, the unstamped miscellany published by Charles Knight for the Society for the Diffusion of Useful Knowledge, came to an end in 1845 when it was superseded by a number of family magazines which offered romantic and sensational fiction as well as the necessary instruction in the virtues of domestic economy.[42] Some radical incorruptibles, however, refused to compromise with popular taste. Richard Carlile, the longest suffering martyr in the struggle for press freedom, continued to believe that the superstitious, the sensational and the irrational would be eradicated by the 'multiplication of reason'. Throughout his lengthy imprisonment for the cause, Carlile subjected himself to a rigorous regime of 'temperance by example': self-discipline, physical puritanism, moral improvement and self-education in the quest for a 'second birth of mind'.[43] *'You cannot be free, you can find no reform, until you begin it with yourselves'*, he explained, exhorting the millions to 'abstain from gin and the gin-shop, from ale and the ale-house, from gospel and the gospel-shop, from sin and silly salvation'.[44] His message and example won few converts, save for the handful of 'zetetics' to be found in most towns, practising their ascetic counter-culture of infidel-republicanism in 'temples of reason'.[45] Radical improvement of this purist and extreme form was as alien to popular taste as middle-class useful knowledge and rational recreation.

Substantial numbers of the working class, however, endorsed the improvement ethic without subscribing either to ultra-radicalism or to middle-class norms and values. Some trades – shoemaking and weaving in particular – produced prodigious autodidacts. Among the most accomplished was Thomas Cooper whose lengthy hours at the shoemaker's stall did not preclude the most rigorous programme of self-education 'until compelled to go to bed from sheer exhaustion – for it must be remembered that I was repeating something, audibly, as I sat at work, the greater part of the day – either declensions and conjugations, or rules of syntax, or propositions of Euclid, or the "Paradise Lost", or "Hamlet", or poetry of some modern or living author'.[46] Most autodidacts, John Harrison notes, were narrow in outlook and imagination, unaware of the true perspective of knowledge. Many concentrated either on antiquarianism, recording the local dialect and oral tradition, or millenarianism, searching for texts and calculating the time prophecies, a form of pseudo-learning which provided an attractive mixture of intellectual discovery, mystification and ultimate authority.[47] Solitary and superior, autodidacts kept a proud distance from the pub, the free and easy and the penny dreadful, but they made the most of other developments in leisure and recreation, not least the cheap railway excursions which widened their geological, botanical, entomological and other field studies.

For those who disapproved of 'rough' culture but were not cut out for the lonely life of the autodidact, there were plenty of 'improving' societies in which the tone was set by working-class notions of self-respect, an ethos distinct from the 'respectability' preached by middle-class reformers. The temperance movement was transformed by working-class teetotalism: the occasional meetings of the past, gatherings of influential local worthies summoned to discuss ways of elevating their inferiors, were superseded by convivial counter-attractive functions which enabled working men to insulate themselves from

public house temptation. There were commercial opportunities here
too – the first railway trips organized by Thomas Cook were strictly
temperance affairs, removing the young from temptation on Leicester
race days.[48]

Teetotalism appealed strongly to those who sought self-dependence
and self-respect, virtues upheld in the more democratic of the nonconformist chapels. Workers were not attracted to these chapels *faute de
mieux*, in the absence of any other public and cultural provision. The
decision to attend chapel was a cultural choice, a decision to forgo
many of the pleasures of popular culture, an assertion of independence and self-respect. For artisans, miners, outworkers and others,
popular nonconformity served to express and legitimize their independence, giving them a sense of pride in the face of social superiors
through the encouragement of self-discipline, literacy, hard work
and a generally methodical approach to life.[49] Methodism struck
a particularly successful balance between individual and corporate
requirements: individual   self-improvement   found   institutional
expression in the associated discipline of choir, class and chapel.[50] In
its more democratic forms, chapel offered opportunities for status
and responsibility as preachers, class leaders and Sunday School
teachers, often the best available training for the political and industrial leaders – the 'preacher vanguard'[51] – of the working class.

Chapel was not a refuge, a place of withdrawal, but the centre for
a counter-attractive working-class culture often in fierce competition
with the public house. The 'respectable' chapel-going working class
sought not to prohibit but to appropriate popular cultural forms – it
was by lusty singing in the Primitive Methodist chapel that the
respectable miner clarified and proclaimed his new self-image, just as
his 'rough' Geordie neighbour established his identity and loyalty
through hearty 'Bob Cranky' chorus in the tap room down the lane.[52]
Working-class self-respect developed apace in the Primitive Methodist chapels of the north-east where *extempore* preaching, praying and
testifying broke through the defences of dialect, registered the tone
of an oral tradition and met the taste for excitement and spectacle.[53]
Itinerant women preachers added to the appeal, but the circuits
disapproved strongly of outside competition from unlicensed 'ranting'
preachers, Mormon missionaries and other 'vagabond charlatans'.[54]
In Primitive form, Methodism was not unduly prudish: much of the
old popular culture was incorporated in its millenarianism, with folk
beliefs and communal conviviality transformed into a religious idiom.
One of the strongest congregations was in Cornwall where Wesleyan
superstition matched the indigenous superstition of tinners and fish-
ermen, workers dependent upon chance and luck in their daily life.
Here the Methodists declared holy war on drink, hurling, wrestling,

bull-baiting, cock-fighting and folk superstitions, but replaced them with revivals, Love Feasts, watch-nights, hymn singing, providential interventions and colourful local versions of the cosmic drama between god and the devil.[55] Presented in such entertaining style, the conversionist theology accorded well with popular taste and attitudes, not least the age-old desire to make a fresh start.[56]

Methodist growth was most spectacular in transitional, industrializing communities where religious enthusiasm offered tangible benefits – as well as religious entertainment, newcomers to the chapel community enjoyed practical support and emotional reassurance. This was much more than a chiliasm of despair, consolation to which workers turned only when radicalism failed. Methodist growth cannot be correlated with periods of radical activity: the figures show an independent pattern of oscillation between strong increases and weaker slumps, a cycle of revivalism and decline which historians have yet to connect convincingly with patterns of demographic, economic or political change.[57] At the height of the Chartist challenge, vast numbers attended religious assemblages, new and enduring popular cultural events like the famous Whit-Walks, street processions of witness through the northern towns, when working-class Sunday School children and temperance reformers paraded in their finery behind banners, flags, decorations and marching bands.[58]

The study of popular culture defies a simple class analysis. There was cross-class alliance to defend some of the old sports and pastimes, and pan-class endeavour to effect reform through temperance, sabbatarianism and other means. Within the working class there were many contesting cultural groupings – 'respectable' and 'rough', chapel and pub, autodidact and illiterate – but these and other divisions should not be pushed too far. Popular culture did not polarize around the drunken hedonists at one end and the teetotal self-improvers at the other. For most of the working class, 'commercial' offerings answered the need for humour and relief in the face of adversity, a good-natured stoicism similar to the fatalism which prevailed outside the institutional framework and doctrinal divisions of organized Christianity. Uninterested in legalistic morality, sabbatarianism and doctrinal rectitude, the majority held to a practical Christianity which owed much to superstition and local custom, and placed considerable trust in the expiatory value of present suffering.[59] The challenge which confronted the popular radicals was to transform these populist idioms and fatalist assumptions into a radical critique of early industrial society.

6 Popular Radicalism

Popular collective behaviour in early industrial England has generally been studied within an oppositional framework, celebrating the making of the working class, the creative process which transformed the riotous 'ungovernable people' of the eighteenth century into the organized and political class-based force of the age of the Chartists. An important advance in history from below, this concentration on popular protest, however, has left much of the crowd in history unexamined. Insufficient attention has been accorded to demonstrations and displays which were integrative, not oppositional, in function.[1] During the last decades of George III's reign, national- as opposed to class-consciousness was promoted through public celebrations of loyalty and royalty, spectacular pageants which elicited appreciative popular support for the existing order.[2] Through rival demonstrations and displays, radicals and loyalists competed for the allegiance of the freeborn Englishman, an uneven contest in the politics of public space. The loyalists, of course, enjoyed many advantages. Well-organized and advertised, lavish celebrations of royal anniversaries and military victories were paid holidays, as it were, a treat for vast and grateful crowds who were allowed considerable licence on the streets. Radical demonstrations were less enticing – participants had to sacrifice wages or leisure and risked victimization, dismissal or arrest. Despite these uneven odds, there were brief periods when the radicals held the initiative, times when they managed to appropriate the legitimizing language and symbolism of the loyalist establishment, thereby winning the battle for the popular mind and attracting the crowds to radical reform, a populist platform justified by history, the constitution and the rule of law.

The eighteenth-century crowd: food riots

Food-rioting was the most frequent and characteristic form of eighteenth-century protest, direct action which was motivated and legitimized by a backward-looking *mentalité* which sought the redress of grievances through the restoration of the hallowed (doubtless mythical) ways of the past. Recalled to their paternalist duties, rulers and employers would uphold traditional customs and practices, including the 'moral economy' of fair prices, honest measures and decent, unadulterated quality.[3] Frequent but not ubiquitous, the incidence of such riotous consumer-consciousness was determined by

60

a number of factors: the communications network, the distribution of the manufacturing population and the structure of community politics. There were regular riots in remote infertile areas ill-served by internal transport, but the major outbreaks occurred much closer to the arable counties, at the communication centres or transhipment points from which grain was exported or despatched to lucrative metropolitan markets which were comparatively well-supplied and riot-free. Market towns which served a large non-agricultural population were particularly riot-prone: in the community politics of the older and smaller towns, the protocol of riot was properly observed by patrician and plebeian alike. As soon as prices started to rise, workers located in an 'isolated mass' – Kingswood colliers, Cornish tin-miners, Devonport dockyard-workers, Tyneside keelmen – would 'invade' their local market town in a pre-emptive display of physical strength. Less awesome but just as rebellious were the rural weavers and other out-workers in the clothing trade of the west country and East Anglia, domestic manufacturing workers without a margin of self-sufficiency who thus depended upon local markets for their provisions.[4]

Reliant upon the open market, food-rioters directed their protest against those who transgressed the traditional rules and regulations of the market-place, the speculating middlemen who manipulated the deregulated market at the expense of the poor consumer. Through disciplined use of violence, deployed against property and not the person, the crowd – usually female-dominated – sought to shame and intimidate those who infringed the moral economy. Doubtless there were some petty pilferers around, but there was no indiscriminate looting: captured provisions were either symbolically 'spoiled' or sold at a just price 'maximum', the money being returned to the chastened merchants. The seizure of goods for such *taxation populaire* was not always necessary: demonstration rather than riot was often sufficient to persuade the dealers to lower their prices or to prompt the magistrates into a timely exercise in paternalist intervention. Victory, however, sometimes exacerbated the long-term supply problem: dealers often chose to divert stocks to markets where there was less likelihood of riot and a 'maximum'.[5]

In no way influenced by the political agitation of the Jacobins, the widespread food riots of 1795–6 – which included some spectacular seizures by soldiers and militia encamped along the southern and eastern coast to meet the threat of invasion from revolutionary France – were to be the last major exercise in traditional collective bargaining with magistrates and patricians.[6] The riots of 1799–1801 displayed a new political awareness, a radicalism born of the dearth and distress of wartime existence. Assisted by discontented Volunteers, starving food rioters in Totnes, Newton Abbot, Devonport and other towns set up their own popularly elected Committees of the People, local 'dictatorships of the proletariat' which enforced justice in the market place.[7] Usurped in the south-west, patrician authorities were condemned and reviled up in the north-west where industrial recession followed in the wake of poor harvests and famine prices. Driven underground by repressive legislation, radical and trade union groups acquired new levels of popular support as wages fell and prices rose – by 1799 wartime inflation had reduced weavers' wages to well below half their real value in 1792. Their planning and propaganda led to well-organized riots in which magistrates, clergy and the old paternalists stood condemned with speculators, factors and middlemen as members of the repressive propertied class.[8] Already intertwined with radicalism and trade unionism, food-rioting was soon to disappear as a distinct and separate form of popular protest in industrial Lancashire, a trend which was to spread across the land – in the mining districts of Cornwall, however, the food-riot was to continue in its traditional form until the middle of the nineteenth century.[9]

Industrial disturbances

Wartime politicization also brought an end to 'collective bargaining by riot', the disciplined and ritualized violence by which eighteenth-century workers enforced the moral economy of the workshop. Employers, newcomers and blacklegs were forcefully reminded of the customs and conventions which determined work practices and payment levels by selective and disciplined direct action – the strike, a term which entered the vocabulary in the midst of the seamen's and other disputes of the 1760s,[10] was often preceded and/or accompanied by the destruction of raw materials, finished goods, machinery and other property. An unacceptable cost to small employers, such destruction of capital equipment imposed solidarity on the workforce, ensured against blacklegging and often prompted magistrates to intervene and mediate. Industrial sabotage was thus a functional tactic of early trade unionism, the normal means of putting pressure on employers or putters-out, but in some disputes machine-breaking was the crucial end in itself.[11] Fierce battles were fought over the introduction of various 'devils', labour-saving, deskilling machines, but even here no separate labour consciousness emerged. Rebellious in defence of custom, workers hoped to restore the united interests of masters and men, a unity celebrated in the concluding verses of a popular Liverpool ballad, 'The Rope Maker's Resolution, Or, The Devil's Downfall':

So now to conclude, and finish my song,

I hope that the time will arrive before long,
When Rope-Makers all, will be furnished with means
Whereby they may wholly abolish machines.
When this is accomplished, you'll all find employ,
And each man the fruits of his labour enjoy;
Men and masters united in concord and peace,
May our trade once more flourish, and commerce increase
    Derry down, down with machinery down.[12]

In some cases direct and informal workshop action was reinforced by wider organization based on a network of houses of call, over 40 in the case of the London tailors in the mid-eighteenth century. These pubs provided the facilities for the tramping system and the 'box' clubs, sickness and burial benefit clubs which also collected for 'the defence of the trade'.[13] These links allowed the trades to strike on the most propitious occasions, when labour was at a premium and substantial funds had been accumulated. By the end of the century, calico printers, compositors, papermakers and bookbinders had perfected the tactic of the 'rolling' strike, withdrawing labour from one shop or mill at a time, with those remaining in work supporting those who were out.[14]

Conducted within a shared discourse of custom, tradition and the unity of interests, collective bargaining by strike or riot was ultimately legitimized by the old paternalist legislation governing work practices, apprenticeship and payment.[15] Obsolete as this legislation was, its final repeal during the Napoleonic wars was a devastating blow for the trades, a far more serious reverse than the new legislation prohibiting workers' combination. First to encounter the strident spirit of *laissez-faire* were the Wiltshire shearmen, the skilled elite of the west country woollen trade. Having persuaded the Trowbridge clothiers to withdraw gig mills by a pre-emptive display of physical strength in 1802, the well-organized shearmen – linked to their northern counterparts through the 'Brief Institution' – turned their attention to parliament and the courts, spending more than £10,000 in an unavailing attempt to enforce a complete ban on gig mills in accordance with the terms of 5 and 6 Edward VI c. 22. All the old statutes regulating the woollen trade were repealed in 1809 however, leaving the shearmen defenceless against gig mills, shearing frames and cheap, unskilled, unapprenticed labour. Violence remained their only means of protection, the most effective weapon of craft combination: machinery was not introduced until the 1820s for fear of a repetition of the destruction of 1802.[16]

Cotton handloom-weavers faced considerable distress as their 'golden age' came to an end amid wartime inflation, over-stocking and competition from cheaply-fed peasant workers on the continent.

Parliament, however, refused them the protection previously extended to the riotous Spitalfields silk-weavers of the 1770s. Shunned by the Commons, they turned to industrial action, removing shuttles from some 60,000 looms to prevent blacklegging. Whatever was gained by the 1808 strike was not retained. Forced to petition again for a minimum wages bill in 1811, the impoverished weavers were reminded by parliament that there could be 'no interference with the freedom of trade'.[17] At this point Lancashire weavers turned to Luddism, but their colleagues further north continued with a 'constitutional' approach. Apparently successful at Glasgow, they decided to test the courts south of the border at Carlisle, an important handloom-weaving centre and convenient meeting place for northern and Scottish delegates of the General Association of Operative Weavers. At the Easter Quarter Sessions in 1812, the magistrates were presented with a memorial signed by one third of the town's workforce, asking them to fix an agreed minimum price for weaving in accordance with their duties under 5 Elizabeth c. 4. When the memorial was rejected the redoubtable weavers engaged the services of Henry Brougham who obtained a *mandamus* in the Court of King's Bench requiring the magistrates to fix a rate for weaving, but on the advice of the Lord Chief Justice the writ was held over until the following year, by which time parliament had resolved to repeal the entire wage-fixing and apprenticeship clauses of the Statute of Artificers, thereby nullifying the weavers' expensive legal victory.[18]

The Luddite disturbances must be placed in the context of these unavailing constitutional efforts to secure protection against falling real wages and adverse changes in work practices. During the distress of 1811–12, the worst crisis of the Napoleonic wars, General Ludd's army of redressers first displayed their strength in the east midlands hosiery district. Skilled town knitters and their less skilled country colleagues employed a variety of complementary forms, legal and violent, to protect their interests against custom-breaking hosiers who cut costs, standards and quality, by producing inferior stockings or 'cut-ups' by means of 'colting', the employment of unskilled unapprenticed labour on wide frames. As a powerful adjunct to Gravener Henson's continued efforts to secure parliamentary redress, the offending frames were symbolically smashed in a disciplined exercise in collective bargaining by riot.[19]

As Luddism spread into Yorkshire, industrial sabotage took on a different function, more in line with the popular understanding of anti-machinery Luddite violence. Yorkshire Luddites looked to the vengeance of 'Enoch', the hammer of destruction, to smash the shearing frames and finishing machinery which threatened the croppers with technological redundancy. Forced to adopt direct action – all constitutional channels had been closed in 1809 when parliament spurned the petitions of the Wiltshire shearmen – the croppers soon became involved with underground radical groups and other discontented workers. Attention shifted from the destruction of machinery to the seizure of arms, but discipline proved difficult to impose despite the famous secret oaths – many ordinary criminals turned the crisis to their advantage as robberies became random and diffuse. Not a coherent regional network, the revolutionary underground had some strength and durability at local level, although most notably in non-woollen towns like Sheffield and Barnsley.[20]

Across the Pennines, Luddism was part of a general protest against the hated 'war system'. Political in thrust, Lancashire Luddism was eclectic in tactics. There was no clear-cut division between political protest and industrial pressure, between participation in constitutional reform movements and involvement in underground activity – the constitutionalism of the Manchester committee for peace and reform, formed after the failure of the handloom-weavers' minimum wages campaign in 1811, was a useful cover behind which money and support could be raised for other purposes.[21] Robert Glen's recent work on Stockport has managed to separate and differentiate food-rioters, machine-breakers and the diminutive number of political revolutionaries in a town where thousands took the Luddite oath but very few actually took part in drilling and arms raids. However, this compartmentalist study fails to acknowledge the peculiarity of Stockport itself with its exceptionally large factory population in both spinning and weaving sectors.[22]

Already political in Lancashire, Luddism was a radicalizing experience elsewhere. A functional form of protest in eighteenth-century England, collective bargaining by riot proved disastrous in the Napoleonic war years when parliament repudiated paternalism and committed the full physical power of the state – a greater military force than Wellington had under his command in the Iberian campaign[23] – to crush the Luddites. Defeated and disabused, workers in the Luddite counties turned to radicalism, to the forward-looking struggle for democratic control of the state and the economy.

Similar changes occurred in London during the war, a strike-prone period of unprecedented inflation. Craft workers in the trades, 'artisans' as they started to call themselves, were forced into new levels of militancy simply to maintain their customary standard of living, to ensure that wage rates remained just and fair, determined by custom and status differentials, not by supply and demand. Unhindered by the Combination Acts, inter-trade links were forged in a sustained campaign to enforce and extend the Elizabethan labour code, beginning in 1809 with the appointment of a lawyer to prosecute offending masters.[24] Parliament's decision to repeal the crucial apprenticeship clauses of the Statute of Artificers in 1814 served both to radicalize the trades and to restrict their influence to the diminishing honourable or bespoke sector, leaving most workers unorganized and unprotected against market forces and open recruitment in London's rapidly multiplying number of small and sweated units of production. Strengthened by the war, popular radicalism was proudly artisan in programme and tone, representing and protecting the 'property' of labour and skill.

Parliamentary reform and the urban crowd

New organizations for the extension of the suffrage followed in the wake of the Wilkite affair and the American question, crises which redefined the issue of parliamentary reform, previously discussed – without reference to representation – in 'country party' terms of the purity and independence of the Commons. Little of this new 'associationism' among Commonwealthmen, neo-Harringtonians and other gentlemanly reformers reached down to the streets where the crowd – a troublesome necessity within the eighteenth-century constitutional settlement – enjoyed the saturnalian licence accorded by this 'unofficial opposition', out-groups opposed to established control of court, city and commercial empire.[25]

On the streets, Wilkes, the self-proclaimed champion of 'all the middling and inferior set of people', was fêted as a lord of misrule amid the post-war high prices and unemployment of the late 1760s. The Wilkite affair, a plebeian celebration of the limits beyond which the Englishman was not prepared to be pushed around, left no legacy of political education and organization at the popular level.[26] Some years later in 1780, the absence of any popular political advance was graphically demonstrated by the Gordon Riots, an ugly display of religious intolerance. Here again, collusion and convergence were at work as the city authorities, Wilkite opponents of the King and his ministers, allowed or even encouraged the crowd, already stimulated by Gordon's anti-papist demagoguery, to despoil the property of Catholics. The ensuing orgy of destruction, however, soon acquired a social and political dimension unacceptable to the complicitous authorities who hurriedly took up arms to suppress the rioters. An expression of xenophobia and gut patriotism, the slogan of 'No Popery' belonged to the vocabulary of English libertarianism, to the celebration of the glorious struggle against continental absolutism, papistry and poverty. Articulated in the context of riot, this motto of liberty merged with other sub-political attitudes, most notably the rough social justice favoured by the crowd, the desire to settle accounts with the rich if only for the day. Thus, the riots were no indiscriminate Catholic 'pogrom': poor Catholics were left alone as the crowd ravaged the property of wealthy Catholics, rich supporters of the Catholic Relief Act, and then assailed various symbols of authority from prisons and toll-gates to the Bank of England, at which point they encountered the armed opposition of the city authorities including the musket-bearing John Wilkes.[27]

Throughout the 1790s, the decade of Jacobinism, the loyal and patriotic crowd remained a volatile force, terrorizing alien, deviant and 'revolutionary' elements at one moment, lionizing the 'free-born' victims of ministerial injustice and repression at the next. Church and King rioters, by no means all a hired mob, took the opportunity to impose their own form of popular social justice – rich Dissenters were attacked as much for their wealth as their religious and political views, prompting Anglican employers in Birmingham to place their own works and houses in a state of defence during the Priestley riots.[28] In small towns up and down the country, Church and King riots were spontaneous effusions of popular loyalty, usually triggered by the excitement of a public gathering or holiday – Boxing Day, Easter Monday, Wakes week, royal birthdays and military victories over Revolutionary France were all the occasion for Church and King activity throughout the north-west. Unlike the targets of other forms of plebeian collective violence, the victims of these riots, stigmatized by their political views rather than their social status, risked serious personal injury as well as the ritualized destruction of their property. By the end of the decade, however, such violence was at an end: popular loyalism had lost its rationale and appeal. Trapped between falling wages and spiralling prices, the cotton workers of the north-west rallied behind a new set of slogans – 'No War', 'Damn Pitt' and 'A Free Constitution'.[29]

A similar change occurred in London where 'No Corruption' replaced 'No Popery' as the most popular cry on the streets, a reflection of popular indignation at the mounting cost and incompetence of the protracted war effort. In the early days, the war was greeted with great enthusiasm, although there were 'crimping' riots directed against the nefarious agencies through which the armed forces were recruited or 'kidnapped'.[30] Amid the initial loyalist fervour, radicals who refused to illuminate their windows to celebrate military and naval victories incurred the wrath of the crowd – Thomas Hardy's pregnant wife died shortly after a jubilant crowd rampaged through her house in the course of celebrating the Glorious First of June. In characteristic volatile fashion, the London crowd took the widowed Hardy, secretary of the London Corresponding Society, to its heart a few months later when – the victim of persecution – he was tried and triumphantly acquitted of High Treason.[31] Loyalist at one

moment, radical at the next, the London crowd was an unpredictable
political force until a decade of war-weariness and economic hardship
produced an enduring radical commitment in the early nineteenth
century.

Jacobinism

In the early 1790s *The Rights of Man* opened the reform debate to
'members unlimited'. Tom Paine's all-embracing language of natural
rights and rational republicanism – his 'intellectual vernacular prose'[32]
– repudiated the exclusive conventions of eighteenth-century reform
discussion, the appeal to history and the constitution, to civic virtue,
liberty and property.[33] His uncompromising tone served to divide
democratic radicals from moderate reformers, the plebeian 'Friends
of Liberty' from the refined 'Friends of the People'. But the new
democratic societies failed to attract the labouring poor, despite
Paine's espousal of welfare reform.[34] The LCS, the most famous of
the new societies, had an active membership of less than 1000 for
most of its existence, composed in the main of artisans and tradesmen,
of shoemakers like Hardy and tailors like Place, together with various
representatives of the 'uneasy' middle class – booksellers, printers,
publishers, authors and members of the legal and medical professions.
In the provinces, Jacobin societies took root best in old artisan centres
like Norwich and Sheffield: elsewhere they were often unable to
withstand the onset of conservative reaction.[35]

It was conservatism, not Jacobinism, that won the battle for the
popular mind in the early 1790s. In the short term, the reaction
provoked by Paine and the deist-republicanism of his *Age of Reason*
proved stronger than the radicalism he excited. Compelled to answer
the democratic Jacobin challenge, opponents of reform developed an
intellectual and moral defence of the existing order. Thereafter, they
used every resource available – including Reeves's Association for
the Preservation of Liberty and Property against Republicans and
Levellers, the largest political organization in the country – to spread
the patriotic conservative message in popular and homiletic form
amongst the lower orders. Denied access to public space – 186 publicans in Manchester, for example, signed a declaration banning Jacobins from their rooms – the plebeian radicals were unable to counter
the loyalist propaganda victory. Outcast, harassed and repressed, the
'disloyal' Jacobins had little chance of disabusing and mobilizing the
masses, treated as they were to a number of patriotic festivities and
celebrations.[36]

Jacobinism, however, was not eradicated: the conservative
onslaught compelled the radicals to revise their ways and means in
at least two important respects. First, there was a distinct change in

emphasis and tone as the surviving popular societies judiciously excised the Paineite vocabulary of rational republicanism with its alien and revolutionary stigma from their public political discourse. Henceforth democratic radicalism was propounded and legitimized through the historicist language of popular constitutionalism.[37] Seeking to galvanize populist anti-absolutist sentiment into political commitment, radicals appropriated the establishment vocabulary of patriotism, posing in heroic guise as the true loyalists and defenders of the constitution, the proud descendants of 'that patriotic band who broke the ruffian arm of arbitrary power, and dyed the field and the scaffold with their pure and precious blood, for the liberties of their country, – Hampden, Russell, Sidney'.[38] Confronted by this demo- cratic version of the dominant ideology of history, constitutional freedom and the rule of law, the conservative victory in the battle for the popular mind was far from secure. Propaganda was reinforced by repressive legislation, 'Terror' which began with a series of measures – the Royal Proclamation against Seditious Publications and the Suspension of Habeas Corpus – designed to embarrass and divide the Whigs, successful exercises in 'high politics' which enticed Port- land into the ranks of government.[39] The Two Acts of 1795, however, were a straightforward attack on the new politics from below, in particular the ominous new tactic of the radical mass meeting.

Throughout the provinces, the *crise de subsistence* of 1795 produced a wave of traditional, non-political food-rioting, but in London the radicals stood forward to organize and coordinate popular protest. A considerable triumph for the previously ailing LCS, the orderly mass meetings at St George's Fields (29 June) and Copenhagen Fields (26 October) provided a popular platform from which to broadcast the radical message, to explain how the 'dreadful scarcity and high price of provisions' were caused by the 'cruel, unjust and unnecessary war'. 'Why, when we incessantly toil and labour, must we pine in misery and want?', the Remonstrance adopted at Copenhagen Fields demanded: '*Parliamentary Corruption* . . . like a foaming whirlpool, swallows the fruit of all our labours.' Three days later, when the King drove to open parliament, huge crowds carrying tiny loaves in black crepe and shouting for peace, hooted at him, and someone threw a stone at his coach, thereby providing the government with the requisite pretext for the introduction of the Two Acts.[40]

Repressive legislation accelerated the second main change in the ways and means of plebeian radicalism: involvement in underground insurrectionary politics – some members of the LCS, however, pur- sued an alliance with the moderate reformers, Foxite and gentlemanly 'liberals' who continued in legal opposition to the war and repression.[41] Recent research has confirmed E. P. Thompson's insights:[42] the efficiency of the government intelligence services, the international dimensions of insurrectionary strategy, and the remarkable continuity of the revolutionary tradition at local level, all attest to the importance of the radical underground.

Ministers were kept well informed of insurrectionary planning through an efficient secret service coordinated and collated by the staff of the Home Office and its tiny adjunct, the Alien Office.[43] Spies and informers were generally carefully recruited, vetted and protected, although some unsavoury characters were perforce employed after 1795 to infiltrate the increasingly secret radical societies. The reliable information thus obtained revealed plans for an oath-bound conspiracy of international dimensions, a union of revolutionary forces in Ireland, France and Britain. The naval mutinies of 1797 highlighted the danger as a politically conscious minority, dominated by cells of United Irishmen, tried to persuade their exploited shipmates – driven to mutiny by poor pay and appalling conditions of service – to desert to the enemy and thereby assist a French invasion of Ireland.[44] These Irish and French links continued to dominate underground strategy. Modelled on the United Irishmen, the oath-bound United Englishmen enrolled groups unattracted to the earlier Jacobin societies – the impoverished weavers, spinners and labourers of Lancashire and the north-west. Militant sections of the LCS formed the Society of United Britons, whose central committee – of which Colonel Despard was the most famous member – was entrusted to prepare plans for English and Irish risings to accompany a French invasion. Fully informed of the details discussed in Lancashire and London with Irish delegates *en route* to France, the government pre-empted the conspiracy by arresting most of the leaders. Except in the case of Coigley, successful prosecutions were not secured as the government decided not to reveal in open court its most useful and reliable informants. Through these protected channels of information, ministers learnt of new insurrectionary plans – elaborated after the failure of the Irish rebellion of 1798 – in which the capture of London was to be the first priority after the essential French invasion. On these grounds, habeas corpus was suspended again, a convenient means of locking up the leaders without any embarrassing courtroom defeats; and a parliamentary committee of secrecy was followed by a series of new laws curbing the press, banning the United Societies and the London Corresponding Society by name, and outlawing workers' combinations.[45]

This tightening of repression failed to crush the radical threat, serving instead to politicize the war-wearied masses, to clinch the industrial control, John Foster observes, 'of those who were themselves outlaws, the working-class radicals. In south-west Lancashire almost every labour organization seems to have passed into their hands. "The republicans", reported one agent, "are drinking Mr Pitt's health.'"[46] Previously an elitist affair, conspiracy had potential mass support, but once again the government moved early. While still awaiting French and Irish assistance, Despard was arrested in November 1802 as there was sufficient evidence – without exposing secret sources of information – to secure his conviction. Despard's execution, followed by the failure of Emmet's rising in Ireland, was a severe reverse for the revolutionary underground which might well have attracted considerable popular support in the north had Despard effected a successful *coup d'etat* in the metropolis.[47] Thereafter the underground was in decline, but local studies have uncovered some remarkable continuities in the revolutionary tradition – many of 'Despard's men' were to the fore in Luddism and the risings of 1817 and 1820, proud veterans who bequeathed to the Chartist movement a commitment to physical force.[48]

Burdettite radicalism

After the collapse of the patriotic consensus of the invasion scare years of 1803–5, indignation at the cost and conduct of the war produced what one historian has described as a middle-class revolt against patrician society.[49] As a series of sensational scandals exposed the malversation and incompetence of the 'Pitt System', the radical 'overground' rallied behind the leadership of Sir Francis Burdett. Formerly regarded as a dangerous Jacobin because of his links with the Irish and the Horne Tooke circle, the wealthy Burdett soon mastered the techniques of legitimate oppositional politics. Much in line with the programme and ideology of the old country party, he stood forward for reform as an independent gentleman who sought to purge corruption and oligarchy by restoring 'purity' to the Commons. In 1807, he secured a sensational electoral victory in Foxite Westminster, thanks to the economic efficiency and organizational skills of the *menu peuple* on the new Westminster Committee. The hero of the London crowd, whom he handled with Wilkite theatrical skill, Burdett was revered as the champion of 'real' reform as opposed to the 'mock' reform proffered by the temporizing Whig 'Mountain'. Burdett's programme of a direct taxation suffrage, equal electoral districts and annual parliaments dominated the reform debate until the end of the war when 'Orator' Hunt, formerly his most fervent supporter, was emboldened to mount a democratic challenge to the moderate radicalism of 'Westminster's Pride and England's Glory'.[50]

Hunt's democratic politics owed much to the teachings of William Cobbett, the poor man's friend. The war, Cobbett regretted, had consolidated 'the Thing', the system of political corruption and financial plunder which had been tightening its hold since the late seventeenth century at the expense of the unrepresented and heavily taxed poor. Paper money and inflation were but the latest horrors of this funding system built upon the monstrous national debt, which produced lucrative profits for political peculators and financial speculators – money-men, stockjobbers, government contractors, pensioners and sycophants – but imposed an intolerable, demand-stifling tax burden on the poor. Thus, what separated the economically protected from the economically defenceless in 'Fortress Britannica', the parasitic plunderers from the hard-working plundered, the rich from the poor, was the monopolistic possession of political power.[51]

Amid the distress of the transition from war to peace without plenty, Hunt stood forward to demand the political rights and economic protection of the common people, now the victims of military demobilization, the cessation of government orders, deflation and the weather – the spring and summer of 1816 were the worst in recorded history, the result of unprecedented volcanic eruptions in the Pacific which obscured the sky throughout the northern hemisphere for months on end. To his astonishment, he discovered that Burdett, the acclaimed champion of the people, refused to lend his authority to any democratic extension of the radical programme. The Westminster Committee, long since shorn of its old LCS members, also declined to participate in mass politics. Hunt, indeed, was in constant conflict with the 'Rump', the caucus of '*petty shop-keepers*, and little *tradesmen*, who under the denomination of *tax-paying housekeepers*, enlisted themselves under the banner of Sir Francis Burdett, in order to set themselves up as a sort of privileged class, above the *operative* manufacturer, the artizan, the mechanic and the labourer'.[52] As the constituency became more prosperous, the Committee sought a rapprochement with the popular Whigs and duly opposed any venture into democratic politics from below which would jeopardize their plans to promote Henry Brougham as Burdett's running-mate. Brougham's credentials were impressive: an effective parliamentarian, he was the strategist of the 'petition and debate' campaigns which brought an end to the Orders-in-Council and the Property Tax, important victories for middle-class public opinion in the unreformed parliament. To Hunt, however, Brougham was an unredeemed Whig, an enemy to the democratic cause. By accepting the invitation of the 'revolutionary party' to speak at Spa Fields, Hunt found a platform from which he could expose the apostasy of Burdett and the machinations of the 'Rump', and thereby establish an independent, uncompromising, extra-parliamentary campaign for democratic radicalism.[53]

The postwar mass platform

Tavern debating clubs provided the organizational base for the promotion of Hunt's mass platform and for alternative, ultra-radical strategies in the post war years, from the preliminary inculcation of Spencean orthodoxy to the immediate *coup d'etat*. To this latter end, the 'revolutionary party', heirs of the Despard tradition, hoped to establish a chain of twenty or so taverns, flashpoints for an uprising led by the physically intimidating – canal navvies, sailors, soldiers, dockworkers, the rough, unemployed and other masculine groups fond of their beer. Amid the distress of the transition to peace, they trusted that a well-attended public meeting would serve as the best springboard for insurrection: hence they invited all the leading reform celebrities of the day to address a meeting of 'Distressed Manufacturers, Mariners, Artisans, and others' at Spa Fields. Hunt alone accepted after he had satisfied himself that he was not being drawn into a revolutionary plan to abolish private property in land.[54]

In a private interview with Dr Watson, the impecunious Spencean surgeon, Hunt dictated his terms for mounting the platform at what was to be the first wholly 'unlimited' demonstration of a radical character in London since 1795. There would be no reference to Spencean principles, and no incitement to riot: the meeting would be strictly 'constitutional', a forum at which the distressed masses would enrol in an extra-parliamentary campaign of petitions and memorials to 'save the wreck of the constitution' by the instauration of universal suffrage, annual parliaments and the ballot. Dr Watson, leading strategist of the 'revolutionary party', readily accepted these stipulations. Not a doctrinaire Spencean, he was prepared to shelve the 'plan' for a major redistribution of landed property and power within each parish in order to support a campaign for universal suffrage, the necessary prerequisite for reordering the economic and social system. Although a revolutionary, he was not obsessed with the traditional *putsch* strategy inherited from Despard and the wartime underground: he was prepared to postpone the *coup* in order to concentrate on a campaign which would facilitate mass mobilization, the best preparation for a propitious and decisive confrontation with the authorities. Some revolutionaries, most notably Arthur Thistlewood and Watson's own son, were less pragmatic. They made sure that a second meeting was called so that they could go ahead with their original plans – every detail of which was well known to government informers – to inflame the assembled crowd and storm the Bank and the Tower. It was not until the disastrous failure of precipitate insurrectionism on 2 December that the more recalcitrant members of the revolutionary party came to accept the utility of Hunt's constitutional mass platform.

With their fruit-sellers, gingerbread stalls and fairground atmosphere, the Spa Fields meetings of 1816–17 established the popular context and tone of democratic radical endeavour. Undaunted by the huge crowds, 'Orator' Hunt upstaged the absent moderates and confounded the spy-infested insurrectionists by enrolling the people in mass agitation for their full democratic rights. Under his leadership, those without the political nation stood forward to demand universal suffrage, annual parliaments and the ballot in an open and 'constitutional' manner, relying on mass pressure from below to coerce the otherwise inexorable government, 'peaceably if we may, forcibly if we must'. Such 'forcible intimidation' drew upon the rich rhetoric of popular constitutionalism and 'people's history', a celebration of the glorious struggles of the past which enshrined the ultimate right of physical resistance, the proud inheritance of the sovereign people. The popular format which Hunt introduced at Spa Fields – constitutional mass pressure from without for the constitutional democratic rights of all – continued to inform radical agitation throughout the age of the Chartists. These populist idioms, indeed, were even to prevail in the tavern debating clubs where Thomas Evans, guardian of Spencean orthodoxy, offered a thorough alternative to platform radicalism. While Evans and other ideologues often took personality and pedantry to fissiparous extreme, most of the audience of 'ragged radicals' relaxed in anti-intellectual, blasphemous enjoyment of the ritual 'hullabaloo' of satirical toasts, patriotic songs and didactic debate, a burlesque 'counter-theatre' which mocked and demystified the establishment and its public ceremonial.[55]

Popular radicalism was transformed by the Spa Fields meetings, accomplishing the breakthrough to mass support that the Jacobins of the 1790s had been unable to secure. Open and inclusive, the new mass platform deliberately exploited ambiguities in the law and constitution, a strategy which henceforth prevailed over other ways and means, supplanting both the 'politics of order', the subservient dependence on the parliamentary opposition displayed by the 'Rump' and other moderate reformers, and the 'politics of violence', the futile insurrectionism of Thistlewood and the revolutionary party which served only to facilitate repressive legislation. This was a remarkable achievement at a time when the crime rate soared precipitously, climbing above previous postwar peaks. Among those demobilized into distress were the group most commonly indicted for property offences in times of peace, namely young men in their late teens and early twenties, but these troublesome youths did not sully the mass meetings with crime.[56] After the much-criticized events of 2 December, when demobilized seamen, awaiting their arrears in payment and prize money, took advantage of the 'revolutionary' *putsch* to rummage their way through the Smithfield shops, the platform displayed the utmost self-discipline. It was this very orderliness that made the radical challenge so intimidating to the authorities.

The Hampden Club convention confirmed the decisive change in mood and style. No champion of mass politics from below, Burdett absented himself, leaving old Major Cartwright – veteran of Wyvill's Association movement and pioneer political missionary to the Luddite counties – to defend the official programme of household suffrage against the blunt criticisms of the 'country cousins'. Ardent supporters of Hunt and universal suffrage, working-class delegates from the north, elected at mass meetings held in the wake of Spa Fields, repudiated any 'doctrine of exclusion'. 'They must seek a Power in the Constitution', the delegates agreed at a briefing meeting at Middleton before heading south:

> a Power that will curtail luxury – by diminishing Taxation, and will enable the people to buy shoes, stockings, shirts, coats, hats, etc. and then there will be a demand for labour . . . suffrage commensurate with *direct* Taxation, seems to grant, that property only ought to be represented; whereas, labour makes property, and therefore in the name of common sense ought to be represented.[57]

As the workers mobilized in the democratic cause, the government hastened to impose repression: the new mass platform was crushed by the 'dungeon parliament' of 1817. The spectre of Spencean revolution provided ample pretext for the suspension of habeas corpus, a new Seditious Meetings Prevention Act, and a general clampdown on radical societies and the radical press, which prompted William Cobbett, a belated convert to universal suffrage, to flee the country – until converted by Hunt and the northern delegates, Cobbett had endorsed the Burdettite programme in his 'Twopenny Trash', the cheap edition of his influential *Register*. 'Alarm', of course, proved self-fulfilling, forcing the radicals underground into the milieu of the *agent-provocateur*, but the provincial risings of 1817 cannot be explained solely in terms of the culpability of government and the nefarious spy-system. Plans were first mooted during the Hampden Club convention when William Benbow, Joseph Mitchell and other northern delegates were befriended by members of the revolutionary party at the evening drinking and discussion sessions at the Cock, Grafton Street. The provincial radicals, however, wanted to be sure of mass support and popular legitimacy before taking any physical action.[58]

The March of the Blanketeers, their first response to repression, combined all the advantages of legality with all the opportunities of development into something else – in strict conformity with legislation against tumultuous petitioning, they decided to petition in groups of twenty, ten of which number, bearing blankets on their backs, were to march to London to present the petitions. Fearing that a mass invasion of the capital might ensue, the authorities took swift and decisive action to curtail this pioneer hunger march, although a few poor weavers got as far as Ashbourne. Anger at the detention of Bagguley, Drummond, Johnston and the other Blanketeer leaders prompted some indiscreet radicals to talk of making a 'Moscow of Manchester', upon which grounds the authorities hastily arrested the Ardwick Bridge secret committee and other local leaders, including Samuel Bamford and 'Dr' Healey, but most were discharged within a month or so because of insufficient evidence. Meanwhile, plans for the general rising first discussed at the Cock were taking shape as repression intensified. Central co-ordination was entrusted to delegate meetings at Wakefield, where it was agreed that there should be simultaneous uprisings in the towns of the midlands and the north, a concentration of forces round Nottingham, and then a march on London. To ascertain the support which was likely to be forthcoming, Joseph Mitchell was deputed to tour the country and report back to Wakefield. As is well known, he soon acquired a travelling companion, the infamous Oliver the spy.[59]

Postponed to 9 June, the rising – 'England's last revolution'[60] – was a limited affair. Several district delegate meetings had already been raided and there were considerable suspicions about Oliver, but even so, some radicals braved the hopelessly uneven odds on the night. Clothing workers advanced upon Huddersfield in their hundreds in the Folley Hall rising, but they wisely dispersed before military reinforcements arrived. At Pentrich, home base of Thomas Bacon, the veteran Jacobin who had represented the east midlands radicals at the Hampden Club convention, the discussions at the Cock, and the central delegate meetings at Wakefield, Jeremiah Brandreth heroically led a contingent of men through the pouring rain on the fourteen-mile march to Nottingham, stopping at houses and farms *en route* to demand arms and support: on one occasion, a farm servant was accidentally shot. When they finally reached Nottingham, wet and demoralized, they were immediately overpowered by a force of hussars ready in waiting.[61]

The exposure of Oliver by the middle-class reform press was a severe embarrassment to the government, compounded by the acquittal of the Spencean 'conspirators' and a number of seditious publicists, although Brandreth, Turner and Ludlam were found guilty of high treason and sentenced to death. Significantly, Thistlewood was the solitary 'gentleman' listed in the return of persons arrested, committed or detained on treasonable charges in 1817. Drs Watson and Healey were entered as surgeons. All the rest, some 90-odd names, were artisans, labourers and factory workers: there were large numbers of framework-knitters and weavers, trades where Luddism had formerly been strong; half a dozen labourers; spinners, cloth-dressers, colliers, masons, cutlers, coopers, hatters, cordwainers, shoemakers, tailors, printers, engravers, and various other trades.[62] The creed of the working people, democratic radicalism was hardened not crushed by the repression of 1817. When the radicals started to mobilize again, a process which began before the Seditious Meeting Prevention Act had run its full course, there was a distinct class identity associated with the platform. The language of 'the people' still predominated and the programme remained that of popular constitutionalism, but the working people now took a particular pride in their independent opposition to the corrupt and repressive political system. Without acquiring any new ideology or revolutionary strategy, radical reform took on a working-class tone.

This class identity owed much to the links with the trades forged during the strikes of 1818, when workers took advantage of the brief economic recovery to seek restoration of former rates of pay. As the 'pendulum' theory of labour history attests, working-class activity tended to oscillate between political agitation and industrial action according to economic circumstance, with trade unionism to the fore in 'good' times like 1818.[63] Not divided into mutually exclusive forms, working-class protest in the postwar years was a cumulative process: the trade union developments of 1818 strengthened the radical mobilization of 1819 in a manner that defies reductionist or compartmentalist interpretation.

During the strikes of 1818, traditional sectional and regional jealousies were cast aside. The spinners, 'aristocrats' of the factory labour force, led the way here, providing John Doherty, the great trade union leader of the late 1820s and early 1830s, with his first experience of wider working-class organization in projects for a general union of spinners, a general union of all trades, and an alliance with the radicals for fair wages, better conditions and parliamentary reform. Spinners' delegates, sent on tour to collect funds for the strike, encouraged local groups of trades to form general unions of 'operative Workmen, Mechanics, and Artizans', in accordance with the Philanthropic Society in Manchester, formed by deputies from the calico printers, dyers and dressers, hatters, blacksmiths, jenny spinners, cotton weavers, bricklayers, fustian cutters, colliers, sawyers, shoemakers, slubbers, mule spinners and machine makers.[64] Their visit to London, where they were the guests of Watson's radical group, led John Gast and others to formalize inter-trade assistance through the Philanthropic Hercules. Formed out of sympathy for the striking spinners, these early general unions did not endure, but their brief appearance in 1818, along with the close radical involvement in the strike, caused considerable concern to the authorities. When the spinners' committee were arrested, their cause – 'the cause of every friend of Impartial Justice and every Mechanic in England' – was championed by the radicals. The Blanketeer radicals, Bagguley, Drummond and Johnston, whose daily 'harangues' to the strikers had so alarmed the authorities, were imprisoned for speeches at Stockport where they condemned the arrest of the committee and recommended the people to arm in readiness for a national convention; and Watson brought out a special pamphlet in support of the committee whose forthcoming trial presented yet another call on hard-pressed radical funds.[65]

United in support of the Manchester spinners, the radicals and the trades cooperated in a renewed campaign for democratic reform, once the Seditious Meetings Prevention Act had run its course. At a mass meeting in Palace Yard, arranged by the Watsonites, Hunt was joined on the platform by John Gast, the shipwrights' leader, who implored the 'mechanical classes' to 'go forth' with the radicals 'as the Barons of old with a Sword in one hand and the Bill of Rights in the other and demand your Birthrights'. A strident Remonstrance was adopted, reminding the Regent of the lessons of history and of the workers' right to protection – 'every industrious labourer, manufacturer and mechanic, has a right to reap the ample and substantial fruits of his virtuous and USEFUL TOIL'. To enlist the northern workers in the new campaign, Hunt set off for Manchester in January 1819, taking the Remonstrance – and his radical reputation – with him.[66]

Hailed in the north as 'the intrepid Champion of the people's rights', Hunt attracted thousands to the radical cause. 'Meaney who was Lukewarm jacks before', one of Col. Fletcher's semi-literate informers reported, 'now Comes forward and Idlese hunt'.[67] After Hunt's departure, the momentum was maintained by a number of new radical societies, Oliver-free open organizations based on the Wesleyan class system and the model rules of the Stockport Union for the Promotion of Human Happiness. Through their educational and cultural provision, the societies attracted community involvement in the radical cause, particularly in the predominantly single industry out-townships, where they reinforced the strong social structural foundations for collective action. After the rejection of the Remonstrance, this network of local societies provided the co-ordinating machinery for an unprecedented national campaign of mass pressure from without, a mobilization which coincided with economic downturn, with the unwelcome return of 'General Distress' who was busy 'beating up for Recruits in all the Manufacturing Districts of the Kingdom'.[68] Union Societies and Political Protestants spread from their respective bases in Lancashire and Yorkshire to other manufacturing centres – Birmingham and the west midlands, Newcastle and the north-east. Trades which had earlier eschewed political involvement turned enthusiastically to radicalism, led by the most distressed of all, the handloom weavers of Carlisle, whose only hope previously had been government-assisted emigration to Canada. Particular efforts were made to enlist the growing number of Irish immigrants 'in the cause of Universal Civil and Religious Liberty'. To overcome the problem of size and communication in London and large cities, a system of parochial unions was introduced. Special female reform societies were established to emphasize the extent of community involvement in the movement, and the great mass meetings became outings for whole families, trades and communities. The platform, once the preserve of exclusive groups of property-owners and electors, now became the people's own.[69]

The mass platform derived its strength in 1819 from the ready rapport between radicalism and popular political attitudes. Radical poetasters struck the popular chord:

Shall Englishmen o'ercome each foe
and now at home those rights forgo,
Enjoy'd by none beside?
Degenerate race! ah! then in vain
Your birthrights sacred to maintain
HAMPDEN and SYDNEY died![70]

The radical mobilization was self-righteously constitutional, a celebration of the people's democratic history and rights:

We are perfectly satisfied that our excellent Constitution, in its original purity, as it was bequeathed to us by our brave ancestors, is fully adequate to all the purposes of good government; we are therefore determined not to rest satisfied with anything short of that Constitution – the whole Constitution – and nothing but our Constitution.[71]

Articulated on the mass platform, this populist claptrap proved a powerful and effective political language, allowing the radicals to mobilize the masses and outmanouevre the authorities. The exciting rhetoric – the emotive evocation of the glorious ancestors, the intimation of impending violence and retribution – pulled in the crowds, attracting the normally apathetic if not the beer-swilling, wife-beating, flag-waving workers whom historians are no longer allowed to forget. At the same time, the orators carefully proscribed any departure from moral force until all 'constitutional' channels had been explored, so that the discipline and peaceable good order of the mass meetings established a public image of legitimate extra-parliamentary behaviour which the government had no real right to infringe, a considerable victory for the radicals in the 'politics of public space' since the legal status of the mass meetings was far from certain.[72]

Viewed from Whitehall there were insuperable legal and parliamentary difficulties in establishing new powers to silence a campaign situated on the borderline of legality, to counter what Sidmouth described as the 'unprecedented Artifice with which the Demagogues of the present day contrive without transgressing the Law, to produce on the Public Mind the same effect which used only to be created by means unquestionably unlawful'. In the confrontation of 1819, an early exercise in the politics of modern collective violence, both sides – radicals and government – hoped the other would be the first to overstep the mark, transgress the constitution, and lose public sanction. Here the radicals enjoyed a considerable advantage: they were assured of the discipline and good order of their supporters, vast numbers of whom were drilled with military precision by demobilized servicemen; the government, however, lacked the means to restrain its indignant auxiliaries, the impatient local magistrates.[73]

The mass platform thrived on the lively interaction between orators and the crowd, a complex mutual relationship of expectation, performance and response. The middle class were quite welcome to participate in this democratic arena of those *without* the political nation – radicalism was addressed to all the useful and unrepresented classes in society – but they chose to absent themselves. Not a class-exclusive programme, the radicalism of the mass platform became an expression of class pride once the working-class radicals realized they were perforce on their own. Working-class carnivals for all the family, mass meetings displayed a rich repertoire of rituals, symbols and iconography, a language of class without words.[79] Weavers' meetings at Glasgow, Manchester, Paisley and Carlisle had all been won over from emigration to radicalism, but the great Blackburn demonstration on 5 July was the first radical gathering in a weaving community and it attracted vast crowds. It was the first meeting too at which the new female reform societies took a prominent part: the women arrived in a great procession to present the chairman with a 'most beautiful Cap of Liberty, made of scarlet silk or satin, lined with green, with a serpentine gold lace, terminating with a rich gold tassel'. Once prominent in loyalist iconography, the Cap of Liberty was well chosen as the rallying symbol of the post war radical challenge: the Roman badge of freedom, it was an ancient and revered emblem which had adorned Britannia's spear and the coinage of the realm until the 1790s when it acquired revolutionary connotations as the livery of French anarchy and Jacobin terror.[75]

Community and class pride ensured the discipline and good order of the mass meetings, each of which contributed to the 'national union', a cumulative display of irresistible strength marshalled through a series of huge regional demonstrations, of which that planned for St Peter's Field, Manchester in August, under Hunt's chairmanship, was to be the largest yet, 'rather a meeting of the County of *Lancashire* etc. than of Manchester alone'.[76] Convinced that Whitehall was being unduly circumspect in dealing with the radical challenge, the Manchester magistrates decided to 'bring the matter to issue'. 'If the agitators of the country determine to persevere in their meeting', the stipendiary magistrate announced, 'it will necessarily prove a trial of strength and there must be a conflict.'[77] On 16 August, the magistrates gained their bloody victory. At least eleven people were killed and many hundreds injured when the magistrates sent in the inebriated publicans, butchers and shop-keepers of the local yeomanry to arrest Hunt and the other leaders on the platform, and then ordered in the 15th Hussars to disperse the peaceable crowd.[78]

The Peterloo massacre inflamed radical spirits, aroused middle-class public opinion and unnerved the government. The failure of the radicals to advance beyond this vantage ground pinpoints what was to prove a recurrent critical flaw in popular radical strategy. Situated on the borderline of legality, the mass platform offered a powerful alternative to other patterns of 'collective violence': the unstructured, non-political 'turmoil' characteristic of pre-industrial protest; and the elitist, spy-ridden 'conspiracy' favoured by the revolutionary underground of the war years.[79] But at some point the leaders had to decide whether or not the social compact had been violated, whether the time had come when the oppressed people could and should exercise their sovereign right of physical resistance as sanctioned by history, Blackstone and all other authorities. It was this question of timing, this issue of judgement, rather than any absolute commitment to 'moral force' or 'physical force' which divided the radicals at critical moments like the post-Peterloo crisis. At such times, the emphatic insistence on legitimacy proved self-defeating. As radicals agonized over their constitutional right they lost their physical might: while they hesitated and deliberated, mass support dwindled, excitement was squandered, and the initiative passed back to the relieved authorities.[80]

At the crucial point Hunt refused to sanction the Watsonite plans for a full-scale confrontation through simultaneous mass meetings: indeed, he decided to forgo the platform altogether, choosing to rest the radical case on Peterloo itself, looking to public opinion and the courts of law for vindication and victory. In the forum of public opinion, however, it was the established opposition not the democratic radicals who benefited from Peterloo, while in the courts the authorities were exonerated without question, Hunt's unremitting efforts to bring them to justice notwithstanding. The moral and propaganda triumph of Peterloo thus proved a pyrrhic victory. Back in control, the government asserted its power. Parliament was specially convened in the autumn to pass the infamous Six Acts, an attempt to return to the narrow political participation of the eighteenth century: 'taxes on knowledge' were imposed on the press, and the right of public meeting was limited by a series of measures, prohibiting banners and flags, and restricting attendance to those actually resident in the parish.[81]

Angered by the collapse of mass support and the imposition of repression, the aggrieved Watsonites, now under Thistlewood's leadership, reverted to conspiracy and were promptly entrapped in the Cato Street affair – the plan to assassinate the Cabinet at dinner – by George Edwards, the government *agent-provocateur*.[82] Militants in the provinces, however, still hoped for a display of strength, a popular uprising against the repressive government:

> BRITONS arise, and yet be free
> Defend your rights and liberty!
> Boroughmongers long have shar'd the spoil
> The working class shares all the toil;
> Now, or never, strike the blow
> Exert yourselves and crush the foe!!![83]

Forced underground, the provincial diehards began to plan a national rising, at which point the initiative passed from Lancashire to the West Riding, a pattern repeated in the Chartist crisis of 1839.[84] Links with other areas proved tenuous, unreliable or positively dangerous, but they extended across the border, where the 1820 rising – appropriated by nationalist historians as their own[85] – took the form of a popular but short-lived general strike in the west of Scotland. The numbers involved in the English risings at Huddersfield on the night of 31 March–1 April, and at Grange Moor on 11 April were far less impressive, but this attempt at a general rising was more significant in its way than the better-known events of the futile Cato Street conspiracy, which simply confirmed the government in its new repressive powers.[86] The defiant last act of the post war mobilization, the West Riding rising followed immediately on news of Hunt's conviction at York for his part in the Peterloo meeting: the insurrectionists marched behind banners proclaiming 'Hunt the Intrepid

Champion of the Rights and Liberties of the People'.[87] The mass platform had failed, but with Hunt elevated to martyrdom by his imprisonment, critics of the populist radicalism he personified so well were to find it impossible to dislodge him and redirect radical endeavour.

The 1820s

After the collapse of post war mobilization, Hunt struggled to preserve the hard-won independence and integrity of democratic popular radicalism, to prevent any exercise in reformist opportunism or ideological revisionism. A tireless agitator, he hoped to reactivate the mass platform through the development of popular political organization, by the promotion of 'a SUBSTANTIAL, a PERMANENT, and consequently an IRRESISTIBLE, INVINCIBLE *UNION* OF THE RADICAL REFORMERS OF THE NORTH'. Launched shortly after the Queen's Affair, the Great Northern Union was as an attempt to counteract the renewed influence and popularity of the moderate reformers – the Whigs, Burdettites and city politicians who had orchestrated Caroline's public campaign, an old-style Wilkite exercise in 'collusion and convergence'.[88]

Promoted by the opposition, support for Caroline extended into small market and historic towns untouched by post war radicalism. Throughout the land, the people were able to indulge their appetite for scandal and display, an explosion of popular licence which embarrassed the government and nullified the constrictions of the Six Acts. Writers, publicists and *philosophes manqué*, impoverished by their radical stock-in-trade, discovered a lucrative new line in anti-establishment satire and pornography, while the press prospered from the 'aestheticization' of the Affair – incorporated in the conventions of Gothic melodrama and domestic romance, Caroline's history and grievances were compulsive reading.[89] The Affair also catered to the taste for spectacle and display, previously evinced by the ritual and iconography of the radical platform. Often patronized by the opposition and the reform establishment, public processions in support of the Queen were expensive and impressive spectacles, popular pageants which proudly displayed the organization and craft pride of the trades together with the ritual and decoration of the benefit societies – the shipwrights marched six abreast behind elaborate models of Noah's Ark and first-rate ships of war.[90]

The Queen's Affair, Hazlitt shrewdly observed, allowed the people to enjoy 'the mock equality with sovereign rank, the acting in a farce of state'.[91] Despite the personal unpopularity of the new monarch, Caroline's persecutor, George IV's coronation was itself an occasion for proud display. At the Liverpool procession, the glassmakers wore 'hats of glass, with glass feathers, and each carried a glass vase'; then came the local potters with their 'vases of excellent workmanship, enamelled and painted in China; and numerous beautiful models, decorated with leaves'.[92] The crowds in London were smaller than expected, but they would not allow Caroline to spoil the day, to reduce the state festival to sectional fiasco: she was shunned and jeered when she tried to intrude. But this was by no means the end of the Affair.

When the Queen died the following month, the government hoped to dispatch her corpse to Brunswick without any public display, a plan which outraged the London crowd. After a number of bloody skirmishes, during which a carpenter and a bricklayer were shot dead by the escorting troops, the cortege was finally forced to process through the crowded city, a great victory for the people and Caroline's prominent political supporters. The public funeral of the workmen killed by the troops proved to be the most impressive of all the Queen Caroline demonstrations, a great display of artisan radicalism organized by the men's trade and benefit societies against the advice of the metropolitan reform establishment, and co-ordinated by a committee of radical and trades leaders, including Watson and Gast. The Queen's Affair restored the freedom of political agitation, but it did not reactivate the radical platform despite Hunt's timely and strenuous efforts to promote the GNU. Once the high political excitement of the Affair had dissipated, radicals were unable to reach a mass popular audience.[93]

Disillusioned by the vacillating crowds, some radicals abandoned popular agitation to strengthen their own individual commitment to the cause, subjecting themselves to an ascetic regime of mental and bodily self-improvement, a programme of ideological purification and physical puritanism pursued with exemplary counter-cultural rigour by Richard Carlile, the incorruptible Paineite ideologue. The complete reformer, Carlile dismissed the GNU as mere 'show', a futile exercise in agitational radicalism which would contribute nothing to the advance of political education, to the inculcation of the principles of rational infidel-republicanism. Averse to 'instrumental' politics, Carlile rejected collective organization and concentrated instead on the 'march of infidelity', a mission which placed him at the forefront of the struggle for the freedom of the press, the rational agency which would 'work the great necessary moral and political change among mankind – The Printing Press may be strictly denominated a Multiplication Table, as applicable to the mind of man'.[94] Here he found himself in unwelcome alliance with commercial pornographers, as various private prosecuting societies, evangelical and otherwise, tried to ban the publication and distribution of obscene and blasphemous literature. A martyr to the cause, the imprisoned Carlile inspired an heroic campaign of resistance: an inexhaustible 'corps' of volunteers, male and female, stepped forward to ensure the continued circulation of freethought material, forcing the societies to withdraw from the courts thwarted and bankrupt.[95]

Unlike the pornographers, Carlile and his supporters were libertarians not libertines.[96] In the sanctuary of their 'temples of reason', these students of Paineite republicanism, 'zetetics' as they were called, advocated contraception, female equality and free love, a programme of sexual radicalism articulated in the language of the liberal Enlightenment, of individual freedom and moral respectability.[97] The zetetic ideal of self-development seemed to offer a decisive advance beyond the populist attitudes of the platform but Carlile's ideological radicalism was ill-suited to popular needs and attitudes. Most zetetics belonged to the 'uneasy' middling classes, socially incongruent professionals, intellectual shopocrats and ambitious artisans, although there were exceptions: the local 'Temple of Reason' in Stockport attracted weavers and other 'Friendly Mechanics to Civil and Religious Liberty', working-class republicans who repudiated the GNU and its local lower middle-class leaders.[98]

Whatever their social status, zetetics were expected to conform to Carlile's latest exposition of the Paineite formulary, the interpretation of which he reserved for himself alone. A trenchant critic of the empty bluster and personalized style of Hunt's 'charismatic' leadership, Carlile displayed the worst faults of an 'ideological' leader, provoking innumerable schisms among the votaries with his dictatorial pronouncements on matters of doctrine, so different in tone from the eclectic and undogmatic nature of popular radical argument. Infidel, republican and sexual radical, Carlile, the doctrinaire individualist, was also the proselyte of *laissez-faire* political economy. His advocacy of birth control was motivated by Malthusianism as much as by feminism, by his conviction that distress was caused by the people themselves through their bad and improvident habits and the 'excess of their numbers in relation to the supply of labour that can employ them'. The showman of freethought, Carlile stood widely divorced from popular radicalism, culture and experience, a lone opponent of collective endeavour of 'any sect, party, or society, instituted for any purpose whatever. I carry the principle even to trade societies, and think them injurious to the general interests of the trades.'[99]

As articulated by Carlile, Paineite ultra-radicalism led to an individualism more extreme than that advocated by popularizers of classical political economy. Following Wade's pioneering efforts in the *Gorgon*, Francis Place and the 'philosophic' radicals tried to convert the organized labour movement of the 1820s to utilitarianism, to a rational system of economic and industrial relations based on unimpeded market forces.[100] This programme of political and economic reform introduced a third language of radicalism. Dismissing constitutionalism and natural rights, 'philosophic' radicals propounded the Benthamite principles of self-preference and utility, the felicific calculus which would ensure the greatest happiness for the greatest number. A forceful critique of privilege, corruption and protection, the new language of functional efficiency contributed substantially to the growth of reformist sentiment within the middle classes, but utilitarianism had less appeal to the trades particularly when it acquired a Malthusian inflexion. Where Wade had supported trades unionism as a means to secure a high-wage economy, Place campaigned for the repeal of the Combination Laws simply to remove an unnecessary antagonism between employers and employees, a grievance which engendered conflict and diverted attention away from the real factors governing labour – demographic and market forces beyond the control of legislation or trade unionism. Thus at the same time as he campaigned for repeal, Place was the first – ahead of Carlile – to advocate birth control as the only means by which labour could ultimately improve its lot.[101]

In alliance with Hume, the Radical MP, Place first captured the initiative from Gravener Henson – the Luddite veteran who led the trades campaign for a comprehensive protectionist measure to accompany repeal – and then dextrously steered his own repeal proposals through parliament. Repeal, however, did not improve industrial relations as Place intended. Workers in many trades promptly took strike action to restore postwar wage-cuts, displaying an unprecedented trade union consciousness at a time of high employment and rising food prices, much to the concern of parliament, which decided to reconsider the whole issue. Amid fears of the reimposition of the old combination law or something worse, trades committees were formed in London and major provincial towns to defend union rights, an important and successful exercise in inter-trades cooperation and political endeavour. After the new legislation of 1825 confirmed the legal status of trade unions, the *Trades Newspaper* was established to provide a permanent forum for mutual assistance and development. Important conflicts of control and ideology ensued, similar to the battles fought within the mechanics' institutes of the 1820s, as the trades asserted their independence in the face of middle-class patronage.[102] Place's exposition of the laws and benefits of *laissez-faire* political economy soon put him at odds with other contributors: those who defended the rights of labour in traditional and particularist terms by demanding the return of legislative protection; and the new ideologues, the advocates of an anti-capitalist economics based on the labour theory of value.

Early numbers of the *Trades Newspaper* reprinted lengthy extracts from Thomas Hodgskin's *Labour Defended*, one of the most important texts of the new anti-capitalist political economy which located exploitation and distress within the economic process itself, a marked contrast to the traditional radical condemnation of 'Old Corruption' and excessive taxation. According to Hodgskin and the other Ricardian or rather Smithian socialists,[103] workers were denied the right to the whole produce of their labour because goods were exchanged according to the labour they commanded rather than the labour they embodied, a violation of the natural laws of value which benefited the capitalists and middlemen at the expense of the workers:

> 'Betwixt him who produces food and him who produces clothing, betwixt him who makes instruments and him who uses them, in steps the capitalist who neither makes nor uses them, and appropriates to himself the produce of both. . . . While he despoils both, so completely does he exclude one from the view of the other that both believe they are indebted to him for subsistence. He is the *middleman* of all labourers'[104]

Firmly based on the labour theory of value, the new anti-capitalist political economy marked a decisive advance upon the agrarian radicalism of Spence, Ogilvie, Paine and Hall, an outdated analysis which explained poverty and exploitation in terms of physical shortage and the primal theft of the land. But there is considerable debate among historians about the contribution of this 'new ideology' to the making of the working class, to the emergence of a class-specific programme addressed to the grievances of the industrial workers. Recent studies have stressed its limitations, pointing to the 'reformism' of the labour economists, none of whom challenged existing patterns of property ownership and production.[105] The 'new ideology', however, should not be assessed according to an ideal standard of revolutionary proletarian socialism: it must be studied in its proper historical context, within a discourse of 'natural' economic laws and values in which attention was focused not on the relations of production but on the inequalities of distribution and exchange.

There was no reference to forcible appropriation or redistribution in this 'people's science', because exploitation and distress were to be eliminated through the independent creation of the necessary conditions for equitable exchange, beginning with labour exchanges and labour notes, a natural standard of value and medium of exchange. Here the Owenites set the example. Eschewing the need for class or political struggle, they provided the facilities – often at extravagant expense – where all classes could cooperate in the practical implementation of the labour theory of value, the economic foundation for a new moral world of communitarian socialism to be established independently, without conflict or confrontation.[106]

Previously condemned for its vacuous attitude to class and politics, Owenite utopianism is now applauded by socialists and feminists for its 'education of desire', its morally compelling and attractive vision of a better future. Much more than an economic alternative to capitalism, Owenite socialism offered the vision of a society without competition, oppression or inequality, a cooperative community free from the selfishness and individualism engendered by private property, religion and marriage, a new moral and technological world where housework would be shared and mechanized. A liberating influence on many women, Owenism laid the foundations of feminist-socialism, extending the programme of sexual equality and marriage reform advocated within the individualist confines of Carlile's ultra-radicalism.[107] On the radical and Chartist platform, however, women still did not question traditional gender roles – the female reform societies of 1819 and their Chartist successors pledged support for universal manhood suffrage through the rhetoric of motherhood and domestic responsibility, the invocation of a 'natural' order threatened by economic change and adversity.[108]

Turning from women's history to labour history, Owenite socialism was a less innovative and inspirational force: here the Owenites provided the facilities rather than the ideology for cooperative endeavour. An umbrella movement, the cooperative socialism of 1828–34 cannot be described as Owenite in inspiration or direction, since much of it originated in workshop practice and experience. Retail cooperation, for example, developed out of artisan consumer-consciousness and the practice of exclusive dealing. Adopted by the Owenites as a means to the communitarian end, a method of raising the capital to buy the land, the cooperative store offered its members – respectable artisans not dependent on credit – the immediate benefit of unadulterated goods at bulk purchase price. For those who looked beyond such advantages to the land, communitarianism was seldom the ideal: land purchased with cooperative funds was to be divided among the members, allowing artisans to enjoy their own smallholdings, summer houses or retirement homes. On the production side, Owenite sponsorship of cooperative production and labour exchanges encouraged the trades to expand their self-employment schemes – long associated with strikes – into a practical system of unemployment relief. Workers took advantage of Owenite premises, facilities and funds without compromising their independence or their radical politics – Owen, indeed, was still regarded with suspicion in working-class circles where he was remembered as the Tory poor-law reformer, the proponent of 'parallelograms of pauperism'. His autocratic style of leadership and extreme anti-political stance alienated many working-class cooperators who resolutely refused to separate the rights of labour from the rights of man.[109]

Viewed from a working-class perspective, Owenism and the other anti-capitalist prescriptions of the 1820s, underlined the importance of the traditional radical programme, the struggle for democratic control of the state and the economy. At the popular level, the 'new ideology' did not displace the old political attitudes, concepts and aims: it reinforced them. It was political monopoly, after all, which enabled the idle and unproductive middlemen to control and manipulate the systems of currency, distribution and exchange, a point repeatedly stressed in the radical unstamped press. 'The process is this', the *Poor Man's Guardian* explained:

> The landlords and capitalists make the law, – the law makes the institutions, – the institutions place the producers in such a position that they must either starve or sell their produce for a fraction of its value, that is to say, give up the major portion of it to the landlords and capitalists. Thus are the producers robbed, and thus do the rich acquire their riches.[110]

Thus the radicals persisted in explaining inequality and exploitation in political terms. Just as the war-inflated 'funding system' had been built on the base of political monopoly so it was political power that underpinned the capitalist system and denied the worker the right to the whole produce of his labour. The extraction of surplus value, to use later terminology, was perceived in classic radical fashion as an onerous tax, exogenous to the process of production itself. Thus, the 'new ideology' simply extended the ranks of radical demonology: alongside the fundholders, sinecurists, pensioners and other tax-gorgers, there now sat the cotton lords, millocrats and other capitalists, parasitic middlemen whose privileged and tyrannical position of unequal exchange stemmed from the monopoly of political and legal power possessed by the propertied governing classes. Whether directed against the tax-eaters and/or the capitalists, the radical demand was always the same: an end to the system which left labour alone unprotected and at the mercy of those who monopolized the state and the law.[111]

Reform
The working-class tenor of democratic radicalism was forcefully asserted at the end of the 1820s through conflict with moderate or rather 'liberal' reform. A fashionable addition to the political vocabulary, 'liberalism' introduced a progressive and pragmatic perspective to the politics of reform, attracting considerable middle-

class support, particularly in the large provincial towns where direct parliamentary representation was now the desideratum.[112] In popular liberal propaganda, the new reform initiatives, designed to incorporate the middle classes, were given a suitably gradualist guise, suggesting an on-going process of moderate reform, a rational alternative to futile democratic extremism. To prevent popular delusion on this point, Hunt challenged the radical pretensions of the liberals at every opportunity.

The self-professed champion of the 'working classes', he repudiated 'moderate reform', liberal schemes which would enfranchise the middle classes, 'placing power in the hands of some great Cotton Lords, iron Lords, etc.', while leaving labour, 'the property of the people', unrepresented and unprotected, defenceless against 'class legislation'.[113] Here his uncompromising democratic radicalism remained closely attuned to popular needs and attitudes, to the struggle to preserve traditional customs and practices against middle-class interventionism and 'progressive' reform, a conflict which extended beyond the workplace to all aspects of popular culture and experience, death not excluded. There was considerable controversy over Henry Warburton's 'Dead-Body' Bill, a utilitarian solution to the needs of science which offended against deeply-held popular attitudes towards death, burial and the human body. Supported by the liberals and 'advanced' radicals like Carlile, the Bill proposed to remedy the deficiency of cadavers for dissection and teaching purposes by sending surgeons the bodies of paupers dying unclaimed in workhouses and hospitals, thereby condemning the poor, Hunt and Cobbett protested, 'to undergo the degradation which our forefathers allotted as part of the sentence of the murderer'. A number of old-style Tories supported the popular radicals in denunciation of such blatant discrimination against the poor, an alliance strengthened in the subsequent struggles over factory reform and the New Poor Law, when working-class resentment was reinforced by Tory paternalism.[114]

Tories and radicals were also brought together in opposition to Catholic emancipation. Radicals stood apart from anti-Catholic prejudice, but they were outraged by the 'liberal' settlement which removed civic disabilities from middle-class Catholics at the expense of the poor disenfranchised Irish freeholders. To Hunt and Cobbett, advocates of 'Universal Civil and Religious Liberty', Catholic emancipation was merely the starting-point for tackling the Irish problem, a necessary preliminary to the really important reforms – disestablishment of the Church, abolition of tithes, and the introduction of a proper landowner-financed poor law system.[115] Ultra-Tories condemned emancipation as an act of treachery against which 'radical reform' offered the only protection. Drawing upon the old country party programmes, Blandford and his colleagues called for the abolition of rotten boroughs and other reforms to curb the corrupt and traitorous executive. In the ensuing political crisis the Whigs acquired office, committed to the introduction of parliamentary reform.[116]

As the enthusiasm for the Reform Bill demonstrated, the Whigs could still project themselves as the party of the people and constitutional liberty, undermining the independence and integrity of popular radical endeavour by repossessing the language of reform. The details of the Bill were elaborated by the 'liberal' members of the party, since Grey shrewdly calculated that the best way to conserve the traditional political order was to produce a thorough, once and for all, measure of reform. Having expected so much less from the 'apostate' Whigs, radicals were overawed by the 'Bill of Bills', the implementation of which would surely prepare the way for the rapid triumph of democracy, a popular delusion which Hunt was unable to dispel.[117]

Enthusiasm for 'the Bill, the whole Bill and nothing but the Bill' led the working-class radicals into a temporary tactical alliance with the middle-class liberals, a political partnership strengthened by common anger at the obdurate resistance of 'Old Corruption'. Assured of overwhelming popular support for the Bill, the leaders of the political unions were able to deploy the 'brickbat argument', the middle-class version of 'collective bargaining by riot': by summoning up the spectre of uncontrollable popular fury should the Bill be dropped or diluted, they kept the otherwise indolent Whigs committed to reform despite the die-hard parliamentary opposition. While the middle-class reformers exercised their 'art of revolution', the crowd enjoyed considerable licence on the streets. Spontaneous rioting reached serious proportions at Derby, Nottingham and Bristol, where the political unions offered the civil authorities no assistance, dangerously exposing the thin line between 'order' and 'disorder' in the pre-reform era before the introduction of professional policing. At these moments of constitutional crisis, when crowds took to the streets and the political unions adopted a miltant, almost para-military, extra-parliamentary posture, working-class ultra radicals joined their gradualist colleagues in fervent support of the Bill, anticipating the prospect of a real revolutionary confrontation.[118]

Historians of 'high politics' have questioned the influence of such pressure from without, but in the popular mind it was the sovereign force of pubic opinion which finally carried the Bill, overpowering the Lords and the Tories during the 'Days of May', the myth which inspired all subsequent extra-parliamentary agitation.[119] While coordinating the triumphant campaign, the unions hoped to establish an ideological framework for continuing cross-class endeavour, for harmonious economic and social relations. The Birmingham Political Union led the way, but even here, in this city of small workshops, of friendly contact between worker and master, class unity did not persist much beyond the Reform Bill crisis. Briefly concealed by the political excitement, the divisive impact of structural economic change was apparent within the BPU itself, the ruling council of which was dominated not by the traditional small masters but by those on whom they now depended for credit and marketing facilities, large-scale industrialists, merchants and bankers. Unlike the small masters, none of these powerful capitalists had risen from the workshops, but the local myth of 'organic growth' provided these leaders of the 'productive classes' with a legitimizing language of economic opportunity and social cohesion, virtues imbued with regional pride and popular appeal during the Reform Bill agitation. Through such specious rhetoric, the Union projected the requisite image of political and economic harmony, of united support for the Bill and Attwood's currency reform proposals, an 'inflationist' scheme to boost home demand – and hence the West Midlands economy – by high prices, high wages and high profits. Soon after the political crisis had passed, however, the 'productive classes' were rent asunder by economic conflict. Competitive pressures compelled the once independent small masters to adopt the methods and values of the large capitalists, an alignment reflected in the new structure of municipal government which left the workers excluded, disillusioned and embittered.[120]

In Birmingham and elsewhere, class relations deteriorated rapidly once the Reform Bill was passed. Disabused of their initial enthusiasm, the workers convinced themselves that they had been deluded and manipulated: encouraged to expect benefits for themselves, they had been mobilized as a 'reserve army' to ensure the Bill's safe passage simply for the advantage of others. Another potent myth, this popular disavowal of the reform alliance precluded any further exercise in class cooperation. Henceforth, the radical platform was independent and class-exclusive, true to the memory of Henry Hunt, the democratic champion 'Who boldly said in thirty two/The Bill was a cheat and vain/Have we not found his judgement true/We shall never see his likes again.'[121] Unheeded at the time, Hunt's democratic fundamentalism, his unsophisticated but uncompromising opposition to the Bill – 'a *liberal* measure; it certainly was all very good, very *liberal*; but *would it get the people something to eat?*' – marked the beginning of the working-class Chartist challenge.[122]

Confronted by liberal propaganda, reformist sentiment and popular prejudice, Hunt had secured support only in the radical strongholds, the Lancashire towns with a proud Peterloo connection, textile communities where the handloom-weavers were in irreversible decline following the heavy investment in powerlooms in the early 1820s and the riots of 1826. Here, democratic control of the state offered the only hope of amelioration and legislative protection, of reversing the trend towards factory-based, export-oriented, competitive production.[123] For workers in more fortunate circumstances, there was a wider choice available. Support for the Reform Bill apart, parliamentary reform was not a priority for those involved in other initiatives such as cooperative socialism, general unionism and the factory movement.

In London, these various endeavours were co-ordinated by the National Union of the Working Classes, the ultra-radical body which developed out of the Metropolitan Trades Union, formed to embrace the 'new ideology' of the British Association for Promoting Cooperative Knowledge and the general unionism of the northern-based National Association for the Protection of Labour. Radical politics were not ignored: the new union believed that 'the Working Classes of Great Britain and Ireland must obtain their rights *as men*, before they can possess their rights *as workmen*, or enjoy the produce of their own labour'. Radicalism of this order, with its class exclusive language and anti-capitalist labour theory of value, shocked the liberals and philosophic radicals, the popularizers of orthodox political economy who established the rival National Political Union during the autumn of 1831, 'as a step towards leading the two classes to a better understanding and diminishing the animosity which prevailed among the working people against those who were not compelled to work with their hands for wages'. Through this timely cross-class endeavour, Place hoped to retain the initiative, to prevent a popular swing towards the NUWC and its 'absurd notions', at a critical point in the Reform Bill agitation. As it was, the NUWC 'stood at ease' throughout the crisis. Preoccupied with other endeavours, the London radicals displayed an indifference to the Bill, a lack of interest in political reform which confounded delegates from the north, Huntite radicals who were unable to persuade their metropolitan colleagues to join the campaign for a democratic alternative to the Bill.[124]

There was disappointment and anger when the political unions withdrew from agitation as soon as the courts of revision set to work on the new electoral registers, thereby terminating their commitment to a further instalment of reform. Regional rental variations notwithstanding, the implementation of the Reform Act left the working class alone as the unrepresented people, separated from the middle classes by the uniform £10 franchise, the carefully calculated property qualification by which the 'shopocrats' acquired the vote and joined the ranks of the politically privileged. In Birmingham, the Midland Union of the Working Classes was formed in opposition to the 'tardy policy of the "parent union"', as disaffected working-class groups – the non-electors, the united trades and the unemployed artisans – demanded progress towards the democratic programme, the virtues of which were expounded by Hunt in a lecture to the new society, a self-righteous rehearsal of his criticisms of the Bill, which 'by bringing in the middle classes, was intended to enable the Whigs to carry on the Government as nearly in the old way as possible'.[125]

Wise after the event, working-class radicals displayed little enthusiasm for another exercise in pressure from without against the reformed and much strengthened establishment. Dissatisfaction with the Reform Act led to a temporary disillusionment with political endeavour. There was one final act of defiance when the NUWC, enraged by the Irish Coercion Act, stood forward to confront the 'base, bloody and brutal Whigs'. Plans for a national convention, the traditional revolutionary expedient, were brought to an abrupt and bloody end when the police dispersed the crowds at the preparatory meeting at Cold Bath Fields in May 1833.[126] By this time, however, attention was turning away from politics to other arenas, hence the parlous financial plight of the *True Sun*, an ambitious attempt to provide a radical daily paper.[127] In his last public statement before his untimely death, Hunt acknowledged the change of emphasis. The implacable opponent of liberal reform and orthodox political economy, he called upon radicals and workers to join the trade unions in an overwhelming display of working-class solidarity:

> Let the working classes be but united and steady to their purpose, and their oppressors must give way. One of two things must follow. There are seven millions of men in the United Kingdom, who are rendered so many *political outlaws* by the Reform Bill: by the provisions of that act, they are to all intents and purposes so many political slaves. Therefore the Unionists say, you have deprived us of all share in making the laws, and we will make laws for ourselves, as far as the regulating the hours of our labour and the amount of our wages. Consequently, one of two things must happen, either the workmen must have *more wages* and *less work*, or an *equal share* in making the *laws* that are to regulate the measure of labour, wages, and profit.[128]

Trade unionism in the 1830s

The trade unionism which Hunt commended was neither sectional nor exclusive. These were the years of attempts at general union, of efforts to enlist the unskilled, non-society men and women. Under threat at the workplace, skilled workers initiated a process of vertical and horizontal integration, extending the framework of unionism to defend working-class interests, upholding an alternative political economy of traditional practices, artisan ideals and Owenite aspirations. As in 1818, the spinners, supposed 'aristocrats' of the factory workforce, took the lead in the cotton districts. Already under threat from the self-acting mules, they were forced to accept wage reductions in 1829, although not without considerable local struggle – the Manchester fine spinners held out for six months against a 15 per cent reduction. As cyclical depression deepened, they decided to amalgamate in a federal union to prevent the progressive undercutting of piece prices between and within districts. Inspired by John Doherty, the Grand General Union of Cotton Spinners was a defensive move to safeguard earnings and status through the policy of 'equalization' between different mills, towns, and types of machinery. The Union, however, was unable to secure central discipline and resources: forced to support a number of local strikes against reductions, it was already overstretched before the decisive confrontation at Ashton and Stalybridge, where the employers acted in concert to crush workers' organization.[129]

Similar problems beset the NAPL, the simultaneous attempt at general union. Also inspired by Doherty, this ambitious exercise attracted considerable support in the textile districts, where cyclical depression brought factory spinners and handloom weavers together in defensive opposition to wage reductions – the overstocked weavers also sought protection through 'equalization', uniform rates fixed by boards of trade. By 'missioning' in the Potteries and elsewhere, the NAPL extended its support to other areas and industries, but the vast majority of the membership remained in the Lancashire textile district – one-third of the contributing members, indeed, were concentrated in Rochdale, where the striking flannel weavers were the first to call upon the Association for financial support. There was considerable disenchantment when the NAPL, still marshalling its funds, failed to oblige. Local and personal rivalries hindered further progress – Manchester 'dictation' was much resented in Bolton, centre of the skilled muslin weaving trade; Doherty's leadership was frequently criticized, particularly after the enforced closure of the unstamped *United Trades' Co-operative Journal*, and the virement of NAPL finances into the *Voice of the People*, a radical paper which condemned Hunt's opposition to the Reform Bill. When the cotton spinners withdrew in dismay at the exiguous assistance accorded to the Ashton and Stalybridge strikers, the NAPL went into decline which the resourceful Doherty was unable to reverse. Despite his efforts to incorporate Owenite and cooperative initiatives, the NAPL played little part in the events of 1833–4, an upsurge of general unionism from which the dispirited spinners abstained.[130]

The Owenite influence on trade union development was first evinced in the building trades, the pioneers as it were, of the industrial syndicalism which excited considerable interest in the early 1830s, in the aftermath of the Reform Bill. A federal organization of craftsmen in seven trades, the Operative Builders Union was formed to defend its members against the encroachments of 'general contracting' by demanding equal rates of pay, the prohibition of piecework and a limitation on the number of apprentices. Small masters were prepared to support these claims but not the general contractors who insisted on the 'document', a signed renunciation of the Union. It was at this point that Owen addressed the 'Builders' Parliament', advising the union delegates to form a national guild, a combination of workers and sympathetic employers to compete with the large capitalists through direct cooperative contracting. Owen provided the builders with an ideology which strengthened and legitimized their workplace struggles against the competitive deterioration in status and standards, but there were problems. The OBU lacked sufficient funds to initiate cooperative schemes while continuing to finance industrial disputes, its first obligation; the small masters aligned with the general contractors in what had become 'a sort of struggle in order to ascertain whether the employers or the operatives are to be masters'; and there remained a number of 'exclusives', masons, carpenters and other craftsmen who displayed little enthusiasm for general unionism and wished to return to the ways and means of sectionalism. Beset with difficulties, the OBU collapsed in 1834, by which time Owen, together with Morrison, editor of the syndicalist *Pioneer*, had transferred attention to the Grand National Consolidated Trades Union.[131]

Encouraged by his success with the builders, Owen announced his plans for a Grand National Moral Union of the Productive Classes, a great general union which would co-ordinate cooperative production, distribution and exchange through its member trade societies, cooperative stores and labour exchanges, a comprehensive scheme which would instantly eradicate the old immoral competitive world. During the early 1830s, Owen's millenarianism was expressed through passionate support of cooperative endeavours which, as a utopian and communitarian socialist, he had previously disparaged. The number of stores had increased dramatically to around 500 in 1832, when Owen took personal charge of the establishment of equitable labour exchanges, 'the only True Way to Wealth for the Working Classes'. Here the labour theory of value was put directly into practice. Self-employed trade union and other cooperative workers could exchange their products without middlemen or money, through a system of 'labour notes' representing labour time – goods brought in were valued by a committee according to the number of labour hours judged to be necessary for the making. The National Equitable

Labour Exchange opened with considerable style in a grandiose building in the Gray's Inn Road, where lectures and balls were held on
festival nights, for which purpose Owen added a platform and organ
to the large assembly hall, a classical-style room with an embossed
ceiling and gold ornamentation. Difficulties with the rent forced a
move to more modest premises, but Owen proceeded with his plans
for the Grand National Moral Union. In the *Pioneer*, Morrison added
a syndicalist gloss to the proposals, anticipating the advent of a 'House
of Trades, which must supply the place of the present House of
Commons, and direct the commercial affairs of the country, according
to the will of the trades who compose the associations of industry'.[132]

The GNCTU should not be judged as the institutional climax of
these initiatives. A traditional exercise in inter-trade cooperation, the
London trades were brought together by the tailors to co-ordinate
assistance for the silk-weavers and other Derby workers locked out
by employers who insisted on the 'document'. Previous attempts at
general union had developed in this way, through support for workers
involved in a major dispute – the Manchester spinners in 1818, the
Bradford wool-combers in 1825, and most recently, the Kidderminster carpet weavers whose artisan status was lost in 1828, when a five-
month strike failed to restore the 'shilling', the traditional piece price
in the Brussels carpet trade.[133] The Derby lock-out was the emotional
focus for general union – the money sent to Derby, a town evangelised
by Doherty's NAPL, was used to finance self-employment schemes,
the products of which were sold at Owen's labour exchange. Despite
the Owenite and other influences, the GNCTU remained committed
to traditional artisan preoccupations: mutual support in strikes; sick
and superannuation benefits; and the kind of cooperative self-employment schemes already organized by the United Trades Association
for members out of work or on strike.[134]

Formed at a time of economic upturn, when there was already
considerable union activity, the GNCTU provided the trades with
the financial and organizational framework for a concerted campaign
to reverse the competitive, downward slide into sweated, piece-rate
poverty, a practical objective which owed little to the Owenite plans
for social transformation. As attention shifted away from Derby, the
tailors put themselves forward as the test case for equal pay and
conditions, much to the annoyance of the shoemakers and hatters,
who impatiently awaited their turn.

At the start of the brisk season in 1834, the Grand Lodge of
Operative Tailors, a recently formed, non-exclusive union, called its
members out on strike for the abolition of homework and piece-work.
Having contributed so much to the Derby cause, the tailors were
bitterly disappointed when they were denied the support of the

GNCTU, lately appropriated by the Owenites as the agency for social reorganization. After his dramatic appearance on a white charger at the head of the mass protest against the Dorchester sentences, Owen assumed the leadership, condemning strike action in the interests of class conciliation and non-violence. This placed him at odds with Morrison and Smith, syndicalist advocates of class conflict, of a militant general strike which would destroy competitive capitalism and 'banish the word wages from the language, and consign it with the word slavery, to historians and dictionaries'. Despite their differences, Morrison and Smith aligned with Owen in outright condemnation of the tailors, denouncing the strike as sectional and irresponsible, 'destructive and unsocial'. Denied assistance, the strike soon collapsed, after which the membership of the GNCTU declined dramatically – the shoemakers were among the first to leave only to suffer an equally humiliating defeat in their postponed turn-out.[135]

The various attempts at general union were short-lived and unconnected, but general unionism was the predominant aspiration of the insecure workers of the early 1830s, an experience shared, in one form or another, by factory workers, skilled artisans, distressed outworkers, miners, potters and many others. Unrestrained by the traditional discourse of labour relations, Owenism carried the message of union to farm labourers, women workers and those normally excluded from craft societies and trade organization. With its millenarian language, Owenism contributed to the pervasive enthusiasm for general union, for a federation of workers united in trades and districts by oath, ritual and ceremony to uphold the 'rights of industry'. Some 'aristocratic' and unrepresentative trades, such as the provincial printers, were able to remain aloof, but many craft-conscious groups pledged their support – the GNCTU membership included bookbinders, jewellers, gold beaters, scale-beam makers and saddlers. However, the collapse of the GNCTU was a decisive defeat which brought an end to vertical and horizontal amalgamation. Owenites and workers were compelled to rethink their position.[136]

After the débâcle of 1834, Owenites were convinced that attempts to implement the labour theory of value within the existing social system were doomed to failure – overstocked with handicraft goods and dumped unsaleable items the labour exchanges had collapsed ignominiously. No longer a mass movement, Owenism, or 'rational religion', acquired the 'expressive' characteristics of an exclusive classless sect – new members were expected to undergo a three-month probation during which they were trained in the 'great moral truths' of 'social science', communitarian principles which were put into preparatory practice in the cultural activities of the local branch. At the local level – where there was strong democratic opposition to the authoritarian cult propounded by Owen himself in the name of 'All Classes of All Nations' – Owenism offered a veritable 'counter-culture' in which leisure, ceremony and ritual were recast in socialist form as a counter-attraction to the pub and chapel. By the early 1840s, when national attendance at the Sunday lectures on socialism averaged 50,000, there were over 65 branches, many with their own schools, libraries and meeting halls, but by comparison with other movements, Owenite cultural, recreational and educational facilities were expensive, restricting full participation to well-paid artisans and above.[137]

According to conventional labour history, the trade union movement also withdrew after 1834, retreating into the limited objectives and practical considerations of craft unionism. But there was much activity outside this restricted formal and institutional framework as workers continued to protect the 'mysteries' of their trade by secrecy, ritual and folk violence.[138] Militant trade unionism persisted in some parts. In the Potteries, the National Union of Operative Potters, a general union which mobilized all branches of the trade survived until the strike and lock-out of 1836–7, when the district was ringed with troops. The potters attracted considerable support among the wider trade union movement, but they were decisively defeated in a contest which confirmed the political lesson of 1834 – behind the aggressive employers and the 'document', there stood the power of the law and the newly-reformed parliament.[139] As the 1830s progressed, the workers attributed their various defeats to a single cause, the reformed government which denied them the very right of combination – the Tolpuddle 'martyrs' were by no means the only 'victims of Whiggery'. The prosecution of the Glasgow cotton spinners committee completed this politicization. Following the strike of 1837, during which a blackleg spinner was shot, the committee members were acquitted of murder but were sentenced to seven years' transportation for their leadership of an association engaged in illegal activities. The campaign on their behalf, the struggle to defend union rights, carried the workers into Chartism.[140]

The war of the unstamped

The legal and other moves against the trade unions ruptured what remained of the 'reform alliance', the joint effort to pressure the Whigs into further reforms. Throughout the 1830s relations with middle-class radicals steadily deteriorated as campaigns for common causes were conducted in different ways and for different purposes. Through lobbying, petitioning and the mobilization of pressure from without, middle-class radicals campaigned for the repeal of the newspaper stamp duty, trusting that a cheap and free press would prove an effective medium to instruct and elevate the masses, to inculcate the virtues of popularized political economy. By heroic organization and cunning contrivance, working-class radicals openly defied the law, engaging in the 'war of the unstamped' to promote a rather different political education – 'the only knowledge which is of any service to the working people', O'Brien declared in the aptly-named *Destructive*, 'is that which makes them more dissatisfied, and makes them worse slaves. This is the knowledge we shall give them.'[141]

In 1836, by which time nearly 750 people had been brought before the London courts for selling and distributing unstamped papers, the government decided to reduce the stamp duty from 4d to 1d, a measure endorsed by O'Connell and the parliamentary radicals. Viewed from the working-class perspective, however, the compromise was another act of betrayal, a political bargain which 'made the rich man's paper cheaper, and the poor man's paper dearer'.[142]

Most publishers turned to more lucrative commercial ventures, but the war of the unstamped prepared the way for Chartism. The unstamped press bequeathed an important ideological legacy, a working-class radicalism strengthened by the critical engagement with Whig reform, middle-class political economy, and non-political Owenite and trade union endeavour. Here the most influential journalist was Bronterre O'Brien, the *Poor Man's Guardian*, who elaborated a militant, class-conscious radicalism, directed against the newly-reformed, politically protected 'property system', the unjust power over labour which rent and profit commanded. 'The first step', he explained in his agenda for real reform, 'is to establish a FREE PRESS, that *ignorance* may be removed; the next is, to obtain POLITICAL POWER, that we may be enabled to adopt efficient measures for *the removal of property*.'[143] There was also an important organizational legacy. The national expansion of Chartism was facilitated through the systems of communication and distribution established during the war of the unstamped, the networks of newsagents, booksellers and street-vendors which survived prosecution through the succour of well-organized 'victim funds'.[144]

The most popular radical paper of the 1830s, however, was a stamped publication, Feargus O'Connor's *Northern Star*, the circulation of which exceeded all other provincial weeklies. Through its popular tone, comprehensive coverage, and promotional gimmicks, O'Connor's paper established a commercial formula by which the radical message could be carried to the 'fustian jackets, unshorn chins and blistered hands'. The profits financed a national system of full-time agents and reporters, 'professional' political activists responsible for local Chartist organization.[145]

The *Star* was published in Leeds, the northern stronghold from which O'Connor, missionary of the Metropolitan Radical Associations, hoped to develop a national movement for universal suffrage. London proved unsuitable for the purpose: radicals withdrew into educational activity once the war of the unstamped came to an end. The London Working Men's Association was an exclusive artisan forum of mutual self-improvement, an exercise in 'elite politics' open to 'the *intelligent* and *useful* portion of the working classes'. O'Connor was not opposed to collective self-help – he supported the rival Universal Suffrage Club which offered similar facilities 'to elevate the moral, intellectual, and political character of the Working Classes' – but he disapproved strongly of the continued middle-class alliance favoured by the LWMA, which refrained from criticism of the new Poor Law in order not to offend the parliamentary radicals. As the LWMA passed into the hands of middle-class 'Malthusians', O'Connor turned his energies to the Central National Association, a Tory–radical society established by James Bernard, ideologue of the anti-capitalist landed gentry, to unite the agricultural labourers, small farmers and urban workers in opposition to the monied middle class. There was much to commend in Bernard's programme in which universal suffrage was a prepatory step to the abolition of the New Poor Law, the protection of native industry, shorter working hours, currency reform and the proscription of the power-loom, but his anti-democratic Cromwellian pretensions alienated support and divided the metropolitan radicals.[146] Up in the north, workers were more accustomed to Tory involvement in their campaigns for factory reform and the abolition of the New Poor Law, issues which O'Connor harnessed to the radical cause.

The short-time movement and the anti-Poor Law campaign
The movement for factory reform began in the post war years when the first short-time committees were formed to campaign for a reduction in working hours. The dramatic intervention of Richard Oastler and other Tory-radicals in the early 1830s was greeted with some suspicion in Lancashire, where the short-time movement was closely connected with working-class radical and trade union endeavour. On this side of the Pennines, a Tory-radical alignment was an unlikely prospect, since many of the cotton masters – the 'Midnight Robbers'[147] – were Tories themselves, still reviled by the working class for their involvement in post war repression. Until the development of convivial employer paternalism later in the century, popular Toryism was a neglible force in Lancashire, restricted to the minority tradition of militant popular protestantism, upon which basis the first Operative Conservative associations were established in the mid-1830s.[148]

Across in Yorkshire, however, Tory paternalism displayed considerable popular and rhetorical force, invigorated by Oastler's unrestrained condemnation of hypocritical 'liberals', millowners and middle-class 'saints', the philanthropic abolitionists who overlooked 'those magazines of British infantile slavery – *the worsted mills in the town and neighbourhood of Bradford!!!*'.[149] The 'king of the factory children', Oastler upheld the sanctity of the altar, the throne and the cottage against the godless materialism and 'deadly curse' of the factory system.

Through the pilgrimage to York and other demonstrations organized in compact with the short-time committees, Oastler mobilized extra-parliamentary support for Sadler's Ten Hours Bill, a restriction on hours for children and young people which, it was assumed, would establish a uniform working day for all factory workers. Here the factory reformers were outmanoeuvred by the newly-reformed government, which brought forward legislation for an eight-hour day for children between the ages of nine and thirteen. Humanitarian in appearance, the Factory Act 1833 was phrased in the language of political economy which strictly rejected any legal interference with the hours and conditions of adult workers, whose working day was soon lengthened as employers introduced a 'relay system' of two or more shifts of 'protected' child workers for each adult shift.[150]

Althorp's Act was an important landmark in social policy, introducing the principle of inspection, but it was a bitter blow to the short-time movement which lost impetus and direction. In Lancashire, the movement took an Owenite turn under Doherty's leadership in the National Regeneration Society, a general union which hoped to implement a plan first recommended by John Fielden, the radical cotton manufacturer and MP for Oldham: acting in cooperation with sympathetic employers, the united workers would restrict their labour to eight hours without any reduction in wages, an arrangement which would benefit all except non-producers on fixed incomes. As the necessary employer support was not forthcoming, the Society adopted a more militant stance until the débâcle of 1834 brought an end to all plans for a general strike.[151] Oastler tried to make the most of the Act, 'the Masters' own Law', by insisting on its proper implementation, recommending the use of industrial sabotage against transgressors. 'The day of petition, argument and persuasion was passed', he proclaimed, warning the recalcitrant employers that it was now 'The Law or the Needle'. If they persisted in defying the law of the land, then he would personally 'teach the Factory children to defend themselves, to prevent themselves being murdered, contrary to Law':

I will, in that event, print a little card about Needles, and Sand and Rustynails, with proper, and very explicit directions, which will make these Law-breakers look about them, – and repent that they were ever so mad as to laugh at the Law and the King.[152]

It was rhetoric of this order – the open advocacy of direct action – which accounted for the applause elicited by Oastler and his colleague, Joseph Rayner Stephens, in the parallel campaign against the 'Fiend-begotten Coarser-Food New Poor Law'.

More than any other issue, the New Poor Law, the hated 'Starvation Act', set the working class at odds with the middle-class radicals who provided the ideological support for the 'centralizing' Whigs and their 'Malthusian cant'. The Poor Law Amendment Act introduced the principle of 'less eligibility', a deterrent test of destitution, by which relief for the able-bodied was available only within workhouses where living conditions were deliberately regulated below the lowest standard of independent labourers outside. Within the new union 'bastilles', families were to be separated and the sexes kept apart, a heartless Malthusian stipulation which enraged Oastler and Stephens, implacable opponents of a law which was 'unchristian, unnatural and unconstitutional'. On the anti-Poor Law platform, Stephens introduced himself as 'a revolutionist by fire, he was a revolutionist by blood, to the knife, to the death':

> sooner than wife and husband, and father and son, should be sundered and dungeoned, and fed on 'skillie', – sooner than wife or daughter should wear the prison dress – sooner than that – Newcastle ought to be, and should be – one blaze of fire, with only one way to put it out, and that with the blood of all who supported this abominable measure.[153]

Although generally described as a 'revolutionary Tory', Stephens came from a liberal and radical background – he first acquired notoriety as an advocate of Anglican disestablishment, for which militant dissent he was expelled from the Methodists. Unlike Oastler, he spoke in favour of universal suffrage, but he was an infrequent and equivocal advocate of the democratic cause.[154] This was where O'Connor – proud and worthy heir to Henry Hunt – made his decisive contribution. During the autumn and winter of 1837–8 – by which time the Poor Law Commissioners had turned their attention to the north – O'Connor joined Stephens and Oastler on a major platform campaign, arranged by the South Lancashire and West Riding anti-Poor Law Associations, the regional bodies which co-ordinated the activities of innumerable township groups into which the local short-time committees transferred their energies. Addressed to this labour movement, O'Connor's speeches were a comprehensive condemnation of the politics of the reformed parliament, of the obvious determination of the Whigs and their 'sham' radical allies to suppress and exploit the working people, a concerted policy of which the persecuted Glasgow spinners were the latest victims. The Poor Law was but one aspect of the 'new system of the political economists':

> The auxiliaries to this infernal law are the Factory scheme, the rural police, and the complete destruction of the Trades' Associations, which was the last remnant of power in the hands of the working classes by which supply and demand could be wholesomely regulated.[155]

Through the platform and the press, O'Connor carried the social content and defiant tone of the anti-Poor Law agitation into the new Chartist movement, a working-class campaign for democratic control of the state and the economy.

Early Chartism

At first, O'Connor and the northern radicals regarded the Charter with some suspicion, as a diversionary ploy by those opposed to the anti-Poor Law agitation and militant provincial radicalism. Such fears were not ungrounded. Jointly signed by the LWMA and a group of parliamentary radicals headed by O'Connell, the Charter was a moderately phrased statement of the traditional radical programme, drafted with the assistance of Francis Place on the understanding that the radicals would neither attack the Poor Law nor advocate socialism. In the provinces, the Charter was not adopted as the symbol and focus of radical endeavour until it was linked to the national petition and the national convention, schemes which emerged from the revived BPU.[156]

Having waited patiently for the reformed parliament to implement an 'inflationist' financial policy, the BPU returned to political agitation with the onset of economic depression in 1837. In pursuit of the requisite currency reform, the BPU now advocated universal suffrage, for which purpose a 'national petition' was drawn up, a tactic which took account of procedural changes in the reformed Commons where – to the detriment of 'petition and debate' – the presentation of petitions no longer conferred the right to speak.[157] Throughout the north radicals were weary of petitioning, particularly after the decisive defeat of Fielden's motion for the repeal of the Poor Law Amendment Act, but inertia was swept aside by enthusiasm for the Birmingham proposal. One great mass supplication, the national petition was to be 'the last petition', a final test of the contractual relationship between the government and the sovereign people. Wary of the consequences, the BPU suggested that the presentation of the petition should be entrusted to a national convention, a proposal which immediately aroused the old ultra-radical enthusiasm for an 'anti-parliament'.[158]

The election of delegates, the collection of the national rent, and the other preparations for the convention fused the various local agitations into a campaign of national dimensions, extending the co-ordination already established within O'Connor's Great Northern Union.[159] The Charter, Dorothy Thompson has stressed, was adopted by an already existing network of organizations, radical groupings which owed little or nothing to the LWMA or the signatories of the People's Charter. Some had existed uninterrupted since the days of Huntite opposition to the Reform Bill; most had been formed or reformed since 1836 as working-class radicals protected themselves against the consequences of Whig reform and middle-class political economy.[160]

In the large cities, where collective action was difficult to effect, trade societies provided the framework for political mobilization.[161] Established in 1838 after O'Connell's denunciation of the Glasgow spinners and the convening of the Select Committee on Combinations, the Manchester Combination Committee organized an effective boycott of Victoria's coronation procession (a marked contrast to the trades' prominence in the 1831 festivities), and then marshalled an impressive display of support at the first Chartist demonstration on Kersal Moor, an occasion which attracted a wide variety of insecure and politicized trades: proletarianized artisans – the proverbially radical shoemakers and tailors; the building trades, craftsmen in conflict with general contractors; organized but insecure factory workers, the spinners and dyers; and the smiths and metal workers, engineers whose aristocratic status was as yet unestablished.[162]

The real Chartist strongholds, however, were not the cities but the surrounding towns and out-townships, the typical industrial communities of the manufacturing districts – the textile towns of Lancashire, Cheshire and the West Riding; the hosiery, lace and glove-making areas of the east midlands; the depressed linen-weaving centres of Barnsley and Dundee; and the 'industrial villages' of the mining and ironworking districts, the north-east coalfield, the South Wales valleys and the Black Country. Here occupational ties were reinforced by other loyalties, by networks of mutual knowledge and trust which facilitated powerful and effective political organization.[163]

The diverse localities were united by the press and the platform as Chartism extended the techniques of mass agitation deployed by Hunt and the post war radicals. Local and regional initiatives were accorded national significance through reports in the *Northern Star*, which quickly established itself as the comprehensive and definitive voice of the movement, a role which earlier radical papers had been unable to fulfil. The platform acted as an integrative and cumulative force, as the movement rallied around the indefatigable O'Connor, the itinerant champion of the people. True to the memory of 'ever-to-be-loved' Hunt, O'Connor toured the country, deliberately exploiting his platform appeal as a gentlemanly and charismatic demagogue to connect and unify the movement, to lay the foundations for more regular forms of working-class organization.[164]

Chartism consolidated its hold on the manufacturing districts in the autumn of 1838 through a series of torchlight meetings. These exciting gatherings, held in the dark evenings after work to prevent the victimization of factory workers, stretched the right of public assembly to the very limit, intimidating the local authorities with militant rhetoric and defiant processions – to the accompaniment of small arms fire, 10,000 marched around the township of Hyde 'with torches burning, bands playing, clarions sounding and the cries of Death or our Rights'.[165] The presence of Stephens – the Savonarola of the early Chartist movement – added considerably to popular excitement and the magistrates' alarm, as he advised the torch-lit crowds to arm in resistance to the Poor Law, a righteous battle for which God had provided 'cold lead and sharp steel'. Stephens, it would seem, was deliberately courting arrest and trial, so that the legality of the Poor Law could be tested in the courts.[166] Whatever the intention, his unrestrained and irresponsible language served to identify northern Chartism with physical force, thereby hindering O'Connor's efforts to promote a unified campaign of 'forcible intimidation', in which the intimation of impending violence, the rhetoric of menace, was a standard platform device. For a brief while, he succeeded in conciliating the Birmingham middle-class radicals, the main opponents of Stephens, but when forced to choose between 'moral force' and 'physical force', he pledged his wholehearted support for Stephens, the first martyr of the movement, arrested by the government in late December following the ban on torch-light meetings.[167]

It was not until this point that O'Connor himself recommended the Chartists to arm in 'constitutional' response to government aggression and persecution. Legitimized in defensive terms, by the pervasive fear of repressive and provocative violence, of a repetition of Peterloo, the mass arming of the Chartists challenged the accepted limits of open constitutional agitation, accentuating the apocalyptic mood of 1838–9, the apogee of the mass platform. Excitement and expectation reached fever pitch as Chartists throughout the nation pledged their allegiance to the General Convention of the Industrious

Classes, the anti-parliament which would present the people's 'last petition'.[168]

There was a considerable middle-class presence in the 'People's Parliament'. Several delegates were drawn from the 'uneasy' or 'middling' class, radical members of the petite bourgeoisie and lesser professions, identified by interest and sympathy with the working class below. Financially independent, these lower middle-class 'Jacobins' assumed the offices and functions which economic circumstance denied the working-class rank-and-file: attendance at the Convention was an impracticable proposition for most working men, given the very real risk of victimization, and the uncertain prospect that a job would still be waiting when full-time political duties were finally discharged. Besides these stalwarts, there were a number of middle-class delegates whose interest in Chartism was instrumental and transitory. The Cobbettites were the first to withdraw, once the Convention refused to restrict its competence simply to the supervision and presentation of the petition. They were followed by another group of financial reformers, the Birmingham middle-class radicals, isolated in condemnation of any discussion of 'ulterior measures', the extra-parliamentary methods which they had previously engaged as the 'brickbat argument'.[169]

Their withdrawal marked a decisive shift in the leadership and temper of the movement, reflecting the widespread frustration at the unexpected delay and deliberation which characterized the Convention's early proceedings. A less hesitant tone came to the fore, reinforced by the arrival of new working-class delegates, but the Convention remained critical of the conspiratorial plans of Harney and the small group of ultra-radical delegates, custodians of the insurrectionary tradition. Harney's power-base was the London Democratic Association, an ultra-radical body whose success in recruiting the 'lower trades' of the East End was attributable not to ideology but to the absence of alternative organization in this part of town. Modelled on the Jacobin Club, the LDA, Harney and his co-conspirators trusted, would purge the Convention of traitors and initiate the necessary insurrection. As it was, their revolutionary rhetoric, steeped in images of the French Revolution, attracted little support within the Convention where they were accused of playing into the hands of government agents.[170]

Much as he opposed Harney's insurrectionist strategy, O'Connor did not condemn the LDA representatives. O'Connor, indeed, often appeared deceptively revolutionary as he called upon the Convention to assume the bellicose posture and positive leadership essential to the success of 'forcible intimidation', a militant strategy of confrontation which depended upon the *threat* of co-ordinated nation-wide insurgency. In the absence of such central direction, O'Connor feared the movement would disintegrate in disillusion, with futile and precipitate outbreaks in the most militant localities. The move to Birmingham was an important step to bring the still circumspect Convention up to the mark of provincial feeling.[171]

At Birmingham the Convention at last issued its long-awaited Manifesto of 'ulterior measures', a series of specific extra-parliamentary expedients, most of which were better suited to middle-class pressure from without – the withdrawal of funds from savings banks, the conversion of paper money into gold, and other tactics of the fabled 'Days of May'. But the Manifesto also recommended a 'sacred month' or general strike, a proposal for outright confrontation between producers and parasites according to the scheme elaborated earlier by William Benbow in his *Grand National Holiday and Congress of the Productive Classes*. Enthusiastically endorsed at Whitsun demonstrations, the Manifesto, or rather the 'sacred month', dominated the discussion at the reconvened Convention, where there was a new mood of militancy following the rejection of the Petition and the display of hostility by the newly-incorporated Birmingham authorities. Poachers turned gamekeepers, the local magistrates – prominent members of the BPU – enlisted the muscle of the Metropolitan Police to disperse the crowds which gathered in the Bull Ring in support of the Convention, a violent end to the spurious unity of the 'productive classes'.[172]

As tension heightened, O'Connor and others hesitated to proceed with the 'sacred month', a retraction which revealed the inherent weaknesses of open constitutionalism. For a while, O'Connor succeeded in appearing more revolutionary than he actually was: the leading exponent of the rhetoric of menace, he spoke ominously of a defensive rising, of spontaneous and invincible armed resistance to government repression. Events, however, belied the rhetoric. The Whigs acted with unexpected forbearance, keeping the state and the military out of provocative confrontation, a shrewd policy which left the maintenance of order to the newly-reformed local authorities. Although there were a number of local clashes, there was no major outrage: in the absence of another Peterloo, there was no occasion for a national defensive rising. To maintain momentum and credibility, Chartists were compelled to advocate positive action, to move beyond the 'constitutional' rhetoric of righteous retaliation to the threshold of violence, at which dangerous point they were pulled up short by O'Connor's disavowal of the 'sacred month'.[173]

Not a syndicalist scheme based on organized trade unionism, the 'sacred month' was a radical mobilization predicated on the active involvement of the overwhelming majority of the population, depending upon the disciplined participation of all the unrepresented people throughout the land. In the absence of the required support, a fact sadly confirmed by the Convention's missionaries in agricultural and other districts, O'Connor refused to lead the Chartists into an unequal struggle against the disciplined, organized and loyal armed forces at the government's disposal. Together with O'Brien, he persuaded the Convention to cancel the 'sacred month' and to substitute instead an innocuous three-day withdrawal of labour, starting on 12 August.[174]

This retreat was a bitter and disorienting blow in the manufacturing districts, where Chartists had eagerly armed themselves for the decisive confrontation. The abnegation of central leadership was compounded by the absence of the local leaders, many of whom were arrested at this critical point by the wily authorities. Some localities braved the odds and persisted with their 'national holiday', particularly in the northern and western areas of the cotton districts, but during the course of these three days more Chartists were arrested than at any period before 1842. The abortive 'national holiday', a sorry end to the 'constitutional' phase of the first Chartist campaign, dispelled the myths that had sustained physical-force radicalism, dissipating the strength of Lancashire Chartism. The cotton districts were to play little part in the various conspiratorial schemes of the winter of 1839–40.[175]

After the ending of the Convention, Chartism operated on two levels, as it were, open and secret. In the localities, spirits were maintained through a variety of public activities – exclusive dealing, readings from the *Star*, educational classes and fund-raising exercises for the defence of arrested colleagues and leaders, the support of prisoners' families and the construction of Chartist halls. At the same time, an underground movement developed, through which plans were elaborated for a national rising early in November until Peter Bussey, chairman of the West Riding secret delegates, took his leave of Bradford and sent the word round to desist, an act of treachery and cowardice for which 'Fat Peter' was never forgiven.[176]

While the north was quiet, thousands of colliers and ironworkers, armed with clubs, muskets and pikes, marched on Newport in the early hours of 4 November, the most significant Chartist excursion into physical force. Those involved were not destitute workers driven to insurrection by technological redundancy or industrial decline: the insurgents came from a rapidly expanding industrial region where wages were comparatively high. The Newport rising must be studied within the specific context of industrial south Wales. A class society from birth, social segregation had produced a culture of alienation, sedition and violent protest. The historical sense of nationality together with cultural-linguistic exclusivity shielded the indigenous workers from the forces of social control and the agencies of bourgeois hegemony, but the Newport rising was assertively a Chartist affair not a nationalist attempt to establish an autonomous Silurian workers' republic. Chartism enjoyed remarkable popularity in south Wales, where political radicalism had previously attracted little interest outside of artisan and lower middle-class circles in the established towns. With the arrival of Chartism, working-class radicalism took control of the industrial valleys – in 1839 there were over 25,000 enrolled or committed Chartists in Glamorgan and Monmouthshire, one in five of the total population. Chartism was the first movement to overcome 'valley mentality', to set local and sectional rivalries aside, uniting the workers in a national campaign, a mobilization which extended beyond the colliers and ironworkers to the navvies, canal boatmen and the unemployed. Here there was no loss of momentum following the failure of the Convention and the clampdown by the authorities. Tension continued to increase as the Chartists, protected by family ties, work gangs and other secret channels of communication, proceeded with their plans to rise throughout the region, to occupy all the towns amidst the saturnalia of 5 November, a scheme modified by John Frost who advised an earlier concentration on Newport, the town where he had once been mayor and magistrate. On the fateful night, the Chartists succeeded (albeit sometimes by impressment) in mobilizing the workforce, native and immigrant, skilled and unskilled, in a brave attempt to capture Newport, trusting that they could rely on sympathetic action by workers across the border, where the events in Wales would serve as signal and inspiration. As it turned out, the Newport rising confirmed O'Connor's worst fears: partial outbreaks were doomed to bloody and ignominious failure – delayed by atrocious weather and indecisive leadership, the marchers were finally confronted by the well-prepared military in Newport: 22 Chartists were killed and many more were injured, the greatest casualties inflicted by the military on the British civilian population in the nineteenth and twentieth centuries.[177]

O'Connor led the campaign to save Frost, Williams and Jones from the gallows, an issue which reopened the field of constitutional protest – petitions for their reprieve collected more signatures than the National Petition itself. He called for a 'second convention' to coordinate the legal efforts, the first obligation of the permanent national organization which he hoped to establish to unify and consolidate the movement. Here he found himself at cross-purposes with the physical force militants led by the revolutionary Dr Taylor who wanted a second convention to instigate the insurrection without which Frost could not be saved. O'Connor absented himself from the convention – a gathering of working-class militants closely linked to the underground movement – but he was asked to endorse the plan, first proposed by the northern delegates committee at Dewsbury, for a concerted rising on 12 January. Having bided his time, O'Connor exposed the scheme in the *Star* on 11 January, after which there was no prospect of success, but abortive risings took place in Dewsbury and Sheffield, and the LDA engaged in diversionary activity, spreading rumours of an insurrectionary plot in the capital to prevent the despatch of extra forces to the provinces. A fortnight later, physical force Chartism came to an end with the failure of Robert Peddie's Bradford rising. After the commution of the death sentences – a wise political move by the government – tension subsided but the Chartists still remembered the Welsh leaders and campaigned persistently for their pardon and return from transportation.[178]

The National Charter Association

Chartism survived and adapted but the movement never recaptured the millenial mood of 1839, the confident expectation of decisive confrontation and heroic victory. Chastened by the defeats of the winter, the Chartists regrouped in the summer of 1840 around a permanent organizational structure, the National Charter Association, the first working-class political party, with a national executive, weekly membership payments and elected officers. In establishing a permanent organization on democratic and inclusive lines, the Chartists tried to maintain the essential 'unlimited' character of platform agitation, a principle which distinguished the NCA from other working-class voluntary associations in the general trend towards more sophisticated structures, based on regular subscriptions and the election and payment of permanent officials.

The successful 'new model' organizations of the 1840s relied upon memberships that could attend meetings regularly and pay an assured weekly contribution, requirements which tended to exclude women and unskilled workers. Committed to members unlimited, the Chartists sought to enroll the poorly paid and the casually employed, the otherwise excluded workers who had little or irregular time to spare when in work, and unlimited time but nothing to subscribe when unemployed. Recruitment amongst the poor and vulnerable precluded the traditional methods of democratic self-government, the regular general meeting and the rotation of offices. At local level, popular control was effected by quarterly meetings and elections, a democratic version of the old parish system of local government. At national level, accountability became a critical issue: paid missionaries were hired and controlled by district delegate meetings, and the Executive itself was kept under scrutiny by a short Annual Delegate Convention, an additional cost beyond the means of several localities, a typical example of the poverty which impeded internal democracy and often left the Executive without proper payment and adequate resources. Economic problems were compounded by legal difficulties since self-governing societies were still not allowed to federate: a national movement could exist only without separate branches or divisions, a centralized and undemocratic structure adopted without demur by the Anti-Corn Law League.[179]

In working-class circles, the law presented problems not only for the Chartists but also for the 'new model' organizations which hoped to consolidate their financial and other resources through 'affiliation' or 'amalgamation'. As their funds and functions expanded, working-class voluntary associations sought legal recognition and protection through friendly society legislation, but this was by no means a simple procedure. Within the friendly society movement itself registration was not easy to obtain, particularly for the rapidly expanding affiliated orders, the 'national' brotherhoods which overtook the old local independent societies in popularity in the manufacturing districts during the 1840s. In 1845 the Independent Order of Oddfellows, Manchester Unity boasted 737 affiliated 'lodges' in Lancashire and 600 in Yorkshire, and the Ancient Order of Foresters 332 and 383 'courts'; by 1848, national membership of these affiliated orders stood at 249,261 and 84,472, respectively. The independent ways and means of the local societies were still respected – in accordance with the old tradition of rotating officials, the Foresters were controlled through an annual moveable committee. The Manchester Unity were more centralized and efficient with permanent directors, but the lodges themselves set their own rates of contribution and sickness benefit: the funeral fund, however, was conducted on a district basis, the first step towards an actuarially sound system of insurance which soon led to the abandonment of the 'equal levy' principle.

The social advantages of membership were considerable: following the tradition of the old local societies and box clubs, collective self-help was promoted through a convivial male-dominated culture of monthly club nights and regular feast-days (as well as obligatory attendance at the funeral of a deceased brother). For those who disapproved of such unnecessary social expense, the Hearts of Oak, established in 1842, offered life and sickness insurance through a postal system of contribution and payment, a centralized operation in which there was no personal contact between the members, most of whom were clerks, shopkeepers and tradesmen. But it was the accentuated ritual and ceremonial of the affiliated orders – the regalia, grips, passwords and other elaborate 'mysteries' unmatched by other forms of friendly society – which accounted for their remarkable working-class popularity and appeal. On account of this secret culture, however, the affiliated orders were regarded as dangerous combinations not entitled to the legal benefits of registration. Without legal protection they were vulnerable to peculation and embezzlement – in 1848 the Corresponding Secretary of the Manchester Unity embezzled £4000 entrusted to his care, to be acquitted by the law courts on the grounds that the Unity was both a mere partnership and an illegal organization. New legislation in 1850 specifically permitted the registration of societies with branches, but Tidd Pratt still insisted that each branch should incur the expense of registering as an entirely separate society.[180]

A few years later, the amalgamated trade unions were brought within the framework of friendly society legislation. After the collapse of general unionism in 1834, craft societies had concentrated on strengthening their own resources through internal 'amalgamation', an exercise achieved or attempted in fourteen trades' groups before the establishment of the Amalgamated Society of Engineers in 1851, the famous 'new model' union which continued and completed the process of centralization and control. During the first phase of amalgamation, fixed national officers replaced the rotating or removeable head society, a change which allowed stricter regulation of funds and benefits at a time when unemployment payments exceeded total income in some local societies. Strengthened by amalgamation, the craft unions offered a range of 'friendly society' benefits, through which they were able to exercise some control over the supply and distribution of the labour force. Given the funds involved, the risk of embezzlement was high, but the newly-amalgamated unions believed they had acquired the necessary legal protection by registering under the Friendly Societies Act in 1855.[181]

By this time, the flourishing retail cooperative societies had succeeded in their campaign for special legislation to meet the needs of a movement transformed by the 'dividend'. Introduced by the Rochdale Pioneers at their Toad Lane store in 1844, the 'dividend' – the division of profits among members in proportion to the amount spent – was already in operation in over 200 societies in 1850, heralding a shift from community-building to shopkeeping. From 1846, cooperative societies were able to register as friendly societies, but registration hampered their operations in a number of ways, restricting the sale of goods to members only, until the introduction of the Industrial and Provident Societies Act in 1852, the first of a series of measures which provided the legislative framework for the continued expansion of the movement in retailing and manufacturing. Here again, the advantages accrued to the better-paid workers: the proscription of credit by most societies excluded the poor from the collective self-help which provided members with decent unadulterated goods and

an automatic savings bank. The virtues were much appreciated by
the female clientele, but the complex organizational and committee
structure of the cooperative movement was a male preserve.[182]

The NCA must be assessed within the context of the general
development of sophisticated but exclusive organizational structures,
a trend which extended beyond the legally insecure voluntary associations to the popular religious sects. Within the chapels, the functions
formerly exercised on a democratic basis were gradually monopolized
by professional ministers, a process of 'role differentiation' which
excluded women and left the laymen without influence or control.
As consolidation predominated over mobilization, growth rates
declined, a deceleration which began in the 1820s, by which time
Wesleyanism was no longer a significant force in working-class culture
and politics. The drift into denominationalism, most evident in
Methodism, provoked a number of schisms and secessions, as ranters
and enthusiasts tried to preserve the norms and values of the original
movement. These secessionist groups fared considerably better until
the 1840s when they fell in line with the Wesleyan gradient and were
themselves subject to organizational consolidation. The Primitive
Methodists were no exception: removed from the itinerant ministry
in 1841, women were shuffled to the margins, barred from the offices
of steward, trustee, delegate and superintendent. By the mid-century,
the various Methodist organizations were devoting their resources not
to recruitment but to sustaining denominational life, by satisfying
the needs of existing members and leadership groups.[183]

The NCA fulfilled a similar function, maintaining the spirits of the
Chartist faithful through a lively 'movement culture', but Chartist
organization was not a denominational end in itself. The struggle for
political power remained the essential consideration: the emphasis,
however, changed from confrontation to collective self-provision, a
cultural broadening which would prepare Chartists to make the most
socially beneficial use of the Charter once it was won. In line with this
prefigurative strategy, the 'ulterior measures' of 1839 were redeployed
within a radical branch culture, a stimulating experience of the shape
of things to come. The boycott of excisable articles was transformed
into Chartist teetotalism with tea-parties, soirees and balls; the practice of exclusive dealing developed into the Chartist cooperative store,
the profits of which were often given to the families of imprisoned
comrades; and the 'occupation' of parish churches, the religious confrontation of 1839, was replaced by a non-sectarian form of radical
preaching and worship. The NCA was the cornerstone of a democratic counter-culture of Chartist schools, stores, chapels, burial
clubs, temperance societies, and other facilities for education, recreation and the celebration of radical anniversaries.[184]

Branch culture, a grassroots complement to political struggle, helped to hold the movement together during the lean periods, preserving the structure intact and in readiness for the return of excitement and the next great national agitation. Not an act of withdrawal, 'cultural' Chartism gave the movement its remarkable staying-power, its ability to reactivate the mass platform at the first suggestion of cyclical depression or 'social tension'. Limited funds hindered the expansion of facilities within the NCA, but considerable care was taken to prevent deviation or exclusivism, organizational and denominational characteristics which, George White warned, 'might lead to the establishment of a sort of aristocracy in our ranks or take the attention of our most active men from the great question of the Charter'.[185] When these traits appeared, O'Connor, a tireless agitator in the services of the NCA, issued his famous condemnation of 'Church Chartism, Teetotal Chartism, Knowledge Chartism, and Household Suffrage Chartism'. Misjudged by historians, O'Connor strongly approved of collective self-help, provided such moral improvement was pursued within the democratic and inclusive framework of the NCA: what he opposed was elitism, the establishment of exclusive standards of Chartist membership, the withdrawal from mass action, developments which led back to the middle-class embrace.[186]

The 'New Move' of 1841, to which the 'deviationists' were annexed, developed out of discussions with Place and middle-class radicals about the illegality of the NCA and the possibility of a renewed reform alliance, a return to the elite politics and ideological alignments of the LWMA. For those who disapproved of O'Connor, the NCA and class-conscious 'fustian' Chartism, there was the alternative National Association for Promoting the Political and Social Improvement of the People, formed by Lovett, Collins and other gaol-instructed revisionists. By eradicating ignorance, drunkenness and thraldom, the Association offered the working class the self-respect necessary for the attainment and exercise of the franchise, but middle-class patronage facilitated the requisite instruction in the virtues of working-class self-reliance.[187]

Those involved in the 'New Move' were brought together after the defeat of the Whigs at the general election, an unexpected reverse which united voluntarists, free-traders and parliamentary radicals in defence of civil, economic and religious liberty. This coalescence produced the Complete Suffrage Union, a middle-class initiative which O'Connor immediately denounced as 'complete humbug', a plot to gain working-class support for Corn Law repeal. Against his opposition, plans proceeded for a conference at Birmingham, centre of Arthur O'Neill's Chartist Church, now high on the list of good causes patronized by the philanthropic Quaker, Joseph Sturge, leader of the 'moral radical party'. The conference – dismissed by O'Connor as 'a remuster of the rump of the Old Malthusian London Working Men's Association' – proved surprisingly radical. Delegates rejected the name 'Chartist' but accepted all six points of the Charter. Sturge, an expert in extra-parliamentary agitation, took to the country, mobilizing 'pressure from without' for this democratic programme through the abolitionist techniques of lectures by agents, petitions, lobbying, intervention in elections and the nomination of parliamentary candidates. As economic distress intensified in the summer of 1842, he contemplated a nationwide campaign of passive disobedience, but the next conference of the CSU was postponed until December, by which time O'Connor and the NCA had seized the initiative.

Chartists were in the majority at the conference, but the Charter was ruled out of discussion. The organizing committee presented the six points in the form of a Bill of Rights, a document prepared in typically high-handed manner without even consulting Lovett and the working-class promoters of the 'New Move'. By this tactless assertion of leadership, Sturge and his friends incensed the Chartists who were required to repudiate their past, to renounce their independence, their very identity. In a remarkable outcome, Lovett and O'Connor united to defend the hallowed name of the Charter, a term of pride and honour, 'the legislative text book of the millions'. Defeated by this unlikely alliance, Sturge and his colleagues withdrew from such 'uncongenial fellowship', unable to fulfil their social function 'to do the people a little good'.[188]

Not an act of Chartist folly, the collapse of the CSU was an object lesson in middle-class social arrogance. Humanitarian and liberal, middle-class 'moral radicals' always assumed the right of leadership in accordance with paternalist traditions of philanthropy and Christian stewardship. A successful businessman who put conscience before profit, Sturge was a 'compleat reformer', a 'physical puritan' who placed principle above political practicality. But despite his sincere commitment to democratic government, he refused to acknowledge democratic organization within the movement for parliamentary reform itself, to accept working-class independence and self-sufficiency. 'There was no attempt to bring about a union – no effort for conciliation – no generous offer of the right hand of friendship', Thomas Cooper one of the Chartist delegates recorded: 'We soon found that it was determined to keep poor Chartists "at arm's length". We were not to come between the wind and *their* nobility.'[189]

The failure of the CSU led to a decisive change in middle-class radicalism as exercised in the instrumental fashion of Cobden and the leaders of the Anti-Corn Law League. Officially unconnected with the CSU, they had welcomed Sturge's initiative as 'something in our *rear* to frighten the Aristocracy – And it will take the masses out of the hands of their present rascally leaders'.[190] After the events of 1842 – the Plug Plot disturbances and the CSU fiasco – the ACLL revised its strategy and abandoned the 'brickbat argument'. Cross-class mobilization was replaced by the 'politics of electoral pressure', an avowedly middle-class policy which concentrated on securing the votes of those within the political nation, to whose numbers provident free-trade supporters were appended by the purchase of forty shilling freeholds.[191]

Opposition to the ACLL accentuated the working-class tenor of the NCA, a reactive or dialectic strengthening of class-consciousness characteristic of the 1840s. Ambivalent about free trade, Chartists were unequivocal in their hostility towards the League, the political agency of the 'mushroom' manufacturers who were impoverishing the nation, leaving the home economy distressed in reckless pursuit of profit and markets overseas. Implacably opposed to these 'steam lords' and the 'great moneyocracy', Chartists waited to be joined by the 'industrious portion of the middling classes', the impoverished 'shopocrats' whose economic interests coincided with their own in a stable and prosperous domestic economy. 'The interests of shop-keepers and that of manufacturers are the very antipodes one to the other', O'Connor persistently maintained: 'The interest of the manufacturer is to have cheap labour; while the interest of the shop-keeper is to have dear labour.' Having rejected the CSU, Chartists waited to incorporate and subsume the distressed lower middle class, to enlist the bankrupt, poor-rate defaulting shopkeepers, a timely accretion of strength which would allow them to capitalize on the widely-predicted disintegration of the Whigs.[192] While the leadership prepared for this desirable political conjunction, the rank and file favoured direct action in the form of the postponed national holiday or general strike.

There was no consideration of 'ulterior measures' in 1842, but the 'Plug Plot' strikes followed the rejection of the Chartist petition – a well-organized affair with three million signatures – when the Parliamentary Radicals, professed supporters of universal suffrage, exacerbated class tensions by leading the Commons' attack on demagogic agitation.[193]

The 'general strike' of 1842
During the early 1840s Chartism developed into a labour movement, providing the local leadership for both political and industrial endeavour. Leach, Campbell and McDouall promoted initiatives to strengthen links with the trades, to transform the NCA into a political

parallel of organized trade unionism. In the large cities, the NCA developed through trades' organization – London, indeed, became a major Chartist centre with some thirty localities, twenty of which were established by particular trades. Organizers and spokesmen of the working class, Chartists were involved from the start in the strike movement of 1842.[194]

Amid the most severe distress of the nineteenth century, the stoppages began in the Staffordshire coalfield, brought to a standstill in July by a number of strikes against wage reductions and the truck system. Here the familiar tactics of the 'Plug Riots' were first put into effect: plugs were drawn from boilers to prevent pit engines from resuming work as strikers marched from one establishment to the next, encouraging the workers to join the turnout.[195] In August the initiative passed to the cotton district where the distressed workers, victims of progressive wage-cuts, were threatened with a further 25 per cent reduction. Protest action, organized by local Chartists, persuaded most employers to withdraw the reduction, but the dispute with the recalcitrant masters rapidly developed into a 'general strike', an exercise in economic and political pressure based upon community support and participation. Emboldened to demand the restoration of 1840 wage rates, striking cotton workers were supported by a general turnout of the local labour force – colliers, labourers, hatters, railway navvies, timber-yard workers and building workers – not all of whom had particular wage grievances. From this regional stronghold the strike was to spread across the country, carrying a strong political message: until the Charter was the law of the land there could be no guarantee of 'a fair day's wage for a fair day's work'.[196]

It was at grassroots level that the strike was linked to the attainment of the Charter, a demand ratified by the *ad hoc* trades conference in Manchester, rapidly but democratically convened before the cautious NCA Executive arrived on the scene. The conference developed out of a meeting of the five engineering trades – millwrights, engineers, smiths, iron moulders and mechanics – who were the first to recommend the cessation of labour until the Charter became the law of the land, a resolution subsequently endorsed by a meeting of various trades and millhands, and finally confirmed by the Great Delegate Trades Conference which assembled on 15 August under the chairmanship of Alexander Hutchinson, the smiths' secretary. Most delegates were cotton factory workers (spinners, powerloom weavers, calico printers, dressers and dyers) or members of the engineering and metal-working trades, but the less secure artisan trades were also well represented, particularly in the clothing and building sectors, and there was a small number of distressed textile outworkers, mainly silk-weavers and fustian cutters. Still to acquire full aristocratic status and security, engineers and spinners, the supposed beneficiaries of industrial change, took the lead, rallying workers behind the Charter, their best guarantee of economic protection. Of the 85 trades in attendance, 58 voted immediately for a strike for the Charter, 19 had no mandate but to support the majority decision and only seven were instructed to vote for a strike for wages alone. [197]

Fortuitously, the NCA Executive had planned to meet in Manchester on 16 August, the anniversary of Peterloo, to unveil the memorial to Henry Hunt. On arrival, however, they declined to assume command, to extend the turnout into an all-out confrontation with the authorities, the militant policy advocated by McDouall. Having rebuilt the movement after the disastrous confrontationalism of 1839, O'Connor and the national leadership were fearful of the consequences of partial and incomplete insurgency, an unequal struggle against the adamantine authorities. At the national level, the caution was justified: strong in the cotton district, the strike was patchy and uneven elsewhere – in the words of Hill, editor of the *Star*, 'there was no element of nationality, and consequently, no element of success in it'. To facilitate the necessary withdrawal, O'Connor and the Executive expressed support for the strikers, but then castigated the factory owners of the ACCL, claiming that they had deliberately forced the working class out on strike in a conspiracy to coerce the government into corn law repeal, a myth not entirely without substance. In the absence of central leadership, the political strike quickly collapsed, although the powerloom weavers maintained their action until the end of September: after seven weeks' struggle, somehow sustained on strike relief pay of 4d a week, they returned to work, having at least prevented a wage reduction. [198]

At its height, the strike involved up to 500,000 workers stretched across the country from Dundee and the Scottish coalfields to south Wales and Cornwall. In some places it remained a wages issue, as at Stockport, a particularly depressed cotton town, where there had been a lengthy but unsuccessful weavers' strike in 1840;[199] in several other towns, sympathetic shopkeepers, whose profits had slumped with the progressive wage-cuts, offered strikers credit on the strict condition that wages remained the only demand. Significantly, the strike was most disciplined and peaceable where the Charter was the avowed aim. Organized outside official trade union channels, the strike was administered by Chartist-dominated local strike committees, *ad hoc* democratic bodies which disciplined strikers against attacks on property, persons or machinery, and issued permits to allow necessary work. No such restraint was displayed at Stockport where there were serious workhouse riots and much plunder and pillaging, or in the Potteries, scene of the most violent destruction since the Bristol riots of 1831.[200] The turnout at Hanley – already aroused by Cooper's inflammatory rhetoric – provoked twenty-four hours of desperate saturnalia, a reprise of the old 'pre-industrial' urban riot, as hungry colliers and other workers went on the rampage, an explosion of popular anger which neither the authorities nor the Chartists had the power to control.[201]

Throughout the industrial districts troops and special constables were called in to quash the strike, clashing with the otherwise orderly but intimidating turnout crowds – itinerant plug-drawers were usually led by women singing Chartist hymns. More than 1100 people were tried in connection with the turnouts before Special Commissions at Stafford, Chester, Lancaster, Liverpool, York and Carlisle; in 1842, indeed, more people were arrested and sentenced for public order offences – for speaking, agitating, rioting and demonstrating – than in any other year. O'Connor, the prize catch, was charged in a 'monster indictment' along with other members of the Executive (including McDouall who had fled to France) and the local leaders of the strike in Lancashire: he escaped imprisonment, however, through delay, legal technicalities and a tactical retreat by the Tory government, the first evidence of 'liberalization' by the ruling orders.[202]

Thereafter Chartist influence on the trade unions was probably strongest in the newly-formed National Miners Association, an ambitious attempt at all-grades organization of coal, lead and iron-stone miners 'to equalize and diminish the hours of labour and to obtain the highest possible amount of wages'. Staffed at the centre by committed Chartists, the NMA was a fighting union with low subscriptions and no benefit function.[203] Having learnt the lesson of 1842, the new union cautioned against open political involvement and partial industrial action, but the advice was ignored on the north-east coalfield at the 'binding' of 1844.

Back in the early 1830s, the pitmen of Northumberland and Durham had revolutionized coalfield protest. By systematic action – transferring funds and wages from branches which had settled to those which had not – Hepburn and his 'preacher vanguard' halted years of deterioration in pay and status. In 1832, however, the employers crushed the union with blackleg labour, cottage evictions and the document. After this subjugation – much applauded by the Whig government – the pitmen endured a difficult and humiliating decade until spirits revived with the formation of the NMA and the appointment of the Chartist lawyer, W. P. Roberts, whose courtroom invective exposed the anomalies and absurdities of the Bond. The foolhardy decision to strike in 1844, a time when coal stocks were particularly high, went against the national intentions of the NMA, and the advice of Roberts.

By taking action, pitmen hoped to initiate an alternative Chartist political economy in the pits, securing the full value of their labour, previously withheld by the rents, royalties and revenues extracted in tax-like fashion by idle and unproductive middlemen. Capital was to be accorded fair remuneration, but this did not appease the coalowners who refused to negotiate on any point throughout five months of bitter struggle. Crowd action against non-strikers and imported blackleg labour was disciplined and selective, with women playing a prominent part in the 'rough music' – here, indeed, the night-time activities of 'Rebecca' may well have been undertaken by women and not by men dressed in female costume as was the practice elsewhere. Dignity and restraint were maintained as the employers imposed their will – the evictions were transformed into convivial demonstrations, celebratory festivals at which the dehoused were feted as heroes and victors. Such brave defiance belied the terrible suffering which finally compelled the strikers to return to the pits, forced to accept the employers' terms of the Bond. The culmination of radical and industrial protest in the north-east, the strike of 1844 ended in total defeat and victimization.[204]

Chartism in the 1840s

After 1842, Chartist politics were less open and spontaneous. The movement survived in a structured and organized form which no longer preserved the unlimited character of popular agitation and street demonstration. As open protest declined and the attack on the Poor Law subsided, women withdrew, leaving the routine (and drink-assisted) organization of the NCA localities to the men. Although still encouraged to join the NCA, women were excluded from the higher echelons of the movement – it was most unusual for women to act as officers or committee members other than in specific female localities, which diminished in number in the early 1840s along with other purely female radical and democratic societies. Chartists who advocated women's rights, restricted the vote to unmarried and widowed women only, in accordance with the necessary dominance of the male breadwinner ideal and the consequent sanctification of female domesticity.[205] Once the leading rioters, women retreated to the respectability of the hearth, but social protest – direct action to preserve the living standards of the home and the family – was still perceived as women's work, hence the transvestism of the 'Rebecca' rioters, nocturnal assailants of toll-gates and workhouses.[206]

At the time women withdrew, Chartism at last achieved some success with the agricultural labourers, still the largest occupational category. Unable to participate in open political agitation, farm workers could join the Chartist Land Company without fear of dismissal or eviction. Through the Land Plan, Chartism expanded its support in the agricultural areas and old southern towns, while the administration and organization of the scheme gave a new sense of purpose to existing NCA localities, a much-needed boost after the dispiriting failure of petitions, strikes and platform agitation.[207]

Misunderstood and undervalued by historians, O'Connor's Land Plan enjoyed remarkable popularity at a time of general enthusiasm for spade husbandry and small farms – a gamut of politicians, philanthropists and political economists promoted and patronized a variety of schemes for settling 'surplus' or dispossessed workers on the land. The radicals were no less enthusiastic: here options ranged from utopian communitarianism to peasant proprietorship, but the distinction between communal and private ownership, a split which went back to Spence and Paine, was of little significance – all agreed that misery and oppression were attributable in the first instance to the usurpation and monopolization of the land, 'the people's farm'. In the 1840s, Owenite socialists, Spenceans and the members of the Chartist Land Company shared a common vision of an alternative society, an egalitarian, artisan-based economy of small commodity exchange and labour credit.

Neither backward-looking nor diversionary, the Land Plan was a welcome complement to Chartist agitation in the 1840s. The scheme was populist not paternalist, an individualist tone set by O'Connor who presented himself as 'a beef-and-mutton, a pork and butter and bread and milk and honey Radical. I am an open-air, a work-when-I'm-able-and-work-for-myself-and-my-family-Radical'. Workers on their own plots of land would reap the full fruits of their labour, thereby establishing the real or 'natural' value of labour, upon which basis other workers could then freely choose between entering the factories or working the land. A means of escape from 'artificial' society, the Land Plan was also designed to reverse the downward competitive pressure on urban wage rates.[208]

O'Connor's plan was distinguished by its democractic and participatory nature. Access to the land was neither dependent on upper-class patronage nor restricted to the high wage 'aristocracy of labour' through the conventional priority system of 'first pay first served'. Shares were payable in small weekly instalments: when an estate became available, a 'ballot' or lottery was used to allocate the farms and homesteads, a fair and exciting procedure. Furthermore, a Land and Labour Bank was established to attract working-class deposits and mortgage the estates so as to give the Land Company more cash in hand with which to purchase more land more quickly. At this stage, legal registration was essential, but once again, Tidd Pratt refused to allow certification under the terms of Friendly Society legislation. Attempts to register under the Joint Stock Companies Act were no more successful: the courts declined to extend limited liability to a company based on mass shareholding among poor people.[209] These legal problems added to the practical difficulties experienced on the estates where most of the allottees were industrial workers with no knowledge of agriculture. Perplexed and confounded by the persistent legal obstacles, O'Connor lost his health and wealth in promoting the company which, the Commons select committee discovered, he subsidized to the sum of over £3000 before it was finally dissolved in 1851. The difficulties and problems notwithstanding, the Land Plan enjoyed remarkable popularity in the 1840s when Chartists dreamt of joining the lucky allottees on the first estates – 'With their freehold for their empire/ And their fireside for their throne.'[210]

Rural protest

The Land Plan apart, Chartism failed to enroll the agricultural workers, pauperized labourers whose protest was perforce covert and violent – nocturnal incendiarism not platform politics was their safest (and most satisfying) form of protest. Often the carefully prepared final act of the traditional trilogy of threatening letter, disguised avenger and burning stack, incendiarism reached its peak in East Anglia in 1843–5 when villages in Bedfordshire and Cambridgeshire were left desolate by the most spectacular blazes. Community support ensured that few arsonists were caught or convicted despite the offer of lucrative rewards for information. On some occasions, indeed, the fires were accompanied by community celebration, as hundreds of labourers came to jeer, cut hoses, roast turnips in the heat, and steal dead animals and property.[211]

Protest of this form – violent but limited in objective – had been a feature of rural life since the inflationary 1790s, although some scholars maintain that wartime polarization allowed new and open forms to develop. According to Andrew Charlesworth, social and spatial segregation produced separate and insulated communities of labourers, the foundation for collective action through which the aggrieved workers, stirred by memories of a pre-war 'golden age', put pressure on the still paternalist gentry and clergy for the restoration of traditional standards and practices.[212]

The open protest of the post war years, however, revealed the weakness of the labourers as an independent force. In East Anglia, the 'Bread or Blood' riots of 1815–6 were a complex amalgamation of disturbances, involving townspeople, industrial workers, fenmen and agricultural labourers. Amid food riots and wage demands, attention was drawn to the farmworkers' plight by the symbolic and ceremonial smashing of mole ploughs and threshing-machines, technology which threatened winter employment. Disturbances were particularly persistent in the fenlands, where the various groups were united in protest against the 'improvements' which, by drainage and other means, were undermining the traditional 'peasant' economy of the area. In the strong loam and claylands of Essex, Suffolk and Norfolk, where the labourers demonstrated alone, open protest was brought to a swift halt by the decisive action of the authorities, a display of strength which forced the riotous labourers to revert to covert and arsonist forms. There were further disturbances in the region in 1822, this time solely directed against agricultural machinery, which the rioters, all agricultural labourers, wished to abolish: once again, vigorous action by the authorities quickly suppressed the revolt.[213] In 1830, however, there was no such response from the authorities: the Captain Swing riots, which began with a wave of incendiarism, spread unimpeded across the southern and eastern counties, engulfing the cereal-growing part of the country.

What set the Swing riots apart from earlier rural disturbances was not greater misery but the unprecedented political context. Unnerved by the reform crisis of autumn 1830, the authorities were slow to move against the rioters who were themselves far from immune from the political excitement. Carters, drovers and drivers, the linkmen of the road, kept the villagers informed of latest developments, as did itinerant workers on the tramp, adding to the knowledge available from the politically conscious village craftsmen, artisans connected with the radical clubs and trade societies of the southern market and county towns. Not a co-ordinated exercise in physical force politics – many of the 1400 or so reported disturbances highlighted specific and particular local grievances – the Swing riots occurred at the conjuncture of reform excitement and economic distress, unique conditions in which agricultural labourers could protest openly and defiantly, supported by other groups in rural society.[214]

Sawyers, papermakers and other workers, 'sworn foes to machinery of all kinds', joined the riotous labourers in the destruction of threshing-machines, a course of action which hard-pressed small farmers did not oppose – having mediated in the wage riots at Overton, Henry Hunt continued on his business trip to Salisbury, scene of extensive machine-breaking, where local farmers distributed money and liquor, encouraging the men to 'Smash away, let us all be on all equality'.[215] With opportunist guile, farmers aligned with the rioters to wrench tithe and rent reductions, to make the landlords and clergy bear the anger and cost of the labourers' demands. Rural artisans and petty tradesmen, impoverished by the long depression in the agricultural districts, often supported the riotous labourers in their demands for beer, food and 'payment', and participated to the full in the ritual humiliation, or 'mobbing', of Poor Law officials and other victims of charivari. Traditional and saturnalian in form, the Swing riots cut across occupational and class divides, but it was the labourers who felt the full force of the repression finally imposed by the new Whig government anxious to dissociate reform from rural riot and European revolution: 1976 prisoners were tried before 90 courts and special commissions sitting in 34 counties; well over 600 were imprisoned, nearly 500 transported and 19 executed. Ruthlessly repressed, the riots were not without effect: the widespread introduction of the threshing-machine was delayed for twenty years and a modest advance in wages was achieved in many parishes.[216]

The political and social alignments of Swing did not endure. Rural society was finally and decisively polarized by the New Poor Law, the cost-effectiveness of which delighted farmers and other ratepayers. A cruel solution to permanent rural unemployment and underemployment, the Act enraged the labourers who violently opposed the implementation of 'less eligibility' and the workhouse test. Violent resistance to the Act reached a climax in the Great Bircham area, where hundreds of armed labourers were 'bound in blood and blood' in a minor peasant war.[217] Direct action was accompanied by a number of attempts at organized opposition. The well-run anti-Poor Law campaign at Wickford, Rayleigh and Rawreth developed into the Rawreth Working Men's Association, the first radical organization administered by farm labourers.[218] Resistance was also organized through agrarian trade unions, the dimensions of which extended well beyond the well-known society at Tolpuddle. Throughout the southern counties the United Brothers amassed a fighting fund during the spring and summer of 1835, but its power was crushed by the 'document' and an employers' lockout, before the planned industrial action in the crucial harvest and hopping season. After this reverse, there was a massive outbreak of incendiarism, animal maiming and other forms of 'malicious damage' directed against the guardians and others connected with the Poor Law.[219]

Covert protest directed against the whole sectrum of 'upper-class' rural society – landowners, farmers, clergymen, guardians and magistrates – remained the norm in the agricultural districts throughout the age of the Chartists, but there were alternatives. The most fortunate labourers were able to insure themselves through friendly societies which, in the East Riding at least, were by no means the preserve of skilled urban workers:[220] it was not until the 1860s, however, that the Foresters, with their comparatively low subscription, were able to recruit heavily in the largely agricultural southern and western counties.[221] The less secure labourers often opted for deference and subservience, hoping thereby to retain favour and employment, to escape the horrors of the union workhouse. A few were more heroic and joined John Thom, alias Sir William Courtenay, the charismatic millenarian leader, in righteous condemnation of the Poor Law, the Established Church and the 'present ignorant House of Commons'. Blessed with a striking resemblance to the traditional likeness of Christ, Thom proudly identified himself with 'the poor labourers and working mechanic', but like other millenarian leaders he drew most of his support from people of moderate social standing, including a number of farmers and a small circle of adoring female disciples. Fearing that he was enticing labourers from their work and inciting them to violence, the Kent magistrates ordered his arrest, but the constable who served the warrant was shot and then impaled to death on Thom's sword. Troops were despatched to Bossenden Wood where the millenarians were encamped: in the desperate fight which ensued, Thom and ten of his followers were killed.[222]

The Rawreth WMA apart, few farm labourers took a prominent and conspicuous part in organized radicalism. The Ipswich Chartists tried to spread the message through a series of rallies in small market towns, where they hoped to establish WMAs to evangelize the surrounding villages, but the hostility of local landowners and employers soon forced them to abandon the programme. There was one area of rural Suffolk, however, where Chartism was strong: John Goodwyn Barmby, the local country gentleman, helped to establish a number of WMAs in the villages around Saxmundham, where Chartist rallies attracted thousands of labourers until the movement collapsed in 1840. In the absence of a figure like Barmby, the first person in England to call himself a communist, landlord and employer pressure was incontestable.[223]

In rural counties, Chartism was a minority creed of the local town-based artisans – journeymen rather than masters – who displayed considerable generosity in their contributions to the various victim funds, in recompense as it were, for their inability to participate in militant activities themselves. Moral-force radicals, the rural Chartists were loyal supporters of O'Connor and the NCA, an indication of their bitter hostility to the liberals, damned in the agricultural districts by their support of the Poor Law. Never a mass movement, rural Chartism was rejuvenated by the Land Plan, a revival of interest and enthusiasm which pre-dated the exciting events of 1848.

1848

The success of the Land Plan apart, there seemed little prospect of a revival of Chartist agitation in the late 1840s, by which time the economy had acquired a new stability. The worst trough had been experienced amidst the cyclical crisis of 1839–42: thereafter a number of growth factors carried the economy through the commercial crisis of 1847 with remarkable resilience and strength. There was some temporary distress in the manufacturing districts but industrial Britain was now out of sequence with continental Europe (and famine-stricken Ireland), where catastrophic economic depression – the combination of famine prices and high unemployment – immediately preceded the revolutions of 1848.[224]

The mass platform creaked into motion, however, before the first news from revolutionary Paris. Impressed by the response to defend O'Connor's parliamentary seat, recently won at Nottingham in the general election of 1847, the NCA Executive introduced the third national petition. A revivalist exercise, the campaign relied upon established leaders and traditional tactics. Pride of place went to O'Connor, the 'Lion of Freedom', whose credentials were enshrined in the past history of the movement, the oft-repeated chronicle of 'our wars, our struggles, and our conquests'.[225] A comparative newcomer to the platform, Ernest Jones revitalized the rhetoric of forcible intimidation. 'By showing a bold physical front, they would prevent the necessity for physical action', Jones insisted as he outlined the required programme of organized agitation:

> We must agitate and organize! One simultaneous meeting, at one hour of one day all over the United Kingdom, to shew our organization. One vast petition, to prove the people themselves how strong they are in numbers. One vast procession of the men of London to present it, while a Convention watches the debate, and keeps piling the pressure from without, till every town in England and Scotland rallies with the same spirit . . . we are not men of non-resistance and passive obedience; we will not be the aggressors – but if we are struck, will return the blow and they must stand the consequence.[226]

Harney added a further note of menace in an article entitled 'The War of Classes', where he sought to direct the campaign away from 'the great-trodden path – the beaten round of the towns in the manufacturing districts' to the enrolment of the physically strong part of the working population, the railway labourers, miners, soldiers and the like – 'those masses of physical force, which, even at present, though deplorably wanting in mental power, strike alarm into the minds of the supporters of the existing system'.[227] There was no such breakthrough in Chartist recruitment, but the 1848 campaign, a shadow of the great agitation of the previous decade, induced near-hysterical alarm in middle-class circles when the platform became identified with European revolution and Irish insurgency.[228]

The Chartists greeted the news of the February Revolution in

France with unbounded enthusiasm. 'We have been meeting, talking, and writing for the last ten years', Harney observed, 'and have not got our Charter; the French, with three days' work, have obtained the Charter and something more.' Since the mid-1840s, Harney, a passionate internationalist, had been trying to strengthen the radical platform by incorporating 'red republicanism', the creed of the revolutionary European artisans exiled in Britain. Known to Marx and Engels as 'Citizen Hip-Hip Hurrah!', he managed to unite diverse nationalities (and social philosophies) in the Fraternal Democrats, an important advance beyond the convivial round of meetings, dinners and toasts at which the otherwise quarrelsome emigres joined the Chartists in cosmopolitan celebration of popular and democratic national anniversaries. Forerunner of the First International, the Fraternal Democrats was envisaged as a pressure group within the NCA, the internal force which would hasten the necessary changes in programme and agitation – 'henceforth mere Chartism will not do, ultra-democracy, social as well as political, will be the object of our propaganda'. Ironically, progress was curtailed by the outbreak of revolution: the repatriation of the political refugees and the introduction of a tough new Alien Act in 1848 deprived the Charter-Socialists of their red-republican allies.[229] Rival internationalist bodies suffered a similar loss as aristocratic nationalists and other non-socialist exiles rushed home to enjoy the 'springtime of the peoples'. The People's International League, the Mazzinist successor to Lovett's Democratic Friends of All Nations, was reduced to a domestic rump of advanced middle-class liberals, social reformers and dissident Chartists, 'rational reformers' who regrouped as the People's Charter Union, an avowedly 'moral force' association which condemned the 'violent' Chartist platform but applauded physical revolution abroad.[230]

Anti-socialist and anti-liberal, O'Connor did not participate in organized internationalism, a metropolitan preoccupation which was given inordinate coverage in the columns of the *Star*. 'Let Frenchmen work for France, Russians for Russia, and Prussians for Prussia', he protested in suitably populist prose: 'I WILL WORK FOR HOME SWEET HOME.'[231] For O'Connor, of course, 'home' included Ireland, an oppressed nation whose desperate plight was often overlooked by those who pursued more exotic continental connections. A vigorous critic of Irish coercion, O'Connor won much respect for his parliamentary denunciation of the Crimes and Outrages Bill, a spirited stance which prepared the way for the formal alliance between the Chartists and the Irish Confederates, the long-awaited agreement which dramatically strengthened the radical challenge in 1848.[232]

Until this time, an open alliance between the Irish and the Chartists had been blocked by Daniel O'Connell's commanding presence.[233] Among Irish immigrants, however, there was considerable support for Chartism, the Liberator's proscription notwithstanding. Some rejected O'Connell's constitutionalism in favour of the republican alternative, a proud tradition revered by the Chartists – the *Northern Star* took its name from the journal of the United Irishmen, from whom Feargus O'Connor traced his radical ancestry; re-enactments of the trial of Robert Emmett were the dramatic highlight of Chartist counter-culture.[234] Many immigrants simply ignored O'Connell's injunction, as ineffective at local level as the 'no-politics' rule of trade unions: in the eclectic conviviality of Chartist localities there was a bewildering overlap in the membership of supposedly discrete and competing movements.[235]

The O'Connellite stance of the Catholic Church was a countervailing influence, but it was not until the second half of the nineteenth century that religion emerged as the defining element in working-class communities. Unlike the unskilled and socially homogeneous post-Famine immigrants, earlier arrivals were not compelled to group together in collective self-defence around their local priest and church. Within each district there could be Irish families from several periods of immigration – some that had come by way of other English or Scottish districts, some who were Protestants, some who had drifted away from the Catholic Church, some who had deliberately broken with the Church.[236] The flow of immigration increased in the 1820s, most notably among artisans (tailors, masons, shoemakers) and workers from the textile industries, victims of de-industrialization in the peripheral areas. Weavers from north-central Ireland migrated to continue their employment in textile production, but those from the north-west – excluded from the tight linen economy – were treated as unskilled labourers.[237] 'Multitudes are daily poured upon our shores ready to invade the work of every labourer and operative,' the *Trades Free Press* warned, but there was no anti-Irish feeling, no xenophobic reversion to 'No Popery'. While campaigning for social justice in Ireland – a policy which would stem immigration – radicals and the trades welcomed the immigrants into their organized ranks.[238]

A heterogeneous mixture, pre-Famine Irish immigrants were not a single out-group facing a stable population, but simply one such group among many. Typical inhabitants of the rapidly expanding industrial areas, these exiles of Erin participated fully in the great protest movements of the early nineteenth century. This is not to suggest that every immigrant was an ardent Chartist. Seasonal migrants – young workers from Ulster and Connacht who managed to dovetail employment on both sides of the Irish sea – lacked the time to participate: their overriding objective was to supplement the subsistence production and inadequate income of the family unit, a unit that remained firmly based in Ireland. Other migrants, often frustrated in their plans to proceed to America, persuaded themselves that their stay in Britain would be temporary, on which grounds they eschewed integration and politics.[239] But for the most part, the Irish displayed greater militancy than their hosts. This was certainly the case in Liverpool where the Irish hod-carriers were the driving force in the industrial disputes of the early 1830s. 'The late turn-out of mechanics and labourers has been almost entirely organized by Irish,' Holme informed the Parliamentary Inquiry on the Irish poor in Britain: 'although the Irish were the poorest mechanics, they took the lead in the turn-out. The English submitted in the most singular manner to be led by the nose.' The Irish remained at the forefront of unskilled strike activity in the 1830s and 1840s, despite the strident condemnation of O'Connell and the local Catholic clergy, who feared that the unions with their secret oaths were linked to Ribbonism, a movement strongly supported in the city. Irish to a man, the corn porters were the most militant section of the dock labour force.[240]

By 1841 the Irish comprised 17.3 per cent of the population of Liverpool, but sectarianism – the characteristic feature of the city's later history – was as yet unpronounced. Native workers were not attracted to the early Orange lodges, the preserve of immigrant Ulster Protestants. Local artisans regarded the Welsh, not the Irish, as their economic rivals. Predominantly unskilled, the Irish in Liverpool competed only amongst themselves, reducing wage rates and employment levels in the worst-paid labouring jobs to which they were largely consigned.[241] Elsewhere, there was some violent conflict between English workers and Irish immigrants, but the famous fights between rival gangs of railway navvies have been accorded undue historical significance at the expense of the more important Liverpool experience.[242] In Barnsley, where Irish and English linen-weavers worked together in their trade society and radical organizations with very little awareness of religious and ethnic differences, the Chartists even managed to recruit the local Catholic priest, the Revd Patrick Ryan![243] By an ironic tragedy, however, the formal alliance between the Chartists and the Irish, delayed by O'Connell until 1848, proved detrimental and divisive, aggravating the hostility to radicals and immigrants.

Following O'Connell's death in mid-1847, the leadership was assumed by the Irish Confederation which immediately widened the Repeal programme to embrace land reform, the social radicalism of Finton Lalor and Young Ireland. Population was falling in Ireland but agrarian 'outrages' increased in number: the ratio of 'protest' crime to indictable crime in general reached 17.7 per cent in 1848, more than double the highest figures recorded in England and Wales during the Swing riots (1831: 8.5 per cent) and the 'Plug Plot' disturbances (1842: 7.5 per cent).[244] Emboldened by news of successful revolution in Europe, the Confederation finally revoked O'Connell's proscription of physical force and an alliance with the Chartists.

'For now thirteen years', O'Connor reminded the Saint Patrick's Day audience in the Manchester Free Trade Hall, 'I have been advocating the very union which you have thus tardily confirmed.' So began 'three glorious days' of joint Chartist – Confederate celebration in Lancashire, culminating in a monster demonstration on Oldham Edge where the assembled thousands swore a solemn oath to set England and Ireland free.[245] Harnessed to the third Chartist campaign, Confederate orators in England restored ominous rhetorical force to the otherwise devalued device of the 'last petition'. Based in Liverpool, Dr Lawrence Reynolds, a graduate of the Royal College of Surgeons in Dublin, introduced himself to audiences as 'a Young Irelander – one of that class of men who detested and hated, and spurned the word "petition"'. 'The only way to proceed', his platform colleague, the provisions dealer Matthew Somers insisted, 'was with a musket over the shoulder and a pike in the hand' – implements available from Dr Reynolds, 'the Chartist ironmonger', at knockdown prices. 'The present movement', *The Times* warned on the morning of the Kennington Common demonstration, 'is a ramification of the Irish conspiracy. The Repealers wish to make as great a hell of this island as they have made of their own.' Along with the fear of continental 'red republicanism', it was the spectre of Irish violence that impelled the middle classes to protect the established order through enrolment in the special constabulary.[246]

A model of confidence and competence in the 'year of revolution', the British government was deeply disturbed by the security implications of the Irish–Chartist alliance which, it was feared, would overstretch military resources by simultaneous and diversionary insurrectionary activity. There were new anxieties about the loyalty of the army which contained large detachments of Irish troops, previously deployed in Chartist trouble-spots, a Habsburg-type strategy to prevent fraternization with disaffected native workers. Confronted by the three-pronged threat of revolutionary Paris, insurgent Ireland and revitalized Chartism, the government was compelled to act decisively: hence the massive display of coercive power on 10 April when troops, police and enrolled pensioners were supported by thousands of special constables in defence of English freedom and constitutional liberty.[247]

The security preparations were preceded and legitimized by a sustained press campaign which stigmatized Chartism as unEnglish and unconstitutional, condemned by association with riot, revolution and repeal. Lurid cartoons of the Parisian *lumpen proletariat*, implementing their 'levelling' theories through plunder, pillage and licentious excess, confirmed the villainous folly and criminal irrationality of red republicanism and the 'right to work'.[248] But it was the Irish alliance rather than the French connection which was the main target of anti-Chartist propaganda, which featured 'Paddy', the stereotype Irishman, in a new and defamatory guise, without his former benign and redeeming features. Now depicted as racially inferior, the uncivilized Irish Celt, incapable of rational economic behaviour, was portrayed as more ape-like than man, a despised simian with ludicrously exaggerated prognathous features.[249] The image was to persist as the volume of anti-Irish propaganda increased dramatically in ensuing years – the dissemination of such material was a particular feature of 'liberalization' in Oldham where the Anglo-Irish political solidarity of the 1840s was to give way to anti-Irish riots in the 1860s.[250] In the early months of 1848, 'press-gang' propaganda was directed to a specific audience, the shopkeepers, clerks and other borderline occupational groups, members of the lower middle class who proudly confirmed their status by joining the forces of order against the Chartist challenge.

Among the 85,000 or so special constables assembled in London in the middle-class *levée en masse*, there was some working-class representation, but few workers, it would seem, enrolled voluntarily. Subject to quasi-military discipline at the best of times, railway employees were in no position to object when conscripted by their employers, an example followed by the gas companies. Domestic servants were similarly powerless to protest when they were enrolled along with their masters: in some instances, crackshot gamekeepers were brought up to town from country estates specially for the purpose. Darlings of the anti-Chartist press, the burly Thames coal-whippers were an exceptional case. Although many had been conscripted by their labour superintendent, their services were lauded as a mark of gratitude and loyalty, following the introduction of legislation in the trade. When the demonstration was over, however, they demanded full compensation for their loss of earnings, a payment which the much-embarrassed government decided to meet. Voluntary enrolment was limited, but some workers who refused to serve were prepared to act within their own works to protect the premises against attack.[251]

Against the barrage of hostile propaganda, Chartists tried to present an orderly and legal public image, a task which exposed the ambivalence of the radical leadership towards street protest and the crowd. Direct action by distressed and unemployed workers – such as the northern and Scottish workhouse riots in March – added to the political excitement, but Chartists refused to endorse violence and disorder, to sanction any departure from the requisite discipline and legality of the 'constitutional' mass platform. But platform meetings themselves were often the occasion for disorder, detrimental 'turmoil' provoked by trouble-making youths, pickpockets, criminals and other members of the 'dangerous classes' attracted to the gathering. The March events in Trafalgar Square were a case in point. Abandoned by its middle-class promoters, the anti-income tax meeting was addressed by the maverick G. W. M. Reynolds, whose Chartist speech was followed by sustained rioting, during which the capital's petty criminals delighted in 'equalising the contents of each others' pockets, and taking from their neighbours a purse, a watch, or a handkerchief, as a token of fraternity'. The NCA Executive disclaimed all responsibility, but henceforth the press refused to distinguish between rioter, revolutionary, Chartist and criminal. After the 'Trafalgar Square Revolution', *Punch*, an accurate barometer of middle-class opinion, 'felt it to be his duty to exert all his powers of ridicule, even to a pardonable exaggeration, in the cause of order and loyalty'. In an effort to convince the crowd of the need for discipline and organization, the Chartist Executive sent Ernest Jones to address the Kennington Common meeting on 13 March, the largest of the flurry of gatherings in the wake of Trafalgar Square. But the day ended in a repeat performance of the previous week's proceedings, as a 'mob' of about 400 foraged its way through Southampton Street, relieving the local shopkeepers and pawnbrokers of a thousand pounds-worth of stock. As the Chartist delegates assembled for the Convention in fortified London, considerable misgivings were expressed about the 10 April demonstration which, Bronterre O'Brien feared, 'would let loose hundreds of rogues and thieves upon society, thus bringing down upon themselves the indignation of the reflecting people of this country'. Under O'Connor's resolute leadership, however, the Chartists decided to proceed with the meeting despite the various risks.[252]

The 'myth' of Kennington Common notwithstanding, O'Connor served the movement well on 10 April: it was 'Feargoose', indeed, who ensured that the day's events were not a fiasco. Many delegates, Harney included, contemplated the cancellation of the entire proceedings after the authorities banned the procession to parliament, but O'Connor was not prepared to surrender the right of assembly, despite the unfortunate location south of the river. Considerable crowds were attracted to Kennington Common – on police instructions, the anti-Chartist press reported the total as 15,000, a figure ten times lower than the latest historical estimate. Thanks to O'Connor's oratorical skills, unpropitious confrontation was avoided, a personal achievement expunged by the mythology. The procession was called off without a murmur of dissent as he proclaimed the meeting 'a great and glorious step achieved', an object lesson for the government in 'your courage and your resolution . . . your love for order, and your respect for the law'.[253]

Having salvaged some self-respect for the movement on 10 April, O'Connor soon abandoned the Chartist platform when the Commons Committee reported that the National Petition had not been signed by 5,706,000 as the Chartists alleged, but by 1,975,496, a figure which included many bogus, fraudulent and obscene signatures. Compelled to withdraw his motion for the Charter amid considerable contumely, O'Connor refused to sanction an escalation in extra-parliamentary pressure from without. As the Convention dissolved in embarrassed disarray, several delegates questioned both the legitimacy and expediency of further agitation, of proceeding to a National Assembly, but O'Connor's sudden renunciation of 'forcible intimidation' was the most damaging blow to the proposed 'anti-parliament'. No longer prepared to appear more insurrectionary than he actually was, he rejected confrontationalism to concentrate on propaganda and discussion, the promotion of his practical programme of social regeneration 'to make the rich richer and the poor rich'. A rational alternative to the visionary and ephemeral schemes, his solution to the 'labour question' would 'take the stink off Chartism', attracting shopkeepers and the trades.[254]

Divided and dispirited, delegates to the sparsely attended Assembly, the last vestige of the anti-parliament as an operative idea in radical politics, displayed more than the usual lack of self-confidence. The movement, however, did not wither away in languishing discussion of tactical and constitutional niceties. Wherever there was a strong Irish presence, Chartism actually grew in strength. There were impressive demonstrations of increased support in Bradford, the town with the highest concentration of Irish-born in the West Riding, where the distressed wool-combers, native and immigrant, were under threat from the introduction of machinery. Home base of George White, a militant Chartist leader of Irish immigrant stock, Bradford established a Chartist 'National Guard', an awesome body which drilled openly on the streets in bold defiance of the newly-incorporated and inept liberal authorities. Encouraged by the example of 'noble Bradford', other towns in the region mobilized in similar fashion until the authorities were accorded sufficient reinforcements at the end of May to reassert their control. A thorough military investigation revealed that half the Bradford Chartists were Irish, nationalist radicals who were preparing to 'make a diversion should Mitchel be convicted, in order to prevent the government from sending more troops to Ireland'.[255]

After Mitchel's conviction, the enraged immigrants refused to conform to the discipline and order of the Chartist platform. Editor of the *United Irishman*, Mitchel was the first victim of the new Crown and Government Security Act, the much-resented 'Felon Act' which introduced the offence of felonious sedition, a charge which extended to 'open and advised speaking'. News of his transportation brought crowds onto the streets in a number of unruly nocturnal processions through city centres, a display of spontaneous and unstructured protest which alarmed the authorities and cut across official Chartist plans for a great Whitsun demonstration – an exact count of heads was to be taken at meetings throughout the land on 12 June, a great moral demonstration which would make good the discredited National Petition. As the street violence continued amid much loose talk of 'private assassination and Moscowing', Ernest Jones stood forward to rehearse the Chartist argument for discipline, order and organization. On 4 June, following several nights of running battles with the police around Clerkenwell Green, he cautioned the crowd on Bishop Bonner's Field against partial and premature physical action. 'Show us your organization', he exhorted, 'and you will have a glorious opportunity on the 12th':

> Only preparation – only organization is wanted, and the Green Flag shall float over Downing Street, and St. Stephen's. Only energy is wanted – only determination – and what will be the result? Why? John Mitchel and John Frost will be brought back, and Sir George Grey and Lord John Russell will be sent to change places with them.

As the crowd began to disperse, the police – under strain from continuous overtime – emerged from concealment with ferocious violence. At this point, with public opinion still firmly behind the forces of order, the government decided to crush the surprisingly persistent Chartist challenge: the Whitsun demonstration was declared illegal; the Executive were prohibited from presenting a Memorial to the Queen; and warrants were issued against Jones and other leaders. 'The reign of terror is established', Harney expostulated, 'we live under Martial Law.'[256]

The tough policy delighted the middle-class press which had viewed the events on Clerkenwell Green with the greatest alarm – *Punch* portrayed Chartism transmogrified into Irish rapine, pillage and massacre, while *The Times* was appalled by 'that extravagance of wild sedition which, for want of any other adjective, must be denominated "Irish"; London, the paper warned, was endangered by 'the Irish love of knife, dagger and poison bowl'.[257] While the press refused to distinguish between the Chartist platform and Irish street violence, the government could be confident of the prompt conviction of Ernest Jones and the other arrested leaders.

As in the past, repression and arrests pushed some militants towards physical force, a course discountenanced by the official Chartist leadership – the first plans for conspiracy were quashed by the NCA Executive within 72 hours of the abandonment of the Whitsun demonstration.[258] Still committed to the platform, Chartists persevered with their hopes of mounting an overwhelming display of popular support, of mobilizing the Irish immigrants in disciplined and open formation. To this end, new papers were published by leaders of Irish stock – Bernard Treanor's *Truth Teller* and James Leach's *English Patriot and Irish Repealer*, edited with the assistance of George White and George Archdeacon – in a final effort to channel the anger and indignation of the Irish in Britain into open and organized 'pressure from without'. By this time, however, a secret Confederate system of organization and communication was well established, quite outside any public Chartist framework.[259]

The extent of Confederate organization was dramatically revealed by unannounced demonstrations of silent protest against the Suspension of Habeas Corpus in Ireland. Caught unawares elsewhere, the authorities were fully on their guard in Liverpool where the number of secret clubs was estimated at between 30 and 50, each of which comprised 100 armed men, all of whom were ready to raise a 'sympathetic rebellion'. Having failed to persuade the government to include Liverpool in the terms of the Suspension, the anxious authorities swore in 9270 special constables to supplement the large military presence already in the town, encamped in tents at Everton. After a rigorous watch for arms shipments, Joseph Cuddy, a prominent Confederate employed by Dr Reynolds as a salesman-courier, was arrested on 24 July in possession of 31 pikes. Further arrests followed, including the contrite Matthew Somers who offered to turn queen's evidence, but Reynolds escaped to America before his cache of 500 cutlasses and several cannisters of gunpowder was discovered in a cellar. Contained by the authorities, the power of the Merseyside movement was effectively broken by the end of the month, before news arrived of the rising at Ballingarry, where those arrested included Bellew McManus, leader of the Liverpool Irish community.[260]

First news from Tipperary raised the emotive question, 'IS IRELAND UP?' Throughout the north, Confederates and militant Chartists were at last drawn together in secret conspiracy. But there were still some objections to immediate diversionary activity. At Rochdale, the Chartists decided to wait and abide by the Executive, to reject plans to 'do a 1842 again'. In Manchester and Bolton, there were considerable misgivings about the precipitate haste of the local Irish who insisted on 'an immediate outbreak of a serious nature'. Chartists were reported to be 'withdrawing' after the riots in Ashton on 14 August during which a policeman was killed – murdered not by the convicted Radcliffe, leader of the Chartist National Guard, but by one of the disreputable witnesses who were hurriedly given a free passage to Australia after testifying against him. All things considered, however, there is much to suggest that Manchester was intended to be the centre of co-ordinated action on either 15 or 16 August. Having failed to receive their last-minute instructions, the Bradford Chartists despatched a delegate across the Pennines: on his return, he showed one of the local informers a note – 'it said that that all was broken up and come to an end.' On the night of 15 August, the Manchester magistrates had struck a 'decisive blow', arresting fifteen Chartist and Confederate leaders, the beginning of an exhaustive round-up of prominent northern radicals.[261]

Events in London are easier to unravel because of the evidence provided by Thomas Powell, an informer-cum-*agent provocateur*, who infiltrated Chartist circles shortly after Kennington Common. Having ingratiated himself with the more militant elements by his denunciation of O'Connor as 'a . . . coward, for he recommended peaceable measures, and that the National Assembly should be postponed', Powell was privy to the deliberations of the insurrectionary committee. Disbanded after Whitsun, the committee reconvened in July, on the eve of the trial of Ernest Jones. Encouraged by Powell, the Orange Tree conspirators – Mullins, Payne, Rose, Brewster, Bassett, Lacey, Ritchie, Cuffay and others – proceeded with their plans for a rising on 16 August when Manchester was expected to be 'up'. At the eleventh hour, as groups of Irish Confederates and others assembled at Shouldham Street and Praed Street to await final instructions from 'delegates', the police raided the Orange Tree, thereby forestalling the 'Anticipated Disturbances'.[262]

Untroubled by Powell's treachery, the authorities cast the net as wide as possible – with Home Office approval, the Manchester magistrates drew up a 'monster indictment', a true bill which 'listed all the leading agitators who have for some time past infested this City and the neighbouring Towns'.[263] The trials followed a standard format well summarized by Harney:

> Place *Fustian* in the dock, let *Silk Gown* charge the culprit with being a 'physical force Chartist', and insinuate that he is not exactly free from the taint of 'Communism', and forthwith *Broad Cloth* in the jury box will bellow out 'GUILTY'.[264]

While the judiciary upheld the virtues of English constitutionalism and political economy against foreign and violent 'red republicanism', the press condemned the radicals for their Irish connections. Cuffay, the veteran black radical, was an easy target for cartoonists, but *Punch* and the press preferred to highlight the Irish element in the August conspiracy, a dastardly affair involving the likes of 'MOONEY, ROONEY, HOOLAN, DOOLAN'.[265] Often at cross-purposes with their Irish allies, the Chartists were indelibly stigmatized by the troubled alliance of 1848.

'The Charter and something more'

Previously weakened by Peelite 'conciliation', the Chartist challenge was ultimately crushed by ruthless coercion. The end of an era in popular agitation, the disastrous defeat of 1848 left the weaknesses of Chartism cruelly exposed. Trapped in the traditional radical discourse, the movement had failed to adjust to changing circumstances. Forceful and relevant in the 1830s, the language of political oppression lost its predictive power when the Peelite state, imbued with a moralized vision of capitalism, abandoned 'class legislation' in favour of beneficial reforms, non-partisan measures addressed to the 'condition of England' question.[266] There was a similar lack of development in Chartist political economy, still phrased in the anti-capitalist 'new ideology' of the 1820s, an underconsumptionist analysis of irreversible slump and deepening crisis, dire predictions which offered no explanation for the violent fluctuations in the trade cycle or for the increasingly obvious resilience of capitalism.[267] Here Owenism proved more adaptable. No longer identified with communitarianism, utopianism and religious controversy, Owenite 'economic socialists' upheld a socialist productivism which promised to out-produce the existing system, to beat it on its own steam-manufacturing terms.[268] By 1848, the Chartist platform was outdated and outmoded. Disillusioned by the futile posturings of the past, many workers were no longer prepared to engage in outright political confrontation. By negotiating in the new language of reformism, they sought amelioration and protection through specific reforms and by legal registration for their autonomous and collective self-help institutions, the repository of the working-class ideal in mid-Victorian England.[269]

The 'liberalization' which steadily undermined Chartism in the 1840s was a two-way process: change from above was modified and accelerated by pressure from below. Out of doors, the successful campaign for the Ten Hours Act of 1847 matched the Anti-Corn Law League in organized singleness of purpose, while the necessary 'pressure from within' was applied by John Fielden, Cobbettite MP for Oldham, a democratic radical well-versed in the politics of parliamentary expediency. Throughout the 1840s, Chartists offered full support to the factory movement and other working-class campaigns for immediate and sectional gains – through their prominent involvement, O'Connor believed, Chartists would educate the workers in the need for political power, the only guarantee of the proper protection of labour. The subsequent abuses and evasions of the Ten Hours Act belatedly proved the point, but the very passage of Fielden's Act had already convinced many workers of the possibilities of reform within the existing order.[270] Forced to revise their ways and means after the humiliating collapse of 1848, the vestigial Chartists modified their programme to incorporate specific economic and social reforms, to seek a social-democratic alliance with social reformers, trade unions, cooperative and other collective self-help agencies.

The advance towards 'Charter-Socialism' was led by Harney and other 'men of the future', members of the revised Fraternal Democrats, the 'red republican' pressure group specially reconstituted to 'push forward a propaganda of social democracy'. Control of the NCA Executive was easily secured as the movement moved forward 'from green flag to red'.[271] The proposed 'fraternal union' with the social reformers proved much more difficult, even humiliating. Encouraged by their Christian-Socialist patrons, social reformers assumed the right to dictate terms at Harney's 'Democratic Conference': Chartists were required to recant their past folly, to renounce their history of political agitation. There were some, however, who were more charitably disposed towards the formation of a National Charter and Social Reform Union. The luminaries of the *Leader*, the influential progressive journal, wished to steer Chartism along a reformist path, combining ameliorative social reform with gradualist political advance, a rational approach to reform personified by George Jacob Holyoake. Editor of the *Reasoner*, Holyoake was a post-communitarian Owenite, a practical secularist who disapproved of demagogic Chartists and other 'foundation reformers', futile fundamentalists who dismissed any progress short of their never-to-be realized 'grand ideal'. For Holyoake, indeed, Cobden was the 'Model Agitator'.[272]

Holyoake, Thornton Hunt and other members of the *Leader* group were largely responsible for the draft programme presented to the famous 1851 Convention, a document much criticized by Bronterre O'Brien who regretted that 'the cloven foot of the old Anti-Corn Law League peeped out in every proposition it contained'.[273] Led by Ernest Jones, the Convention overturned the reformist package: the programme was transformed into the blueprint for a 'socialist' democratic state in which the land, cooperative endeavour, credit and welfare provision were all to be nationalized prior to 'the complete readjustment of the labour question'.[274] 'Henceforth', Harney joyously

proclaimed, 'Chartism is *democratique et sociale*',[275] but the new programme failed to revivify the movement. The initiative, Harney was
soon forced to admit, had passed to the retail cooperative societies
and the new amalgamated trade unions, bodies which had attended
the 'Democratic Conference' simply to enlist Chartist support in
their campaign for legal protection. With the reaction in 'full swing',
Harney was prepared to shelve the name and details of the Charter
in the hope of rendering political reform more attractive. Together
with W. J. Linton and the 'middle-class literati' of the *Leader*, he
sought to institute a 'third force' uniting Chartists, middle-class radicals, cooperators and the trades on the single issue of the suffrage.
By an irony of the times, the campaign for 'The Charter and Something More' ended with the sacrifice of the six points – the original
'whole hog' – abandoned in favour of gradualism, moderation and
expediency, mid-Victorian synonyms for rational politics.[276]
  Despite the eventual liberal outcome, the promotion of Charter-
Socialism provoked the ire of some Chartists, pragmatic proselytes
of a middle-class 'Little Charter' alliance who had no wish to see the
movement progress 'from the idea of a simple *political reform* to the
idea of a *Social Revolution*'. A diminutive but vociferous splinter
group, the National Charter League mounted a rearguard campaign
against 'Communistic Chartism', the 'mongrel Socialism' borrowed
from 'the Parisian school of philosophers'.[277] O'Connor refused to
head this anti-socialist crusade, despite his determination 'never to
allow our Political or Social Movement, or the Land and Labour
Question to be mixed up with Communism or Socialism'. The first
to abandon the mere political platform, O'Connor was overtaken by
Charter-Socialism, but he refused to defer to orthodox middle-class
economy, to reject the protectionism of the past as well as the socialism of the present – Clark, the founder of the NCL, publicly
renounced his participation in 'organized and systematic opposition
to the Anti-Corn Law League'. 'The bugbear of free traders and
middle-class deceivers', O'Connor remained vehemently opposed to
any rapprochement with 'the money manufacturing middle class –
those who live upon labour, who coin your sweat, marrow and bones
into gold'. Through land purchased by poor rates and other funds
he promised the hard-working 'shopkeeping classes' a practical solution to the 'labour question' – the 'unwilling idler' would be transformed into the happy man in his own labour field, 'a better customer,
a better friend, and a better subject, than the system-made pauper
who is consigned to the workhouse and made a burthen upon their
industry'. Unable to support the Charter-Socialists or the NCL,
O'Connor, the 'worn-out warrior', was left stranded in political isolation, seeking the illusive 'union of the veritable middle classes and

the working classes . . . an alliance between mental labour on the one hand and manual labour on the other'.[278]

Having failed to enlist O'Connor, the NCL tried to incorporate the burgeoning retail cooperative movement. Here they encountered the fierce opposition of O'Connor's successor, Ernest Jones, a strident critic of local and divisive self-help endeavour, schemes which were 'likeliest to succeed with the better paid mechanics – with the aristocracy of labour':

> . . . and here the injuriousness of their conduct becomes doubly apparent: THEY ARE THE DECOY DUCKS OF THE MIDDLE CLASS – drawing from us those men, who are, or would be, with us, and *thus throwing the overbalance of power into the hands of our opponents*.[279]

Still committed to mass agitation, Jones refused to acknowledge the refined sensibilities of the ascendant working-class institutions, 'joint-stock' associations which were 'creating a fresh conservative class out of your own order'.[280] 'THE ARISTOCRACY OF LABOUR MUST BE BROKEN DOWN', he decreed as he battled against the 'aristocratic privilege' and 'doctrine of expediency' displayed by William Newton and the ASE.[281] The trades, he insisted, must join the Chartists in demanding political power and the nationalization of the land, the necessary first stage in the 'gradual revolution'. A pupil of Marx and Engels, Jones remained firmly within the English radical tradition: the evils of industrial capitalism were to be eradicated by the abolition of political and landed monopoly, political change which would leave the working class secure in their property, able to enjoy the natural right to the full produce of their labour.[282]

By his unrestrained animadversions on the 'new model' unions, Jones committed the residual Chartist movement to 'political sectarianism', a divisive legacy which long left its mark on the labour movement.[283] These unfortunate divisions followed in the wake of an important but neglected effort to establish a formal alliance between Chartism and the unions through the National Association of Organized Trades for the Industrial, Social and Political Emancipation of Labour (NAOT). This radical trades body must be distinguished from the better-known National Association of United Trades (NAUT), an inter-trades organization established in 1845, at a point which the Webbs located as 'halfway between the revolutionary voluntaryism of 1830–34 and the Parliamentary action of 1863–1875'.[284] Amid the Parisian-inspired enthusiasm for the 'Organization of Labour', the two wings of the NAUT were brought together in 1848: the Association for the Protection of Industry, which dealt with industrial disputes on the principle of 'mediation', merged with the Association for the Employment of Labour in Agriculture and Manu-

factures, which raised capital to establish cooperative workshops and
home colonies:

> the means of drafting from the labour market that 'surplus labour' which
> is the great proximate cause of all reductions of wages, and of setting it to
> work on their own estates, in their own workshops, by means of their own
> capital and machinery, under circumstances which will make those funds
> reproductive and beneficial, which, by the old system of strikes, were
> totally lost, or positively injurious.[285]

Self-sufficient subscription schemes of this order were the preserve
of the better-paid trades, an exclusive 'labourism' rejected by the
rival NAOT.

Formed by a committee representing the 'lower' depressed trades
– ladies' shoemakers, tailors, bootmakers, pressmen, carpenters, cabinet-makers, silk dyers, gold-beaters, painters, silkweavers, carvers
and chair makers, tin-plate workers, plumbers, type-founders,
farriers, paper stainers and upholsterers – the NAOT insisted on
legislative intervention where the NAUT looked to 'self-reliance –
self-respect – self-helpfulness – these will do more for us than all the
governments in the world can'. Delegates adopted an eight-point
programme of political, economic and financial reform, much in line
with Bronterre O'Brien's proposals for 'national regeneration', but it
was soon decided to highlight three points for public agitation: the
suffrage; the establishment of local boards of trade which would
'prevent the ruinous competition among employers and the demora-
lizing and destructive effects on the working classes'; and above all,
a Home Colonies Bill.[286]

These divisions in national trade unionism had unfortunate reper-
cussions on the Chartist movement. Through their identification with
the NAOT, the Charter-Socialists were to be tarred with the brush
of Tory protectionism, a most unwelcome stigma in mid-century
England. At the conference to draft the Home Colonies Bill, there
was much discussion about a proposed prefatory clause to commit
the government to the protection of British industry, a proposal
strongly supported by delegates like Ferdinando, representative of
the Spitalfields silkweavers, who were 'utterly opposed to the philosophy of the Manchester school of economists'. While the conference
was adjourned, the NAOT unwisely invited G. F. Young, Tory
shipyard owner and prominent protectionist, to chair a public meeting in Stepney 'in favour of legislative protection for native industry,
against the present unfair and ruinous system of competition'. The
meeting was a tempestuous affair. Clark, founder of the NCL, seized
control of the proceedings with a strident anti-Tory speech from the
floor in favour of 'the removal of all the remaining impediments to

the free exercise of industry'; Young was forced to quit the chair; Oastler was denied a hearing; and the NAOT beat a hasty retreat before putting the protectionist resolutions to the vote.[287]

At the next public meeting of the NAOT, a carefully managed affair, there was no mention of protection until resolutions had been passed in favour of universal suffrage and home colonies, when delegates clearly explained that 'they did not seek the same kind of protection as that which was given before the introduction of free trade; what they wanted was protection for their own labours'. But the damage of Stepney could not be repaired, despite the support for the protectionist cause provided by Henry Mayhew's investigative journalism. Charter-Socialists castigated Clark for the harm he had caused the radical movement: it was 'absolutely dishonest and unfair', George White protested, 'to confound "Protection to Labour", with "Protection to Landlords"'. But having once promised to effect a new social-democratic departure in the labour movement, the protectionist NAOT rapidly degenerated into a small rump of trades which renounced radical politics and supported Oastler's campaign for 'regulation'.[288]

Trapped in the fierce debate between free trade and protection, Chartism was hindered by its protectionist leanings and its liberal sentiments. Where employer protectionism remained strong – as in silk towns like Macclesfield – working-class Chartism was unable to make headway against popular Toryism.[289] A similar pattern applied in ports and coastal towns – South Shields is the best known example[290] – where the struggle to maintain the Navigation Acts determined the Tory political allegiance of seamen and shipwrights, workers whose livelihoods were threatened by foreign competition in the carrying trade and the lucrative ship-repair business. Protectionist but not Tory, Chartism failed to establish a distinct radical identity capable of transcending 'party' divisions – Liverpool was unable to develop a strong radical movement because of the conflict of interests between the influential but 'Tory' shipwrights and the 'liberal' dockside workers, the stevedores, dockers and porters for whom free trade meant more trade through the port.[291]

Chartist protectionism was directed against the 'monopolizing, combining, speculating, taxing, loan-jobbing *commerce*' which Cobbett had condemned in his famous 'Perish Commerce!' articles of 1807. Subsequently expanded, the unregulated export trade had produced excessive profits for large capitalists at the expense of small masters and the exploited workers, victims of over-competition, over-work, declining wages and the abuse of machinery.[292] Some industrialists acknowledged the logic of the argument. Already forced to diversify, John Fielden was acutely aware of the dangers of over-production and dependence upon fickle and precarious overseas markets. By regulating hours and wages, he hoped to curb competition and restrict production, to redirect the cotton industry to the security and stability of a prosperous home market. Fielden, however, was a political oddity, a Cobbettite radical committed to the political rights of labour. Little other support was forthcoming for radical protectionism.[293]

Chartism undoubtedly suffered from the public equation of protectionism with Toryism, but a more telling weakness was its proximity to popular liberalism. At times of reverse, Chartist self-confidence was undermined by liberal versions of reform, practicable programmes presented in a popular constitutional format. Without an alternative language of its own, Chartism was powerless to stem the seepage, the weary and disheartened drift to liberalism.

In the early days, however, Chartist language was remarkably powerful and successful, mobilizing large numbers of the otherwise non-political majority. Here context was as important as content. 'Rational recreation' failed to draw popular support but crowds flocked to the Chartist mass meetings with their star orators, fairground atmosphere, colourful spectacle and show. There was no ascetic barrier, no improvement ethic – and unlike Owenism, no expensive admission charges – to deter popular involvement in the Chartist cause. For all its ideological and intellectual weaknesses, the populist language of the mass platform effected an impressive mobilization of the masses.[294] The strength of the early Victorian state, however, was greater still.

Despite their pride in the new language of class, middle-class social commentators were deeply disturbed by the absence of discipline in a society devoid of traditional orders and ranks.[1] In the troubled period after the Napoleonic wars, labour discipline and public order appeared everywhere in crisis. The casualization of the agricultural proletariat in the south-eastern counties was followed by rapidly rising rates of vagrancy, pauperism and petty crime. In the factory towns of the north, peace and order were seemingly unenforceable at times of cyclical downturn and mass unemployment. In London there was an urgent need for a professional police force both to control politically motivated crowd disturbance and to contain juvenile delinquency – masterless apprentices, orphans, under-employed youths, child prostitutes, all seemed to symbolize a breakdown in the order of the family, the parish and the workshop. Hence there arose the fear of what was soon to be called the 'dangerous classes' – a term borrowed from the French – an alliance of vagrants, criminals, political agitators and the unemployed, an ominous collective presence which threatened to corrupt and contaminate the entire working class.[2]

Through a number of 'total institutions' – penitentiary prisons, union workhouses, juvenile reformatories, industrial schools and the like – humanitarian and administrative reformers sought to isolate the deviant dangerous classes, trusting that the regime of enforced asceticism, hard labour and religious instruction would effect their individual reformation and salvation.[3] In practice, much of the rigour rubbed off on the needy and unfortunate. Applied within the general mixed workhouse, the principle of less eligibility – a self-acting test of destitution designed to differentiate the pauper from the poor – had the perverse effect of stigmatizing the entire body of the poor, able-bodied and 'impotent' alike.[4]

To complement the coercive aspects of social control,[5] middle-class reformers offered a range of facilities for 'rational recreation' and 'self-improvement', social and cultural provision which would protect the otherwise vulnerable working class against infectious contact with the dangerous classes. Education was the main agency here, although some conservative critics feared the revolutionary consequences of popular literacy. Established at the end of the eighteenth century, the Sunday schools, mostly undenominational in origin, attracted large numbers of working-class children – by 1851, indeed, there were over two million Sunday scholars, representing 75 per cent of working-class children between five and fifteen. Planned as an exercise in social control, Sunday schools offered the working class tangible benefits, including the prized acquisition of literacy, for which they were prepared to endure middle-class patronage – significantly, however, there was no increase in formal religious adherence: according to Laquer's calculations, no more than 4 per cent of total Sunday school enrolment belonged at any one time to a church or chapel. The schools succeeded best where teaching was provided by homegrown talent, the curriculum extended beyond pious catechisms, and local autonomy prevailed over denominational encroachment.[6]

Government intervention in elementary education began in 1833 with the first annual grant of £20,000 – about one per cent of national income – to the religious voluntary societies which provided weekday education through the cost-effective monitorial system, recently imported from Madras. When the grant was increased to £30,000 in 1839, its administration was placed in the hands of the Committee of the Privy Council for Education, of which the Secretary was James Kay-Shuttleworth, pre-eminent exemplar of the 'administrator as statesman'. A social engineer, he looked to the schools to 'raise a new race of working people – respectful, cheerful, hard-working, loyal, pacific and religious'. His plans were considerably hampered by denominational antagonisms and public parsimony, but these difficulties were of little consequence to the vigorous working-class private sector, the lost elementary schools of Victorian England.[7]

Working-class private schools flourished despite the animadversions of middle-class critics. Expunged from the historical record of progressive state interventionism, the scale of private provision is difficult to establish, but at the time of the Education Act 1870, by which point the annual grant to the public sector had risen spectacularly to £895,000, at least a quarter of all working-class children at elementary school were still attending private schools. Beyond the reach and control of the Inspectorate (until 1870), these self-financing 'people's schools', run by local, mainly female, working-class teachers, embodied an educational culture quite distinct from that which was officially prescribed from above. Private elementary schools responded to demand from below, the pressure to obtain prized basic skills as rapidly as possible. Here, parents were able to exercise some control over the content and organization of education, a power they were denied in the publicly provided alternative. Attuned to the broader working-class culture, private elementary schools were able to respond to the constraints of everyday living, to concentrate learning time, when it could be afforded, upon basic instrumental skills, without the unwelcome and time-consuming element of moral regulation that formed a crucial part of the public sector curriculum.[8]

During the 1830s, middle-class reformers and educationalists turned their attention to social investigation, an active and interventionist strategy which brought missionaries and investigators, the agents of organized virtue, into direct contact with the working-class community and family life. The new Statistical Societies pioneered the door-to-door survey to investigate 'the other nation', to establish the moral and intellectual condition of the working class, the lurid details of which were elucidated by a stock questionnaire about overcrowding, domestic management, religious affiliation, church-going, literacy and school attendance.[9] Spiritual almoners to the 'neglected poor', the Unitarian domestic missionaries were similarly entrusted to investigate the state of social discipline among the slum-dwellers, 'to bring them into a permanent connection with religious influences – and, above all, to promote an effective education of their children, and to shelter them from corrupting agencies'. Not envisaged as poverty surveys, these investigations nevertheless uncovered disturbing and intolerable facts about the economic realities of working-class life, shocking revelations which challenged the ideological security of the socially-concerned middle class.[10]

Drawing upon the evidence of the various investigations, administrative, scientific and religious, the 'industrial' novelists explored the disturbing contradiction between the dominant ethic and lived experience, adding literary force to a structure of feeling which struggled to reconcile middle-class ideology with the blameless realities of working-class poverty. As with all Condition of England literature, the novels were written for a middle-class audience – they possessed little interest for the poor themselves who much preferred Newgate and Gothic novels which portrayed their own kind in the most villainous terms.[11] In the absence of an alternative ideology, the novelists condemned the vulgar materialism and ruthless individualism which accompanied contemporary political economy, vices which were spiritually impoverishing, socially divisive and morally repugnant. Salvation lay through paternalism and philanthropy, the provision of the succour, compassion and guidance which the poor both needed and deserved. Charitable and sympathetic, this condescending judgement conflicted with the evidence of working-class self-sufficiency, the collective endeavours which the novelists, in their otherwise factual descriptions of working-class life, chose either to exclude or travesty.[12]

The new paternalism demanded a degree of personal commitment quite beyond the temporary display of concern in traditional charitable exercises, the emergency measures which helped to contain riot and disorder in Georgian England.[13] Mid-Victorian paternalism was to be an ambitious exercise in comprehensive supervision and guidance, a permanent display of benevolent concern best exemplified by the northern factory owners who provided works dinners, 'treats', trips and all manner of social and cultural activities over and above the 'mere cash nexus', in line with Trafford's practice in *Sybil*, and Thornton's aspirations in *North and South*.[14] In rural areas, the gentry reappeared to supervise ploughing matches, labourers' fetes and other revived popular festivities, recreating a hierarchical '*pseudo-gemeinschaft*' through their active participation and patronage.[15] Throughout the country, there was a revival of interest in the district visiting scheme of organized charity pioneered by Chalmers in Glasgow in the 1820s.[16]

Among the most strident critics of the new philanthropy was Henry Mayhew, literary bohemian and investigative journalist:

> The poor are expected to become angels in an instant, and the consequence is, they are merely made hypocrites . . . It would seem, too, that this overweening disposition to play the part of pedagogues (I use the word in its literal sense) to the poor, proceeds from a love of power than from a sincere regard for the people.

While conducting his survey into the London trades for the *Morning Chronicle*, he was engaged in fierce altercation with Ashley over the Ragged School Union, a much-vaunted charitable exercise in the social reformation of the poorest, vagabond children. The schools, Mayhew's investigations indicated, were actually nurseries of delinquency, in no way responsible for the decline in juvenile crime.[17]

Predisposed against philanthropic initiatives, Mayhew was compelled to question political economy itself as he continued with his methodological scrutiny of *Low Wages, Their Causes, Consequences and Remedies*. Here the problem was not surplus labour but the sweating of labour, an uncontrolled competitive system in which 'over-work makes under-pay' and 'under-pay makes over-work'. Mayhew, however, failed to elaborate an alternative political economy, a characteristic weakness in a writer who seldom completed his major projects. A member of the 'uneasy' middling class, he was both rebellious and respectable: at times innovative and radical, his journalism was often highly commercial, well suited to the market of bourgeois opinion. As he turned from the trades to the street-folk, intended simply as the introductory material for a comprehensive study of *London Labour and the London Poor*, Mayhew's remarkable powers of observation and investigation served to confirm, not to challenge, middle-class prejudices, no longer disturbed by the distant memory of Chartism, cholera and continental upheaval.[18]

Mayhew's work always relied heavily on a biological system of classification, a meticulous scientific procedure to distinguish – often with exaggerated precision – the innumerable categories of occupational groups and income levels. Applied to the street-folk, variegated as they were, biological science provided the single explanation for the persistence of residual and irreducible poverty. Peculiarly poor, the street-folk, with their distinctive 'moral physiognomy', were a regressive 'race' apart, a primitive 'tribe' surviving in the very heart of civilization. Poverty in mid-Victorian London, Mayhew confirmed, was a form of social pathology, a cultural rather than an economic condition. Concern about the Condition of England and the dangerous classes was thus reduced to the residuum, the common term to describe the refuse of humanity and the refuse of the sewers, contamination that could now be contained.[19]

Henceforth the attention of the police and other coercive agencies was concentrated on the residuum, a separate and discrete minority outside the main body of the working people, leaving the working-class communities largely to discipline themselves, a mutually respected tacit agreement characteristic of the new class relationships in mid-Victorian England.

PART TWO:
1850–75

8 'The Mid-Victorian Boom'

Previously perceived as problematic or catastrophic, industrial capitalism acquired in the course of the 1840s the stability which ensured its subsequent permanence. Economic and psychological, this transformation owed much to the railways, their diminished importance in counterfactual econometric analysis notwithstanding. Following the crisis of 1837–42, heavy investment in railway-building exercised a steadying as well as expansive influence, rectifying the dangerous imbalance between the industrial sector and the rest of the economy. More than any other factor, the railways resolved the crisis of profitability, lessened the impact of cyclical downturn and stimulated production in coal, iron and the other capital goods industries, thereby ushering in the 'second phase' of diversified industrialism. The 'workshop of the world', Britain then enjoyed a quasi-monopoly position in overseas markets as other countries sought to industrialize by importing capital goods on an unprecedented scale. The secular expansion of the British economy reached its highest levels between the 1840s and the 1870s.[1]

By no means a uniform period of growth, prosperity and euphoria – the image first projected at Crystal Palace in 1851 – the 'Great Victorian Boom' included 'spells of rising, falling and stable prices; uncertainty as well as speculation and optimism; pressures on profit margins as well as windfall gains; checks to output and idle resources, competition, expansion and high levels of employment; stagnant and rapidly rising real wages'.[2] The economy continued to grow in a markedly uneven manner: different sectors experienced different price trends; profitability and investment patterns diverged widely between and within industries; and regional wage differentials persisted and widened as new economic activity clustered around the original 'growth-poles' – capital was not drawn to low-wage backward and peripheral regions in the fashion postulated by neo-classical equilibrium theory.[3]

Dominated by the culture of the factory, 'the rule of tall chimneys', the textile districts continued to set the pace.[4] Here alternative modes of production – outwork and artisan – were finally eradicated. Even in the woollen industry, mass-production factories steadily replaced the cooperative or company mills where artisan domestic clothiers took their own materials through the mechanical processes of scribbling, carding, fulling and so forth.[5] In some instances, the extinction of artisan-based systems marked the end of production: the 'cottage factories' of the Coventry ribbon-weaving trade, for example, closed amid the local distress of the 1860s when new free trade policies, compounded by changes in fashion, sacrificed the industry to the flood of foreign silk imports.[6]

Once completed in cotton, the transition to mechanized factory production was never in doubt. But there was no dramatic increase in scale: between 1850 and 1890, the numbers employed in the average spinning, weaving and combined firms rose respectively from 108 to 165, 100 to 188, and 310 to 429. Small and medium-sized firms appear to have persisted as the representative units of production, but these figures obscure the large size of many firms and the high concentration of ownership in the main centres of the industry.[7]

Previously confined to the spinning belt, male employment in the cotton factories re-stabilized the family economy on the basis of traditional gender roles and functions. The reconstitution of the family unit, Patrick Joyce contends, enabled employers to pursue successful paternalist strategies, transforming the factory into the centre of settled community life.[8] Less prone to the violent cyclical fluctuations of the past, this factory culture weathered the crisis years of the 'Cotton Famine' with remarkably little turbulence.

Size was the key determinant of the new paternalism. New model employers were large, well-established masters, the 'industrial clans' who owned the huge combined firms of the south, and the wealthy 'dynasties' who dominated Preston and Blackburn, the old weaving centres of the north.[9] Beneficiaries of the stability and prosperity of mid-Victorian England, these large employers were able to afford concessions from above, to experiment with new methods of efficient labour management. The substitution of 'intensive' for 'extensive' labour utilization brought greater productivity through shorter hours and higher wages, concessions which pre-empted disruptive strike activity as trade and profits boomed.[10] Lancashire mill-workers were the first to enjoy *la semaine anglaise*, the 5½-day working week which spread throughout the workforce in the third quarter of the nine-teenth century, allowing a great expansion of sporting and popular cultural provision on the Saturday half-holiday.[11] The employers themselves provided a number of trips and treats for the loyal and deferential workers, sound investments against the recurrence of Chartist class-conflict and worker insubordination – trips to the countryside and seaside, the annual works dinner, and workplace libraries, reading rooms, canteens and baths.[12]

The consolidation of the factory system had important psychological, cultural and political consequences. For the vast majority of workers outside the stable environment of the factory, the struggle for economic survival continued unimproved. Trades which had already lost their honourable status descended further into sweating as a consequence of increased sub-division of tasks and the introduction of intermediate technology.[13] Introduced in the 1850s and 1860s, the sewing machine led to intense specialization in the slop sectors of the clothing and shoemaking trades.[14] In the ready-made workshops, cutting-out, basting, machining, button-holing and pressing were carried out by different employees, while among the female home workers there was a corresponding concentration upon one kind of garment. Technical change led to the proliferation of small workshops and the 'feminization' of the trades, a debased system of 'pre-industrial' domestic production particularly prevalent in mid-Victorian London, where East End sweating enabled small masters to offset the high overheads of the capital in competition with semi-skilled provincial factory production, a serious challenge from the late 1860s. Industry declined in London in the second half of the nineteenth century, leaving the metropolis as a finishing centre for consumption goods. Here, the new mass market for ready-made goods – established by rising working-class prosperity – was supplied through the exploitation of an overstocked, unskilled labour market of women and immigrants prepared to work at sub-subsistence wages. Increasingly casualized, large sections of the London labour force were denied the stability and prosperity of the mid-Victorian boom.[15]

9 Living Standards

At the material level, working-class improvement during the mid-Victorian boom owed more to greater stability in employment than to a marked increase in wages. The last to benefit from the prosperity, workers did not achieve substantial and lasting advances in real wages until the late 1860s.[1] During the high price years of the Crimean War, the real wages of Black Country miners fell by a third, not to recover fully until 1869, after which there was a major advance, carrying real wages some 30–40 per cent above the 1850 level.[2] Money earnings in the cotton industry displayed a similar chronology: advances in the 1850s were generally of a modest order, but some spectacular gains were secured after the Cotton Famine. Between 1860 and 1874, weavers earnings rose by 20 per cent; spinners, piecers, blowing and cardroom hands, throstle and ring spinners, winders, reelers, warpers, dressers and sizers by 30–50 per cent; strippers and grinders 55 per cent; and drawing-frame tenters by 81 per cent. These figures suggest a widening of differentials, but not on a simple gender and skill basis. Female operatives not employed as weavers seem to have fared much better than male spinners.[3]

As a general rule, however, the craftsman's differential increased in mid-Victorian England – the wage ratio between the skilled and unskilled probably approached 2:1. In terms of actual earnings the skilled fared better still since they were less vulnerable to unemployment: for skilled trade unionists in the engineering, metal and shipbuilding trades, there were only two occasions (1858 and 1868) when the unemployment rate reached double figures.[4] The greatest gains were made by skilled workers in high-wage regions, a premium on upward mobility which accelerated the redistribution of labour, the changes in occupational structure which were responsible for something like one-third of the overall increase in real wages between 1850 and 1900.[5]

For agricultural workers, whose numbers now fell absolutely, the mid-Victorian boom, the golden age of English agriculture, brought no amelioration. Somewhat ironically, the improvement in their standard of living was delayed until the 1870s and 1880s, a period of falling profitability. Published in 1874, George Bartley's study of *The Seven Ages of a Village Pauper* calculated that no less than three-quarters of the inhabitants of the typical village would require public relief at some stage in their lives.[6] In some industrial areas there was a similar lack of material advance. Despite peak production in the local coal and iron industries, the skilled building trades alone enjoyed an increase in real wages in the Black Country where earnings in the domestic nail, lock, chain and key making trades continued to fluctuate around a downward, sweated gradient.[7] On Merseyside, wage rates for skilled and unskilled workers remained stable until the early 1870s, when the general advance was eroded by particularly high food prices.[8] Women workers in sweated and casual employment probably gained least from the mid-Victorian boom, but there is some evidence of an improvement in day rates for charring and washing in the 1870s.[9]

Not a period of continuous price inflation, the mid-Victorian economy was characterized by high, relatively stable prices, intervening between the spectacular inflationary spells of 1853–5 and 1870–3.[10] With the occasional exception, food prices rose less than most others, resulting in marked increases in the consumption of tea, sugar and other 'luxuries'. In dietary terms, however, there was no significant advance in the standard of living until the falling prices of the 1880s. Brewing apart, food remained an unrevolutionized industry in production and retailing until the end of the century.[11] Real wages kept pace with food price rises, but rent, the other major item in the working-class budget, proved increasingly expensive, with particularly sharp increases in the mid-1860s.[12]

Few working-class families rose above economic insecurity and bouts of periodic poverty, despite the greater stability of employment and the belated improvement in earnings. At critical moments in the family cycle, indeed, the differential enjoyed by skilled workers was often inadequate to prevent considerable hardship. For those in critical family circumstances, penury was particularly severe at times of general distress when a downturn in the trade cycle or a harsh bout of winter weather led to short-time working and unemployment.

The most notable depression was the Lancashire Cotton Famine, 1861–5, a protracted period of distress and unemployment which, Neville Kirk insists, resulted from the over-production of the late 1850s boom and the consequent saturation of markets, and not simply from the Federal blockade of Confederate ports as contemporaries believed. At its worst in the winter of 1862–3, 49 per cent of all operatives in the 28 poor law unions of the cotton districts were unemployed in December 1862, with a further 35 per cent on short-time and only 16 per cent in full-time work. The depth and persistence of such mass unemployment was quite remarkable: at Ashton, the worst-hit town where there was little industrial diversification, 60 per cent of the operatives remained out of work as late as November 1864, while at Salford, at the opposite end of the league table, the unemployment rate still stood at 24 per cent. Unemployment of this order had a catastrophic impact on the standard of living, although some disingenuous observers pointed to a possible improvement in health: 'it was not a case of starvation when a man was deprived of beer, gin, or even tea', Chadwick opined, 'it was the case of men having bread, simple food with better air, as against a high or ordinary diet with impure air.'[13]

The dire distress in Lancashire posed considerable problems for the relief agencies, both Poor Law and philanthropic, once the independent and thrifty operatives had exhausted their savings in cooperative, friendly society and other collective self-help institutions, the means by which 'Rochdale Man' maintained working-class pride and respectability. Unsuited to the needs of unemployed factory operatives, the Poor Law and the charities were already under critical scrutiny following the events in London during the extremely harsh winter of 1860–1 when the temperature remained below freezing for a solid month, causing severe privation particularly for the casual labour force – apart, that is, from the enterprising chestnut sellers who flocked to Hyde Park where the Serpentine, frozen thirteen inches thick, proved a popular venue for impromptu ice-skating competitions. Across in the East End, the Poor Law system broke down as the number of paupers increased from 96,752 to 135,389.[14] To meet the emergency, charitable funds had to be distributed without investigation, an unwise exercise in indiscriminate 'stray charity' condemned by the investigative journalism of Hollingshead's *Ragged London*, which portrayed the pauperized working class as 'low, wanting in self-reliance and self-respect, demoralized by much charity – always ready to receive'.[15] Under investigation by a parliamentary select committee, the Poor Law Board was determined to prevent similar pauperization in the Cotton Famine north by insisting on strict compliance with the Outdoor Relief Regulation Order, but local Guardians refused to force the respectable unemployed to perform demeaning work tasks in the company of idle and dissolute paupers. The Guardians paid out small weekly allowances of between 1s and 2s a head on the assumption that this meagre non-pauperizing sum would be augmented from other sources – short-time earnings, income from other members of the family or charitable aid [16]

Charity was more stringently controlled through the Central Executive Relief Committee which issued strict instructions, drawn up by Kay-Shuttleworth to the 180 local relief committees in the distressed cotton districts. Well below normal working income, relief was to be paid partly in kind in the form of tickets to be exchanged at certain shops, a system which would prevent squandering and the misuse of funds. Recipients were to be regularly visited to ascertain needs and to detect impostors. Furthermore, there had to be some form of work in return for the relief granted, but not the degrading tasks of oakum-picking and stone-breaking traditionally associated with the Poor Law. The Committee advised educational classes for men and boys and sewing classes for girls – by inculcating the skills and virtues of domesticity in the sewing classes, philanthropic middle-class ladies hoped to remedy the servant recruitment problem, an occupation shunned by urban working-glass girls. Serious riots ensued when the officious Stalybridge Relief Committee reduced its relief rate and tightened its supervisory practices. In imitation of 1842, 'turn-out' crowds marched to Ashton, Hyde, Dukinfield and other nearby towns to encourage the unemployed to quit the schools and join the protest. The disturbances reached as far north as Preston, uniting Irish and English workers in indignant anger. These untoward events compelled the government to introduce the Public Works (Manufacturing Districts) Act, an interventionist measure in direct contradiction with the individualist premises of the Poor Law: too late to eradicate the bitter memories of 1863, this public works programme prevented the outbreak of further unrest.[17]

After the Cotton Famine, Lancashire operatives began to benefit from the mid-Victorian boom. Others were less fortunate. Workers in the East End were hit hard by the crisis of 1866–8, a most unfortunate conjuncture of calamities. Precariously dependent on government favour and foreign orders, the ship-building industry collapsed after the banking failures of 1866, a financial panic which brought an end to the boom in building and railway construction. Another harsh winter, accompanied by high food prices and the return of cholera, added to the hardship, causing the breakdown of the seasonal economic equilibrium. The overall effect was to augment the casual labour problem. Only skilled and young unmarried operatives were able to emigrate or move to alternative centres like Tyneside, leaving behind, the chairman of the Poplar Guardians regretted, the 'second class men, who were the first thrown out of work, and who would be the last to be taken on again were there any revival of trade'. Married men with children preferred to stay put in the hope of weathering the bad times through the casual earnings of the wife; ageing workers also remained, relying on some financial help from their grown-up children.[18]

10 Housing

Housing standards remained low in the mid-Victorian period, by which time over half of the population were classified as urban, a term which lacked statistical precision until the advent of the urban sanitary district in the Public Health Act 1872. High transport costs protected the exclusive character of suburbs, satellite towns and resorts, middle-class developments which were to outpace the urban centres of iron and steel production, shipbuilding, railway engineering and heavy manufacture, the nodal points of the second phase of industrialism.[1]

Unrelieved by urban migration, rural housing continued to decline except in a few carefully controlled 'closed' parishes where philanthropic landowners erected model cottages. Commissioned by John Simon in 1864, the sample survey for the first national inquiry into rural labourers' dwellings revealed that the average air-space a person in cottages worked out at 156 cubic feet, whereas the law required a minimum of 250 cubic feet in common lodging-houses providing only temporary accommodation, and 500 in workhouses and other 'less eligible' Poor Law institutions. Public concern about the 'cottage question' led to some new building, but this was brought to an abrupt halt by the onset of agricultural depression in 1873.[2]

In urban areas, the lengthy building cycle reached a peak in the late 1870s, but productivity in the industry remained abysmally low, a fundamental obstacle to better working-class housing.[3] However, an important change in residential style was tentatively introduced in the 1860s, the early days of 'by-law housing', the first attempt at 'planning' in working-class urban areas. Under the Form of By-laws which accompanied the Local Government Act 1858, regulations were drawn up respecting the width and construction of new streets, the structure of walls, the adequacy of air space about buildings and their drainage and sewerage; some specific clauses related to room heights, the area of windows and the construction of flues. An alternative to expensive local Acts, the by-laws were offered as a model for local authorities to modify in accordance with local custom and building practice, providing a useful guide for the more progressive towns, and an important precedent for national involvement in housing matters.[4]

Applicable only to new buildings, these permissive regulations were often ignored or evaded, but they heralded the shift from a 'cellular and promiscuous' style to the 'open and encapsulated'. Directed

160

against back-to-backs and enclosed courts, the regulations stipulated that all new houses should have an area of open space – usually interpreted to mean an exclusive back yard, a private patch of rear territory which would accommodate an individual privy – related to the height of the building. The improved standards of construction and sanitary convenience suggested in the mid-Victorian by-laws were to become standard features of late nineteenth-century terrace housing.[5]

Conditions in inner-city areas, however, continued to deteriorate as the immobile casual poor were crowded closer together by 'displacement'. The commercialization of city centres gathered pace with the conversion of houses into workshops, offices, shops and warehouses, forcing the former domestic occupants into the immediately adjacent districts. In London, the problem was compounded by dock development, the extension of the railway network and the construction of vast railway termini – during the railway boom of 1859–67 at least 37,000 were displaced from central areas. Despite the claims of the promoters, these commercial developments were not beneficial exercises in slum clearance: those evicted did not disperse to distant and healthier neighbourhoods. The city centre remained the strategic focus of the casual labour market, where meagre incomes could best be supplemented through the black market, crime and other means, not least female earnings in laundering, charring, office cleaning, flower-selling and other sweated labour. Many artisans, too, were compelled to live close to their employment in central locations: in the Clerkenwell jewellery and watchmaking trade, for example, local residence was essential as expensive tools were shared between craftsmen. In the absence of cheap transport and industrial relocation, the commercialization of central areas led to serious overcrowding in the contiguous districts, where the desired residential distinctions were soon under threat. Previously segregated, the residuum and the respectable working class were forced together in dangerous proximity.[6]

Metropolitan 'improvement' compounded the problem. Planned to eradicate the rookeries, the foci of crime, cholera and Chartism, street clearance and sanitary reform schemes simply created new slums in the surrounding neighbourhoods. Redevelopment and rehousing were undertaken on strictly commercial lines, at rents beyond the means of poorly compensated evicted tenants. The Cross Act 1875 was a misguided attempt to remedy these defects through the newly fashionable 'levelling-up theory'. Following the demolition of insanitary areas, rehousing was to be entrusted to model dwellings associations who would provide decent tenement accommodation for artisans on the commercial basis of 5 per cent philanthropy, allowing the displaced casual poor to occupy the housing vacated by the artisans.[7]

Back in the 1840s and 1850s, the first model dwellings associations, patronized by royalty and aristocracy, fulfilled an exemplary role, demonstrating to speculative builders that decent sanitary accommodation for the working class could be made to pay a modest return on capital. During the 1860s, however, a number of model dwellings companies undertook to relieve accommodation pressure in central London themselves by the construction of tenement blocks which were to yield a dividend of 5 per cent a year. The accommodation was self-contained with a decent standard of sanitation, but the tenements proved unpopular with artisans who disapproved of the institutional atmosphere of the blocks, where 'moral rules' and petty regulations were enforced with paternal vigilance. As rents continued to rise, the tenements became a form of lower middle-class charity, increasingly occupied by policemen, poor clergymen, clerks and shop assistants. Established in 1862 with a gift of £150,000 from an American merchant, the Peabody Trust was intended to provide tenement accommodation for the poorer sections of the working class, but here too the rules and regulations excluded all but the self-supporting and the regularly employed. Despite the predominantly seasonal character of metropolitan employment, rents had to be paid in advance and no arrears were allowed; sub division was strictly forbidden as were 'offensive' home-based trades, including the taking in of washing, an indispensable contribution to many working-class budgets. Out of the reach of the casual poor, the Trust nevertheless treated tenants as members of the 'degraded classes'. Vaccinated on arrival, they were kept under constant supervision until the outside door was locked at 11 p.m. when the gas was turned off, ensuring that the tenants went to bed at a respectable hour.[8]

The Octavia Hill system, regarded as the solution to the housing problem of the casual poor in the 1860s and 1870s, was no less meddlesome. Tenants in poor and overcrowded courts were to be 'trained' in punctuality, thrift and respectability by the 'moral force' of the lady rent-collector. A kindly and personal interest in those who 'improved' – who were thus entitled to repairs – was accompanied by an uncompromising sternness to those who could not achieve regularity, the precondition for a satisfactory return of 5 per cent on housing for 'the destructive classes'.[9]

The levelling-up theory failed to operate in overcrowded London as artisans shunned the model dwellings and failed to move out to the suburbs, where rents were cheaper but everything else was dearer, restricting migration to those with guaranteed earnings in excess of 30s a week. Extra costs, together with the inconvenience of overcrowded and badly timed workmen's trains, forced some workers to return to the centre and deterred many more from moving out in the 1870s.[10] Where possible, however, better-paid workers were proud to display a new status-oriented choice in housing. Family circumstances permitting, the enhanced income differentials of the mid-Victorian boom enabled the artisan elite to distance themselves from socially unacceptable neighbours. In the 1850s, Stourbridge glassmakers began to move to the more select area of Amblecote, north of the town.[11] Around the same time, specifically artisan residential areas – poorly built but with flourishes of architectural respectability – were developed in Greenwich, Deptford and Woolwich, the Kentish London towns dominated by the growth industries of the mid-Victorian economy, engineering, shipbuilding, metal working and armaments.[12]

By moving to 'respectable' areas, artisans confirmed their status *within* the working class as superior working men. They wished to distance themselves from the rough residuum but they had no wish to cross the class divide, to join the ranks of the lower middle class. Status aspirations within the working class were by no means incompatible with consciousness of belonging to that class or with repudiation of middle-class values. Although restricted to those who could afford guaranteed regular subscriptions, artisan building societies were democratic and convivial exercises in mutualism, fundamentally different in spirit in ethos from the new permanent societies promoted by middle-class dignitaries. Although encouraged by the middle class, the aspiration to house ownership was an expression of artisan independence, the heartfelt desire to escape from conditions of degradation and dependence within the housing market.[13]

Marriage patterns tended to reinforce this internal stratification. In towns and cities where trades and industries were well established, residence and marriage often followed occupational lines, a reflection of traditional craft exclusiveness. Where new industrial skills dominated, better-paid workers from various occupations were drawn together in many ways. For a bridegroom from a skilled working-class background in Kentish London, the probability of marriage into the skilled working-class or non-manual strata ranged between 60 per cent and 70 per cent in the 1850s, while the chances were generally even higher in the 1870s. In contrast, the chances of marrying into those strata for someone of the labourer background were 29 per cent in the 1850s and 36 per cent in the 1870s: at this level, the great probability was marriage into the unskilled working class.[14] An important exception to this pattern should be noted, however: of the three towns studied by John Foster, Oldham had the widest income differentials *and* the highest level of inter-marriage between labouring and craft families.[15]

While the artisan elite moved up into socially acceptable areas, the flood of post-Famine Irish immigrants were confined to the worst residential quarters, but there were no formal urban ghettos. In London, 'exiles of Erin' were relegated to the side-streets and back alleys of working-class neighbourhoods, within which narrow confines they were constantly on the move. There was little internal conflict in the London slums where the various constituent groups, ethnic and otherwise, largely ignored the others – each group followed the Irish example and lived and married within its own network of kin, friends, shops and services.[16]

Up in the cotton districts, however, the Irish were forced together in defensive separation: even in the mixed streets there was a strong tendency towards ethnic clustering with distinct Irish and non-Irish ends. Direct competitors in the factory labour market, the Irish were reviled as subversive aliens imbued with Fenianism and Catholicism, the horrors of which were revealed by a succession of Protestant demagogues. The sectarian riots provoked by the likes of the apostate Baron de Camin and the inflammatory William Murphy, were foreshadowed by the violent events in Stockport in 1852, the most destructive disturbance of the decade – two chapels were badly damaged, over 100 people were seriously injured, and a man was killed before order was restored.[17]

Conflicts were often triggered by the provocative actions of teenagers, but working-class adults, many of them 'respectable' factory operatives, were heavily involved in all the major disturbances of the period. The Tories built up a mass following around the single issue of 'No Popery', a force which displayed its strength at election riots in many Lancashire towns in 1868, by which time anti-Catholic sentiment had been hardened by Fenian 'outrages', Murphy's demagoguery and the severe economic distress of the preceding winter.[18]

Where competition in the labour market was less direct, the incidence of ethnic conflict was less pronounced. In Liverpool, where the casual labour market dictated the pattern of Irish residence close to the docks, most violence continued in factional and regional form, feuds within the immigrant community itself.[19] However, here and elsewhere the proverbial Irish reputation for drinking and fighting amongst themselves was often deliberately distorted by law enforcement agencies. At Wolverhampton, for example, the local constabulary concentrated its resources on the 'rough' Irish quarter around Stafford Street, a poverty-ridden, overcrowded and insanitary district, marked by a profusion of lodging houses, pubs and beershops. Here prosecutions for minor offences were easily effected, producing crime figures which suggested an impressive level of police efficiency! The Black Country police found in the Irish a natural target for their attentions, and the Irish reciprocated with attacks in kind. Anti-police riots, a common feature of the Chartist period, became an Irish speciality in mid-Victorian England. Seemingly sectarian, the famous 'Garibaldi riots' in Birkenhead in 1862 were more in the nature of these regular clashes between the victimized Irish immigrants and the police.[20]

Irish violence was retaliatory in nature, but given their 'belligerent fidelity' to the Catholic faith, they were easily provoked. Despite their lowly and inferior position, they maintained an exalted notion of their own religion, and a sovereign contempt for the 'haythen' by whom they were surrounded. This religious loyalty owed much to the priests who provided community leadership, religious and secular, from their humble abodes in the poor missions. Revered and respected, the local Catholic priest displayed none of the condescending censoriousness of the Anglican clergy and other philanthropic 'visitors to the poor', such as Octavia Hill's lady rent collectors. Frequently repeated, the priest's intervention in such matters as drinking and fighting carried no expectation of permanent moral reform. The priests, Booth shrewdly observed, were 'lenient judges of the frailties that are not sins, and of the disorder that is not crime'.[21] The cotton district apart, Catholicism ultimately served to integrate the Irish immigrants, to institutionalize their sub-culture within mainstream social and political developments, through identification with the Liberal Party and the policy of Home Rule.[22]

11 Work

Against the logic of deskilling technology and 'machinofacture', craft-like control persisted in amended form in the mid-Victorian factory, a privilege enjoyed by a new aristocracy of labour. Sharply differentiated from the old and autonomous craft elite, the new aristocrats, John Foster contends, derived their status from a change in employer strategy. Stripped of their former craft control, skilled workers were incorporated in a new authority structure designed to strengthen discipline and increase production – 'While the self-imposed work routine of the craft worker served to insulate him from employer control, that imposed by the technological demands of the new industry equally firmly identified the skilled worker with management.' The introduction of the 'piecemaster' system in the engineering factories brought the skilled engineer into active involvement in the work of management as pacemaker and technical supervisor. In the cotton factories, spinners retained skilled status as the crucial pacesetter group after the introduction of the long-awaited self-acting mules. Responsive to piece-rate incentives, these male workers forced an intensification of labour from juvenile and female time-paid assistants, an effective adaptation of traditional gender and family roles to the factory environment.[1]

The new aristocrats, Gareth Stedman Jones insists, were less secure than Foster's analysis suggests. Left untouched, distinctions of status were purely formal: real control had passed to the employers with the restabilization of the labour process on the basis of modern industry. Thereafter skilled workers were defensive and collaborationist, seeking to preserve their insecure status and differentials through the goodwill of their employers within the now permanent framework of industrial capitalist production.[2] Much as they differ, Foster and Stedman Jones both assume that changes in the labour process involved technical deskilling, but this was not necessarily the case. Old skills were often reconstituted in new forms by workers whose technical knowledge and experience remained indispensable to production. In the cotton factories, for example, the craft of mulespinning was transformed by the introduction of the self-actors, but it was not deskilled. The mechanical adjustment and supervision of the new machinery – quadrant nut adjustment, cop formation, and the oversight of humidity, temperature, twist and roving variations –

were crucial tasks of skilled labour mastered only by long practice by those already experienced in the handicraft trade.[3]

In the absence of technical expertise, employers were often forced to concede considerable autonomy to skilled workers, although they generally derived some benefit from the arrangement. By allowing spinners to appoint their own piecers, they were relieved of direct responsibility for labour recruitment and discipline. Apprenticeship rules operated in a similar way, providing the employer with a skilled workforce trained at worker expense. Craft pride and respect were also acceptable when they served as a form of quality control – like many craft trades, the boilermakers had rules on proper working and fined those who cheated their employers by shoddy work.[4]

The pragmatic compromise between skilled workers and employers was usually negotiated locally and informally, in a discourse of mutual rights and shared interests, language which acknowledged the triumph of capitalist market relations. Capital made production possible, but the actual details of production, the workers insisted, were the responsibility of labour. However, there were a number of major conflicts at the frontier of control. In the engineering industry, for example, the claims of employer authority and craft independence were in outright confrontation during the strikes and lock-out of 1851–2. United in opposition to the expansion of piecework, systematic overtime, and semi-skilled 'illegal' labour, regional unions combined to form the ASE, which immediately took industrial action to prohibit the new cheapening practices. Employers retaliated with a national lock-out, a co-ordinated exercise to enforce their authority, their 'right to do what they wish with their own'. They secured a formal victory in April 1852 when rules restraining overtime, piecework and the labour supply were deleted from the ASE rule-book as the men returned to work. In the ensuing years, however, the engineers regained the lost ground through local and district workshop action: by 1876 only 7 per cent of engineering workers were on piecework and only 15 per cent worked systematic overtime.[5]

Acquiescent subordination prevailed in the paternalist cotton factories but workers retained a residual independence. Grateful for the new facilties which transformed the factory into the centre of social life – the trips, treats and lavish celebrations which marked such rites of passage as the coming of age of the master's son – workers displayed a deference that was no more than instrumental in form. They were not prepared to be unduly patronized, to accept employer authority – or 'affectionate tutelage' – beyond certain limits. When the paternal bargain was transgressed in these ways, deference was withheld until acceptable, negotiated relations were restored.[6]

Outside the factories, skilled workers in handicraft trades still enjoyed genuine independence provided they could enforce union control of recruitment and craft regulation of the labour process. Most aristocratic trades included a semi-skilled sector providing a useful buffer at critical phases in the life-cycle, when skilled workers were otherwise forced down into the insecure mass of the unskilled. Workers in the unregulated sweated trades toiled in garrets and workrooms often without direct capitalist supervision, but theirs was a degraded form of independence. Lacking control of the labour market, they were mercilessly exploited by a multi-layered sub-contracting system of production.[7]

Where no independence was allowed, workers were generally reluctant to enter employment, whatever the material advantages on offer. Domestic service, a comparatively well-paid occupation uninterrupted by cyclical or seasonal unemployment, was shunned by working-class girls in factory districts and urban areas, despite the in-house benefits of decent food, accommodation and medical attention. On call for long hours, servants were stripped of all individual identity in a culture of ritualized social subordination which compelled them to wear uniform, use separate entrances and regulate their hair, speech and demeanour. In the process, servants acquired savings and a modicum of middle-class polish, but contrary to belief, these did not improve their marriage prospects. According to the Lancashire marriage registers, servants tended to marry husbands of a lower social-economic status than their peers, an indication of the social stigma attached to service in an area where alternative female employment was readily available. The resident bourgeoisie of the factory districts had to depend on rural migrants, although at the bottom end of the scale, small shopkeepers, clerks and even some working-class families obtained cheap live-in servants from the local workhouse. Rural girls were more expensive but less fractious: lacking access to the urban labour market, they were prepared to accept social subordination and the irksome restrictions of life in the employer's home. When this labour supply began to decline, there was a real 'servant problem'.[8]

Less demeaning than domestic service, factory employment offered women some independence, but they seldom attained the most lucrative and responsible jobs. Under the new paternalist regimes, they were deemed ineligible for the crucial supervisory tasks, the jobs which carried skilled status and workplace authority, male preserves jealously protected by 'closed' trade unionism. There was some physical and technical basis for this hierarchical structure of gender and skill which denied women access to the well-paid spinning sector. In physical terms, women were quite capable of operating the new self-actors but they lacked the necessary technical skills and experience, having been removed from the spinning factories a decade or so earlier when the use of 'doubled' mules put a premium on male physical strength. Without recent hands-on experience, women were the victims of a cultural discontinuity in the transmission of craft skills and knowledge from one generation to another.[9]

But there was a further factor which hindered the acquisition of workplace skills, the cult of domesticity which sought to limit female paid employment to the brief period before marriage. In some parts of the cotton districts, married women went out to work in substantial numbers, but not in the southern spinning belt, where the well-paid spinners and engineers now feared a loss of status should their wives return to paid employment. For the most part young and unmarried, female cotton operatives were concentrated in the weaving sheds where in theory there was equal pay for men and women. In practice, however, the men enjoyed a differential of up to 4s a week by monopolizing the large looms.[10]

Unable to restrict labour supply through closed and exclusive organization, the weavers, male and female, united in 'open' trade unionism, a development deplored by paternal employers. The Preston lock-out of 1853-4 was an unrestrained confrontation between masters and workers, provoking the last attempt at a Chartist revival. Amid the struggle to reverse the 10 per cent wage cuts of 1847, Ernest Jones canvassed support for a Labour parliament, which would levy a penny rate on wages to render financial assistance to workers in dispute, and to purchase land and machinery for cooperative employment. The Preston struggle for 'Ten Per Cent and No Surrender' exhausted all available funds, however, and the scheme soon collapsed. The cotton workers themselves were starved back to work after 28 weeks, a decisive defeat which marked a turning-point in union strategy. Henceforth, politics were completely excluded as the leadership strengthened its central and bureaucratic control, disciplining local activists against ruinously expensive industrial militancy. While husbanding the funds, the leadership cultivated an image of moderation and respectability, a public relations exercise to secure recognition from reluctant employers. In districts where competition was particularly stiff, this pragmatic moderation elicited the requisite concessions from employers: Blackburn employers granted union recognition and negotiating rights on the strict understanding that responsible union officials would 'police' the agreement, ensuring that uniformity and parity were observed by weavers throughout the district. Elsewhere, union recognition and arbitration were delayed until the 1880s, but the Blackburn weavers pointed the way forward towards modern collective bargaining.[11]

In industries which were already unionized, similar conciliation and arbitration schemes enjoyed a considerable vogue in the late 1860s and early 1870s. First introduced in the Nottingham hosiery industry, the schemes were of mutual benefit to unions and employers, an institutional expression, as it were, of the mid-Victorian compromise in labour relations. Unions were accorded full recognition and negotiating rights, in return for which employers secured settlements which would not be disrupted by unpredictable workshop disputes. The new sliding wage-scales were welcomed in the coal and iron trades where wages disputes had broken many unions: conciliation boards now automatically adjusted wages to product price. Some of the other schemes clearly favoured the employers: in the building industry, for example, masters took advantage of mutual negotiation to reassert and redefine managerial prerogatives, thereby curtailing the autonomous regulation of the trade. An important advance in modern collective bargaining, the craze for conciliation and arbitration schemes came to an end with the collapse of the mid-Victorian boom.[12]

12 Popular Culture

Commercial investment in leisure and recreation proceeded apace in mid-Victorian England. New facilities appeared and prospered in advance of significant gains in leisure time and money, benefits withheld from most of the working class until the end of the boom, when the Saturday half-holiday and the nine-hour day were established as the norm. The trend towards the capitalization of leisure was best exemplified by the lavish, purpose-built music halls of the 1850s and 1860s. Entertainment was still on offer in innumerable 'smalls', 'spitoons' and other pub rooms, but the new people's palaces soon dominated the business – by 1866 there were 33 large halls in London with an average capitalization of £10,000 and an average seating capacity of 1500. Within the sham opulence, the halls offered a variety of escapist delights, pleasures enjoyed by artisan and labouring families alike. Performed by artistes with strong working-class roots, the entertainment was promoted on the populist and profitable basis that 'a little of what you fancy does you good'.[1]

Rivalling the halls, large-scale investment in circuses and fairs was prompted in part by the new excursion trains which enabled untold numbers to visit permanent sites of amusement and recreation, a method of popular access which proved its worth during the Great Exhibition.[2] The railways also assisted the distribution of commercially produced popular literature and journalism, hastening the decline of the old itinerant broadsheet and ballad trade. Newspaper sales soared, rising by no less than 600 per cent between 1856 and 1882, with the salacious Sunday press leading the way, offering a repackaged version of the old chapbook and broadsheet formula of crime, sex and sensationalism.[3]

In some areas, however, commercial capital was slow to perceive popular demand. Apart from the pier-building boom of the 1860s and 1870s, seaside resorts displayed no inclination to profit from the day-tripper trade, despite the ever-increasing numbers who arrived by popular excursion train. An unwelcome intrusion, trippers threatened the otherwise carefully controlled social tone of resort development. But there was no stopping the popularity of travel for pleasure, whether to the sea, a sporting fixture or a brass band competition. By the late 1860s, the excursion train had become routine and unremarkable, a known and essential ingredient in the leisure life of the people.[4]

Commercial developments were supplemented by public provision as money became available for the previously poorly supported schemes of the rational recreationalists. Through public purchase and private donation land was set aside for public parks and open space in most large towns and cities. Ratepayers were less forthcoming where public libraries were concerned: by 1867 only 24 libraries had been built under the 1850 Act, but here too local philanthropists were often prepared to remedy the deficiency. Baths and washhouses were the most popular of the new public buildings: constructed in the interests of public health, they allowed the working class to indulge their pleasure in swimming.[5]

Positive encouragement was accorded to sport and organized recreation by the Christian Socialists and other exponents of the new paternalism, sponsors of cross-class initiatives which marked a decisive change in middle- and upper-class attitudes to popular leisure. As the threat of disorder receded, physical recreation and organized leisure provided the arena for what Hugh Cunningham has described as 'a reconciliation of classes, a recreation of community, a reassertion of paternalism'. A conscious appropriation of old and idealized gentry values, the new middle-class patronage drew upon an archaic language of social harmony – cricketeers wore belts inscribed with the motto, 'The prince and peasant by cricket are united'. Middle-class amateurs, trained in the revitalized public schools, dominated cricket and football, sports which acquired codified rules and social respectability, virtues transmitted on the field to the working class at large. Established on an amateur basis, many of today's professional league clubs were sponsored by paternalist employers, religious groups and other middle-class missionaries of organized sport. In the absence of any alternative, the working class accepted such sponsorship but without any deference to middle-class values or ideology. As soon as circumstances permitted, the clubs dispensed with the patronage of the rich, securing their independence in the mid-1880s when professionalism was legalized.[6]

A similar pattern applied in the working men's clubs of the Club and Institute Union. Established in 1862 by the Revd Henry Solly, the clubs – a respectable alternative to the pub – attracted considerable middle-class patronage, but working-class recruitment was not forthcoming until the original temperance stipulations were abandoned. Once drink was allowed, members imposed strict sanctions against colleagues who abused the privilege, a typical mid-Victorian balance between paternalism and independence. Recruitment, however, was still inhibited by the prominent presence of patrons and parsons until the Hackney Club and other new branches led the move towards complete independence 'from any class of society other than their own', a policy adopted throughout the CIU in the mid-1880s.[7]

Working-class members of the Volunteer Force, founded in 1859, were similarly resistant to middle-class values despite their participation in a cross-class initiative which proudly reproduced the social structure of the workplace on the parade ground. While officers proclaimed a new spirit of class harmony, recruitment to the ordinary ranks depended upon the provision of recreational facilities for physical training, shooting, music and many other non-military activities, none of which brought the men close to the officers and their ethos. By the 1870s, the Volunteers had a membership of 200,000, but by this time the Force no longer paraded the hope of class conciliation.[8]

The new paternalist initiatives were almost exclusively male-oriented: there were few attempts to break down the barriers of both class *and* sex. Women were expected to enjoy confinement at the hearth, the centre of family affection and domestic leisure. Extra-curricular activities, organized by middle- and upper-class ladies, endorsed these domestic virtues within the context of religious instruction, a formula adopted at the popular Mothers' Meetings of the 1860s. But here too the practical requirements of the working-class membership came to the fore: secular self-help activities soon dominated the weekly proceedings. The meetings, a forum for information about child health and other matters, provided the facilities for clothing clubs, thrift and provident schemes. Applauded by the patrons in the language of respectability, these temporal activities were welcomed by the members on more material grounds, as helpful tactics in the struggle for family survival and self-respect.[9]

Thus the working class took practical advantage of new facilities for recreation and advancement without deferring to middle-class leadership and social norms. As practised and reformulated by the working class, self-improvement pointed to independent self-respect not to deferential respectability. There was no embourgeoisement, no assimilation of middle-class values: through industry, thrift and sobriety the working class struggled to free themselves from poverty, dependence and deference, to secure independence and respect within the newly-stabilised economic system.[10]

Better-paid workers were able to pursue these goals through their own mutual improvement societies – adult education institutes, temperance societies, co-ops, building societies and the like – independent bodies which required no heavy-handed patronage from above. These were not, as John Foster has suggested, narrow and protective institutions, shielding the supervisory workers – the new aristocracy of labour – from cultural contact with the undermass of workers.[11] Full benefits were limited to regular subscribers, but mutual improvement societies were convivial and democratic, a collective means to self-respect alien to the individualist culture of the lower middle class. Although not inclusive, these exercises in mutualism served as an example for the rest of the working class to follow.[12]

Respectability was thus deeply embedded in what Trygve Tholfsen has called the working-class sub-culture of mid-Victorian England, 'values and attitudes that were very much of the culture as a whole and yet distinct from the dominant middle-class version of the prevailing ethos'. The distinction, however, proved increasingly difficult to uphold. Political independence was steadily undermined by the liberal advance, as progressive middle-class groups added an amiable gloss to the dominant language of respectability and improvement.[13] Labour leaders, indeed, soon found themselves united in sentiment with the reforming forces which brought the Liberal party into being in the constituencies.[14] At the same time, the old class solidarity of the Chartist days was cast aside as respectable workers censured the unorganized poor in their midst for failing to apply the improvement ethic – the aristocracy of labour remained proudly within the ranks of the working class, but they displayed a critical lack of sympathy for those less fortunate than themselves. Once championed as the unfortunate victims of the system, the poor were now condemned by radical leaders for their excesses and irregularities, their lack of industry, thrift and sobriety.[15] There was thus considerable ambiguity and contradiction in mid-Victorian working-class attitudes, between the assertion of working-class independence, and the adoption of a consensual language shared with dominant groups in society.[16]

Labour organizations were brought into the Liberal alliance through the cult of respectability, but for other members of the working class incorporation in the mid-Victorian party system took a different cultural and political form. In party terms, the new paternalism usually succeeded best where there was a whole-hearted return to old squirely values of enjoyment and festivity, to a relaxed and expansive Tory style which mocked the moral restrictiveness of the respectable Liberals. This old-style paternalism was more evident in the factories than in the countryside itself, where landlords awarded prizes and certificates to encourage industry, thrift and loyalty.[17] In the factory districts, Tory employers, often of landed origins or connections, remained close to the customs of the rural past, a culture idealized in the memory of the workers. Proper squires, Tory masters displayed an easy mastery of the common style, championing the working man's right to his glass of beer and his idle pastimes. There was no condescension or moral preaching in the manful paternalism of 'Sir Harry' Hornby, the latest 'gamecock' of the Hornby dynasty, a family of squire-employers whose Tory politics were proudly followed by their loyal and devoted Blackburn workers.[18]

The difference in paternal styles was reflected in popular political behaviour. Liberalism developed in the narrow confines of 'elite politics', within the abstinent institutions for working-class self-advancement. The Tories favoured a more open and enjoyable brand of politics which encouraged the workers onto the streets with their bands, banners and processions. Spectacle and ritual – essential characteristics of the radical mass platform – were incorporated into party politics under Tory aegis, as factory and community loyalties were strengthened and celebrated in public display. The process of incorporation was extended through Tory working-men's clubs, which in Lancashire at least were more popular than the non-political CIU alternative. Here there was no resistance to the demand for drink and entertainment: members were happy to accept middle-class patronage and political direction when they were left free to enjoy the benefits of cheap 'bacca, billiards and beer'.[19]

The strength of popular Toryism in Lancashire cannot be explained simply in terms of ethnic conflict. 'No Popery' was a frontal assault on the Irish immigrants, competitors in the factory labour market, but this regional blend of militant Tory-Anglicanism gave vent to other prejudices and populist attitudes, not least the popular dislike of narrow and restrictive nonconformity, the moral creed of the Liberals. Defenders of the faith, the Tories were also the guardians of a robust popular culture which mid-Victorian respectability failed to amend.

13 Reformism and the Labour Movement

Shorn of its idealist connotations of deviance and betrayal, the term reformism best describes the character and tone of the mid-Victorian labour movement. By contrast with the Chartist mass platform, organized endeavour was limited, narrow and not without practical success. As workers adjusted to the unexpected stability of industrial capitalism, exclusive and autonomous self-help institutions – financed by regular guaranteed contributions – offered security and advancement without structural or political change.

The cooperative movement abandoned millenarian community-building schemes to concentrate on dividend-paying retail associations which were in themselves the promise and fulfilment of a better world. Much applauded by the middle class, their virtues were proclaimed in the new 'Co-operator's Catechism': 'I believe in good weight and measure, in unadulterated articles, in cash payments, and in small profits and quick returns.' For those who could afford the no-credit rule, the co-op served as a useful lever for social advancement, enabling them to become savers and investors, respectable property-owning citizens. The movement was led by the skilled elite, many of whom moved up in a world of Liberal connections, but the co-ops remained working-class in character and custom, a prosperous and respectable institution which all operatives aspired to join once wages permitted. Membership continued to grow at a rapid rate – by 1867, a few years after the establishment of the Co-operative Wholesale Society, the *Co-operator* enumerated 560 societies in England and Wales with a total of 173,000 members.[1]

The amalgamated new model unions offered an extensive range of benefits to protect their members' interests: the ASE undertook 'to exercise that same care and watchfulness over that in which we have a vested interest – i.e. our skill – as the physician does who holds a diploma'. Militant confrontation was avoided on tactical, not ideological, grounds as full-time national officials, responsible for husbanding the funds, pursued cheaper and more efficient bargaining techniques. When the union rule-book was infringed, the offending employer was brought to heel by the gradual withdrawal of labour, a discreet and cost-effective 'strike-in-detail' financed by the union's central unemployment fund, thereby avoiding the crippling expense and adverse publicity of an outright confrontation, a procedure reserved for exceptional cases. In an industrial policy of 'defence not defiance', funds were needed to adjust the market, to restrict the supply of labour through emigration and other schemes, an important supplement to the friendly society benefits. These activities required a firm legal base, hence the public relations exercise to court public approval and official recognition, without which there could be no further progress in collective bargaining. Having adjusted to the rules of the game, unions negotiated in the language of common interests and improvement, but they remained committed to basic working-class aspirations, the right to work and a fair day's wage for a fair day's work.[2]

Previously laggards in matters of general concern, the craft unions joined together to head the campaign for labour rights, following the building disputes of 1859–61, the watershed of mid-Victorian labour history. London building workers were locked out in 1859 for demanding a nine-hour day, the first large-scale attempt to control working conditions by the modern device of an hour's reduction. This simple demand left sectional and wage differences undisturbed, thereby facilitating united action throughout the trades. Behind the façade of improvement – in their public language the workers stressed the moral and social benefits of a shorter working day – the dispute was a struggle for workplace control. By reducing hours, the men hoped to spread work evenly and stabilize the trade, to regain some of the autonomy recently lost by the introduction of machinery, systematic overtime, piecework, tyrannical foremen and other employer encroachments. Forced back to work after eight months, they were soon engaged in another unsuccessful contest as the triumphant employers introduced an hourly system of payment.[3]

These disputes led to important new alignments in labour and politics: the adoption of exemplary new model unionism in the building trades; the formation of the London Trades Council; the establishment of the *Bee-Hive*; and the active involvement of the Positivists in the workers' cause.[4] Proponents of Comte's religion of humanity, the Positivists hoped to moralize existing property relations, to reconcile capital and labour through the incorporation of the working class. In marked contrast to the Christian Socialists and other groups associated with the unions and cooperative production, these middle-class intellectuals sought to radicalize the labour movement, to rally the unions as a powerful and progressive political force. Professor Beesly, chairman of the inaugural meeting of the First International, was a tireless agitator for a new political departure within the LTC, a cause which gradually gathered momentum through public interest in international events – the American Civil War, the Italian Risorgimento and Polish freedom. A strident critic of Southern sympathizers – the old-fashioned, anti-capitalist Tory radicals – Beesly hoped that support for the North would effect a progressive alliance between modern trade unionism and advanced middle-class radicalism under the inspired and indispensable leadership of John Bright.[5]

Within the trade union movement itself, there was less enthusiasm for internationalism and radical politics. Affiliation to the First International was largely an industrial matter as unions took advantage of the arrangements to prevent foreign blacklegging during disputes.[6] Dominated by union bureaucrats, the LTC was slow to abandon its official non-political stance, hindering the progress of independent radical initiatives. The Trade Unionists' Manhood Suffrage and Vote by Ballot Association, established in 1862, attracted little support and was eventually subsumed in the Reform League.[7] The League was formed in more propitious circumstances, at a time when parliamentary reform had become practical politics, but interest remained low among the rank and file. Funds were made available by an obliging group of 'influential gentlemen', advanced Liberals who looked to the unions to work up an earnest agitation, to supplement the pressure applied by the middle-class Reform Union for household suffrage.[8] This accommodation with middle-class radicalism was welcomed by the 'Junta', the côterie of full-time leaders and bureaucrats who dominated labour politics, but their control of the League was challenged by industrial militants and extra-parliamentary radicals, heirs to the independent Chartist tradition. By sheer force of rhetoric, Bright remained above these disputes, preserving some unity in the Reform Bill agitation.[9]

George Potter, champion of the small, non-amalgamated, militant trade unions, established the rival London Working Men's Association to challenge the moderate ways and means of the Reform League. Having already antagonized the Junta by his defence of the pro-Southern editor of the *Bee-Hive*, Potter, staunch supporter of all striking workers, was finally forced out of the LTC.[10] Through the LWMA, he campaigned for manhood suffrage and labour legislation, but by the time he arranged the first Trades Reform Demonstration, the militant political radicals had already seized the initiative. At weekly outdoor meetings on Clerkenwell Green, Benjamin Lucraft, a Chartist veteran, condemned the limitations of Gladstone's Reform Bill, a moderate measure reluctantly endorsed by the League in deference to their middle-class financial sponsors.[11]

When the Bill was defeated, the radical demonstrations were transferred to Trafalgar Square, a provocative move which the League felt compelled to match, to capitalize on the popular indignation aroused by the disparaging anti-democratic remarks of the Bill's parliamentary opponents. A programme of official demonstrations was arranged, culminating in a national gathering in Hyde Park on 23 July, plans which involved the League in the controversial question of the right of assembly in London's public spaces – there had been violent clashes when the police tried to clear the park during the Sunday trading demonstrations of 1855, and the Garibaldi festivities of 1862.[12] Under pressure from the militants, the League decided to proceed, despite the ban imposed by the authorities. Denied entry to the park, Edmund Beales, president of the League, led the first column of the procession peaceably away to Trafalgar Square, but many demonstrators remained at the scene, gaining access to the forbidden territory when the dilapidated railings collapsed under the pressure of numbers. There followed three days and nights of intermittent skirmishing as the police tried to seal the area, but order was not restored until Beales returned to the scene, an intervention which Spencer Walpole, the Home Secretary, welcomed with tearful relief.[13]

Parliament was prorogued for several months but public interest in reform remained at a high and irresistible level as Bright toured the country addressing huge working-class audiences. When parliament reassembled in 1867, the militant radicals convened a series of meetings in Trafalgar Square at which Potter and other orators advocated a 'universal cessation of labour', reviving the old Chartist rhetoric of a 'Grand National Holiday' and a 'People's Parliament'. Unwilling to be upstaged, the League announced another official demonstration in Hyde Park, overruling the cautious advice of Beales and Howell. The government immediately banned the proceedings and mobilized the forces of order, but this time it was they who capitulated. Led by the Clerkenwell branch of the Reform League, carrying a red flag surmounted with a Cap of Liberty, some 150,000 demonstrators marched through the open park gates on 6 May to attend a peaceable and triumphant meeting. The hapless Walpole, scapegoat for this humiliation, resigned his ministerial post.[14]

In these circumstances, the minority Tory administration could not withdraw from parliamentary reform, but it was 'high politics' not extra-parliamentary pressure that prompted Disraeli to accept radical amendments which transformed the government Bill into an extensive household suffrage measure by enfranchising lodgers and removing the distinction between compounders and personal ratepayers. By conceding these points, Disraeli was able to outmanoeuvre Gladstone and 'dish the Whigs'. With radical support he maintained command of parliament, keeping control of the redistribution of seats, enabling the Tories to exploit and develop their strength in the counties – in these party political terms, the urban franchise was of little significance, since the large urban constituencies were mostly Liberal already.

As it emerged from parliament, the Reform Act awarded the vote to 'registered and residential' male householders, the respectable urban working class on whose behalf the League had campaigned. The Act thus vindicated the middle-class alliance, a Lib-Lab arrangement which labour leaders wished to continue in pursuit of legislation on trade union rights. Here again they were challenged by radical militants who hoped to advance to an independent labour politics, to establish a third party by extending trade unionism throughout the ranks of the working class.[15] Unable to counter the institutional power of the Lib-Lab leaders, the radical-republicans also lacked a new ideology to inspire and sustain this major leap forward: new unionism among the unorganized in the early 1870s was brought to an abrupt halt by the onset of the 'Great Depression'.

Soon after the Reform Bill was passed, Howell, full-time secretary of the League, entered a secret agreement with Glyn, Liberal chief whip, by which a 'special fund' was made available for certain services at the forthcoming general election. Using the extensive organization of the League, Howell undertook to investigate the intentions of the much enlarged urban electorate, to promote designated Liberal candidates and thereby prevent independent working-class candidates from splitting the radical vote. An ex-bricklayer turned professional labour leader, Howell lacked a permanent union post and was thus dependent on precariously financed political appointments: the agreement with Glyn and the Liberals ensured the flow of funds necessary to maintain his current office. Too susceptible to Liberal blandishments, Howell sacrificed the independence of the League without securing any real concessions over policy and working-class representation – a handful of League members, Howell included, were encouraged in their candidacies in hopeless constituencies, but other labour leaders were compelled to withdraw in favour of Whigs and other official party nominees. As negotiated by Howell, Lib-Labism was a poor deal for organized labour, but a great asset for the Liberals who secured a remarkable electoral success in 1868.[16]

The Reform League was disbanded in post-election recriminations, but Lib-Labism was by no means discredited. Through the formation of the Labour Representation League, Howell and the moderate trades leaders hoped to renegotiate the terms of the pact, to prevail upon the Liberals to accept a small band of working-class labour MPs in return for electoral support throughout the land.[17] This limited objective was briefly but dramatically revised when the government introduced the Criminal Law Amendment Act, an unexpected reverse which underlined the radical argument for an independent labour party to guarantee trade union rights.

In the midst of the Reform Bill agitation the legal status of the trade unions was called into question by adverse court decisions and a hardening of middle-class attitudes. The notorious Sheffield 'outrages' were a local anachronism, the final protest of the old artisan culture against the new dominance of the big steel companies, but the violence – terrorism and 'rattening' directed against non-unionists – inflamed middle-class opinion against the entire trade union movement.[18] In the courts, the *Hornby* v. *Close* decision deprived unions of their imagined legal status under the friendly society legislation of 1855: the Boilermakers' Society was ruled in restraint of trade, an illegal association with no power of redress against defaulting officials. A few months later, a group of striking London tailors were convicted of conspiracy, a judgment which undermined trade union freedom in industrial disputes. By this time a Royal Commission had been appointed to investigate the Sheffield outrages and examine the general workings of the trade union movement.

At this critical juncture, the unions were unable to unite in self-defence. The Junta organized a Conference of Amalgamated Trades to uphold the interests of the new model unions, whose moderate and respectable image was not to be compromised by association with militant provincial unions. Here Potter stepped forward with a rival national conference in London in March 1867, well attended by provincial unions, several of whom were already members of the United Kingdom Alliance of Organized Trades, established in 1866 'for the purpose of effectually resisting all lock-outs'. Of far greater long-term significance, the Manchester and Salford Trades Council called for an annual congress of trade unions and trade councils: when the first TUC convened in Manchester in 1868 to discuss the Royal Commission and the legal plight of the unions, the Junta were conspicuously absent.[19]

Avoiding other trade groups, the Junta worked in close alliance with two sympathetic members of the Commission, Frederic Harrison, a leading Positivist and Thomas Hughes, novelist, sportsman and Christian Socialist. Through joint manipulation of witnesses, the Commission was steered away from the violence of the old, local societies to a laudatory examination of the actuarial soundness and friendly society functions of the amalgamated unions. Having feared the worst, the unions emerged in favourable light, particularly in the minority report signed by Harrison, Hughes and the Earl of Lichfield, which served as the basis for government legislation in 1871. Legal recognition and financial protection were accorded to unions, privileged bodies which could not be sued as corporate entities. However, the new trade union law was accompanied by the Criminal Law Amendment Act, a forceful restatement of anti-strike legislation which made those on the picket line liable to prosecution for intimidation, molestation and obstruction. The Junta were thus betrayed by their own moderation. Having projected themselves as friendly societies, they gained legal status precisely on those terms, without any advance on legal rights during disputes.[20]

Furious with the Liberal government, labour leaders called for an independent labour party to secure full trade union rights, a policy briefly endorsed by Howell – 'we must create a Working Class Party', he wrote in anger, 'for Whig, Tory and Middle-Class Radicals ignore our wants and requirements'.[21] Lacking substantial support in the provinces, the Labour Representation League could find no way of raising the necessary finance. The TUC was similarly hamstrung: provincial leaders opposed any political levy, fearing that it would lead to an unacceptable accumulation of money and power in the hands of the Parliamentary Committee, newly formed to lead the campaign to repeal the Criminal Law Amendment Act. As its full-time secretary, Howell soon reverted to his former professional practices and tried to secure partial concessions through private negotiations in the lobby of the House – the TUC, however, was in no mood to compromise, particularly after the imprisonment of striking Gas Stokers on a series of charges under the new Act and other legislation. Despite their initial enthusiasm for independent working-class politics and the creation of a 'third party', the Positivists subsequently confused the issue by supporting Joseph Chamberlain's 'firmly drawn quadrilateral' – Free Church, Free Land, Free Schools, Free Labour. As the 1874 election approached, the Positivists, Royden Harrison critically notes, 'wavered between a conception of a third party organized *de novo* in the country and a reconstruction of the Liberal Party on the basis of Chamberlain's programme'. Lacking clear leadership, delegates at the 1874 TUC decided against any specific commitment on labour representation, leaving themselves free to adopt whatever policy seemed most appropriate in their own constituencies.[22]

The Liberals were badly defeated at the election as middle-class 'faddists', disillusioned by other legislation, withheld their support, but they were saved from disaster by the absence of a coordinated labour challenge – working-class estrangement, it has been calculated, cost the Liberals no more than ten to fifteen seats. The two labour candidates elected, Burt at Morpeth and Macdonald at Stafford were returned without Liberal opposition on orthodox programmes unexceptionable to middle-class radicals. During the campaign, Conservative candidates had appeared the more responsive to trade union pressure, but the new government decided against an immediate repeal of the Criminal Law Amendment Act in favour of another enquiry, the Royal Commission on Labour Laws (1874). Under pressure from the unions, the government decided to ignore the Commission's limited and unhelpful recommendations, and introduced the Conspiracy and Protection of Property Act, which repealed the Criminal Law Amendment Act and confirmed the legality of peaceful picketing. This was followed by the Employers and Workmen Act which removed the legal and linguistic inequalities of the existing Master and Servant legislation, a cause of much union discontent. However, the Conservatives gained little by way of gratitude. Once the labour legislation was safely on the statute book, the unions rallied behind the Liberals, supporting Gladstone's moral crusade against the wicked Turk and the 'prestige politics' of Beaconsfieldism. The Lib-Lab tradition was firmly enshrined in the TUC when Henry Broadhurst replaced the exhausted Howell as secretary of the Parliamentary Committee.[23]

By the time labour legislation was secure, the economic upswing of the early 1870s had come to an end, terminating the radical initiatives based on new unionism. The speculative climax of the mid-Victorian boom, the early 1870s – when unemployment in the organized trades was well below 2 per cent – witnessed the first great British strike wave, the number of strikes increasing from a mere 30 in 1870 to about 350 in both 1872 and 1873. This strike wave, James Cronin has suggested, was probably the first of those major explosions of militancy and union organization that have characterized the subsequent history of British industrial relations. Not merely an escalation of overt conflict between workers and employers, this militancy – like the waves of 1889–90, 1911–13, and 1919–20 – registered a shift towards more inclusive organization of less skilled workers, together with an upsurge of rank-and-file activism, a rejection of the cautious advice of established officials, and a renewed emphasis upon the efficacy of strike activity.[24] But there was to be no such advance in political radicalism. While closely involved with the First International, the Land and Labour League – founded after the disbandment of the Reform League by radicals and republicans, members of the democratic clubs which had persisted in Soho and other parts of London since Chartist times[25] – remained committed to Bronterre O'Brien's formulations for national regeneration. Inequalities in the industrial means of production were still unexamined as radicals persisted in the condemnation of 'property', the monopoly control of land, money and credit. Of its nine-point programme, a medley of old Chartist, Owenite and currency reform schemes, land nationalization and home colonies were given particular prominence at unemployment demonstrations in Trafalgar Square in 1870. Just at the point where it threatened to challenge the discredited Lib-Lab leaders by mobilizing the unorganized and unemployed, the League fell victim to sectarianism, left-wing divisions prompted by events in France.[26]

The defeat of Napoleon III and the establishment of the new French Republic had been greeted with great enthusiasm and considerable anti-monarchist agitation against 'Mrs Brown', Queen Victoria's sobriquet. Meritocratic middle-class republicans withdrew, however, when events took a different turn: the radicals were left to argue amongst themselves about how best to emulate the social and democratic Communards. One faction led by John Hales tried to regroup the radical forces through the International, by establishing an English section, a Federal Council which would unite trade unions and O'Brienite republicans in an independent political party. The attempt fell victim to other sectarian disputes as Marx decided to transfer the International to New York to prevent a takeover by Bakunin and the anarchists.[27]

While internal wrangles occupied the energies of some members of the Land and Labour League, others continued to agitate among the unorganized, encouraged by the success of the Nine Hours League. Having started as an unofficial movement among Tyneside skilled engineers, the League secured notable victories in the northeast by uniting various grades of workers, unionized and non-unionized, skilled and unskilled, an example which London radicals were keen to follow. Assisted by Patrick Hennessey of the Land and Labour League, London dockers organized themselves in the Labour Protection League which pursued a vigorous policy of short sharp selective strikes, a successful tactic for casual and unskilled labourers in the booming economic conditions of the early 1870s. By October 1871 there were over 30,000 members, mainly dockers, although recruitment extended to engineering labourers, dustmen, slopmen and scavengers. Shortly afterwards, there was an attempt to form a great transport workers federation, an Amalgamated Labour Union of dockers, carmen, lightermen and railway workers, but cyclical downturn and the return of unemployment brought an end to such ambitious schemes of general unionism. By the end of the decade, the Labour Protection League had less than 2000 members: the relatively skilled stevedores were the only group able to maintain a stable trade organization, an important base for the revival of mass unionism on the waterside in 1889.[28] In Liverpool, the collapse of new unionism was hastened by the absence of indigenous radical leadership. Dockers and labourers relied for guidance and arbitration on an eccentric local philanthropist with pronounced anti-union views, and a local new model employer whose experience of craft unionism was of little relevance to striking unskilled workers.[29]

Attempts at general unionism proved abortive, but some success was achieved by new unions of a sectional or industrial type. Despite rigorous company discipline, railway workers registered an important advance with the establishment in 1871 of the Amalgamated Society of Railway Servants, an all-grades union. By the end of 1872 there were 17,000 members, but this early momentum was not maintained: ten years later, membership had dropped back to 6000, less than 2 per cent of the workforce, and by this time the aristocratic drivers had split off to form the Associated Society of Locomotive Enginemen and Firemen.[30] On the coalfields, the moderate Miners National Association was briefly challenged by the militant Amalgamated Association of Miners. Led by Alexander Macdonald, the existing Association – dominated by the county unions of the 'sliding-scale' export coalfields of the north-east – concentrated on parliamentary lobbying to improve pit safety, and made no attempt to coordinate industrial action between the coalfields. Miners on other fields took advantage of the coal boom of the early 1870s to demand a minimum wage, a cause championed by Thomas Halliday's new Amalgamation. Action began in south Wales, where owners were paying wages 20–30 per cent below the English average. Striking miners were supported by levies on working Lancashire miners while a vigorous campaign deterred the Staffordshire miners from blacklegging. After this carefully co-ordinated victory, miners on other fields gained wage advances without recourse to strike action. Membership of the Amalgamation topped 100,000 in the spring of 1874, but economic circumstances were already on the turn. As wages fell on every field, it proved impossible to maintain national and tactical unity. The various districts seceded to cut their costs and regain autonomy by reaffiliation to the National Association, into which the Amalgamated was itself dissolved in August 1874.[31]

The most famous of the new unions of the early 1870s, Joseph Arch's National Agricultural Labourers Union, displayed a similar chronology of rapid rise and sudden collapse. Established in 1872, the Union developed at a remarkable pace in the labour-intensive corn counties, assisted by the leadership of rural and small town craftsmen, tradesmen and nonconformist preachers, outside figures independent of the tyranny of squire, farmer and parson. By 1874, the union boasted a membership of 100,000, many of whom enjoyed wage rises of 20–30 per cent, thanks to favourable market conditions and selective strike action. The onset of agricultural depression and the return of a Conservative government led to a dramatic reversal of fortune as the power of the union was crushed in conflict with farmers' Defence Associations and the imposition of a lock-out in the eastern counties. Defeated and demoralized, the union abandoned industrial action to concentrate on emigration schemes, friendly society activities, and the campaign for land reform and the vote. The persistence of agricultural depression prevented any subsequent revival: by the mid-1880s, agricultural unionism was largely extinct, and earnings had fallen back to the level of the late 1860s.[32]

14 The Working Class Observed

During the mid-Victorian decades, the condition of England question was reformulated to reflect the material and moral progress of the nation. Improvement was everywhere to be seen, not least on the streets where there was a welcome decline in crime and violence. Caution was still required in some areas. Sanctioned and protected by their fellow casual labourers, Liverpool 'cornermen' continued to extract largesse from outside intruders, fair game for mugging.[1] In London, alarmist newspapers fabricated the occasional garrotting panic, particularly after the end of the transportation system, but mugging and other forms of street crime were definitely on the decrease.[2] Crime, middle-class social observers were reassured to report, was a residual activity, restricted to an hereditary criminal class – statistics, indeed, indicated an increase in the number of re-offenders and in the average age of those convicted.[3] Poverty, too, was at an acceptable or rather irreducible level amongst the residuum, as the broad advance of industrialism enabled workers to improve their lot by diligence, industry and thrift.[4]

Mid-Victorian economic growth clarified the distinctions within the working class, a tripartite grouping for whom old inclusive terms like the labouring poor were no longer appropriate. Interest focused on the strategic intermediate group, located between the residuum of demoralized labour and the respectable workers capable of combination and cooperation, into whose ranks it was hoped they would rise.[5] Through paternalism and philanthropy the middle class encouraged and supervised this upward movement, while social policy isolated and disciplined the residuum. Assisted by new professional expertise, the mid-Victorians confidently distinguished between the deserving and undeserving poor.

The new professionalism in social science was tried and tested in the East End of London, an area denied the benefits of mid-Victorian prosperity. Excluded from new industrialism, the East End was in a state of crisis throughout the 1860s with the decline of staple industries, the expansion of casual and sweated trades, increased overcrowding, poor health, harsh winters, prolonged unemployment and chronic poverty. The local Poor Law broke under the strain, an inevitable consequence of the exodus of the rich to more salubrious districts, since each metropolitan Poor Law Union was wholly responsible – until 1867 – for the relief of its own poor, a system which presupposed a rough balance between rich and poor. Residential segregation saddled the poorest unions with the highest burden, often aggravated by the influx of the casual poor displaced from the rich and low-rated districts. Having reached the limit of local taxation, hard-pressed unions abandoned expensive workhouse provision in favour of meagre doles, relying upon charity – the guilt money, as it were, of the West End in default of its legal obligations – to supplement the inadequate amounts of outdoor relief. At the end of the 1860s, it was calculated that £2 million or so was annually expended in legal relief in London, and over £7 million in private charity. Indiscriminately distributed, this charitable bounty produced pauperism and demoralization among the working class, dangers identified by Hollingshead's survey of *Ragged London*:

> They increase and multiply, and all for what? To become paupers; to glut the labour market; to keep their wages down at starvation point, to swell the profits of capital. They look to everyone to relieve them, but make few efforts to relieve themselves.[6]

Depersonalized and indiscriminate, alms-giving failed to encourage the poor in the path of virtue. The separation of classes had produced 'the deformation of the gift'. As the relationship between persons had disappeared, so had the essential elements of prestige, subordination and obligation.[7]

The need for social leadership in the East End prompted Edward Denison to take up residence in Stepney after the London 'season' of 1867. A staunch critic of indiscriminate charity, Denison called upon the middle class to offer the poor 'something better than money . . . help them to help themselves, lend them your brains'. Denison died in 1868, shortly after leaving the East End, but his example served to inspire the settlement movement of the 1880s.[8] In the absence of a resident gentry, middle-class philanthropists relied upon regular inspection to ensure that charity was properly implemented, a task undertaken with improving zeal by Octavia Hill's lady rent-collectors. New standards of professional expertise were applied to charitable distribution with the establishment in 1869 of the Society for Organizing Charitable Relief and Repressing Mendicity, better known as the Charity Organization Society, an investigative agency committed to 'scientific charity'.[9]

'Charity requires a social discipline', C. S. Loch, secretary of the COS explained, 'it works through sympathy, it depends on science.' Through meticulous investigation and casework, the Society aimed to identify specific needs in order to direct applicants to the charitable agency best qualified to help them back to independence. In these positive respects, the COS pioneered the methods and techniques of the modern social work profession, but the main purpose of investigation and scrutiny was to detect and deter the undeserving poor, in particular the 'clever paupers' who made an easy living out of indiscriminate and overlapping charity. Unworthy of further assistance, they were to be despatched to the workhouse, to suffer the full rigours of 'less eligibility'. The COS, indeed, was in the forefront of the campaign for stricter workhouses, for a return to the principles of 1834.[10]

The methods and philosophy of the COS were formulated by members of the liberal professions, the new urban gentry who sought to legitimize their newly-defined status through philanthropy and public service. Social problems were studied with scientific precision, a professional procedure encouraged by the National Association for the Promotion of Social Science, but the fundamental assumptions of orthodox political economy remained unquestioned. As exemplified by the COS, the 'professional ideal' of social service and scientific standards served to strengthen, not to moderate, the entrepreneurial ethos of economic individualism. New methods endorsed old attitudes. Precise and professional classification of the poor enabled the proper implementation of the deterrent principles of 1834. The state was to discipline the feckless and work-shy, while the deserving poor were to be assisted by voluntary agencies under middle-class patronage.[11]

The determining influence on philanthropy, the professional ideal was also the dynamic factor in mid-Victorian government growth. New technocrats like Sir John Simon secured money and powers denied Chadwick and other Benthamite administrators. Through the irrefutable language of science and professional expertise, Simon persuaded politicians to accept minimum standards of public health, duly enforced by inspection as the national norm. But there was no move forward into a constructive and positive role for the state. Insanitary housing was compulsorily demolished but the provision of new sanitary accommodation was left to market forces and 5 per cent philanthropy. Personal medical services were available only within the pauper framework of the Poor Law, with the single exception of state vaccination, a free, national and compulsory health service administered by professionally qualified local government officials.[12] Various professional and philanthropic associations protested against the scandalous conditions in workhouse wards – 'Sickness and poverty are different things', *The Times* proclaimed in 1866: 'To confound them or to treat them alike is bad system or bad administration or a general confusion of ideas.' Shortly afterwards, the metropolitan Poor Law Unions established separate infirmaries and dispensaries for the sick poor, but those who sought medical assistance were treated as paupers, symbolically deprived of their civil rights until the Medical Relief Disqualification Act of 1885.[13]

Through further investigation of specific needs, philanthropists and policy-makers were gradually able to remove various classes of the poor from dependence on the Poor Law, the inadequacies of which were revealed in a number of ways during the 1860s. But there was no relaxation of 'less eligibility' for the undeserving poor, consigned to the new 'test' workhouses, where they were subjected to strict discipline and irksome labour.[14]

It was this new precision in classifying the working class which facilitated the second Reform Act. Incorporated in the political nation, the respectable working class would be rewarded for their virtue and drawn away from dangerous and contaminating contact with those below them. Their enfranchisement would thus strengthen the garrison, to use an image much favoured by Bright. Not indoctrinated with middle-class views, the aristocracy of labour accepted the vote on these terms and conditions. Old Chartist notions of working-class unity had been undermined by the dominant ideology of respectability and improvement. Lack of sympathy for the rough and 'undeserving' poor extended down the social scale into the upper ranks of the working class.[15]

PART THREE
1875–1900

15 'The Great Depression'

After the boom of the early 1870s, prices, profits and interest rates fell on trend for the next twenty years or more, but this period, traditionally labelled the 'Great Depression', lacked specific unity or significance within the secular process of British economic decline and industrial retardation.[1] Doubt and disenchantment were promptly dispelled when trade values surged up after 1896, but productivity, capital accumulation and production, the key ratios of economic strength, failed to display a commensurate advance. Production and productivity nearly stagnated as the economy moved further down the U-curve, the characteristic feature of modern British economic growth. Fundamental problems remained unaddressed as the export boom of the Edwardian years, the Indian summer of the free trade system, concealed the need for industrial reconstruction in a final flourish of the traditional export economy.[2]

The 'myth of the Great Depression' notwithstanding, the late Victorian decades were the crucial period of economic transition, the climacteric which led to sluggish and conservative industrial decline. Once the leading and most dynamic industrial economy, Britain failed to respond to the 'second industrial revolution', the new growth generated by a cluster of innovations based on applied science and research, on prudent investment in education and science. Neighbours and competitors assumed the initiative, latecomers who had earlier looked to Britain for industrial leadership and capital. Unable to accelerate its productivity growth, the British economy dropped further behind, heading towards industrial failure.[3]

The slowdown in productivity growth was first evident in agriculture, where previous high levels had allowed the early release of labour, a pattern of development which distinguished Britain from the rest of Europe. Migration from the land acquired a more desperate momentum during the late Victorian decades, a period of protracted depression and extensive structural change – the numbers employed in agriculture fell from 962,000 in 1871 to 621,000 in 1901. Wheat prices slumped after the 1872 harvest, bringing severe distress to farmers in the heavy wheat lands, high-cost areas where there was little flexibility in switching crops. Farmers in the pasture counties generally fared significantly better, cushioned by low prices for grain feeding-stuffs – land values dropped by a third in cereal areas between 1880 and 1895 but the decline in Cheshire was less than 10 per cent.

Here too competition from mass imports was less severe: domestic markets for high-quality meat and liquid milk remained unchallenged. Remunerative and secure, milk-production accelerated the shift from arable to pasture, at the expense of the agricultural labour force. Other changes in land use, including fruit growing and market gardening, labour-intensive but profitable, were a restricted option, dependent upon soil, situation and marketing facilities: only a small number were able to benefit from the new mass production jam industry and the beginnings of commercial canning.[4]

The first sector to slow down, agriculture accounted for about half the total decline in productivity growth between 1856–73 and 1873–1913. Manufacturing continued its steady growth on trend until 1899, after which output and productivity growth decelerated dramatically, a disturbing development at a time when other countries continued to advance. Not a zero-sum game, industrialization offered untold possibilities for new developments, but Britain failed to progress beyond its initial vantage-ground, to utilize its accumulated capital, expertise and commercial dominance to keep abreast of new competition. Still the reputed 'workshop of the world', Britain remained overcommitted to the narrow range of export industries which had proved so lucrative during the mid-Victorian boom, depending upon the continuing sale and shipment of cheap cloth, cheap iron, machinery and coal. Traditional markets declined as new industrial nations began their development with these same commodities, applying tariff barriers and the latest technology to the mechanization of textiles and basic metals. Eased out of Europe and America, British exporters turned to the underdeveloped world, the network of formal and informal colonies which, in the short term at least, provided a guaranteed market for traditional manufactures.[5]

Distorted by crude statistics, Britain's relative decline has been questioned by cliometricians, econometric historians who have mounted a neo-classical defence of the late Victorian economy which apparently measured up to contemporary 'best practice'. The economy, McCloskey contends, was 'not stagnating but growing as rapidly as permitted by the growth of its resources and the effective exploitation of the available technology'.[6] In retrospect, no calculations, counterfactual or otherwise, can conceal the climacteric as the economy failed to respond to the technological and organizational innovation of the 'second industrial revolution'. Old export industries continued in unmodernized form, dominating the economy at the expense of advance in chemicals, electrical engineering, motor cars and transport equipment, fast-growing sectors of world trade in which latecomers set the pace. The fundamental faults and failings, however, were by no means apparent at the time when there was neither the incentive nor the mechanism to modernize the economy. Profits remained at a satisfactory level, so individual firms were reluctant to undertake the risk and expense of major innovation, to scrap old plant and methods which still provided the lowest-cost production. Repair and replace remained the obvious managerial policy, a striking contrast to the American predilection for root-and-branch re-equipping.[7]

Technological lag soon ensued. In the steel industry, for example, it was overseas competitors who exploited the Gilchrist-Thomas 'basic' process, a breakthrough which the British were reluctant to adopt given the existing investment in acid steel production – as Eric Hobsbawm has commented, heavy investment in obsolete plant in obsolete industrial areas anchored the British industry to an obsolete technology.[8] There were similar institutional rigidities in the cotton industry, where the organizational structure of vertical specialization favoured the retention of the mule and the power loom, superseded elsewhere by the ring-frame and the automatic loom. Old methods proved satisfactory until the First World War, after which Lancashire was unable to compete either with cheap labour economies such as India and Japan or the high-throughput methods of the United States and other advanced economies.[9]

Individual firms were not jolted out of their old practices by economic concentration and rationalization. A powerful force for modernization and technological efficiency in Germany and the United States, cartels and trusts were less common in Britain, where they were introduced simply to share the market and set the price, enabling the least efficient firm to make profits without changing its ways. Despite the merger mania of 1888 and 1899–1900, most firms remained small in size, family-controlled and self-financing, relying for their capital on ploughed-back savings and profits, a marked contrast with Germany where the finance capitalism of the banks provided the capital and progressive impetus for the development and integration of the country's large-scale growth industries.[10]

In England, financial wealth stood proudly aloof from industrial capitalism, a geographical and cultural divide which gentrified indus-trialists failed to traverse, despite their exaggerated conformity to the non-entrepreneurial values of public schools and the south.[11] Powerful and prestigious, the financial institutions of the City protected the rentier interests of the Establishment, 'gentlemanly capitalism' in which domestic industrial needs were of little account. After the 1870s, the banking system withdrew from long-term industrial involvement, from the risky business of modernization and inno-vation, requirements which stretched the limits of traditional self-finance. Channelled through the City, investment flowed overseas, into safe and secure infrastructure projects, many of which were no longer linked with export orders to British industry.[12] These capital exports were not necessarily harmful, a squandering of resources at the expense of industrial modernization. Much of the criticism of the 'haemorrhage of capital' overlooks the fact that Britain was a net gainer on capital account from the early 1870s because of interest payments on earlier foreign investments, on the loans which had bridged the sterling gap during the mid-Victorian boom. Britain, Sidney Pollard notes, 'never had to "find" any net capital for abroad out of current production after *c*. 1874; the burden was in principle on the borrowing countries, as the latter were only too well aware.' Had this capital been diverted to home purposes, modernization might well have ensued, but here too there was no incentive or interventionist mechanism. Satisfied with existing returns, individual investors gave little thought to Britain's long-term industrial future.[13]

Rentiers not industrialists, the Victorian elite derived their wealth from the City, through their control of political, legal and financial services, the monopoly against which radicals had always protested. The profits of 'Old Corruption' fell victim to reform and 'cheap government', but overseas trade and investment, the 'invisible empire' of finance, proved a lucrative alternative. Relatively unburdened by the heavy tax costs, the City elite gained most from the Empire, although there were more profitable areas of overseas investment.[14] Remunerative and prestigious, employment in the City allowed financiers to enjoy gentlemanly status and ready access to political power, much to the envy of provincial industrialists. By the end of the century, London's financial dynasties had achieved equality of wealth and prestige with the landed aristocrats – City investors themselves – who still occupied the highest positions in political and social life.[15]

Along with the credit and institutions of the City, the global extension of the sterling standard increased 'invisible' earnings substantially, continuing to make good the deficit in the balance of payments. Banker and carrier to the world's commerce and trade, Britain managed to offset its declining industrial competitiveness. Wealthy and expanding, the City injected considerable impetus into the regional service economy of London and the south-east, the most dynamic area of change after 1870, with the highest rate of growth of employment and the largest per capita incomes. This prosperity ensured the commercial success of the new 'multiples' and other retail developments, a trade where there was no lack of entrepreneurial enterprise. In the late Victorian decades, London reasserted its pre-eminence, briefly appropriated by the industrial provinces earlier in the century.[16]

Juxtaposed with industrial deceleration, the dynamism of the City was the first symptom of 'Dutch disease', the debilitating oblivion with which finance undermined domestic industry.[17] No longer competitive, Britain became a parasitic economy of trade and finance, living off its past monopoly and accumulations of wealth, providing financial and commercial services which hastened the advance of actual and future industrial rivals. Geared to the needs of the rentier class, the City denied itself the most profitable long-term benefits of overseas development. The gentlemanly capitalists of Edwardian England were reluctant to risk funds in direct investment in industrial concerns, the lucrative overseas policy later pursued by the United States. The City favoured low-risk securities with a steady guaranteed income, the fixed-interest return obtainable through transport undertakings and other infrastructural development. Politically entrenched, these rentier attitudes were to persist well beyond the chastening experience of the First World War, as the City endeavoured to regain its former dominance through the most cautious financial orthodoxy, a fundamental hindrance to domestic industrial reconstruction.[18]

16 Living Standards

A time of doubt and uncertainty in middle-class circles, the Great Depression was in statistical terms at least an unmixed blessing for the working class. Real wages rose dramatically, while unemployment remained close to the levels of the mid-Victorian boom, enabling workers to enjoy a greater share in the distribution of national income – according to Saul's calculations, the share of wages in the sum of profits plus wages rose from 52.3 per cent in 1870–4 to 62.2 per cent in 1890–4.[1] Sticky in bad years, money-wages continued upward at other times, but the decisive factor in improved living standards was the dramatic fall in prices, a lengthy 'Kondratieff' cycle, most marked in food and other staples, goods which accounted for much of the working-class budget. Prices tumbled by over 40 per cent, drawing real wages up in the most substantial and sustained increase of the nineteenth century. Allowing for unemployment, the real wages of the average urban worker stood some 60 per cent higher in 1900 than in 1860. In some regions, the advance was delayed until the 1890s, as in the Black Country, then in the process of major structural change as engineering finally asserted its dominance over mining, iron-making and the sweated domestic trades, which had long been in decline. By this time, however, prices were beginning to move up slowly, bringing an end to the increase in real wages, the relative level of which fell thereafter against other industrial nations.[2]

The advance in living standards was neither uninterrupted nor evenly spread. All grades of workers, from well-paid boilermakers to seasonal casual labourers, had to endure economic fluctuations of one kind or another, not least the cyclical troughs of 1878–9, 1884–7 and 1892–3, but the frequency and severity diverged markedly. Ship-building, the industry which replaced railway construction as the central pivot of the nation's heavy industries, felt the full impact of the world trade cycle. Demand was highly inelastic for a product which was long in construction and tailor-made to specific require-ments – there was frequently an over-supply of ships at exactly the time when the boom was most vulnerable, while stockpiling was not an option during the ensuing depression. In these conditions, employers limited their overheads by continuing with labour-inten-sive techniques, placing the burden of the recurrent intense depressions squarely on the backs of the labour force. Boilermakers and shipbuilders appear high on the list of Hobsbawm's aristocratic trades with over 20 per cent earning 40s or more in 1906, a prosperous phase of the cycle, but the income actually available for consumption was substantially less than these wages suggest. At such times of full employment, skilled men worked hard to pay off debts incurred during the last spell of unemployment and to save for the next interruption in earnings.[3]

Workers in the building industry were subject to a different rhythm, longer in duration than the 5–7-year trade and investment cycle experienced in capital goods industries. Local variations aside, swings in the building industry lasted 20 years or more: after the peak of 1876, earnings and work outlets were reduced until the mid-1890s, the start of the next boom, which reached a double peak in 1898 and 1903. During the up-turns, fully-employed builders' labourers, the elite of unskilled labour, reached economic independence, able to live above the poverty line without supplementary income, an indispensable resource at all other times. Within the long cycles, building activity remained at the mercy of the weather, with a seasonal trough from November to February, an annual reverse which pushed those without savings – discharged unskilled labourers and their families – back into poverty.[4]

Winter remained the slack season in many other trades, bringing hardship and deprivation to the casually employed in the docks, on the streets and in the sweatshops. Distress was particularly severe when trade continued depressed after the weather improved, an unfortunate conjuncture which upset the seasonal mechanism of credit in 1879 and 1886, a time of unemployed riots and demonstrations. In 1895, when floating blocks of ice immobilized the Thames, parliament appointed a commission to investigate seasonal distress which extended beyond riverside and building industries into casual trades, glutted by surplus female labour as wives and daughters sought employment to make good the male breadwinners' loss of earnings.[5]

In the East End and other urban centres, the pool of casual labour continued to expand, a vast reserve of underemployed workers whose irregular work and earnings denied them any escape from economic hardship – in Charles Booth's survey, it was broken time rather than low rates of pay which accounted for working-class impoverishment. The ubiquitous deployment of the sewing machine led to increased outwork and specialization, but employment in the clothing trades was still seasonal and sweated. Averaged out over the year, female workers in the cheap 'slop' end of the London tailoring trade worked no more than two and a half days a week, at a daily rate of 2s 6d to 4s for machinists, and 1s 6d to 3s 6d for button-holers. Wages were higher in the West End bespoke trade – up to 30s a week in brisk periods – but the 'season' exerted a greater tyranny. Milliners, dress-makers and tailoresses, Sherwell regretted, were 'frequently driven upon the streets in the slack season, returning to their shops with the advent of the new season's trade. In other words, *morals fluctuate with trade.*'⁶

Irregular earnings and employment were the norm for other female workers – box-makers, paper-bag makers, hook- and eye-carders, artificial flower-makers, and other sweated labour conducted at home or in small unregulated factories. The female casual labour market reached its peak during this period as elderly single women, widows, wives of irregularly employed labourers and others sought work at any price whenever available, no matter how brief or monotonous. There were notorious squabbles outside the new jam factories during the short busy season when extra hands were hired 'sometimes for a day, sometimes for a few hours only, as occasion requires'. This was an area, however, where seasonality was soon to decline as cost-conscious employers used their premises to produce sweets and potted meats during the winter months after the summer peak of jam and marmalade production. The same economics were applied in provin-cial shoe and garment factories which aimed as far as possible at continuous production in order to minimize overheads. Despite these developments, seasonal factors still determined the earnings and living standards of many workers at the end of the century, although by then there were well-established patterns of interlocking occu-pations. Dismissed from lemonade bottling plants in the autumn, resourceful female hands promptly transferred to pickle factories, or to washing and charring. Some winter labouring work was available for men in the gas industry, while the expansion of the mass consumer market increased the demand for sandwich-board men, deliverers of handbills, newspaper sellers and the like, streetwork undertaken for the most part on daily hire. At the bottom of the casual hierarchy, down in the 'nether world', were those who spent most of their lives in the workhouse, except for the fruit-, pea- and hop-picking season, and those who preferred to sleep rough, forlorn individuals prepared to attempt any task which was offered to them.⁷

These unfortunates, William Booth discovered, were the victims not of moral fecklessness but of adverse personal circumstances, ill-health, disability, age and other factors which devalued their worth in the labour market. The remarkable stoicism of these homeless outcasts was perhaps best articulated by 'No. 12', interviewed by an officer of the Salvation Army on a wet night on the Embankment in 1890:

Says he can't say he does like it, but then he *must* like it! Ha! ha! Is a slater by trade. Been out of work some time; younger men naturally get the work. Gets a bit of bricklaying sometimes; can turn his hand to anything. Goes miles and gets nothing. Earned one and twopence this week at holding horses. Finds it hard, certainly. Used to care once, and get down-hearted, but that's no good; don't trouble now. Had a bit of bread and butter and cup of coffee today. Health is awful bad, not half the size he was; exposure and want of food is the cause; got wet last night, and is very stiff in consequence.[8]

From homeless outcasts to aristocrats of labour, adverse personal circumstances, particularly at critical phases in the family and life-cycle, aggravated the fluctuations in living standards occasioned by cyclical, seasonal and other economic factors. Family size began to fall in this period – the marriage cohort of 1861–9 had an average of 6.16 children, that of 1890–9 had 4.13, and the 1920–4 cohort had 2.31 – but fertility rates diverged markedly between social classes and within the working class itself. During the Great Depression, the middle class were the first to practise family limitation, a timely adjustment to the increasing cost of children, servants and the para-phernalia of conspicuous gentility. Between 1880 and 1911, the fer-tility rate in middle-class Hampstead fell by nearly 30 per cent while in working-class Poplar the decline was a mere 6 per cent. Miners apart, the working class were split along income lines: marital fertility declined substantially faster for families headed by skilled, semi-skilled and textile workers than for those headed by miners, agricul-tural labourers and the unskilled, among whom family limitation did not really take hold until after the First World War. The last to adjust, low-waged groups maintained an earlier demographic profile, enduring considerable hardship until the children contributed to the family income.[9]

Despite compulsory education, children were still able to earn at an early age. From nine or so, boys sought out-of-school hours employment as delivery-boys, newspaper sellers, hawkers and coster-mongers, 'streetwise' occupations which allowed these 'young bar-barians of the slums' to outwit unsuspecting middle-class customers through a variety of ingenious short-change techniques. The proceeds were handed straight to the mother, chancellor of the family exch-equer, who would generally allow a penny in the shilling as pocket money. Ill-gotten gains were handled in similar fashion – parents accepted the bounty without asking too many questions. Juvenile crime, oral evidence suggests, was often inspired by a sense of family duty, a moral determination to provide for the family whatever the legal consequences.[10]

Often dependent upon the supplementary income of their children, poor parents regarded compulsory education as an economic threat and unwelcome intrusion, particularly as the state system left no room for community-controlled private elementary schools. In London, the attendance officers, the unpopular School Board men, had to struggle hard to raise attendance rates from 76.7 per cent in 1876 to 88.2 per cent in 1906. Non-attendance, or subsistence truancy, remained high in large families where the father was either dead, unemployed or unskilled, circumstances which compelled the elder children to undertake paid employment and/or assist overworked mothers.[11] The half-time system proved an acceptable compromise in the textile districts, although twelve-year-olds who spent long mornings in the mill were in no fit state to be taught in the afternoon. For those on low incomes, the overriding concern was to get children working and earning as soon as possible – the MP for Middleton was spat upon by angry local women for supporting legislation in 1899 to raise the school leaving age to fourteen.[12]

Children were still regarded as an economic asset, except in areas of substantial female employment, where their future earnings were offset by the higher opportunity-cost of pregnancy and childcare. In the textile districts, where fertility was comparatively low, there were significant local variations in female employment. The vast majority of women in the spinning towns south of Rochdale left the mill on marriage or when the first child was due, as their husbands – mule spinners, engineers and miners – prided themselves on their family wage. In the weaving districts to the north, however, wives often continued working, much to the detriment of male wage rates throughout the local economy – since employers calculated that wives would work and earn a wage, labouring wages were significantly lower than elsewhere. Women in these areas were thus trapped in what Elizabeth Roberts describes as a vicious circle. They worked because they had to, but by working they ensured that they and other women would have to continue working. Important as it was, their net contribution to the family income was reduced by the high cost of convenience foods, childcare and other domestic services, unless, of course, they had obliging kin or neighbours.[13]

Married women's employment was poorly remunerated, incurred costs and carried social stigma. Such were the unfortunate consequences of the dominance of the male breadwinner ideal, the official policy of organized labour. 'It was their duty as men and husbands', Broadhurst assured the Trade Union Congress in 1874, 'to use their utmost efforts to bring about a condition of things, where their wives would be in their proper sphere at home, instead of being dragged into competition for livelihood against the great and strong men of the world.'[14] As a bargaining ploy, the invocation of female domesticity was not without success, hastening the advance in male wage rates towards an adequate family wage through the supportive mobilization of bourgeois ideology. But the gains were sectional and divisive, leaving the employers with a pool of cheap female labour conditioned to accept low-status, low-paid work. Denied workplace equality, working women were condemned as unfair competition, undercutting wages and workshop practices.[15]

Antagonism was particularly acute in the Potteries where the old patriarchal system of subcontracted family labour was abruptly terminated by technological innovation at the potbank which brought new opportunities for women in occupations previously defended as skilled male preserves. Paid at no more than two-thirds the rate for the job, female flat-pressers were set to work on the lighter, smaller ware, while the embittered men struggled to maintain former wage rates on the larger, more difficult articles. Unrestrained in their castigation of women, the male craftsmen attacked a symptom not the cause of their predicament. Having disdained to accept women as peers, to unite with them to secure the best terms for the new machines, they were deskilled and displaced. During the 1890s, the number of male potters decreased while female employment increased by 10.9 per cent; in 1901, women constituted 21,000 of the total workforce of 46,000.[16]

Denied domesticity, working wives were exploited as cheap labour by the male breadwinner ideal, but the economic struggle was harder still for widowed and divorced women with children to support. In these circumstances, intergenerational downward social mobility often ensued, as the pressure of poverty pushed the children into unskilled, dead-end jobs where high initial rewards brought much needed additions to the family purse at the expense of future earnings, restricted by the lack of craft training or apprenticeship. Sons of working-class widows seldom moved up the occupational hierarchy which contributed much to the aggregate rise in real wages.[17]

Families with a skilled male breadwinner were best placed to benefit from improved living standards, but illness and advancing age denied them permanent economic security. Many trades remained dangerous and unhealthy, inflicting a variety of debilitating diseases and occupational disabilities. High earnings were often interrupted by ill-health – the ovenmen, the best-paid potters, were frequently ravaged by heat and dust.[18] Earning capacity was restricted by age, with a marked fall in income generally in the late forties when the highest-paid workers, prematurely old, moved down the job hierarchy – miners took on surface work, spinners became sweepers – or set themselves up in a corner shop or some other 'penny capitalist' venture, the traditional resource at times of difficulty. During critical periods, many families relied on the 'penny capitalist' acumen of the women, employment which could be arranged around the housework, offering a variety of community services, including dressmaking and alterations, childminding, washing, board and lodgings, and home-produced food and ale served from the 'parlour' shop.[19]

Income and expenditure fluctuated erratically, but through credit and thrift working-class families struggled to maintain decent standards, whatever the circumstances. The corner-shop 'tick book' remained the most common form of credit, generally available from pay-day to pay-day, extended to longer periods for seasonal workers and at times of particular distress. During short-term emergencies, respectable aristocrats of labour received financial assistance from the Co-op, credit disguised as a drawing upon savings, being limited to some fraction of their paid-up share capital. Disdainful of credit for the weekly shopping bill, better-paid skilled workers were heavily committed to borrowing at the top end of the market, relying upon credit-purchasing to acquire furniture, a piano and other durable symbols of respectable status.[20] Lower down the scale, many working-class families depended upon mutual savings networks to ease the expense of costly necessities and little luxuries, such as boots and clothes, Christmas and holidays. The 'diddlum' operated through regular weekly contributions, distributed at fixed intervals on a rotating basis by ballot or lot, less a small commission for the enterprising, 'penny capitalist' housewife who organized the scheme. Local churches, chapels and shopkeepers encouraged the formation of weekly clothing clubs, but the initiative soon passed to commercial interests alert to the rise in wages and the new mass market.[21]

The easy payment check system was pioneered by the Provident Clothing Company in 1881, a rapid success which altered the traditional market for credit. Pawnbroking declined from its 1870s peak, after which the trade diversified into the retail business with new and fashionable lines sold for check, cash or credit. Fashion-conscious customers often pawned their check-purchased clothes soon after purchase, leaving them unredeemed as shoddy and outdated items.[22] Poorer families, however, continued to use the pledge shop in the conventional way, as a source for cheap second-hand clothing, and a substitute savings bank. Expensive items purchased with seasonal earnings – 'thrift in reverse' – were subsequently pawned off one by one to tide over hard times. Symbols of domestic respectability, these goods and ornaments were a readily realizable store of value, more liquid and accessible than deposits in the Co-op, the Post Office Savings Bank or a building society.[23]

Pledgeable articles were the most basic form of insurance against adversity. At the other end of the scale, the friendly societies offered systematic cover against the costs of sickness, accident and death, but at a price still beyond the means of some working-class households. No Oddfellow, it was calculated, earned less than 20s a week, while some of the smaller societies specified a minimum wage for members, aimed at excluding all but the most regularly employed. Despite such restrictions, membership increased rapidly, particularly in the affiliated orders, no longer discriminated against in friendly society legislation: between 1872 and 1899, the Manchester Unity of Oddfellows increased from 427,000 to 713,000, and the Ancient Order of Foresters from 394,000 to 666,000. The ritual and regalia which once ensured secrecy and self-protection were now proudly displayed as a cultural badge of status, respected and admired throughout the working-class community.[24]

In insurance terms, sickness benefit was the most important advantage of membership, paid at a rate of between 10s and 14s a week, a sum supplemented in some cases by trade union benefit, the double cover of the aristocracy of labour. By the end of the century, however, the friendly societies were on the verge of actuarial crisis as an increasing number of elderly members relied upon sick benefit in lieu of a pension, an unforeseen burden on the funds. In these circumstances, young members proved difficult to recruit, particularly as their immediate interests were better served by the popular new dividing societies or 'Tontines', slate clubs which offered sick pay and death benefit, the fund remaining at the end of the year being divided among all surviving contributors.[25] As well as sick pay, friendly society members were entitled to medical treatment from a general practitioner, employed on an annual part-time contract reviewed by the local lodge or court. Complaints were common, but patients generally received value for money as the organized consumer power of the societies outmatched the monopoly pretensions of the medical profession. When doctors proved obstructive or neglectful, lodges often pooled their resources to establish medical institutes, self-sufficient health centres with full-time medical, nursing and dispensing staff, whose services were also available on subscription to wives, children and other dependants – by 1885, 42 medical institutes were affiliated to the Friendly Societies Medical Alliance, with a total membership of 211,000.[26]

Other forms of medical treatment depended upon philanthropy, employer paternalism or the overworked services of the Poor Law. Free outpatient treatment was available from the voluntary hospitals, but these were unevenly spread with a heavy concentration in London and the larger cities. Elsewhere, provident dispensaries operated on a subsidized, semi-charity basis, insisting on a small contribution from the patient to eradicate the pauperizing tendencies of the original free dispensaries of the eighteenth century. Works clubs or medical aid societies were encouraged by new model employers, who deducted a weekly sum from pay to finance the scheme, the benefits of which usually covered the worker's family. By the end of the century, it was common practice for the workers to select and appoint the medical practitioner. Inadequate and overstretched, Poor Law medical facilities lost some of their stigma following the Medical Relief Disqualification Act 1885.[27]

Despite these advances, the medical establishment was still regarded with hostility and suspicion in some working-class circles, where various forms of alternative medicine were favoured, ranging from homeopathy, mesmerism and spiritualism, practices based on natural remedies, gentle treatment and the active cooperation of the patient, to the latest patent pills advertised in the press, quack commercial substitutes for old superstitious remedies. Poor families without access to charity or friendly society insurance were forced to rely on the Poor Law, unless they could muster sufficient funds for private treatment, the much-preferred alternative, available at rates related to rent or income, but still at a level which precluded regular or adequate treatment – surgery consultations cost 1s–2s 6d, and home visits 1s 6d–3s 6d. Although poor and unprotected, these families were not necessarily destitute, a fact appreciated by the commercial insurance companies, quick to capitalize on the spare penny or two now available in quite humble working-class budgets. Medical treatment was offered as an enticing loss leader to the lucrative burial insurance business until the General Medical Council prohibited the advertising and canvassing of medical services.[28]

With or without medical cover, burial insurance was considered obligatory, particularly for wives, children and those with no independent income of their own. Most of the business was conducted on an expensive commission basis by large and inefficient collecting societies, Liverpool-based bodies registered under section 30 of the Friendly Societies Act 1875. Contributions were low, a penny or a halfpenny a week, but expenses were high – 40 per cent of income as compared with 10–15 per cent in friendly societies – as was the rate of lapsing – 13 per cent per annum in the Royal Liver as compared with 3 per cent in the Oddfellows. The industrial life assurance companies were more efficient: the Prudential kept its collectors under close supervision and tried to prevent unnecessary lapses, but the company was far more selective, declining to accept Irish-born or inhabitants of certain neighbourhoods. For all its deficiencies, burial insurance enabled the poor to escape the shame of a pauper funeral, to display at the end their independence and self-respect, prized values within the working-class community. What mattered was the judgement of neighbours and peers, not the opinion of middle-class outsiders, incredulous critics of such unnecessary squander. Without show and display – the ostentatious funeral, the immaculate front parlour – respectability would be unacknowledged. Used only as Sunday best, the front room was for the benefit of passers-by, displaying the conspicuous expenditure on furniture and ornaments which, together with the increasingly elaborate certificates of friendly society and trade union membership hanging on the walls, established status and worth within the community. Only those whose status was already secured by ritual display made use of savings banks, where assets accumulated in anonymous secrecy. Against all kinds of adversity, late Victorian working-class households tried hard not simply to make ends meet but also to keep up appearances, to maintain a show of respectability.[29]

Management of the household budget was generally the housewife's responsibility. After deducting a sufficient sum for beer, tobacco and other personal needs, most husbands readily parted with their wage packets, leaving the wife to arrange all the affairs, relying on her unpaid expertise to balance the budget without compromising the family's social standing. Food was the principal item of expenditure, a disproportionate charge on working-class incomes – according to Levi's calculations in 1885, the working class spent 71 per cent of their earnings on food and drink, while the middle class spent only 44 per cent. By this time, however, food prices were falling, facilitating a major advance in living standards – between 1877 and 1887 the retail price of food in a typical working-class budget fell by 30 per cent, the most significant price change of the century.[30]

The lower prices, a consequence of the large-scale import of cheap wheat and meat, the progressive reduction of taxes on food, and the belated industrial revolution in food manufacture, soon led to changes in working-class diet. Bread consumption fell, a phenomenon widely associated with a rising standard of living, as more money was spent on meat. Eschewed by prosperous artisan families, imported meat, tinned or frozen, was good value, cheap and appetizing when embellished with one of the new commercial sauces. Consumption of tea, sugar and other English weaknesses rose spectacularly as housewives found themselves with more money to spare. New technology and factory production led to a dramatic increase in biscuit, jam, chocolate and cocoa manufacture – Chivers, Rowntree, Cadbury and Fry were soon established as household names. Jam sold particularly well as there was a huge popular demand for a sweet, highly-flavoured spread that was cheaper than butter and made margarine more palatable. Sauces, relishes and essences based on salt, sugar, spices, starches and artificial colours and flavourings also emerged as mass-consumption items.[31]

Some of the new developments were of dubious nutritional value. Roller-milling produced a finer flour and a whiter loaf much esteemed by working-class consumers, but the process removed the wheat germ, principal source of protein, vitamins, mineral salts and fats. Margarine was vitamin-deficient, as were cheap and convenient dairy products, hence the prevalence of rickets among children fed on canned condensed and evaporated skimmed milk. More nutritious, but much criticized by middle-class observers, was the tasty fare on offer at the new fish and chip shops, a popular outgrowth of the old hot-pie shops, vanquished in competition with the new supplies of cheap cod. The outstanding example of a gastronomic institution designed principally for the working class, the fish and chip shop made an important contribution to the inadequate protein content of urban diet. For working mothers, fish and chips was a welcome and affordable convenience, saving time, effort and cooking costs – fuel was an expensive item for the working class, unable to buy coal at bulk discount, while few households were yet equipped with cheap gas ovens on penny meters.[32]

The extent of dietary improvement in late Victorian England should not be exaggerated. Agricultural labourers, particularly in the low-wage south-western counties, seldom enjoyed meat, apart from their own fattened pig, 'the live savings bank', most of which had to be sacrificed to pay the tradesmen who had supplied its meal, leaving the family with a little bacon and just enough cash to buy another 'suckling'. Shorter working-hours, however, allowed labourers to spend more time on the vegetable allotment, while the new touring vans from nearby cooperative societies offered decent supplies in rural recesses.[33] In the urban household, gains were unevenly shared: the male breadwinner was accorded priority at the table, a practice which often resulted in the underfeeding of women and children. Women's diet remained one of bread and tea, while almost all men consumed a main meal of meat or bacon or fish and potatoes. The fall in prices notwithstanding, families with incomes less than 30s a week were perforce undernourished, the consequences of which were graphically revealed by contemporary social surveys and the subsequent investigation of the nation's 'physical deterioration'.[34]

Viewed with historical hindsight, this was a period of transition in the nation's health, as the age-old pattern of mass morbidity and mortality occasioned by infectious diseases, poor nutrition and heavy labour, was gradually replaced by the modern assemblage of functional disorders, viral disease and bodily decay associated with old age. Two factors hastened the change: the increased survival rates of susceptibles who formerly would have been lost in infancy or childhood; and the new diet with its excessive sugar and salt content, the deleterious consequences of which were aggravated by increased addiction to cigarette smoking, encouraged by the introduction of the penny-per-five packet in 1888.[35] Harmful or not to the bodily constitution, the quality of food undoubtedly improved, assisted by new legislation against adulteration and by higher standards of retailing, promoted by the Co-op, which secured its biggest advance in members in the 1880s and 1890s, and the new multiple stores pioneered by Lipton's.[36] But those who depended on 'tick' still had to suffer the high prices and low quality of the small corner-shop, while other poor families eked out a diet on the offal and otherwise unsaleable items knocked down in price at Saturday night markets.

The financial benefit of cheaper foodstuffs was not always sufficient to offset the inexorable rise in rents, the one major exception to the general downward movement in prices. Rowntree's figures for York in 1899 underlined the inequitable correlation between income and rent – a mere 9 per cent of the income of the most prosperous working-class families earning as much as 60s a week, rent absorbed 29 per cent of the income of the very poor with family earnings under 18s a week. In London, where a single room near the centre cost upwards of 4s a week in the 1890s, 85 per cent of working-class families paid out at least one-fifth of their total income on rent.[37] This was the economic context of the housing crisis, perceived by commentators and critics as the social problem of the age.

17 Housing

House rents were pushed up by the increase in urban land values, a lucrative area of investment at a time of otherwise declining growth-rates. Commercial pressures soon filtered down to low-income rents as capital moved into property, and aristocratic landlords, feeling the pinch of the agricultural depression, concentrated on their urban holdings. The bottom end of the market was managed and manipulated by a complex web of lease-holding middlemen, small capitalists who rack-rented the tenants, a practice which ground landlords were happy to ignore until exposed by investigative journalism, radical propaganda and the 'plays unpleasant' of G. B. Shaw. The coming of the tram added further to the disproportionate rise in land values, both in prime commercial sites close to the central termini and out in the suburbs where extensions to the network pushed up the price of building land so new house rents were often beyond the means of modest working-class budgets.[1]

Delayed by technological difficulties and powerful opposition, the 'tram revolution' – pioneered in Birkenhead – brought an end to the golden age of exclusive middle-class suburbia, now within reach of lower middle-class clerks and aristocratic artisans, unwelcome new-comers who attached themselves like limpets around the edges of elite areas, often infilling between an original village-suburb and the continuous built-up area. Exclusiveness was best preserved by moving out to a remote dormitory town, but social contact was easily avoided by separate travelling times, a form of temporal social segregation which awaits detailed historical study. Access to improved transport facilities was a graduated process, slowly extended to successive lower income groups, but stopping short of the inner-city poor. In the provinces, the tram network determined the pattern of artisan suburban development, areas of 'by-law' terraced housing, located round tram termini some two or three miles distant from the city centre, as at Sherwood in Nottingham. In London, where distances were greater, the introduction of workmen's trains facilitated the growth of similar working-class suburbs – between 1851 and 1891, Willesden grew from 3000 to 114,000, West Ham from 19,000 to 267,000 and Leyton from 5000 to 98,000.[2]

Significant numbers of better-paid working-class households took advantage of new transport and suburban developments, moving out of the juxtaposed mixture of differently rented dwellings in central courts and in-fillings. Housing standards slowly improved in this process of residential differentiation, as 'by-law' suburban developments, rectilinear in layout, progressed through an upward cycle of increasing expectations and tighter regulations. Dissatisfaction with some of the poorer quality provision in the initial 'free enterprise' stage, prompted the introduction of new by-laws which led to a period of 'controlled building' when most housing just met the regulations but little substantially exceeded them. As living standards improved, this uniform and monotonous provision proved unacceptable, leading to the final stage, 'divergence from minimum standards', when variety of building heralded the free enterprise stage of the next cycle. Despite this upward momentum, housing standards overall failed to rise as quickly as rents or real wages, and there was little increase in average house size.[3]

Here again, it was the better-paid aristocrats of labour who gained most from the improvements. Top of the hierarchy, they occupied recently built suburban houses with five rooms or more, accommodation which displayed their status through a number of highly prized features: small gardens to front and rear; bay windows to the front parlour where the piano, chiffonier, marble fireplace and other expensive luxuries were on display; and 'architectural' decorations to the front, such as coloured string courses, plinths, eaves details, ceramic tiles and coloured-glass door panels. Below this level, in houses without gardens, separate hallways or prominent bay windows, there was no simple correlation between housing quality and occupational status. Household income, the life-cycle and other family factors were crucial variables. Uniform housing stock, terraced or back-to-back, accommodated working-class households of widely different status and income. Upward mobility was an attractive prospect, but many families preferred to remain in the neighbourhood, since nearly all of them depended at some time or other on the support services of the community, on the goodwill of neighbours and local tradesmen to see them through periods of temporary poverty.[4]

Community replaced kin as the crucial welfare network for the urban working class in this 'classic' period. Settled and stable, most envisaged a future spent within the narrow confines of the town or city in which they had been brought up, secure in the protection of the customs and mores of a particular district.[5] A creative experience of social interaction among those with similar attitudes, beliefs and interests, community was not necessarily defined in territorial terms. Welsh migrants in Liverpool were bonded together by strong cultural ties despite their relative lack of residential concentration – families travelled long distances to worship together in Welsh-speaking Calvinistic chapels, Welsh newspapers circulated in the city, and the

National Eisteddfod was held there on several occasions. Other ethnic communities were less dispersed. In Liverpool and elsewhere, the Irish lived close together in poor-quality housing areas adjacent to casual labour markets. Residential concentration was even more pronounced in the rapidly expanding Jewish immigrant communities, isolated in ghettoes in the East End – Whitechapel's population was 31.8 per cent alien in 1901 – and in several northern cities: by 1900, the Jewish community in Leeds had grown to 10,000, nearly all of whom were concentrated in Leylands, a low-lying area of poor terraced housing, cut off from east Leeds by a perimeter wall.[6]

For the most part, community was a mixture of spatial and social factors, as pubs, churches, clubs, co-ops and various special-interest groups were locality-based, serving the needs of relatively independent, self-sufficient urban villages, demarcated districts within which the working class moved and married. Housewives, indeed, rarely ventured beyond the boundary lines of their particular 'village' within which there were strong family support networks linking mothers and married daughters, sometimes supplemented by the services of a 'connecting relative', an aunt or unmarried sister who could be counted on to travel from house to house, lending a land whenever required. Men who travelled out of the neighbourhood to work hurried back home for a drink at the 'local', now patronized in preference to the trade pub close to the workplace. The 'open and encapsulated' style of by-law housing encouraged domesticity, but it also fostered a sense of community, a convivial communality of interests.[7]

There was a similar, self-sufficient community spirit in inner-city slums, despite the high level of internal mobility and 'moonlight flits'. Even when escaping the rent-collector, casual labourers seldom left the neighbourhood, which still offered the best prospects for employment or relief. Credit, charity and public works schemes all required a residential qualification of some kind, a form of 'settlement' which poor families were unwilling to relinquish by moving farther afield. Swollen by migrants seeking casual employment in consumer goods industries, services and utilities, this immobile labour force lived in a diminishing stock of overcrowded central accommodation – the decline in the average number of persons a house decelerated markedly between 1871 and 1891.[8]

Despite the building boom in the suburbs and the gradual introduction of cheap transport, the 'levelling-up' theory failed to filter down to the casual poor, trapped in inner-city locations where pressure on land was most intense. A further factor of displacement, the Cross Act demolitions aggravated the housing crisis, as Gareth Stedman Jones has shown:

In fact the operation of the Act was disastrous. Instead of alleviating overcrowding, it intensified it. Instead of penalizing slumowners, it rewarded them substantially. . . . The Act was particularly disastrous because it was directed with such accuracy against the housing of the casual poor – the class least likely to find better accommodation.[9]

Andrew Mearns' *Bitter Cry of Outcast London*, a damning indictment of landlordism, overcrowding and the failure of organized religion in 'Horrible London', brought the hard-core slum problem to the forefront of public attention.[10] Henceforth, housing was the social problem of the age, the main threat to social stability as displacement and overcrowding forced the casual poor and criminal classes back into dangerous proximity with respectable artisans. This alarming prospect prompted a barrage of pamphlet literature, press reportage and parliamentary investigation, culminating in the Royal Commission on Housing in 1885.[11]

In line with the Commission's report, the Housing of the Working Classes Act 1890 consolidated and extended existing legislation, but new powers were accorded to the newly-reformed local authorities, allowing them to take a more constructive role in the housing market. Under Part 3 of the Act, they were empowered but not encouraged to build new housing, a provision which was widely ignored – of all new houses built between 1890 and 1914 less than 5 per cent were provided by local authorities, the great majority of whom were reluctant to enter the field of property-owning when the whole expense had to be borne from the rates. Most preferred to adopt the cheaper alternative of the repair and improvement of existing unfit property, the cost of which fell upon the owner, the authority only having to meet administrative charges. Here Birmingham set the example with an extensive improvement policy implemented at minimal cost to ratepayers. At the other extreme, Liverpool, the first provincial city to embark on council housing as early as 1869, undertook an ambitious programme of subsidized building on the rates to rehouse the poor, displaced by slum clearance schemes.

The new London County Council was the most adventurous authority in housing matters until the Conservatives gained control in 1907. In the early days of Progressive power, the authority, aware of the failure of market forces, experimented with two possible solutions to the problem of working-class housing. Multi-storey flats in central areas, a modification of the tenement schemes of the Model Dwellings Companies; and garden villages in the suburbs, an extension of the new style of employer housing. In the 1880s and 1890s, at a time when philanthropic building in depressed agricultural villages came to an end, employer housing entered a distinct and influential phase with Lever's Port Sunlight, Cadbury's Bourneville and Rowntree's New Earswick, planned communities, mock-bucolic in style, which offered decent and aesthetic housing for the industrial wage-earning class, the vision which inspired the garden city movement and the architects of the LCC, until the Tories came to power.[12]

18 Work

Given the residential and industrial complexities of large towns and cities, work-based friendships were increasingly less significant than neighbourhood connections, but the workplace remained an important social institution in itself. Skilled or routine, work could still provide craft satisfaction or convivial company, with horseplay, practical jokes and other sociable devices serving to alleviate the most monotonous tasks. In isolated communities, work relations remained of primary importance. Coalfield communities, for example, varied in character according to the career pattern, authority structure and working practices of the local pits. Up in the north-east, where hewers had to work their way up the job hierarchy to acquire workplace autonomy and social respect, there was considerable variety in income and privilege within each pit village. But the distinctive feature of these parts was the strength of workplace relationships, a consequence of the double-shift system which linked the pitman to his 'marra', the friend who shared the stall on the other shift. The men would divide their joint earnings, alternate between the fore- and back-shifts, and 'cavill' together, preserving the practice by which work was fairly and evenly distributed in the old bord-and-pillar system despite the quirks of geology and the wishes of management.[1]

Culture and community in the factory became the concern of 'scientific management', a comprehensive strategy significantly in advance of former paternalist gestures. The working environment improved considerably as employers implemented new factory legislation and extended the range of welfare programmes, but other initiatives were less benevolent. Pioneer forms of Taylorism, the new managerial techniques were designed to raise labour productivity and curb the power of organized labour, complementary aims pursued with some vigour as international competition increased and prices fell. Divorced from execution, the design and planning of production processes became a managerial prerogative, a task undertaken by new production engineers and draughtsmen, while shopfloor operatives were kept under constant surveillance by foremen, non-commissioned officers of the new regime.[2] Supervision was often accompanied by new methods of payment, elaborate incentive schemes such as the premium bonus system. Through control of the labour process and social association at work, employers hoped to effect the maximum division of labour, to take advantage of the technological developments of the 'second industrial revolution', semi-automatic machines, standardized and interchangeable parts, and the increasing use of semi-skilled labour on tasks hitherto the preserve of a skilled elite. Taken together, these managerial and technical initiatives threatened to undermine skilled status and craft organization, producing an increasingly homogeneous working class, the inevitable consequence of the logic of capitalist development as outlined by Braverman and others. In the English context, however, skill and craft were to prove remarkably resilient, protected by pragmatic sectionalist struggle.[3]

The outcome of the attempt to reorganize production varied from industry to industry according to the balance of power and authority at the workplace, the 'bargained' context of industrial relations. As a general rule, craft organization remained strong where employers were inhibited by market factors, by the relative inelasticity of demand for the product or its perishable nature. Hand compositors in the newspaper industry captured control of the new linotype machines for their own exclusive 'craft' use, a jealously guarded trade privilege extorted from pliant employers in a competitive market for a perishable product.[4] Some employers decided against reorganization when confronted by the threat of craft resistance, a sensible enough short-term attitude for family-owned firms making satisfactory profits in guaranteed markets. Furthermore, the product market for British-made capital goods was often highly differentiated, a significant obstacle to the introduction of standardized mass-production techniques – ships, machines, railway engines and the like were constructed to the bespoke needs of individual customers. At the domestic level, a broad-based demand for a product with standardized, interchangeable parts did not emerge until the bicycle boom of the mid-1890s, at which point engineering employers began to introduce American-style machine tools, turret and capstan lathes, milling and grinding machines, precision gauges, and other technology designed to replace expensive skilled labour and 'speed up' production.[5]

This new mechanization was implemented in the midst of workplace conflict, as employers combined in a national organization, the Engineering Employers Federation, to reverse the gains secured by the ASE during the craft militancy of the 1889–92 boom. In the lockout of 1897, the EEF insisted on the absolute right of management, but their victory did not portend the crushing of the union or the thorough transformation of the division of labour. There was no breakthrough into a new rationalizing Taylorist mode, simply an extension of previous strategies for work intensification and cost-cutting: the most popular innovation, the premium bonus system, was designed to boost output and reduce labour costs without major capital expenditure. Craft regulation was temporarily curbed in the new system of collective bargaining which the ASE were forced to accept, unable to continue in isolated struggle without the support of other unions and non-organized engineering workers, the unfortunate legacy of previous policies of demarcation and exclusivism. Employers looked to the union executive to discipline its members, to prevent unofficial local efforts at craft resistance, but rank-and-file militancy soon revived in the workshops, sanctioned by the executive, itself quickly captured by craft militants and socialist allies.[6]

Throughout the 1890s there were similar disputes in other major industries as employers reasserted their authority in pursuit of more efficient labour utilization and lower labour costs – between 1892 and 1898 the number of working days lost each year averaged 13.2 million compared with 2.3 million between 1899 and 1907 when new systems of national collective bargaining, similar to that in engineering, took effect.[7] Conflict was particularly intense on the coalfields, where resistance was led by the Miners' Federation of Great Britain, a militant organization formed in the buoyant trade of the late 1880s to unite the inland coalfields against the conciliatory policies favoured in the north east by the Miners' National Union. The 1893 lock-out, a vast dispute involving some 300,000 miners, prompted the first direct intervention in industrial relations by politicians and government, following the death of two miners, shot by troops at Featherstone. Demands for a minimum wage and an eight-hour day were decisively rejected in the final settlement which created a Conciliation Board for the entire federated area, collective bargaining which guaranteed a limited role for the MFGB while enabling employers to reduce labour costs by short-time working and other non-negotiable expedients.[8]

The new system of collective bargaining in the boot and shoe industry, introduced after the lock-out of 1895, was strictly limited to wages and hours, leaving work organization to the absolute discretion of management. Here too, trade unionism was accorded a role in the bargaining process, following the defeat of socialist-led workplace resistance to new systems of supervision and increased production.[9] In cotton-spinning, unions and skilled workers enjoyed new privileges in the system of collective bargaining introduced after the lock-out of 1892–3. The Brooklands Agreement cut the wage reduction demanded by employers, limited the annual wage round to 5 per cent adjustment in either direction, withdrew the masters' objection to the closed shop, and established a grievance procedure which confirmed the privileged position of senior minders in relation to the large majority of operatives in the trade, victims of a system of 'co-exploitation'. But employers were accorded the right to use whatever cotton they wished, however poor the quality, and work had to go on while complaints went through the lengthy procedures; as a further boost to labour intensification, employers were no longer obliged to pay for time lost due to breakage, a feature of poor quality yarn.[10]

The collective bargaining arrangements of the 1890s, the outcome of national strikes, recognized and confirmed the role and function of craft trade unionism, while enunciating the power and prerogatives of employer authority, a suitable compromise in the struggle for workplace control. Some skilled workers sensibly shed some of their exclusivism to strengthen their position against modernizing employers. The aristocratic boilermakers set the example, preventing a major reorganization of steel ship production by a flexible union policy which kept the boundaries of membership under constant review. When the need arose, semi-skilled caulkers, holders and other independent groups central to production were granted membership, prior to the union establishing a virtual closed shop in these areas. Attitudes to unskilled helpers depended on circumstance: holders-on and rivet boys were admitted but platers' helpers were strictly excluded.[11]

As a rule of thumb, skilled workers who were prepared to redefine their boundaries of exclusion, to admit previously prohibited groups, succeeded best in retaining aristocratic status in the new conditions of late-Victorian England. The lesson was well learnt by the Alliance Cabinet-Makers' Association but not by the older Friendly Society of Operative Cabinet-Makers, which withered away in narrow craft restrictionism.[12] Old-fashioned prejudice was probably most difficult to abandon where gender was concerned. Craft organization in the Potteries remained narrow and sectional, powerless to prevent displacement, as cheap female labour was put to work on new machines.[13]

The persistence of privilege depended upon various contingent factors which differed from industry to industry, reflecting the interplay between 'genuine skill' – the necessary exercise of dexterity, judgement and knowledge – and 'socially constructed skill' – the specious status upheld by organizational prowess. Previously located on the shopfloor, technical expertise became a function of management with the new distinction between planning and execution, the implementation of which depended on supervisory workers, trained technicians who owed their position to knowledge acquired at night school, one area of educational provision where Britain was not outmatched by competitors.[14] Shopfloor skills were increasingly limited and specialized, but knowledge of the trade was still passed on through apprenticeship, an exclusionist practice which proved remarkably resilient. Formal, indentured arrangements in the older crafts steadily declined, but apprenticeship expanded in several growing industries – engineering, shipbuilding, woodworking, building and printing – where there was apparently considerable agreement between employers and workers over training methods. The ratio of apprentices to journeymen and the terms of their employment, however, provoked recurrent and bitter conflict. With the greater specialization of work and skill, apprentice labour was quickly turned to profit for the employer, a source of cheap labour which undermined the position of adult men in the labour market. Capable of keeping the new machine technology in operation, apprentice labour was of strategic importance at times of strikes and disputes, hence the employers' reintroduction of a form of indenture, a private disciplinary contract without the old reciprocal obligations.[15]

As implemented in late Victorian England, scientific management and new technology did not portend the degradation of work, the deskilling of labour. The persistence of craft organization apart, skill in one form or another extended down the labour market, as workers in industries without formal apprenticeship acquired dexterity and knowledge through migration, 'following up' and hands-on experience. New unions of semi-skilled workers in transport, utilities and other growth industries, were quick to appreciate the market value of this technical know-how, skill which employers could not readily replace. In casual trades, too, there was a premium on proficiency, a useful adjunct to strength and stamina. Those with the knack were the first to be taken on, irrespective of ethnicity, religion or politics, crucial considerations in casual labour markets like the Liverpool docks. Acquired in a variety of ways, skill was an important bargaining asset, rewarded by differentials which remained sharply pronounced until the inflation of the First World War. In 1913, unskilled workers in coal, cotton, building and engineering, earned 34–49 per cent less and semi-skilled workers 12–29 per cent less than colleagues who could boast a skill.[16]

Despite the persistence of skill differentials, the working class became more homogeneous in appearance in late Victorian England. As the proportion of the occupied population engaged in agriculture was halved from 15 per cent in 1871 to 7.5 per cent in 1901, rural immigrants entered the most rapidly expanding sectors of the domestic economy, transport and mining, a major shift from worse to better-paid jobs, from less to more regular employment.[17] Small units continued to proliferate in some sectors of the economy, but the factory was finally established as the predominant form of organization, even in the sweated clothing and shoemaking trades, leaving some poor outworkers stranded in old centres of petty workshop production.[18] Factory tailoring developed rapidly at Leeds where power-driven machinery completed the 'feminization' of the trade, although some of the work was still contracted out to smaller workshops and sweated homeworkers.[19] In the Leicester hosiery industry, cost-conscious factory employers pursued a policy of labour substitution, but there was none of the acrimony experienced in the Potteries and elsewhere. In deference to the male knitters, women were at first restricted to new types of automatic knitting machines, while the expansion of the local boot and shoe industry provided an alternative source of factory employment at wages which recognized the male breadwinner's status. Through different forms of modern factory employment, men and women continued to find work at customary wages in accordance with the gender differentials of the old domestic system.[20]

Traditional or otherwise, differentials within the working class were less pronounced than the sharp social and cultural divide – the veritable class boundary – which separated the aristocracy of labour from marginal non-manual groups of the lower middle class. The number of clerks increased dramatically from 95,000 in 1850 to 843,000 in 1914, an expansion which soon exposed their market weakness. Access to office employment was virtually unrestricted once progressive urban school boards improved the quality of elementary educational provision, while opportunities for advancement, a potent occupational myth, were further curtailed by the commercial rationalization which accompanied the Great Depression. Beset by these market pressures, routine office clerks, respectable but otherwise unskilled, lived in fear of a precipitate fall in status, a collapse into the ranks of the lower working class. Unable to secure professional status or other institutional protection, they chose to affirm their gentility through censorious rejection of manual employment, erecting a new caste-like division between those who worked with their 'hands' and those who worked with their 'brains'. Isolated in 'villa Toryism', they segregated themselves from the culture of collective mutuality, street-life and pub-centred leisure enjoyed by well-paid skilled workers and manual labourers alike. The expensive display of certain material trappings, symbols of individual respectability, confirmed the requisite image, a considerable financial burden for those whose salaries barely matched the wages of labour aristocrats. White-collar workers, however, generally enjoyed relative security of employment and the promise of some form of salary scale, advantages denied their financial equals, the best-paid members of the working class.[21]

Obviously, there was some upward mobility into the lower middle class, but many working-class families, particularly at the top end of the scale, did not regard white-collar employment as an attractive escape from manual labour, a desirable aim for their children. Puny and parasitic, clerks were viewed with derision by skilled workers proud of their transmissible craft and workplace skills. A cultural gulf between two different ways of life, the social separation of skilled workers and clerks reinforced the cultural and political identity of the working class, as the aristocracy of labour, repulsed by lower middle-class pretensions, turned back to align themselves with their semi-skilled and unskilled manual colleagues. Unappealing to the skilled working class, clerical employment was a boon for single and 'surplus' middle-class women who sought respectable office jobs with the greatest alacrity at salaries which afforded decency but not comfort – the number of female clerks rocketed from 2000 in 1850 to 166,000 in 1914.[22]

19 Popular Culture

Mass culture came of age in late Victorian England, a time of lavish commercial investment – much of it counter-cyclical – in leisure, sport and recreation, cross-class activities offered for enjoyment in common but segregated markets. Pleasures were shared, but differential pricing kept the classes suitably apart, an arrangement best exemplified in the redesigned internal architecture of theatres and music-halls. At seaside resorts, brought within reach of the masses by rising real wages, there was a clear spatial pattern of 'social zoning'. Each resort had its own social tone, finely adjusted to the status of its clientele – those which catered for a wider range were divided into class-specific areas, as at Blackpool where the select north shore attracted the more refined visitors, anxious to distance themselves from the working-class crowds on the central pier. At sports grounds, middle-class directors enjoyed professional football from the comfort of boxes, away from contact with crowds on the terraces. On the county cricket field, a mirror of social stratification, gentlemanly amateurs and professional playe.. _merged from different dressing-rooms and passed through separate doors on to the ground in order to play for the same team. Not sa isfied with such segregation, some members of the middle class sought complete exclusivity, hence the search for distant holiday locations; the development of tennis, badminton and land-hungry golf, individualist games different in character from the team sports favoured by 'muscular Christians' and advocates of class conciliation; and the appropriation of pedestrianism and rowing, low pastimes which acquired social cachet as athletics and sculling through the proscription of professionalism.[1]

Populist in pursuit of profit, commercial investment freed popular leisure from the mid-Victorian ethic of improvement, the rational and moral restraints of paternalist provision. Limited liability replaced the old religious and employer patronage, transforming football into the people's game, played and enjoyed on an open professional basis – the change in style and ethos was symbolically prefigured by the teamwork and preparation which brought Blackburn Olympic victory over the Old Etonians in the 1883 FA Cup Final, a remarkable triumph for the working-class side who gave their aristocratic opponents an average 28 lb a man. The working class provided the talent and paid at the gate – by 1903 the average cup tie attendance was over 20,000 – but they exercised little participatory control.

Shareholders and directors were drawn overwhelmingly from higher ranks. Tony Mason's study of 46 professional clubs from 1885 to 1915 calculates that only 0.5 per cent of the directors were unskilled manual workers and 5.7 per cent skilled manual workers; most directors, indeed, were top-hatted not flat-capped – small employers, wholesalers and retailers, publicans and hoteliers. A mass spectator sport, professional football was a shrewd investment, pulling in crowds – some 3 or 4 per cent of the population – on a regular weekly basis, assisted by the introduction of football 'specials' for away matches and the spread of the Saturday half-holiday, the enjoyment of which was brought forward to noon in the 1890s thanks to successful trade union pressure.[2]

Capitalization continued apace in the music halls, encouraged by new licensing regulations which favoured the large and 'respectable' establishments, lavish and baroque variety theatres offering family entertainment, at the expense of the smaller halls, many of which were forced to close. By no means a metropolitan phenomenon, the first superdromes appeared in the provinces, but they were soon a ubiquitous presence, financed and managed through syndicates like the Moss Empires, capitalized at nearly £2 million in 1900. With the concentration of ownership, the individual proprietor or 'caterer', an amalgam of sporting publican, showbiz impresario and respectable citizen, disappeared from flamboyant public display to be replaced by the faceless bureaucracy of modern business management. The entertainment itself suffered a similar loss of vitality as commercial calculation transformed the pattern of social and visual space in the halls. Powerful lighting, introduced in the 1880s, emphasized the dominance of the stage over the auditorium, where the removal of the old promenade areas and the introduction of permanent tip-up seats ensured a disciplined and stratified house – 'shopkeepers and publicans in the orchestra stalls and dress circle, artisans and regular workers in the pit stalls, and the low class and no class on the "top shelf" or balcony'.[3] Some managements even obliged their performers to sign contracts forbidding the direct address of the now distant audience, since repartee and extemporization played havoc with the tight timetabling necessitated by the turn system, twice-nightly houses, and the advertized scheduling of performances to tie in with specific bus and train times. By the end of the century, other characteristics of the original interactive halls had all but disappeared – the sale of alcohol was restricted to the relative quarantine of ante-room bars, while Walter Leaver of the Royal Albert was the last remaining chairman, an office rendered redundant by the elevation of the stage and curtain control of entrances and exits.[4]

As the star system developed, songs became the exclusive property of individual artists, purchased with the performing copyright direct from the writers, whose market formula was the concrete and familiar. Courtship, marriage, old age and other comic disasters of working-class life were chronicled by warm-hearted, pearly-suited costermongers and the experienced-yet-wholesome Marie Lloyd, stage cockneys who replaced the 'heavy swells' as the celebrities of the halls. Stars of this ilk were expected to remember their origins, to accept the social obligations of success, a duty enforced by claques in the gallery – Jenny Hill, a working-class girl who achieved stardom in the early 1890s as the Vital Spark, was stopped dead in one performance by a voice from the gallery demanding: 'Why don't yer pay yer coachman?' Stoic and mundane, the songs confirmed the harsh immutability of working-class life, relieved by occasional visions of sudden windfalls and ensuing whoopee, otherwise restricted to seaside excursions and bank-holiday outings, a ritual pleasure following the Holidays Extension Act 1875.[5]

Jingoism enlivened some of the lyrics, but here theatrical convention triumphed over political manipulation. War had always figured prominently in popular art, which relished the juxtaposition of heroism with comic cowardice, a traditional device rehearsed in 1878 when the famous jingo song was matched in popularity by Herbert Campbell's parody:

I don't want to fight, I'll be slaughtered if I do!
I'll change my togs and sell my kit and pop my rifle too!
I don't like the war, I ain't no Briton true,
And I'd let the Russians have Constantinople.[6]

Other military songs bemoaned the ingratitude accorded to common soldiers once surplus to requirements. Destitute heroes dependent upon the workhouse and casual wards, their sad fate was personified by Charles Godfrey's old Crimean veteran in 'On Guard', one of the most popular songs of the 1890s. Up in the West End, where the music hall now catered for a new audience of upper-class rowdies and middle-class jingoes, the workhouse scene was curtailed from the act because officers from the household brigade complained that it was bad for recruiting.[7]

Judged simply by its songs, music-hall offered a culture of consolation, an inward-looking, class-bound inflexion of the stoic fatalism characteristic of late Victorian thought. But the commercial halls were genuine variety theatres, offering an array of exotic delights. The new prominence of the stage facilitated the most extravagant tableaux and spectacles, while the auditorium itself, stratified as it was, generated a lively drama of individual and collective acts of display and competition. Condemned to a life apart, working-class audiences were doubtless consoled and reassured by some of the acts and songs, but the whole commercial package offered something much more exciting, the chance to see and learn about 'life' outside familiar and domestic confines, and all for a shilling a night.[8]

Ally Sloper's Half-Holiday, the top-selling illustrated paper with a circulation in excess of 340,000 in the late 1880s, offered further knowledge of the expanding world of pleasure and leisure, hedonistic holiday delights within reach of the masses, an opportunity seized by the eponymous hero, a festive underling with access to the high life. A vade-mecum for the uninitiated, the *Half-Holiday* attracted a large middle-class readership who relished every solecism in the catalogue of graceless manners and taste, comic art which alleviated anxieties about cultural penetration from below – exclusivity was quite secure against the lumpen leisure class personified by A. Sloper, Esq., 'Most Frequently Kicked Out Man in Europe'.[9]

Pleasure in Ally's good-time world was regular but episodic, joyous delights snatched in defiance of domestic constraints. For many, leisure hours were spent cosily at home, a haven of recuperation in which to enjoy the piano – by 1910 there were between two and four million pianos in Britain, one for every 10–20 people[10] – or simply to peruse the popular press. New papers like *Tit Bits* (1881), *Answers* (1888), and *Pearson's Weekly* (1890), complemented the old favourite, the *News of the World*, essential pre-prandial Sunday reading.[11] However, the home-centredness of working-class life did not necessarily lead to domestic isolation, internal burrowing in the face of a harsh and hostile world. Home-based hobbies were often linked to a vibrant associational culture, collectively organized without managerial or middle-class intervention – pigeon, dog and canary breeders developed national organizations to promote the hobby within a context of fierce competition similar to that displayed at flower and vegetable shows. Hobbies were a prized area of working-class autonomy, a competitive outlet for lives otherwise circumscribed by group loyalties and mechanized work routines. They also encouraged a socially acceptable level of intellectual activity: the mastery of a craft-hobby or sport demanded accuracy, knowledge, discipline and skill, qualities which the elementary educational system failed to instil.[12]

New organizational opportunities were on offer for troublesome adolescents, but membership of the scouts, boys' brigades and other 'paramilitary' youth movements, products of the age of imperialism, was restricted to the few who could afford the uniform.[13] On the streets, gangs reigned supreme, unformulated youth clubs with rules of their own. Here the new imperialist ethic was subsumed in old cultural traditions of territorial rivalry and male assertion, loyalties which ensured a degree of protection and safety for local inhabitants, however delinquent the gang. Violence or 'scuttling' between rival gangs generally took a ritualized form, involving customary constraints that prevented serious injury, except when newly-arrived immigrant groups were the unfortunate victims.[14]

Some youths were able to earn a bit extra by working on the margins of betting, the best-organized street-based activity, recently described by Ross McKibbin as 'the most successful example of working-class self-help in the modern era'. Operated in defiance of the law and middle-class censure, gambling on the horses was a recurrent but strictly controlled element in such disposable income as the working class enjoyed. A rational alternative to saving – another example of 'thrift in reverse' – a well-placed wager offered hope of temporary relief from the debt–credit cycle of most working-class budgets. Assiduous readers of the sporting press, working-class punters relied not on luck but on carefully studied knowledge and form. Betting was a popular intellectual activity, an absorbing hobby open to all through a ubiquitous but informal organizational network remarkable for its honesty and proletarian self-sufficiency. Misunderstood by censorious labour leaders and middle-class moralists, mass betting extended into territory beyond the reach of voluntary, religious and political associations.[15]

Religious, political or whatever, voluntary associations faced stiff competition from commercial and other forms of cultural provision. Those who followed a purist line made no concession to popular taste, concentrating their expressive energies on ideological edification and individual commitment. The more pragmatic bodies were less exacting, offering a variety of popular amusements in the instrumental hope of retaining and attracting ordinary members. They introduced clubs on the CIU model to complement their intellectual and ascetic activities, but as in the CIU itself, 'free and easy' entertainment soon became the main attraction – a survey of 1904 confirmed that the large majority of the 992 affiliated clubs were social in nature, congenial gatherings for 'talking, drinking, smoking and association', although some older members tried to preserve the clubs for serious political debate.[16] Incorporated in religious and voluntary associations, drinking and entertainment clubs offended the scruples of the incorruptible, particularly the earnest and respectable disciples of rational freethought. The 'beer question' aside, secularists were agreed on the need for a popular denominational culture, a 'chapel' life of education, elevation and entertainment, in which new opportunities for organized sport, cycling trips and other outings were put to good effect in a calendar of practice and observance appropriated from orthodox religion. Even so, secularist societies fell into rapid decline after the brief golden age between the Knowlton trial in 1877 and Bradlaugh's admission to parliament in 1886, rendered redundant by the secularization of society. Secularism was not the complement to religion, advancing as religion retreated, but a supplement to it, dependent upon it for its rise and fall.[17]

Confronted by the late Victorian crisis of plausibility, churches and chapels obscured their institutional and recruitment difficulties by concentrating their energies, evangelical and cultural, on internal constituencies, on those already within their influence. Much attention was accorded to children, captive or endogenous recruits, while at the adult level, membership standards were relaxed, a form of 'lateral growth' which drastically reduced the once considerable reservoirs of partially committed adherents.[18] Those who hoped to reach the wider external audience were forced to make further concessions to the secular, presenting the religious message in cultural and recreational guise through initiatives like the Pleasant Sunday Afternoon movement. Averse to orthodox worship, large numbers of the working class were prepared to attend 'services' in which interesting talks on social questions, Biblical subjects and educational matters were preceded by musical entertainment – the Hull Excelsior Minstrels proved a great draw at Scunthorpe in 1896 attracting a crowd of 600, over 450 more than the membership of the local Primitive Methodists who organized the service. The nonconformist establishment, however, condemned all such attempts to 'brighten the hours of the day of rest at the expense of its sacredness'.[19]

Direct evangelizing provoked hostility, particularly in the form practised by the Salvation Army, formed by the Booths, dissatisfied Methodists, on the plausible assumption that the working-class poor could be saved for Christ only by 'people of their own class, who would go after them in their own resorts, who would speak to them in a language they understood, and reach them by means suited to their own tastes'. Enlivened by brass bands and other crowd-pulling gimmicks, outdoor missionary activity was boisterous and brash, expounding in graphic detail *The Up Line to Heaven and the Down Line to Hell*, but the formula, which also included militant teetotalism, served to antagonize not to convert. In 1882 alone, 643 Salvationists were physically assaulted by indignant crowds in what was to prove a favourite pastime of the 'Skeleton Army', a band of pre-Edwardian Teddy Boys who parodied and harassed the Salvation Army at every opportunity.[20]

At an institutional level, the churches failed to attract a large working-class congregation, but non-attendance (Sunday schools apart) did not necessarily imply widespread religious apathy or indifference. Formal, sectarian and socially exclusive, organized worship was alien to the working class, but absence from church was not tantamount to heathenism as the Booths assumed. At community level, the working class practised their own form of religion, a 'practical Christianity' of mutual aid and self-respect, reinforced by the traditional fatalism which helped them accept the disasters of life as the irrefragable will of God. Few working-class people would admit to not being Christian – in pubs and workshops, Robert Roberts recollected, outright atheists were 'looked upon as tempters of Providence, very odd fish indeed' – but the churches were unable to transform this residual religious sentiment into denominational commitment.[21] Here the labour movement promised a new beginning with John Trevor's Labour Church, which extended the hand of ethical fellowship to all classes and creeds in a gospel of social amelioration, celebrated in music and texts, religious, democratic and socialist. An initial success – there were 54 Labour Churches by 1895 – the movement soon peaked, unable to compete with yet more convivial forms of socialist fellowship, such as the new Clarion Cycling Clubs.[22]

Sponsored by Robert Blatchford, the clubs took the urban working class out into the country, where healthy exercise was combined with political propaganda: members dismounted to distribute socialist literature and hold impromptu meetings, disturbing the 'sabbath quiet' of remote country villages. Despite the politics, the clubs conformed to the pattern of English associational culture, united by friendship and good cheer not by party discipline and organization. Given the plethora of working-class associations, it was impossible for the labour movement to establish a comprehensive labour alliance, to subsume the various forms of working-class mutuality within a counter-cultural party network. Socialism took deepest root in isolated districts, as in the new labour clubs of Colne Valley where trade unionism and other forms of working-class association were relatively weak. Elsewhere socialists had to compete for popular support. Here was a marked contrast with Germany where the establishment of the Social Democratic Party preceded and controlled the development of working-class associations, industrial, social and cultural. In the increased leisure time and rising real wages of late Victorian England, labour's advance was hindered not only by commercial mass culture, but also by working-class traditions of collective but autonomous convivial mutuality.[23]

20 Labour's Turning-point?

Independent labour representation became a political and organizational reality in late Victorian England, as union membership exploded to incorporate (temporarily at least) semi-skilled and unskilled workers. Socialism, it has often been assumed, was the necessary catalyst, the ideological inspiration for this great leap forward, fulfilling the radical aspirations of the early 1870s, the false dawn of new unionism. Crucial as it was, socialist inspiration was unofficial and pragmatic, stronger in some regions than in others. Socialist ideologues, doctrinaire and sectarian, shunned all contact with trade unions and other reformist bodies. But at grassroots level, where ethical fellowship and socialist unity prevailed, practical activists pursued a wide labour alliance. By tapping union funds and other resources, they hoped to secure independent labour representation, at the earliest opportunity, thereby replacing Lib-Labism, a discredited creed in the industrial districts.

Previously restricted to continental exiles, socialism entered radical discussion through the Manhood Suffrage League and other O'Brienite clubs. The Labour Emancipation League, established in 1881, carried the process a stage further by adding socialism – the collectivization of the instruments of production and means of employment – to its traditional programme of Chartist and radical demands. Thereafter the socialist revival gathered considerable momentum, fuelled by dissillusionment with Gladstone and enthusiasm for Henry George, celebrated American author of *Progress and Poverty*. No socialist himself, George opened the way for socialism by his passionate and oft-repeated challenge to the 'invisible hand' of orthodox political economy, as he toured the country campaigning for 'Single Tax' on the incremental value of land. Disillusioned radicals, outraged by Gladstone's Irish and imperial policies, quickly passed beyond land nationalization, once the *ne plus ultra* of radical social democracy, to the full socialist programme, the Marxist exposition of which was now widely available in English translation.[1]

As interpreted by H. M. Hyndman, founder of the Social Democratic Federation, scientific socialism was a rigidly mechanistic creed. Dictatorial and dogmatic, Hyndman, a former army officer and county cricketer, assumed the role of ideological apostle, imposing a socialist orthodoxy of inflexible determinism, enlivened by some Tory-radical jingoism, a legacy of his past – *England for All* contained chapters lifted straight from Marx alongside demands for a strong navy to protect the colonies, special heritage of the English working class. A fierce critic of reformism and the 'trade union fetish', he refused to cooperate with existing working-class organizations, labourist bodies led by 'stodgy-brained, dull-witted, and slow-going time servers'. Aloof from the labour movement, 'the chief drawback to our progress', Hyndman and the SDF sought public attention through opportunist agitation on the issues of the day, tactics which soon split the socialists and undermined the hopes for a united front of radicals, secularists and socialists. William Morris was among the first to secede, disgusted by such 'adventure, show and advertisement', financed by 'Tory gold' during the general election of 1885.[2]

Inspired by Carlyle, Ruskin and the romantic critique of bourgeois industrialism, Morris found in socialism the promise of a qualitatively different way of life, the attainment of which was not to be compromised by electoral politics or premature violence. Morris left the SDF to found the Socialist League, committed to a policy of educational-revolutionism, making true socialists of the working class before the decisive struggle for power. Socialist consciousness was to be inculcated with purist rigour, untainted by contact with lesser ideals, a high-minded exercise in expressive politics. But the strategy proved futile, as the most likely socialist recruits were left untutored, denied socialist leadership and instruction in their struggles for limited reforms. Having eschewed active involvement in the labour movement, Morris was soon displaced in the Socialist League which fell into the hands of anarchists who looked to the bomb, not the organized working class, as the agency of human liberation.[3]

Morris failed to provide a viable alternative to Hyndman's agitational antics, sham insurrectionary tactics which created a considerable stir during the unemployed demonstrations of 1886. Unemployment, a word which first appeared in the *Oxford Dictionary* in the 1880s, was a recurrent feature of the late Victorian economy, a corollary of intensified labour utilization and low levels of domestic investment in industry. The unemployment rate among trade unionists, still a privileged minority of the workforce, reached 11.4 per cent in 1879, 12.6 per cent in 1883 and 10.2 per cent in 1886.[4] From the outset, the SDF agitated amongst the unemployed, taking the lead in protest marches and deputations to East End Boards of Guardians, but the Tory Protectionists were no less active, mounting a number of rallies and demonstrations coordinated by the London United Workmen's Committee. When the Fair Traders called a demonstration in Trafalgar Square on 8 February 1886, the SDF decided to sabotage the proceedings, to capture the crowd for the socialist cause, symbolized by the red flag brandished by John Burns.

Behind this makeshift banner the SDF led the crowd away in a counter-demonstration, but they soon lost control of events. Provoked by denizens of London clubland, the crowd rioted its way through Pall Mall and adjacent streets, smashing windows, looting shops, attacking all forms of wealth and privilege. 'Black Monday' provoked a display of middle-class hysteria, a mixture of guilt and fear, as thousands of pounds suddenly poured into the Mansion House Fund for the unemployed, while insurrection was expected at any moment, a *grande peur* which brought business to a halt. Confidence was not restored until the dense fog lifted a couple of days later when the imaginary armies of avenging paupers were nowhere to be seen. Feared by the middle class, the casual poor remained undisciplined and unorganized, a volatile force which the socialists had yet to marshal – participants in the Pall Mall riot returned to the East End singing 'Rule Britannia!'[5]

'Black Monday' aroused anxiety among socialists critical of Hyndman and the SDF, but they joined together in a broad-based campaign to defend the right of open-air public assembly, threatened by the return of a Tory government and the appointment of a new metropolitan police commissioner. 1887 was a crucial year in the politics of public space, confirming the power of the authorities through festival and repression. Blessed by fine weather, Victoria's Golden Jubilee in June offered the crowds a stage-managed package of 'jingoism, circuses and guff'. The pageant of monarchy, always a holiday crowd-puller, was now enriched with imperial exotica, as Maharajas and African tribal chiefs were paraded in the streets, as at a Roman triumph.[6] Once the celebrations were over, however, Trafalgar Square and other public places were occupied by the homeless unemployed. These outdoor camps, refuge of 'outcast London', were soon the scene of rival initiatives, philanthropic and socialist. As hot summer gave way to chilly autumn, charitable agencies distributed food and lodgings tickets, while the SDF rallied the unemployed in meetings and demonstrations under the slogan 'Not charity, but work'. Despite repeated attempts, the police failed to clean up the Square, much to the anger of local residents and businessmen, outraged and inconvenienced by the smells and disorder. When Sir Charles Warren, the new commissioner, took decisive action in early November, banning all public meetings in the Square, socialists, radicals, secularists, Irish nationalists and members of the Salvation Army united to defend the right of assembly. The Metropolitan Radical Association announced a monster demonstration on 13 November to defy the ban and protest against William O'Brien's imprisonment in Ireland. On the fateful day – 'Bloody Sunday' – mounted police and troops broke up processions heading for the

Square and dispersed the assembled demonstrators with brutal ease and ferocity, inflicting lethal injuries on three of the crowd. A week later, the authorities confirmed their control in a further show of force, during which Alfred Linnell, an innocent radical bystander, sustained fatal injuries. Tens of thousands lined the route of his funeral procession, a united and defiant demonstration of protest.[7]

Radicals, secularists, socialists and others were united in outrage at police brutality and the suppression of free speech – among the pall bearers at Linnell's funeral were Annie Besant and W. T. Stead, leading figures in the new Law and Liberty League, William Morris whose 'Death Song' was sung over the grave, and Frank Smith of the Salvation Army.[8] But 'Bloody Sunday' added further to internal dissension, as socialists were forced to take account of the overwhelming physical power of the state. George Bernard Shaw immediately abandoned all thoughts of working-class revolutionary insurrectionism – 'I object to a defiant policy altogether at present', he wrote to Morris: 'If we persist in it, we shall be eaten bit by bit like an artichoke.'[9] Other Fabians were similarly shaken by the events of Trafalgar Square, after which 'permeation', working through existing institutions, seemed the only route to socialism. Having adjusted Marxist theory to English circumstances, the 'Hampstead Marx Circle', the Fabian think-tank, elaborated a strategy of gradual socialism, concentrating their efforts on the rational conversion of politicians and administrators. Committed to 'permeation', tactics which met with some local success in the Progressive politics of the new London County Council, the Fabians made no contribution to labour's turning-point, to the development of an independent working-class movement.[10]

Unconcerned with the ideological rigour and strategic prescriptions of official policy, many members of the socialist societies campaigned for change through the labour movement, concentrating their efforts on independent representation and the extension of trade unionism. Through the *Labour Elector* and the Labour Electoral Committee, established by the TUC in the wake of the 1884 Reform Act, H. H. Champion built up an electoral machine to secure the return of a group of labour MPs who would represent the working-class cause at Westminster in the same single-minded spirit as the Irish nationalists. Forced to quit the SDF, Champion supported a number of independent candidates, most notably Keir Hardie at the Mid-Lanark by-election of 1888, the beginning of the 'labour revolt' against Liberal domination of constituency politics.[11]

By no means a mere personal protest at Liberal control of the selection process, Hardie's candidature was a test of the Liberal Party's willingness to recognize 'Labour', and what it stood for, as a separate political force. Teetotaler and 'advanced' radical, Hardie underwent a rapid political education in the years immediately preceeding the by-election, a time of bitter industrial dispute on the Lanarkshire coalfield, scene of extensive socialist propaganda. J. L. Mahon, Champion's counterpart in the SL, was the most energetic and influential missionary, eschewing ideological niceties to pursue a united front of trade unions and other working-class bodies, the necessary foundation for a broad-based socialist party. Supported by Champion and Mahon's Scottish Land and Labour League, Hardie managed to secure a mere 8.4 per cent of the vote at Mid-Lanark, but sufficient interest was generated to establish a Scottish Labour Party.[12] South of the border, progress was blocked by vested interests and internecine disputes. Under Broadhurst's leadership, the TUC remained a bastion of Lib-Labism, opposed to independent parliamentary initiatives. Socialists and others, proponents of a labour alliance, wrangled over ideology, religion, finance and much else beside. Hardie's 'ethical socialism', vague in detail, nonconformist in spirit, offended against the secular and theoretical propensities of metropolitan and middle-class socialists. Caught in the middle of these and other polemics, the hapless Champion emigrated to Australia after the closure of the bankrupt *Labour Elector*, previously assisted by Tory funds.[13]

Despite these dissensions, socialists secured a foothold in the trade unions, a vantage point from which to promote political independence. Working-class activists, educated in socialist societies, refused to dismiss the trade unions out of hand. Working from within, socialists like Burns and Mann hoped to transform the unions into an inclusive and militant political force, committed to a programme of 'palliatives', worthwhile reforms to reduce unemployment, poverty and labour exploitation. The campaign for the eight-hour day, initiated by Mann's Eight Hour League, not only attracted considerable support within existing unions but also inspired new initiatives among the unskilled, such as the Tyneside-based National Labour Federation, established in 1886.[14]

With or without socialist involvement, new unionism was developing apace in the 1880s, well before the dramatic events at the end of the decade. In the textile districts, women workers were organized in the Northern Counties Amalgamated Association of Cotton Weavers (1884), and the Amalgamated Association of Card and Blowing Room Operatives (1886), a prototype new union which aimed to recruit tens of thousands of poorly paid workers ignored by craft unions.[15] Other important developments included the British Steel Smelters' Association, open to workers shunned by the Association of Ironworkers, the National Amalgamated Union of Seamen and Firemen, and the National Amalgamated Labour Union, based in Swansea docks.[16]

Trade union membership in 1888 stood around 750,000, still far below the 1874 peak of over a million, but a considerable recovery from the trough of 1881, when less than half a million were affiliated to the TUC. In a sudden and dramatic burst between 1889 and 1891 membership doubled. As in the early 1870s, union expansion coincided with cyclical upturn and a tight labour market – by 1889 unemployment had fallen to 2 per cent. This time round, there was no shortage of suitable leadership or advice, as socialists, Georgeites and others came forward to organize the unskilled. Striking match-girls at Bryant and May secured the catalytic victory in 1888, encouraged and inspired by Annie Besant and W. T. Stead, co-publishers of *The Link*, a socialist-radical journal established in the wake of 'Bloody Sunday'. The next advance, the gasworkers' attainment of a three-shift system, an eight-hour day, was organized by Will Thorne, worker at Beckton Gas Works and member of the SDF. Not fully literate, Thorne was assisted by Eleanor Marx and an array of socialist intellectuals and activists – precursor of the General Municipal Workers, Thorne Gas-workers Union was the most militant left-wing union of 1889, the nearest thing to a 'red' body before the foundation of communist parties.[17]

From the gasworks it was a short route to the docks, where large numbers of gasworkers, Thorne included, annually sought employment during the summer lay-off. Lightermen and stevedores apart, London dockers lacked organization, save for the diminutive Tea Operatives and General Labourers' Union formed by Ben Tillett in 1887. As spontaneous strikes spread along the waterfront in the favourable market conditions of 1889, Tillett stood forward to organize comprehensive action among 30,000 workers with little tradition of solidarity and discipline, and no funds. Here too, the socialist engineers, Burns and Mann, offered invaluable assistance, mobilizing the strikers in disciplined and dignified fashion, much to the approval of middle-class opinion. Purged of the political fears of 1886, Londoners applauded the dockers' orderly demonstrations, trusting that the strike – and such responsible trade unionism – would hasten decasualization. Supported by public opinion and much-needed funds from Australia, the dockers held out until the dock companies accepted terms recommended by the Mansion House Committee headed by Cardinal Manning, a settlement which awarded the strikers union recognition, a virtual closed shop and 'the full round orb of the dockers' tanner'.[18]

A sensational triumph for new unionism, the London dock strike encouraged other workers, unskilled, semi-skilled and previously unorganized, to mobilize for increases in wages and reductions in hours. The national strike-wave even extended to school classrooms, where militant working-class pupils, keen to emulate their parents, demanded flexible attendance requirements and non-authoritarian teaching methods.[19] In 1890, in response to the call from the founding Congress of the Second International, May Day demonstrations were held in London and other cities to demand the legal eight-hour day. A few months later, the TUC, briefly in tune with the new mood, decided to promote an eight-hour Bill, and elected the first socialist, John Burns, onto its parliamentary committee. The socialist societies, however, still remained aloof: the SDF officially dismissed the trade union work of Thorne, Burns and Mann as 'a lowering of the flag, a departure from active propaganda, a waste of energy'.[20]

Realists not revolutionaries, socialist activists offered the new unions practical assistance not ideological instruction – Champion, indeed, reckoned they were accepted in spite of, rather than because of, their views.[21] Above all, they encouraged semi-skilled and unskilled workers to exploit their bargaining strengths, to adopt structures and strategies alien to the craft-based traditions of conventional trade unionism. The initial impetus towards general labour unions was doubtless unintentional, as new unions in particular industries were besieged by other workers clamouring to join. Founded to organize semi-skilled platers' helpers in the Tyneside shipyards, the National Amalgamated Union of Labour was soon catering for dockers, gas and chemical workers, builders' labourers, and less skilled workers in engineering, glass, iron and steel. The trend, however, was strengthened by socialist commitment to open unions, a structure which allowed new unions to spread risks between industries and areas, not all of which were liable to attack at the same time. Thorne's Gas-workers Union, where socialist influence was most marked, was probably the least exclusive despite its title, taking in among others rubber workers, dyers in the Yorkshire woollen industry, local authority workers, workers in the Birmingham metal trades, in chemicals, clay-pits and quarries.[22]

Economic circumstances prevented most new unions from offering friendly society benefits to their low-paid members, but here too socialist influence made a virtue of necessity. Not craft unions or 'coffin clubs', new unions were mobilized by socialists for all-out industrial militancy, intimidating blacklegs and employers alike, as continuous production processes were brought to a halt. The success of such tactics depended on high employment and a tight labour market. When conditions changed, unions were forced to reverse the policy, to offer friendly society benefits as a means of retaining members, an option restricted to those who catered for better-paid, semi-

skilled workers. A similar mixture of tactical and ideological considerations applied to legislation and independent labour politics. Unable
to enforce craft regulation at the workplace or restrict the labour
supply, new unions were compelled to advocate legislation – socialist
palliatives like the statutory eight-hour day – to consolidate gains
won by militant industrial action in favourable market conditions.[23]

The success of new unionism thus depended on full employment,
police tolerance of vigorous picketing, and the absence of concerted
employer opposition, factors which were not to persist beyond the late
1880s. Relieved by the orderly demonstrations of London dockers,
middle-class observers turned harshly against new unions when other
disputes led to violent clashes between strikers and blacklegs. Quick
to sense the change in mood, employers mounted a counter-attack,
combining to uphold the rights of 'free labour' against the 'tyranny'
of the closed shop. Organized by the Shipping Federation and other
employers' associations, blackleg labour was dispatched to trouble-
spots throughout the country with full police protection. Gunboats
stood by in the Humber when the power of waterfront unionism was
finally broken in a stormy seven-week strike at Hull in 1893, last of
a series of violent confrontations.[24]

Abruptly halted in the early 1890s, the forward march of new
unionism failed to capture control of the labour movement. It was
the old Lib-Lab unions which benefited most from the membership
explosion, sustaining their growth after the boom collapsed in 1891
– at the end of 1892, they accounted for some two-thirds of total
union membership. Those new unions which managed to survive
adjusted their ways and means to conform to established trade union
practice, adopting an industrial policy which Hobsbawm has
described as 'cautious, limited, conservative and sectional'. Little
different from the old, they restricted their membership to those
overdue for organization, the better-paid, regularly employed semi-
skilled workers, many of whom worked for local authorities,
employers unconcerned about productivity but much influenced by
workmen's votes.[25]

Prompted by the weakness of new unionism, the formation of the
Independent Labour Party was a political reaction to the failure of
industrial action. The initiative passed to the Yorkshire woollen
towns, custodians of the old Chartist tradition, best preserved in this
region of small-scale production units where factory unionism and
employer paternalism were never strong.[26] Woollen workers were hit
hard by the Great Depression, a time of declining wages and increasing workloads, conditions which deteriorated further with the imposition of foreign tariffs. In December 1890 workers at Manningham
Mills, Bradford, encouraged by the recent success of the socialist-

organized Leeds gas-stokers, decided to take action against the latest piece price cuts. A bitter five-month lock-out ensued, a class struggle as it were in which Tory employers were staunchly supported by the local Liberal authorities. Repressed and impoverished, strikers and their families were defended by socialists and workers throughout the region, but defeat was inevitable. The political lesson endured with the establishment of the Bradford Labour Union in which radicals and trade unionists combined with local members of the SL and other socialists to promote labour representation at Westminster and on the town council 'irrespective of the convenience of any political party'. Similar Labour Unions and Clubs, offering education, entertainment and political propaganda, spread throughout the West Riding, joining the new Trade Councils in demanding independent political action and an end to Lib-Labism.[27]

Impressed by these and similar initiatives elsewhere, John Burgess and Robert Blatchford advocated a national federation to link these local independent labour parties of non-sectarian socialists, disaffected radicals, and politicized trade unionists. As a further boost, independent candidates polled well at the 1892 general election, not least at Bradford where Ben Tillett came near to victory in a three-cornered contest. John Burns and Havelock Wilson, the seamen's leader, were elected at Battersea and Middlesbrough respectively, but both were to seek an accommodation with the new Liberal government. Cloth-capped and proud of it, Keir Hardie remained defiantly independent, shocking the Commons with his proletarian manners and headgear when he arrived to take his seat, won at West Ham on an independent, anti-unemployment platform of land nationalization, municipal workshops and the statutory eight-hour day. At the TUC later in the year, Hardie chaired a small unofficial meeting which decided to call a national conference to unite the 'Independent Labour Parties in Great Britain'. In January 1893, the foundation conference of the Independent Labour Party assembled in Bradford, an appropriate venue.[28]

In marked contrast to the socialist societies of the 1880s, the composition and ethos of the Bradford conference was overwhelmingly provincial, working-class and pragmatic. More than one-third of the 120 delegates came from Yorkshire, working-class representatives of local labour unions, profoundly suspicious of the handful of middle-class London socialists, G. B. Shaw included, who had travelled north. The object of the new party, delegates readily agreed, was 'to secure the collective ownership of the means of production, distribution and exchange', but the term socialist was not to appear in the party's title or its manifesto, a programme of reforms little in advance of progressive liberalism. Here the important practical consideration was not to offend the trade unions, whose support was indispensable if independent labour representation, the desideratum of the ILP, was to be achieved at the earliest opportunity.[29] A short-cut to political effectiveness, this 'Labour Alliance' with the unions was pursued with single-minded instrumentalism as Hardie exerted his influence over the new party. Alternative strategies were squeezed out of consideration, much to the chagrin of Blatchford and the Lancashire socialists, advocates of a United Socialist Party, a fusion of groups including the ILP and the SDF, belatedly purged of sectarianism.[30]

Excluded from political and strategic planning, socialism was reduced to a vague ethical creed of fellowship and good cheer, a brotherhood congenial to radical nonconformists and secularists alike. The counter-culture of intense aspiration, the 'religion of socialism' still practised in Colne Valley, was undermined elsewhere by pragmatic concern with electoral politics and party machinery. Blatchford tried to resist this process of goal displacement with his popular vision of a socialist (and autarkic) *Merrie England*, a million-seller penny text in which 'making socialists' still took priority over courting allies and winning votes, sole considerations of the ILP.[31]

Despite such pragmatism, the ILP failed in the first instance to attract the official labour movement or the electorate – all 28 candidates, Hardie included, finished bottom of the poll at the general election of 1895. To make matters worse, the TUC introduced new standing orders which strengthened the old brigade, block-voting big battalions, at the expense of socialist trades councils, radical new unions and independent labour politicians, troublesome proponents of a labour alliance.[32] Four years later, however, a majority of unions were converted to the cause: in 1899 the TUC agreed that trade unions, cooperative societies, Fabian societies, the SDF and ILP should confer together 'with a view of securing united political action'. At the conference the following year, Hardie and the ILP steered a skilful course between Lib-Lab attempts to restrict the new organization to limited trade union matters and the SDF's insistence on a clear socialist objective. The labour alliance was given institutional form as the Labour Representation Committee, subsequently the Labour Party, but many obstacles remained to its electoral success.[33]

Political attitudes within the trade union movement reflected the geography of industrial location. Lib-Labism was strongest on the coalfields, separate parliamentary constituencies dominated by miners whose interests and needs could not be ignored. Unlike elsewhere, working-class candidates were encouraged to stand on the Lib-Lab platform, an arrangement which Ben Pickard, president of the MFGB, had no wish to alter. Adequately represented in parliament, the MFGB kept apart from the LRC, fearing that miners' funds would be purloined to support extraneous candidates.[34] Scattered throughout the length and breadth of the land, railwaymen had no such clout at constituency level, a considerable disadvantage for workers in an industry without adequate safety legislation or union recognition. Along with the surviving new unions, the ASRS led the call for independent labour representation, not to promote a socialist millennium but simply to protect the interests of workers ignored by Lib-Labism. By 1899, most unions shared this position, converted to political independence out of dissatisfaction with the Lib-Lab alliance.[35]

As dissatisfaction spread, socialists came to the fore in political and industrial struggles, hastening organized workers towards independence by force of example. With or without 'progressive' Liberal support, socialist local councillors and elected officials demanded the implementation of permissive legislation on housing, sanitation, and unemployment relief, and the inclusion of 'fair wage' clauses in municipal employees' contracts. By 1900, the ILP boasted 106 local councillors, 66 members of School Boards and 51 Poor Law Guardians, numbers which included a handful of women, otherwise excluded from political office – in 1894 Mrs Pankhurst was nominated by the Manchester ILP on a programme of free education, free preschool breakfasts and 'equal pay for equal work, irrespective of sex'. This local advance was strongest at West Ham, where Hardie and his labour colleagues gained control in 1898 to promote certain specific demands, a compulsory eight-hour day, improved housing and the transfer of the tramways to public ownership.[36]

At the workplace, socialists acquired influence and respect amongst craft workers, former critics of new unionism, by their defiant stand against employer prerogatives and the reorganization of production. Shortly before the lock-out of 1897, George Barnes, a declared socialist and member of the ILP, was elected general secretary of the once-exclusive ASE. Over the next five years, some 20,000 planers, borers and other semi-skilled workers were admitted to union membership, practical socialist tactics to extend the culture of control.[37] Socialist activists, proponents of independent labour representation, emerged from obscurity in the Leicester footwear and hosiery industries as 'disciples of St. Crispin', defenders of skilled workers threatened by mechanization and new work practices.[38]

Presented in such a way, independent labour politics promised protection to craft and other workers, security no longer provided by the Lib-Lab alliance, now strained to breaking-point by the employers' legal counter-attack on organized labour. Employers turned to the courts not simply to crush new unionism – a task

undertaken with considerable zeal by various free labour associations
– but also to affirm their rights and authority at a time of critical
change in the labour process and collective bargaining. Union immun-
ities were drastically curtailed in a number of adverse decisions,
case rulings which implied the principle of representative action, the
responsibility of one person for the action of the whole. Unions, it
seemed, could now be regarded as corporate bodies which could be
sued for tortious acts committed on their behalf, a point expressly
denied by previous legislation. The principle was put to the test in
a famous case in 1901 when the Taff Vale Railway Company was
awarded damages against the ASRS for actions by its members during
the strike of the previous summer. The Taff Vale decision virtually
destroyed the right to strike, but some trade union leaders were
reluctant to press for its reversal, since the ruling addressed the
crucial question of internal trade union authority, the control over
militants and troublemakers necessary for the effective operation of
new collective bargaining arrangements. Union leaders, however,
finally rallied behind the LRC and the campaign to reverse Taff Vale,
a change of heart prompted by the strength of rank-and-file protest,
the scale of the award (the ASRS settled two years later at a cost of
£42,000), and the intransigence of the Tory government. This was
the moment of 'final breakthrough': union-affiliated membership of
the LRC rose from 375,000 in February 1901 to 861,000 in 1903,
when it was decided to raise a fund for the payment of Labour MPs
– a practical necessity previously ignored by the Liberals – by means
of a compulsory levy on the unions.[39]

But the labour alliance remained fragile and vulnerable. Union
leaders were for the most part staunch supporters, looking to the new
party to provide the political and legal framework for 'voluntarism'
or free collective bargaining. Many of their members, however, were
reluctant to abandon their old Lib-Lab habits – nearly 40 per cent
of the membership of the nine largest unions voting in ballots for the
political levy in 1913 were opposed to funds being used to support
independent Labour candidates. In the absence of a distinctive socialist ideology – a precondition of the final affiliation of the miners in
1908 – the Labour Party struggled to retain an independent identity
as junior partner in the Progressive Alliance of Edwardian Britain,
all but subsumed by the remarkable Liberal revival.[40]

Rejuvenated in programme and personnel, Liberals polled well in
industrial Lancashire, London and elsewhere, on a platform of social
and welfare reforms, but the strength and vitality of Edwardian 'New
Liberalism' was by no means the only factor hindering Labour's
advance. In its residence and registration requirements, the electoral
system reflected a systematic bias against the working class: as well

as all women, some 40 per cent of adult males were excluded from the electoral rolls, even after the reforms of the 1880s.[41] Labour, it would seem, was denied much of its natural constituency, but the franchise factor did not operate entirely to its disadvantage, hence the absence of pressure for change. Unable to organize the urban poor, the labour movement ignored the disfranchised, impoverished itinerants constantly on the move between tenement accommodation and the Boards of Guardians. Excluded from unions, friendly societies and other institutional forms of collective mutuality, the poor remained vulnerable to charity, patronage and beer, traditional electoral devices of the corrupt old regime. Among the poor Irish immigrant communities, a higher level of enfranchisement would have helped the Liberals not Labour.[42]

The question of women's suffrage, however, could not be ignored, but here the inequities of the existing electoral system, together with the suspicion of women's innate conservatism, led Labour to oppose enfranchisement under the present arrangements. Those who agitated on these terms, the suffragettes of the Women's Social and Political Union, were increasingly isolated from working-class politics – dominated by Mrs Pankhurst's autocratic daughter Christabel, the WSPU abandoned links with the ILP to mount a militant but socially conservative campaign of middle-class womanhood to coerce the political establishment into conceding 'Votes for Ladies'.[43] Less spectacular but more significant were the radical suffragists, working-class women trained in the trade union and cooperative movement, peaceful campaigners for the vote within a wider framework of political and industrial rights. Female trade unionism was gradually breaking loose from middle-class philanthropy, instigating force of the Women's Trade Union League, formed in 1874 as the Women's Provident and Protective Society. The full-time organizers of the 1890s, talented working-class women like Helen Silcock and Ada Nield Chew, were quick to recognize the importance of the vote, but for the WTUL the priority remained industrial, the struggle to organize and sustain female trade unions. Free from dependence on the goodwill of the male trade union establishment, the Women's Co-operative Guild took a more positive line on the suffrage. Founded in 1883, the Guild provided a forum for working-class women to discuss issues and grievances beyond the confines of kitchen and home. For Sarah Reddish and others, it offered training and encouragement to stand in local elections for School and Poor Law Boards, further political experience to strengthen the claim to the parliamentary franchise. By the end of the century, the ground was well prepared for a radical suffragist campaign led by working-class women from the Guild, the League, the new Clarion and Labour groups, and the recently strengthened textile unions. A working alliance was subsequently achieved with the Labour Party which benefited substantially from suffragist support in pre-war by-elections, an early indication of the crucial role women were to play in building up constituency organization after the war and the fourth Reform Act.[44]

Hindered or not by the pre-1918 electoral system, Labour had to contend against the powerful appeal of popular Toryism. Masters of the politics of recreation and entertainment, the Tories offered a range of attractions which radicals and socialists, divided over temperance and other ascetic considerations, were unable to match. Populists like Blatchford had no inhibitions, attracting a wide audience to the socialist cause through the various Clarion clubs – cycling, camera, field and glee – but his latent 'Tory' instincts (the 'Blimp' within) drew him towards racism, xenophobia and imperial expansionism during the Boer War. Clarion clubs, however, were no match for the Primrose League. The popular wing of Conservatism, the League was by far the largest political organization of the time – in 1906, the Bolton branch with 6000 paid members matched the total paid membership of the ILP! Extensive leisure and benefit facilities attracted the widest possible membership, non-voters as well as voters, the apathetic as well as the political, women as well as men, but party purpose was not forgotten. Led by a captain and a lieutenant, each local branch of the Primrose League Cycling Corps helped ensure the remarkable stability of the Conservative vote by tracing removals on the electoral register, contacting isolated voters and conveying messages between committee rooms. Not a matter for apology, class was a positive virtue in the League, deliberately emphasized by a hierarchical system of membership and fees. Social unity of this order allowed working-class Tories (and others) to indulge their fascination with the lives of the high-born and wealthy, dignitaries who graced the lantern-shows, concerts, tea parties, garden parties and other social functions organized by the local 'habitation'.[45]

In electoral terms, the League's strength derived from its lack of a specific programme or 'fad' – the Tories, indeed, were to poll disastrously in Edwardian England when they committed themselves to tariff reform, an ambitious policy of industrial reconstruction which infringed the hallowed doctrine of free trade, linked ineluctably in the working-class mind with the defence of free collective bargaining. In its late Victorian heyday, before the tariff reform controversy, the League propounded an uncontentious, vague and popular brand of patriotism, imperialism and monarchism, the Tory 'spirit of the age'. Criticism of the Queen, a marked feature of former decades, gave way to admiration of her seeming immortality, celebrated in *Chatterbox* and other cheap magazines full of royal trivia. Long since withdrawn from active politics, the monarchy was imbued with a repertoire of ritual, participation in which was a proud national right. Only a committed socialist few, most notably Keir Hardie, wanted no part in the 'sham and cant' of the Diamond Jubilee, although there were some local arguments between the classes about how best to celebrate the occasion. Come the day, disputes were reconciled in a ritualized display of consensus, enjoyed by the crowds as another holiday treat. Such dazzle and ceremony confirmed the legitimacy of monarchy, now respected as the guardian of fair play, the even-handed guarantor of the class neutrality of parliament.[46]

The growth of patriotic-imperialist sentiment, a consequence of increasing international rivalry and the commercialization of the Empire, similarly favoured the Tories at the expense of socialist and radical internationalists – at the popular level, internationalism had long been eradicated by racism, forcibly displayed by the reaction to the Indian Mutiny and the flood of post-Famine Irish immigrants. Along with the efforts of the League, popular imperialist propaganda took a variety of forms in late Victorian Britain, from music-hall songs and juvenile comics to advertising slogans and commercial packaging, with the benefits of Empire depicted on biscuit tins, cigarette packets and other symbols of the retail revolution. Despite this barrage, large numbers of the working class remained indifferent to the message as the Boer War was to reveal.[47]

Neither the jingo crowds nor the early recruits were working class in composition: it was the lower middle class, avid readers of the *Daily Mail*, who took the most prominent and rowdy part in breaking up anti-war meetings. By the same token, there was little working-class enthusiasm – socialist Battersea apart – for the anti-war movement, lacking charismatic leadership, populist style and a programme of immediate economic relevance. Indifferent to empire and the war, the working class nevertheless flocked onto the streets on Mafeking night to enjoy some fun, for once unrestrained by the forces of law and order, an opportunity not to be missed. The open mingling of classes on the streets, an exceptional occurrence, entered historical consciousness as the true spirit of the nation.[48] Myths of this order – along with other invented traditions – have served the establishment well, suggesting a fundamental patriotic and social unity, glossing over the divisions of a class society. Seldom accorded the licence for 'Mafficking', the late Victorian working class kept themselves proudly and defensively separate. Their strategy for survival was a life apart, protecting their interests, enjoying their fun in a self-enclosed world of work and community into which politics, labour or otherwise, was generally an unwelcome intrusion.

21 The Working Class Observed

The Great Depression undermined confidence in the progress of the nation, prompting middle-class observers to re-examine the 'Condition of England', to question the attitudes and assumptions of economic and social policy. A new generation of investigative journalists, novelists and social explorers exposed the squalor and deprivation of Darkest England, bringing elements of sociological analysis to their personal forays into the East End and other notorious inner city slums. By the end of the century, the scientific language of poverty cycles and subsistence levels replaced the graphic vignettes and exploration imagery of the past. Poverty, not the poor, became the subject of study.[1]

Not a mere methodological advance, the development of social criticism in the 1880s and after owed much to a new historical perspective which located the origins of intolerable social conditions in the 'industrial revolution', cataclysmic theme of Arnold Toynbee's famous Oxford lectures:

> a period as disastrous and terrible as any through which a nation ever passed; disastrous and terrible, because side by side with a great increase of wealth was seen an enormous increase of pauperism; and production on a vast scale, the result of free competition, led to a rapid alienation of classes and to the degradation of a large body of producers.[2]

Across the political spectrum, late Victorian critics of contemporary economic performance and social conditions traced the problems back to the political economy of the industrial revolution, an unrestrained system of *laissez-faire* which had to be abandoned in the interests of national efficiency, social imperialism and a guaranteed 'national minimum' for the deserving poor.[3]

As phrased in the language of the 1880s, the condition of England question expressed

> a new consciousness of sin among men of intellect and men of property . . . a growing uneasiness, amounting to conviction, that the industrial organization which had yielded rent, interest and profit on a stupendous scale, had failed to provide a decent livelihood and tolerable conditions for a majority of the inhabitants of Great Britain.

This middle-class sense of guilt, Beatrice Webb recollected, led some of the socially aware to a life of self-sacrificing public service, following the example set by Toynbee whose memory was perpetuated in the most famous East End settlement of the 1880s, Canon Barnett's Toynbee Hall. Having lost faith in conventional religion, orthodox economics and scientific charity, middle-class progressives among the urban gentry confronted an acute social crisis in the 1880s. Guilt was aggravated by fear, prompted by the revival of the old Chartist spectre of popular insurgency.[4]

The internal working-class stratification which had ensured mid-Victorian social stability, appeared to be breaking down in the housing crisis of the 1880s. No longer segregated and confined, the residuum threatened to contaminate those above them. Employing the latest techniques, a number of surveys assessed the danger. In many respects, their findings were reassuring, confirming the old mid-Victorian assumptions about the structure and progress of the working class. Charles Booth purged one great fear of the 1880s, a spectre first raised by Henry George, by limiting his Class A, the lowest class of occasional labourers, loafers and semi-criminals, to less than one per cent of the capital's population:

> The hordes of barbarians of whom we have heard, who, issuing from their slums, will one day overwhelm modern civilization, do not exist. There are barbarians, but they are a handful, a small and decreasing percentage: a disgrace but not a danger.

At the other end of the scale, Booth reported that large numbers of the working class, some 51.5 per cent of the population of London, were living 'in comfort', headed by the independent aristocracy of labour and the 'non-commissioned officers of the industrial army', foremen and other well-paid supervisory workers. Class E, the largest single category, enjoyed 'regular standard earnings – above the line of poverty', and were thus capable of collective self-help: 'This class is the recognized field of all forms of co-operation and combination, and I believe, and am glad to believe, that it holds its future in its own hands.' Booth's findings confirmed the possibility of continuing social progress through the incorporation of the respectable working class, but his survey shocked the middle class into a greater awareness of the size and structure of the casual labour market.[5]

According to Booth, some 30.7 per cent of London's population were in poverty or in want, a figure which could be reduced only by the forcible removal of the very poor, the 'unfit' casual labourers of Class B (7.5 per cent). By their withdrawal – Booth recommended transportation to labour colonies outside the capital – the labour market would be much improved for the 22.3 per cent 'in poverty', with increased employment for the insufficiently employed of Class C and higher wages for the regularly employed of Class D. Through drastic state intervention – 'taking charge of the lives of the incapable' – Booth proposed to isolate and discipline the residuum, a rigorous approach to an old social problem.[6]

Booth's 'State Socialism', similar in tone to the proposals of Marshall, Barnett and others, marked an important shift in attitudes to urban poverty, no longer perceived as pauperism in disguise. The characteristic traits of individual demoralization – drink, early marriage, improvidence, irreligion, idleness – were now regarded merely as symptoms of inescapable poverty, the inevitable consequence of lengthy exposure to the degrading conditions of city life, ecological conditions which threatened to emasculate the race. The new biologism, an offshoot of Social Darwinism, provided scientific verification for a comprehensive theory of hereditary urban degeneration, the consequences of which were all the more alarming as rural workers, migrants from agricultural depression, were flocking into unhealthy cities. Differential birth rates compounded the problem as the degenerate casual poor with their 'low cerebral development' had yet to emulate the middle-class practice of family limitation. No longer a revolutionary threat, the fecund, inferior residuum were a dangerous and unacceptable source of weakness in a nation which required maximum efficiency to uphold its economic, military and imperial pre-eminence at a time of increasing international rivalry. Seen in these terms, state action to eliminate the casual unfit was an urgent necessity, whether in the form of compulsory labour colonies or the 'sterilization of the failures', the eugenic approach favoured by Wells, Shaw and other Fabians.[7]

In the new pseudo-scientific discourse, social problems were neither moral nor economic in origin. It was the abundant supply of physically degenerate labourers which accounted for the prevalence of the casual labour market, a convenient rationalization as harsh and false as the old moralism. Similarly with crime, biological explanations came to the fore, embellished by theories of criminal anthropology imported from the continent. Classified as abnormal individuals, criminals were to be found in all social classes, but for Morrison, Ellis, Rylands and other criminologists the prime focus remained the working class, or rather the degenerate residuum within the urban slums.[8] Stimulated by the social crisis of the 1880s, the vogue for Social Darwinian thinking – with its drastic policy prescriptions – simply provided a new vocabulary for old attitudes and prejudices. Shortly afterwards, amid the outrage over British weakness in the Boer War, some Social Darwinians abandoned their support for social reform, now held responsible for the nation's deterioration, 'penalizing the fit for the sake of the unfit'.[9]

Away from public gaze, alternative approaches were developed in the course of the 1890s, innovation which brought a sense of context to the study of social problems. Unemployment was broken down into its component parts, with seasonality and casuality recognized as separate social phenomena.[10] Rowntree's poverty line -- meticulously calculated at 21s 8d a week for a man, wife and three children – enabled a distinction to be drawn between primary poverty, resulting from an income insufficient to provide even the bare necessities of physical well-being, and secondary poverty, following the unwise expenditure of income which, given highly disciplined budgeting, could have kept the family above the poverty line in physical terms. No less important was his concept of the poverty cycle, a mechanism which took account of changing family and domestic circumstances, the crucial variable in working-class living standards.[11]

Such advances, together with the Boer War debates and the competing claims of tariff reform, prepared the way for the Liberal welfare reforms, a legislative drive against poverty supported by independent Labour. As James Hinton notes, there was a convergence of interest between labour aristocrats, disdainful of the moral incompetents in the slums, and progressive middle-class liberals, social engineers who regarded the poor as less than responsible citizens.[12] But when reform extended beyond the 'unfit', the class contradictions of the 'Progressive Alliance' were promptly exposed. Through state-promoted welfare capitalism, new Liberals hoped to revive the ailing economic system and outmatch Chamberlain's ambitious protectionist programme of industrial regeneration, social reform and imperial economic unity. But in seeking to establish minimum standards, they took insufficient account of basic working-class attitudes – ingrained suspicion of the state and preference for voluntarism.[13] Beset with actuarial problems, friendly societies welcomed government assistance but not state control, a political intrusion inimical to the proud traditions of working-class autonomy and collective self-help. National insurance was an unhappy compromise, allowing a limited role for approved societies, but the inclusion of commercial insurance companies undermined the democratic and participatory spirit of collective mutuality.[14] Liberals were ultimately unable to retain the non-Tory working-class vote, a political commitment determined by institutional and class loyalty. Proud of their unions and friendly societies, the working class voted for the party which best respected their autonomy, their own Labour Party.[15]

Notes

Place of publication London unless otherwise stated.

Introduction

1. M. Berg, *The Age of Manufactures: Industry, innovation and work in Britain 1700–1820* (1985), and N. Crafts, *British Economic Growth during the Industrial Revolution* (Oxford, 1985) provide the best text book introductions to the new economic history of the industrial revolution. See also Raphael Samuel, 'The workshop of the world: steam power and hand technology in mid-Victorian Britain', *History Workshop Journal*, 3 (1977), 6–72.
2. Richard Price, *Labour in British Society: An interpretative history*, (1986), 1–12. Raymond Williams, *Marxism and Literature* (Oxford, 1976), ch. 9.
3. L. A. Clarkson, *Proto-Industrialization: The First Phase of Industrialization?* (1985) provides a useful introduction to this complex area.
4. Alan Fox, *History and Heritage: The social origins of the British industrial relations system* (1985), 52–4. Peter Mathias, *The First Industrial Nation. An economic history of Britain 1700–1914* (2nd edn, 1983), 31–47. For a useful introductory comparative study, see Tom Kemp, *Historical Patterns of Industrialization* (1978).
5. W. D. Rubinstein, *Men of Property. The very wealthy in Britain since the industrial revolution* (1981).
6. D. Nicholls, 'Fractions of capital: the aristocracy, the City and industry in the development of modern British capitalism', *Social History*, xiii (1988), 71–83, provides an excellent critique of Perry Anderson, 'The figures of descent', *New Left Review*, 161 (1987), 20–77. See also P. J. Cain and A. G. Hopkins, 'Gentlemanly capitalism and British expansion overseas II: new imperialism, 1850–1945', *EcHR*, 2nd series, xl (1987), 1–26; and M. J. Wiener, *English Culture and the Decline of the Industrial Spirit 1850–1980* (Penguin edn, 1985).
7. See Eric Hobsbawm's essays on 'The formation of British working-class culture' and 'The making of the working class 1870–1914', in his *Worlds of Labour: Further studies in the history of labour* (1984). Hobsbawm's starting-point, of course, is E. P. Thompson's monumental study of *The Making of the English Working Class* (Penguin edn, 1968).
8. Asa Briggs, 'The language of "class" in early nineteenth-century England', in Asa Briggs and John Saville (eds), *Essays in Labour History* (1967 edn), 43–73.
9. R. S. Neale insisted on theoretical rigour in *Class in English History 1680–1850* (Oxford, 1981), 100–19.
10. Ibid. For an introductory discussion of the issues involved here see R. J. Morris, *Class and Class Consciousness in the Industrial Revolution 1780–1850* (1979).
11. G. Claeys, 'The triumph of class-conscious reformism in British radicalism, 1790–1860', *Historical Journal*, 26 (1983), 969–85. Sociologists have carried this revisionism further, see Craig Calhoun, *The Question of Class Struggle: Social foundations of popular radicalism during the industrial revolution* (Oxford, 1982).
12. Such is the method employed in R. Glen, *Urban Workers in the Early Industrial Revolution* (1984). Glen and his supporters are taken to task in Neville Kirk's critical review 'The myth of class', *BSSLH*, 51, i (1986), 39–42. Kirk's own study of *The Growth of Working Class Reformism in Mid-Victorian England* (1985) adopts a cautious and qualified materialist approach.

13. Michael Mann, *Consciousness and Action among the Western Working Class* (1973), 13.

14. This is the range covered in David Montgomery's study of *The Fall of the House of Labor. The workplace, the state, and American labor activism, 1865–1925* (Cambridge, 1987).

15. New studies by Phil Gardner, *The Lost Elementary Schools of Victorian England* (1984) and David Green, *Working-Class Patients and the Medical Establishment: Self-help in Britain from the mid-nineteenth century to 1948* (Aldershot, 1985) have added considerably to the work of P. H. J. H. Gosden on *Self-Help: Voluntary Associations in the Nineteenth Century* (1973).

16. Ross McKibbin, 'Why was there no Marxism in Great Britain?', *English Historical Review*, xcix (1984), 306–10.

17. Gareth Stedman Jones, 'Working-class culture and working-class politics in London, 1870–1900: Notes on the remaking of a working class', in his *Languages of Class. Studies in English working class history 1832–1982* (Cambridge, 1983), 179–238.

18. Standish Meacham, *A Life Apart: The English Working Class 1890–1914* (1977), passim.

19. W. H. Sewell Jr, *Work and Revolution in France: The language of labour from the old regime to 1848* (Cambridge, 1980), 1.

20. Charles More, *Skill and the English Working Class, 1870–1914* (1980), 13–26. Royden Harrison 'Introduction' in Royden Harrison and Jonathan Zeitlin (eds), *Divisions of Labour. Skilled workers and technological change in nineteenth-century England* (Brighton, 1985), 1–18.

21. William Knox, 'Apprenticeship and de-skilling in Britain, 1850–1914', *IRSH*, xxxi (1986), 166–84.

22. Barbara Taylor, *Eve and the New Jerusalem. Socialism and Feminism in the Nineteenth Century* (1983), 110–13.

23. Elizabeth Roberts, *Women's Work 1840–1940* (1988) provides a useful introduction to the subject. See also Sally Alexander, 'Women's work in nineteenth-century London: a study of the years 1820–50', in A. Oakley and J. Mitchell (eds), *The Rights and Wrongs of Women* (1976), 59–111; Angela John (ed.), *Unequal Opportunities. Women's Employment in England 1800–1918* (Oxford, 1986); and Jane Lewis (ed.), *Labour and Love. Women's Experience of Home and Family 1850–1940* (Oxford, 1986).

24. See the collection of essays edited by Patrick Joyce on *The Historical Meanings of Work* (Cambridge, 1987). For a spirited reassessment of institutional labour history, see Jonathan Zeitlin, 'From labour history to the history of labour relations', *EcHR*, 2nd series, xl (1987), 159–84.

25. Clive Behagg, 'Secrecy, ritual and folk violence: the opacity of the workplace in the first half of the nineteenth century', in R. D. Storch (ed.), *Popular Culture and Custom in Nineteenth-Century England* (1982), 154–79.

26. Patrick Joyce, *Work, Society and Politics. The culture of the factory in later Victorian England* (1982 edn).

27. Craig Calhoun, 'Community: toward a variable conceptualization for comparative research', *Social History*, v (1980), 105–29. Michael Savage, *The Dynamics of Working-Class Politics* (Cambridge, 1987), 56–61.

28. Richard Dennis, *English Industrial Cities of the Nineteenth Century: A Social Geography* (Cambridge, 1984), chs 6–9.

29. John Foster, *Class Struggle and the Industrial Revolution. Early industrial capitalism in three English towns* (1974).

30. Michael Anderson, 'The emergence of the modern life cycle in Britain', *Social History*, x (1985), 69–87.

31. David Levine, 'Industrialization and the proletarian family in England', *Past and Present*, 107 (1985), 168–203. Wally Seccombe, 'Patriarchy stabilized: the construction of the male breadwinner wage norm in nineteenth-century Britain',

Social History, xi (1986), 53–76. The male family wage is a controversial topic among socialists and feminists, see M. Barrett and M. McIntosh, 'The "family" wage: some problems for socialists and feminists', *Capital and Class*, xi (1981), 51–72.

32. My approach is similar to that of Paul Johnson, *Saving and Spending: the working-class economy in Britain, 1870–1939* (Oxford, 1985), and 'Credit and thrift and the British working class, 1870–1939', in Jay Winter (ed.), *The Working Class in Modern British History: Essays in honour of Henry Pelling* (Cambridge, 1983), 147–70; and Melanie Tebbutt, *Making Ends Meet: Pawnbroking and Working-Class Credit* (1984). Readers who prefer a statistical approach should consult in the first instance R. Floud and D. McCloskey, *The Economic History of Britain since 1700. Volume 1: 1700–1860* (Cambridge, 1981).

33. Gareth Stedman Jones, 'Rethinking Chartism', in his *Languages of Class*. See also Noel Thompson, *The People's Science: The popular political economy of exploitation and crisis 1816–34* (Cambridge, 1984).

34. John Belchem, 'Radical language and ideology in early nineteenth-century England: The challenge of the platform', *Albion*, xx (1988), 247–59. See also Neville Kirk, 'In defence of class', *IRSH* xxxii (1987), 2–47.

PART ONE: 1750–1850

Chapter 1: The industrial revolution

1. M. Fores, 'The myth of a British industrial revolution', *History*, lxvi (1981), 181–98. Rondo Cameron, 'A new view of European industrialization', *EcHR*, 2nd series, xxxviii (1985), 1–23.

2. Crafts, 68–9.

3. Ibid., 2, 137–40 and 156. For an introduction to the debate on enclosure, see Michael Turner, *Enclosures in Britain 1750–1830* (1984), and K. D. M. Snell, *Annals of the Labouring Poor: Social Change and Agrarian England, 1660–1900* (Cambridge, 1985) ch. 4.

4. E. A. Wrigley, 'The growth of population in eighteenth-century England: a conundrum resolved', *Past and Present*, 98 (1983), 121–50, conveniently summarizes the relevant findings of E. A. Wrigley and R. S. Schofield, *The Population History of England, 1541–1871: A Reconstruction* (1981).

5. N. McKendrick, 'Home demand and economic growth: a new view of the role of women and children in the industrial revolution', in N. McKendrick (ed.), *Historical Perspectives: Studies in English Thought and Society in honour of J. H. Plumb* (1974). See also N. McKendrick, J. Brewer and J. H. Plumb, *The Birth of a Consumer Society: The Commercialization of Eighteenth-Century England* (Bloomington, 1982).

6. Crafts, ch. 7.

7. This was particularly the case in Stockport, see Glen, 38–43.

8. V. A. C. Gatrell, 'Labour, power and the size of firms in Lancashire cotton in the second quarter of the nineteenth century', *EcHR*, 2nd series, xxx (1977), 95–139.

9. Stewart A. Weaver, *John Fielden and the Politics of Popular Radicalism, 1832–1847* (Oxford, 1987), 19–24.

10. Samuel, 'Workshop of the world', 19.

11. L. D. Smith, *Carpet Weavers and Carpet Masters. The Hand Loom Carpet Weavers of Kidderminster 1780–1850* (Kidderminster, 1986), 48–51.

12. Berg, 11 and passim, for a forthright rejection of the once fashionable determinism of David Landes, *The Unbound Prometheus. Technological Change and Industrial Development in Western Europe from 1750 to the Present* (Cambridge, 1969).

13. D. Bythell, *The Handloom Weavers: A Study in the English Cotton Industry during the Industrial Revolution* (Cambridge, 1969), ch. 3.

14. Samuel, 'Workshop of the world', 45–60.

15. H. Perkin, *The Origins of Modern English Society 1780–1880* (1969), 183–95. Fox, 52–4.

16. Clive Behagg, 'Custom, class and change: the trade societies of Birmingham', *Social History*, iv (1979), 463–66.

17. David Cannadine, 'The past and the present in the English industrial revolution', *Past and Present*, 103 (1984), 131–72 traces four generations of economic historians.

18. Noel Thompson, 53–6.

Chapter 2: Living standards

1. M. V. Flinn, 'Trends in real wages, 1750–1850', *EcHR*, 2nd series, xxvii (1974), 395–411; G. N. Von Tunzelman, 'Trends in real wages, 1780–1850, revisited', *EcHR*, xxxii (1979), 33–49; P. K. O'Brien and S. L. Engerman, 'Changes in income and its distribution during the industrial revolution', in Floud and McCloskey, 164–81.

2. L. D. Schwarz, 'The standard of living in the long run: London, 1700–1860', *EcHR*, 2nd series, xxxviii (1985), 24–41.

3. P. H. Lindert and J. G. Williamson, 'English workers' living standards during the industrial revolution: a new look', *EcHR*, 2nd series, xxxvi (1983), 1–25.

4. E. H. Hunt, 'Industrialization and regional inequality: wages in Britain, 1760–1914', *Journal of Economic History*, xlvi (1986), 935–66.

5. E. H. Hunt and F. W. Botham, 'Wages in Britain during the industrial revolution', *EcHR*, 2nd series, xl (1987), 380–99.

6. P. Linebaugh, 'Labour history without the labour process: a note on John Gast and his times', *Social History*, vii (1982), 319–27, and his conference paper published in *BSSLH*, 25 (1972), 11–15.

7. Snell, ch. 4.

8. C. Fisher, 'The free miners of the Forest of Dean, 1800–41', in Royden Harrison (ed.), *Independent Collier: The Coal Miner as Archetypal Proletarian Reconsidered* (Hassocks, 1978).

9. Bob Bushaway, *By Rite: Custom, Ceremony and Community in England 1700–1880* (1982), 21–7.

10. Gail Malmgreen, *Silk Town: Industry and Culture in Macclesfield 1750–1835* (Hull, 1985), 41.

11. Clive Emsley, *Crime and Society in England, 1750–1900* (1987), 117.

12. David Philips, *Crime and Authority in Victorian England* (1977), 213.

13. Peter King, '"Stout women . . . dare to contend the right." Gleaners, farmers and the failure of legal sanctions 1750–1850', forthcoming.

14. J. Ginswick (ed.), *Labour and the Poor in England and Wales 1849–51. The Letters to 'The Morning Chronicle' from the Correspondents in the Manufacturing and Mining Districts, the Towns of Liverpool and Birmingham, and the Rural Districts* (8 vols, 1983), i, 100.

15. John Rule, *The Labouring Classes in Early Industrial England 1750–1850* (1986), ch. 4.

16. Bythell, *Handloom Weavers*, ch. 5.

17. Eric Hopkins, 'Working hours and conditions during the industrial revolution: a re-appraisal', *EcHR*, 2nd series, xxv (1982), 59.

18. *Reports from Assistant Hand-Loom Weavers' Commissioners*. Part V, (1840), 615–17.

19. John Rule, *The Experience of Labour in Eighteenth-Century Industry* (1981), ch. 3.

20. E. P. Thompson and E. Yeo (eds), *The Unknown Mayhew: Selections from 'The Morning Chronicle' 1849–50* (Penguin edn, 1973), 420–1.
21. Rule, *Experience of Labour*, 195.
22. Ibid., 195 for details of Thomas Manby Smith.
23. *Labour and the Poor*, ii, 29, 66–77. R. Colls, *The Pitmen of the Northern Coalfield. Work, culture, and protest, 1790–1850* (Manchester, 1987), 29–33, 48.
24. *Unknown Mayhew*, 81–2.
25. Pat Hudson, 'Proto-industrialization: the case of the West Riding', *History Workshop Journal*, 12 (1981), 34–61.
26. W. Cooke Taylor, *Notes of a Tour in the Manufacturing Districts of Lancashire* (1842: rpt 1968), 119.
27. *Unknown Mayhew*, 508–10.
28. J. H. Treble, *Urban Poverty in Britain 1830–1914* (1979), 72–5.
29. Rule, *Experience of Labour*, 51–2.
30. *Labour and the Poor*, i, 136.
31. David Jones, *Crime, Protest, Community and Police in Nineteenth-century Britain* (1982), 183–4.
32. R. Samuel, 'Comers and goers', in H. J. Dyos and M. Wolff (eds), *The Victorian City: Images and Realities* (1976 edn), i, 123–60.
33. Eric Hopkins, 'Working-class housing in Birmingham during the industrial revolution', *IRSH*, xxxi (1986), 92. *Unknown Mayhew*, 570.
34. Colls, 112, 134.
35. Eric Hobsbawm, 'Artisan or labour aristocrat', *EcHR*, 2nd series, xxxvii (1984), 355–72.
36. *Unknown Mayhew*, 285, 509.
37. *Labour and the Poor*, ii, 32.
38. *Black Dwarf*, 9 September 1818.
39. Rule, *Labouring Classes*, 111.
40. 'Public meeting of manufacturers and weavers, Sessions Room, Bolton, 3 March 1823', handbill in Bolton Library, reference ZZ/250.
41. *Reports from Assistant Hand-Loom Weavers Commissioners*, 530–40.
42. Ibid., 473–5, 592–8.
43. Rule, *Experience of Labour*, 142.
44. *Reports from Assistant Hand-Loom Weavers Commissioners*, 585.
45. Malmgreen, 23.
46. Joseph Lawson, *Progress in Pudsey* (Stanningley, 1887; rpt Firle, 1978), 84. Rule, *Experience of Labour*, 142.
47. 'Beauties of a cotton factory', *Poor Man's Advocate*, 4 February 1832.
48. *The Autobiography of Joseph Gutteridge*, reprinted in V. E. Chancellor (ed.), *Master and Artisan in Victorian England* (1969), 120.
49. *Labour and the Poor*, ii, 52–4.
50. J. Norris, 3 February 1819, HO 42/184 ff90–2. Mathias, 139.
51. 'An old potter' (Charles Shaw), in J. Burnett (ed.), *Useful Toil. Autobiographies of working people from the 1820s to the 1920s* (Penguin edn, 1977), 303.
52. E. P. Thompson, *Making*, 270.
53. Eric Richards, 'Women in the British economy since about 1700: an interpretation', *History*, 59 (1974), 337–57.
54. Levine, 168–76.
55. Sonya Rose, '"Gender at work": sex, class and industrial capitalism', *History Workshop Journal*, 21 (1986), 113–31.
56. Berg, 172–4.
57. Rose, 121–2.
58. P. E. H. Hair, 'The Lancashire collier girl, 1795', *Transactions of the Historic Society of Lancashire and Cheshire*, 120 (1968), 63–84.
59. Colls, chs 6 and 8.
60. *Reports from Assistant Hand-Loom Weavers Commissioners*, 369–75.

61. N. G. Osterud, 'Gender divisions and the organization of work in the Leicester hosiery industry', in John (ed.), 45–70.
62. Snell, ch.1. D. Bythell, *The Sweated Trades: Outwork in Nineteenth-century Britain* (1978), 119–23.
63. Snell, ch. 6.
64. F. Hunt, 'Opportunities lost and gained: mechanization and women's work in the London bookbinding and printing trades', in John (ed.), 71–94.
65. Seccombe, 63–5.
66. Barbara Taylor, ch.4. *Unknown Mayhew*, 220–3.
67. J. J. Bezer, 'The autobiography of one of the Chartist rebels', reprinted in D. Vincent (ed.), *Testaments of Radicalism: Memoirs of Working-Class Politicians* (1977), 176.
68. Peter Gaskell, *Artisans and Machinery: The Moral and Physical Condition of the Manufacturing Population* (1836; rpt 1968), ch. 6. *Labour and the Poor*, i, 47–8.
69. M. Anderson, *Family Structure in Nineteenth-century Lancashire* (Cambridge, 1971), 71–4.
70. Richards, 348.
71. Snell, 64–5.
72. Lindert and Williamson, 19. See also E. H. Hunt, *British Labour History 1850–1914* (1981), ch.3; and A. J. Taylor (ed.), *The Standard of Living in Britain in the Industrial Revolution* (1975), xxvii.
73. 'The autobiography of Thomas Wood', reprinted in Burnett (ed.), 304–12. See also the excellent chapter on 'The family economy', in D. Vincent, *Bread, Knowledge and Freedom: A Study of Nineteenth-century Working Class Autobiography* (1982), 62–86.
74. *Labour and the Poor*, i, 105.
75. Snell, ch. 7.
76. R. A. Sykes, 'Popular politics and trade unionism in south-east Lancashire, 1829–42', unpublished PhD thesis, Manchester University, 1982, 39–40.
77. *Labour and the Poor*, ii, 62–3.
78. Eric Hobsbawm, 'The tramping artisan', in his *Labouring Men. Studies in the History of Labour* (1968), 34–63.
79. M. Anderson, *Family Structure*, 152–60.
80. Snell, ch. 7.
81. *Labour and the Poor*, i, 79.
82. B. Disraeli, *Sybil. Or the Two Nations* (1845), Book 3, ch.3.
83. J. L. and B. Hammond, *The Town Labourer* (1978 edn), 46–8. Bythell, *Sweated Trades*, 125–6.
84. *Labour and the Poor*, ii, 105.
85. Rule, *Labouring Classes*, 110.
86. Gaskell, 119–21. F. Engels, *The Conditions of the Working Class in England* (1892; Panther edn, 1969), 100–2.
87. *Labour and the Poor*, i, 80.
88. Tebbutt, 11; Meacham, 75; and Hunt, *British Labour History*, 89.
89. M. Anderson, *Family Structure*, ch.5; Foster, ch.4; and J. Burnett, *A Social History of Housing 1815–1985* (2nd edn, 1986), 6.
90. Gaskell, 300–9; Engels, 210–11. For a contrasting view of the country mills, see Cooke Taylor, 25, 138–41 and 164.
91. *Labour and the Poor*, i, 189.
92. Ibid., i, 35, and 190.
93. Colls, 262–6.
94. *Labour and the Poor*, ii, 95.
95. Hopkins, 'Working-class housing in Birmingham', 85, 90.
96. E. Yeo, 'Some practices and problems of Chartist democracy', in J. Epstein and D. Thompson (eds), *The Chartist Experience: Studies in Working-Class Radicalism and Culture, 1830–1860* (1982), 368.

97. *Labour and the Poor*, i, 90, 95.
98. D. Jones, *Crime*, 157.
99. Malmgreen, 83. 'Good Mrs Brown' practises her trade in *Dombey and Son*.
100. Tebbutt, chs. 2 and 3. V. Neuberg (ed.), *Henry Mayhew: London Labour and the London Poor* (1985), 494–5.
101. Tebbutt, 59–64.
102. See the evidence of W. Spicer, Birmingham pawnbroker, in T. Clutton Salt, 10 July 1819, HO 42/189 ff. 171–9.
103. M. E. Rose, *The Relief of Poverty 1834–1914* (1972), 29.
104. M. Anderson, *Family Structure*, ch.8. Vincent, 66.
105. *Labour and the Poor*, ii, 62–3. Malmgreen, 74–5.
106. See W. T. Greg's review of *Mary Barton* in *Edinburgh Review*, lxxxix (1849), 402–35. James Winter, 'Widowed mothers and mutual aid in early Victorian Britain', *Journal of Social History*, xvii (1983–4), 115–16.
107. J. Mokyr and N. E. Savin, 'Stagflation in historical perspective: the Napoleonic wars revisited', in P. Uselding (ed.), *Research in Economic History*, 1 (1976).
108. Clive Emsley, *British Society and the French Wars 1793–1815* (1979), ch.8.
109. J. D. Post, *The Last Great Subsistence Crisis in the Western World* (Baltimore, 1977), xii–iii, 14, 16, 27 and 84–5.
110. Eric Hobsbawm and George Rudé, *Captain Swing* (Penguin edn, 1973), chs 2–4.
111. Glen, 272–3.
112. R. G. Kirby and A. E. Musson, *The Voice of the People: John Doherty, 1798–1854* (Manchester, 1975), 41–4.
113. Bythell, *Handloom Weavers*, 104–11.
114. *Leeds Patriot*, 19 December 1829.
115. For the full report see the handbill in Bolton Library, reference ZZ/250/3. Gaskell, 382–3 provides a summary. The criticism of the figures by Bythell, *Handloom Weavers*, 126–9 has been ably refuted by Weaver, 66–7 and 120.
116. John Burnett, *Plenty and Want. A social history of diet in England from 1815 to the present day* (1979 edn), 71–3.
117. Eric Hobsbawm, 'The British standard of living 1790–1850', in his *Labouring Men*, 74–7.
118. *Report of the Committee of Metropolitan Trades* (1848), 1.
119. Eric Hobsbawm, 'Economic fluctuations and some social movements since 1800', in his *Labouring Men*, 129.
120. Bristol Record Office: Letters and Miscellaneous Papers, box 1816.
121. Philips, 145–6 and 163–4.
122. Emsley, *Crime*, 32–35 and 245.

Chapter 3: Housing

1. M. J. Daunton, 'Public Place and Private Space: The Victorian City and the Working-Class Household', in D. Fraser and A. Sutcliffe (eds), *The Pursuit of Urban History* (1983), 212–33.
2. D. Cannadine, 'Victorian cities: how different?', *Social History*, ii (1977), 457–82.
3. Engels, 78–80. Thomas Carlyle, *Chartism* (1840: rpt Penguin edn, 1971), 228.
4. Dennis, 73–7.
5. *Labour and the Poor*, ii, 141.
6. Hopkins, 'Working-class housing in Birmingham', 82. Gutteridge, 83.
7. Dennis, 76–7.
8. A. Sutcliffe, 'Working-class housing in nineteenth-century Britain: a review of recent research', *B.SLH*, 24 (1972), 40–50.
9. Burnett, *Social History of Housing*, ch.2. Disraeli, *Sybil*, Book 3, ch.2.
10. Anderson, *Family Structure*, 40–2.
11. R. Lawton, 'Population mobility and urbanization: the nineteenth-century British

experience', paper presented to the International Seminar on Comparative Urban Population Development 1750–1920, held at the University of Liverpool, September 1984.

12. Samuel, 'Comers and goers', 126–9.
13. *Labour and the Poor*, i, 74–7.
14. Malmgreen, 86–7.
15. See the essays on Birmingham, Nottingham and Leeds, in S. D. Chapman (ed.), *The History of Working-Class Housing: A Symposium* (Newton Abbot, 1971).
16. Burnett, *Social History of Housing*, 70–9.
17. Glen, 25–6.
18. M. W. Beresford, 'The back-to-back house in Leeds, 1787–1937', in Chapman (ed.), 93–132.
19. J. H. Treble, 'Liverpool working-class housing, 1801–51' in ibid., 165–220.
20. Burnett, *Social History of Housing*, 64–9.
21. Rule, *Labouring Classes*, 95.
22. Hopkins, 'Working-class housing in Birmingham', 86.
23. Glen, 28.
24. *Labour and the Poor*, ii, 38.
25. Dennis, 174–85.
26. *Labour and the Poor*, ii, 38–9.
27. Dennis, 176.
28. Calhoun, *The Question of Class Struggle*, ix–xiv.
29. Lawson, passim.
30. *Labour and the Poor*, i, 87.

Chapter 4: Work

1. E. P. Thompson, 'Time, work-discipline, and industrial capitalism', *Past and Present*, 38 (1967), 56–97. Savage, ch.2.
2. For a recent discussion of these issues, see Joyce (ed.), *Historical Meanings of Work*.
3. J. Breuilly, 'Artisan economy, artisan politics, artisan ideology: the artisan contribution to the nineteenth-century European labour movement', in Clive Emsley and James Walvin, *Artisans, Peasants and Proletarians 1760–1860: Essays presented to Gwyn A. Williams* (1985), 198–9.
4. Behagg, 'Secrecy, ritual and folk violence', and 'Violence and ceremonial forms in the workplace organizations of the 1830s', *BSSLH*, 49 (1984), 14–15.
5. Richard Price, 'The labour process and labour history', *Social History*, viii (1983), 57–75. J. E. Cronin, *Industrial Conflict in Modern Britain* (1979), 38–9.
6. Richard Price, *Masters, Union and Men. Work control in building and the rise of labour 1830–1914* (Cambridge, 1980), 32–9.
7. John Fielden, *The Curse of the Factory System* (1836: rpt 1969), 6–8. *A Memoir of Robert Blincoe* (Manchester, 1832), and *Poor Man's Advocate*, 9 June 1832.
8. Eric Hobsbawm, 'Custom, wages and work-load', in his *Labouring Men*, 352–6.
9. *Poor Man's Advocate*, 'Introduction', and 21 Jan.–4 Feb. 1832.
10. Andrew Ure, *Philosophy of Manufactures*, quoted in E. P. Thompson, *Making*, 395.
11. Gaskell, ch. 4.
12. *Labour and the Poor*, i, 29.
13. For a convenient summary of *Social Change in the Industrial Revolution*, see N. J. Smelser, 'Sociological history: the industrial revolution and the British working-class family', in M. W. Flinn and T. C. Smout, *Essays in Social History* (Oxford, 1974), 22–38.
14. M. Anderson, 'Sociological history and the working-class family: Smelser revisited', *Social History*, i (1976), 317–34.
15. Joyce, *Work, Society and Politics*, chs 2 and 3.

16. M. Ignatieff, 'State, civil society and total institutions: a critique of recent social histories of punishment', in S. Cohen and A. Scull, *Social Control and the State* (Oxford, 1983), 96–7.
17. *Labour and the Poor*, i, 14–15.
18. Joyce (ed.), *Historical Meanings of Work*, 21.
19. J. Burnett, 'The autobiography of work', paper presented to the Centre for the History of Social Policies, University of Liverpool, April 1988.

Chapter 5: Popular culture

1. R. W. Malcolmson, *Popular Recreations in English Society 1700–1850* (Cambridge, 1973); Hugh Cunningham, *Leisure in the Industrial Revolution c.1780–c.1880* (1980); and J. M. Golby and A. W. Purdue, *The Civilization of the Crowd: Popular Culture in England 1750–1900* (1984).
2. Brian Harrison, *Drink and the Victorians. The Temperance Question in England 1815–1872* (1971).
3. Gutteridge, 98. Charles Kingsley, *Alton Locke, Tailor and Poet* (World's Classics edn, 1983), 24.
4. J. F. C. Harrison, *The Early Victorians 1832–1851* (1973), 96–8.
5. W. Lovett, *Life and Struggles of William Lovett in his Pursuit of Bread, Knowledge and Freedom* (1876; rpt Fitzroy edn, 1967), 24–6.
6. Rule, 'Methodism, popular beliefs and village culture', in Storch (ed.), 55.
7. Lawson, 84. J. F. C. Harrison, 98.
8. E. P. Thompson, *The Making*, 157.
9. Lawson, 83–4.
10. D. A. Reid, 'The decline of Saint Monday 1766–1876', *Past and Present*, 71 (1976), 76–101.
11. Brian Harrison, 'Religion and recreation in nineteenth-century England', *Past and Present*, 38 (1967), 98–125.
12. Golby and Purdue, 76–7.
13. Rule, 'Methodism', 53, 59.
14. Mark Harrison, 'The ordering of the urban environment: time, work and the occurrence of crowds 1790–1835', *Past and Present*, 110 (1986), 159–67.
15. Cunningham, ch.3; Golby and Purdue, ch. 4.
16. This account of the holiday calendar in Middleton is based on S. Bamford, *Early Days* (1893 edn), chs 14 and 15.
17. Storch (ed.), 2.
18. A . Delves, 'Popular recreation and social conflict in Derby, 1800–1850', in E. and S. Yeo (eds), *Popular Culture and Class Conflict 1590–1914* (Brighton, 1981), 89–127.
19. A. Howkins, 'The taming of Whitsun: the changing face of a nineteenth-century rural holiday', in ibid., 187–208.
20. J. K. Walton and R. Poole, 'The Lancashire wakes in the nineteenth century', in Storch (ed.), 100–24.
21. Malcolmson, 127–35.
22. Peter Bailey, *Leisure and Class in Victorian England: Rational recreation and the contest for control, 1830–85* (1978), 15.
23. Lawson, 31–3.
24. Bailey, 20. See also Hugh Cunningham, 'The metropolitan fairs: a case study in the social control of leisure', in A. P. Donajgrodski (ed.), *Social Control in Nineteenth-Century Britain* (1977), 163–84.
25. Golby and Purdue, 68–9; Cunningham, 30–5.
26. Golby and Purdue, 69–72. Louis James, 'Taking melodrama seriously: theatre and nineteenth-century studies', *History Workshop Journal*, 3 (1977), 151–8.
27. John Belchem, *'Orator' Hunt: Henry Hunt and English Working-Class Radicalism* (Oxford, 1985), 94.

28. J. A. Hone, *For the Cause of Truth: Radicalism in London 1796–1821* (Oxford, 1982), 183–4.
29. Kingsley, *Alton Locke*, 24, 108.
30. Golby and Purdue, 73–4.
31. *Labour and the Poor*, i, 80–1.
32. Louis James, *Fiction for the Working Man 1830–50* (Penguin edn, 1974), 176–7.
33. R. Colls, *The Collier's Rant: Song and Culture in the Industrial Village* (1977), 51–6.
34. *Labour and the Poor*, i, 83.
35. Bailey, 16–7.
36. R. D. Storch, 'The plague of the blue locusts: police reform and popular resistance in northern England, 1840–57', *IRSH*, xx (1975), 61–90.
37. Golby and Purdue, 150–6.
38. Cunningham, 88.
39. Ibid., 89–105.
40. James, *Fiction*, chs 2–4; Thomas Frost, *Forty Years' Recollections: literary and political* (1880), 85–9; *Labour and the Poor*, i, 61–3.
41. G. Himmelfarb, *The Idea of Poverty. England in the Early Industrial Age* (1984), chs 17 and 18. Engels, 142.
42. Raymond Williams, *The Long Revolution* (Penguin edn, 1965), 72–4.
43. Joel Wiener, *Radicalism and Freethought in Nineteenth-Century Britain: The Life of Richard Carlile* (Westport, 1983), 55–75.
44. *Lion*, 24 July 1829.
45. Belchem, *'Orator' Hunt*, 151–7.
46. T. Cooper, *The Life of Thomas Cooper* (1872; rpt Leicester, 1971), 59.
47. J. F. C. Harrison, *The Second Coming. Popular Millenarianism 1780–1850* (1979), 229–30.
48. Brian Harrison *Drink*, 107–78, 330.
49. A. D. Gilbert, *Religion and Society in Industrial England. Church, Chapel and Social Change, 1740–1914* (1976), 83–93.
50. D. Hempton, *Methodism and Politics in British Society 1750–1850* (1987 edn), 214–15.
51. Colls, *Pitmen*, 189–202.
52. Colls, *Collier's Rant*, 77.
53. Colls, *Pitmen*, 162–76.
54. Malmgreen, 154–9.
55. Rule, 'Methodism'.
56. Hempton, 28–9.
57. Malmgreen, ch.5, cuts a clear path through the controversy over Methodist revivalism.
58. Golby and Purdue, 98.
59. H. McLeod, *Religion and the Working Class in Nineteenth-Century Britain* (1984), 63–4; J. Obelkevich, *Religion and Rural Society: South Lindsey, 1825–75* (Oxford, 1976), 308–17.

Chapter 6: Popular radicalism

1. R. J. Holton, 'The crowd in history: some problems of theory and method', *Social History*, iii, (1978), 219–33.
2. Linda Colley, 'The Apotheosis of George III: loyalty, royalty and the British nation 1760–1820', *Past and Present*, 102 (1984), 94–129; and 'Whose nation? Class and national consciousness in Britain 1750–1830', *Past and Present*, 113 (1986), 97–117.
3. E. P. Thompson, 'The moral economy of the English crowd in the eighteenth century', *Past and Present*, 50 (1971), 76–136; and 'Eighteenth-century English society: class struggle without class?', *Social History*, iii (1978), 133–65.

4. J. Stevenson, *Popular Disturbances in England 1700–1870* (1979), ch.5. J. Bohstedt, *Riots and Community Politics in England and Wales 1790–1810* (1983), 11–22, 202–23.

5. D. E. Williams, 'Morals, markets and the English crowd in 1766', *Past and Present*, 104 (1984), 56–73. R. B. Rose, 'Eighteenth-century price riots and public policy in England', *IRSH*, vi (1961), 277–92.

6. Emsley, *British Society and the French Wars*, 42–3.

7. Roger Wells, 'The revolt of the south-west, 1800–01; a study in English popular protest', *Social History*, ii (1977), 713–44; and *Insurrection. The British Experience 1795–1803* (Gloucester, 1983), 259–60.

8. Alan Booth, 'Food riots in the north-west of England 1790–1801', *Past and Present*, lxxvii (1977), 84–107.

9. J. Stevenson, 'Food riots in England, 1792–1818', in J. Stevenson and R. Quinault (eds), *Popular Protest and Public Order. Six Studies in British History* (1974), 33–74.

10. C. R. Dobson, *Masters and Journeymen. A Prehistory of Industrial Relations 1717–1800* (1980), 19.

11. Eric Hobsbawm, 'The machine breakers', in his *Labouring Men*, 5–22. See also Rule, *Experience of Labour*, chs 6–8.

12. 'The rope maker's resolution, or the devil's downfall' (n.d.), Old Street Ballads, Liverpool City Library.

13. Dobson, ch. 4.

14. Rule, *Experience of Labour*, 182–3.

15. J. Smail, 'New languages for labour and capital: the transformation of discourse in the early years of the Industrial Revolution', *Social History*, xii (1987), 49–71.

16. A. Randall, 'The shearmen and the Wiltshire outrages of 1802: trade unionism and industrial violence', *Social History*, vii (1982), 283–304.

17. J. L. and B. Hammond, *The Skilled Labourer* (1919; rpt 1979), 49–65.

18. J. C. F. Barnes, 'The trade union and radical activities of the Carlisle handloom weavers', *Transactions of the Cumberland and Westmorland Antiquarian and Archaeological Society*, new series, lxxviii (1978), 149–61. A. B. Richmond, *Narrative of the Condition of the Manufacturing Population and the Proceedings of Government which lead to the State Trials in Scotland* (1824); rpt 1971), 6–41.

19. For an introduction to the controversial historiography of Luddism, see John Dinwiddy, 'Luddism and politics in the northern counties', *Social History*, iv (1979), 33–63. Although not siding with E. P. Thompson, *The Making*, 569–659, Dinwiddy rejects the 'compartmental' approach of M. I. Thomis, *The Luddites: Machine-Breaking in Regency England* (Newton Abbot, 1970).

20. Dinwiddy, 51–6.

21. Ibid., 46–51.

22. Glen, ch. 8.

23. F. O. Darvall, *Popular Disturbances and Public Order in Regency England* (Oxford, 1934), 1.

24. Eric Hobsbawm, 'Artisan or labour aristocrat?', 357; Rule, *Labouring Classes*, 278–9.

25. G. Rudé, 'Collusion and convergence in eighteenth-century English political action', in his *Paris and London in the Eighteenth Century. Studies in Popular Protest* (1970), 319–40.

26. G. Rudé, *Wilkes and Liberty* (Oxford, 1962); J. Brewer, *Party Ideology and Popular Politics at the Accession of George III* (Cambridge, 1976), ch. 9; W. J. Shelton, *English Hunger and Industrial Disorders. A study of social conflict during the first decade of George III's reign* (Toronto, 1973), 155–203; and E. C. Black, *The Association. British extraparliamentary political organization, 1769–1793* (Harvard, 1963).

27. Rudé, 'The Gordon Riots: a study of the rioters and their victims', in his *Paris and London*, 268–92.

28. R. B. Rose, 'The Priestley riots of 1791', *Past and Present*, 18 (1960), 68–88; Stevenson, *Popular Disturbances*, 137–42.
29. Alan Booth, 'Popular loyalism and public violence in the north-west of England, 1790–1800', *Social History*, viii (1983), 295–314.
30. J. Stevenson, 'The London "crimp" riots of 1794', *IRSH*, xvi (1971), 40–55.
31. E. P. Thompson, *The Making*, 145–8.
32. Olivia Smith, *The Politics of Language 1791–1819* (Oxford, 1984), 36.
33. H. T. Dickinson, *Liberty and Property: political ideology in eighteenth-century Britain* (1977), ch. 7.
34. A. Goodwin, *The Friends of Liberty: The English Democratic Movement in the Age of the French Revolution* (1979), chs 6 and 7. Gwyn Williams, *Artisans and Sans-Culottes. Popular Movements in France and Britain during the French Revolution* (1968), 13–18.
35. H. T. Dickinson, *British Radicalism and the French Revolution 1789–1815* (Oxford, 1985), 10–13.
36. Ibid., 25–36.
37. John Belchem, 'Republicanism, popular constitutionalism and the radical platform in early nineteenth-century England', *Social History*, vi (1981), 2–3, 6–12.
38. *Memoir of Thomas Hardy*, reprinted in Vincent (ed.), 51.
39. Clive Emsley, 'Repression, "terror" and the rule of law in England during the decade of the French Revolution', *English Historical Review*, c (1985), 801–25.
40. Goodwin, ch. 10.
41. Hone, 117–35.
42. E. P. Thompson, *The Making*, 515–42.
43. Clive Emsley, 'The Home Office and its sources of information and investigation', *English Historical Review*, xciv (1979), 532–61; Wells, *Insurrection*, ch. 2.
44. Ibid., ch. 5.
45. Dickinson, *British Radicalism*, 43–54.
46. Foster, 38.
47. M. Elliott, 'The "Despard Conspiracy" reconsidered', *Past and Present*, 75 (1977), 46–61.
48. J. L. Baxter and F. K. Donnelly, 'Sheffield and the English revolutionary tradition 1791–1820', *IRSH*, xx (1975), 398–423.
49. A. D. Harvey, *Britain in the Early Nineteenth Century* (1978), 245–6.
50. John Dinwiddy, 'Sir Francis Burdett and Burdettite radicalism', *History*, lxv (1980), 17–31. Belchem, *'Orator' Hunt*, 24–41.
51. G. Spater, *William Cobbett: The Poor Man's Friend* (2 vols, Cambridge, 1982), ii, 314–16.
52. H. Hunt, *Memoirs of Henry Hunt, Esq* (3 vols, 1820–2), ii, 75.
53. Belchem, *'Orator' Hunt*, 44–54.
54. Iain McCalman, *Radical Underworld: Prophets, Revolutionaries and Pornographers in London, 1795–1840* (Cambridge, 1988), 97–112.
55. Belchem, *'Orator' Hunt*, 54–70. McCalman, *Underworld*, 113–27.
56. Emsley, *Crime*, 28–9.
57. Belchem, *'Orator' Hunt*, 65–7.
58. Ibid., 71–4.
59. Ibid., 74–5.
60. J. Stevens, *England's Last Revolution: Pentrich 1817* (Buxton, 1977).
61. E. P. Thompson, *The Making*, 711–33. M. I. Thomis and P. Holt, *Threats of Revolution in Britain 1789–1848* (1977), 44–61.
62. *Journals of the House of Commons*, lxxiii (1818), Appendix, 778.
63. For a critical analysis of the pendulum theory, see A. E. Musson, *British Trade Unions 1800–1875* (1972).
64. Kirby and Musson, 18–28.
65. I. Prothero, *Artisans and Politics in early Nineteenth-century London: John Gast and his times* (1981 edn), 99–103.

66. Belchem, 'Orator' Hunt, 86–90.
67. B's report, enclosed in Fletcher, 11 February, and Norris, 3 February 1819, HO 42/184.
68. Nottingham posting-bill, enclosed in Enfield, 2 May 1819, HO 42/187.
69. Belchem, 'Orator' Hunt, 96–9.
70. 'Ode', *Manchester Observer*, 9 January 1819.
71. Resolution at Leeds meeting, reported in *Black Dwarf*, 28 July 1819.
72. Belchem, 'Orator' Hunt, 107–9.
73. Ibid., 109–10.
74. P. Pickering, 'Class without words: symbolic communication in the Chartist movement', *Past and Present*, 112 (1986), 144–62.
75. Belchem, 'Republicanism', 9, and 'Orator' Hunt, 112. See also James Epstein's forthcoming paper on 'Understanding the Cap of Liberty: symbolic practice and social conflict in early nineteenth-century England'.
76. See the intercepted correspondence between Hunt and Joseph Johnson in HO 42/189–91.
77. Norris's letters, 14–31 July 1819, HO 42/188–9.
78. D. Read, *Peterloo: The 'Massacre' and its Background* (Manchester, 1958) remains the best study.
79. For the classification of political violence, see T. R. Gurr, *Why Men Rebel* (Princeton, 1970), 9–13.
80. Belchem, 'Radical language', 257–8.
81. Belchem, 'Orator' Hunt, 112–24.
82. J. Stanhope, *The Cato Street Conspiracy* (1962).
83. Birmingham posting-bill, enclosed in Deputy Postmaster, 14 December 1819, HO 42/201.
84. R. Sykes, 'Physical force chartism: the cotton district and the Chartist crisis of 1839', *IRSH*, xxx (1985), 207–36.
85. P. B. Ellis and S. M. A'Ghobhainn, *The Scottish Insurrection of 1820* (1970).
86. F. K. Donnelly, 'The general rising of 1820: a study of social conflict in the industrial revolution', unpublished PhD thesis, University of Sheffield, 1975.
87. Belchem, 'Orator' Hunt, 131–2.
88. Ibid., 145–8.
89. Iain McCalman, 'Unrespectable radicalism: infidels and pornography in early nineteenth-century London', *Past and Present*, 104 (1984), 74–110. T. W. Laquer, 'The Queen Caroline Affair: politics as art in the reign of George IV', *Journal of Modern History*, 54 (1982), 417–66.
90. Prothero, *Artisans and Politics*, 141–2.
91. Quoted in Colley, 'The apotheosis of George III', 124.
92. K. Moore, '"This Whig and Tory-ridden town": popular politics in Liverpool, 1815–50', unpublished M.Phil thesis, University of Liverpool, 1988, 73.
93. Prothero, *Artisans and Politics*, 147–55.
94. Belchem, 'Orator' Hunt, 151–7.
95. Joel Wiener, ch.5.
96. McCalman, 'Unrespectable radicalism', 103.
97. Iain McCalman, 'Females, feminism and free love in an early nineteenth-century radical movement', *Labour History*, 38 (1980), 1–25.
98. Glen, 264–8. For an excellent analysis of the social composition of the zetetic movement, see Iain McCalman, 'Popular radicalism and freethought in early nineteenth-century England', unpublished MA thesis, Australian National University, 1977, chs 3 and 4.
99. *Lion*, 9–23 October 1829. Belchem, 'Orator' Hunt, 154–5, 197–8; and E. P. Thompson, *The Making*, 838–44.
100. Ibid., 845–51.
101. John Dinwiddy, *From Luddism to the Reform Bill. Reform in England 1810–1832* (Oxford, 1986), 13–18, 43–4.

102. Prothero, *Artisans and Politics*, chs 9 and 10.
103. For the importance of this distinction, see Noel Thompson, ch 4.
104. Thomas Hodgskin, *Labour Defended against the Claims of Capital* (1825; rpt 1922), 71–2.
105. Noel Thompson, chs 5–8. Stedman Jones, 'Rethinking Chartism', 113–46.
106. Noel Thompson, 131–5. See also J. F. C. Harrison, *Robert Owen and the Owenites in Britain and America: the Quest for the New Moral World* (1969), 63–78.
107. Barbara Taylor, ix–xviii and passim.
108. Epstein, 'Understanding the Cap of Liberty'; and Dorothy Thompson, 'Women and nineteenth-century radical politics: a lost dimension', in Oakley and Mitchell (eds), 112–38.
109. Prothero, *Artisans and Politics*, 239–64.
110. *Poor Man's Guardian*, 21 June 1834.
111. John Belchem, 'The politics of Chartism', *History Sixth*, 1 (1987), 16–19.
112. Asa Briggs, 'The background of the parliamentary reform movement in three English cities (1830–2)', *Cambridge Historical Journal*, x (1950–2), 293–7.
113. Belchem, *'Orator' Hunt*, 194–201.
114. Ibid., 189, 198. Ruth Richardson, *Death, Dissection and the Destitute* (1987).
115. John Belchem, 'English working-class radicalism and the Irish, 1815–50' in R. Swift and S. Gilley (eds), *The Irish in the Victorian City* (1985).
116. John Cannon, *Parliamentary Reform 1640–1832* (Cambridge, 1973), 191–203.
117. Belchem, *'Orator' Hunt*, 221–2.
118. Thomis and Holt, 85–99. Stevenson, *Popular Disturbances*, 218–27.
119. D. Fraser, 'The agitation for parliamentary reform', in J. T. Ward (ed.), *Popular Movements c.1830–1850* (1970), 31–53.
120. Clive Behagg, 'Custom, class and change: the trade societies of Birmingham', *Social History*, iv (1979), 455–80; and 'Myths of cohesion: capital and compromise in the historiography of nineteenth-century Birmingham', *Social History*, xi (1986), 375–84.
121. Huntite song, in *Northern Star* 10 November 1838, quoted in Sykes, 'Popular politics', 397–8.
122. Belchem, *'Orator' Hunt*, 226–30.
123. Ibid., 241–55.
124. Prothero, *Artisans and Politics*, 268–92. D. J. Rowe (ed.), *London Radicalism 1830–1843. A Selection from the Papers of Francis Place* (1970) contains a useful selection of documents on both these societies.
125. Clive Behagg, 'An alliance with the middle class: the Birmingham Political Union and early Chartism', in Epstein and Thompson (eds), 63–4. H. Hunt, *Lecture on the Conduct of the Whigs to the Working Classes* (1832).
126. Prothero, *Artisans and Politics*, 293–6; and 'William Benbow and the concept of the "General Strike"', *Past and Present*, 63 (1974), 135–41.
127. Belchem, *'Orator' Hunt*, 262.
128. Ibid., 274–5 – the letter was printed in *Poor Man's Guardian*, 26 April 1834.
129. Kirby and Musson, chs 4 and 5.
130. Ibid., chs 6–8. Robert Sykes, 'General unionism, class and politics: the cotton district, 1829–34', *BSSLH*, 49 (1984), 20–1.
131. Price, *Masters, Union and Men*, 34–6. Rule, *Labouring Classes*, 294–6.
132. J. F. C. Harrison, *Robert Owen*, 197–216. See the extracts from *The Pioneer* in G. D. H. Cole and A. W. Filson (eds), *British Working-Class Movements: Select Documents 1789–1875* (1951), 272–5.
133. L. D. Smith, ch. 3.
134. W. H. Oliver, 'The Consolidated Trades' Union of 1834', *EcHR*, 2nd series, xvii (1964), 77–95. Prothero, *Artisans and Politics*, 302–3.
135. T. M. Parssinnen and I. J. Prothero, 'The London tailors' strike of 1834 and

the collapse of the Grand National Consolidated Trades' Union: a police spy's report', *IRSH*, xxii (1977), 65–107. Barbara Taylor, 114–16.

136. Rule, *Labouring Classes*, 303–07. J. F. C. Harrison, 'Owenism and the unions', *BSSLH*, 49 (1984), 21–2.

137. J. F. C. Harrison, *Robert Owen*, 216–32. Eileen Yeo, 'Robert Owen and radical culture', in S. Pollard and J. Salt (eds), *Robert Owen. Prophet of the Poor* (1971), 84–114. E. Royle, *Victorian Infidels. The Origins of the British Secularist Movement 1791–1766* (Manchester, 1974), 47–101.

138. Behagg, 'Secrecy, ritual and folk violence'.

139. R. Fyson, 'Potters Unions, 1825–1837', *BSSLH*, 49 (1984), 19–20.

140. Robert Sykes, 'Early Chartism and trade unionism in south-east Lancashire', in Epstein and Thompson (eds), 156–8.

141. *Destructive*, 7 June 1834. P. Hollis, *The Pauper Press. A Study in Working-Class Radicalism of the 1830s* (Oxford, 1970), ch. 1. Joel Wiener, *The War of the Unstamped. The Movement to Repeal the British Newspaper Tax, 1830–1836* (Ithaca, 1969), chs 2, 4 and 5.

142. Ibid., 264–77. Hollis, 294–306.

143. *Poor Man's Guardian*, 14 January 1832.

144. Dorothy Thompson, *The Chartists* (1984), 37–42.

145. James Epstein, *The Lion of Freedom: Feargus O'Connor and the Chartist Movement, 1832–1842* (1982), ch. 2.

146. Ibid., 24–59. G. Claeys, 'A utopian Tory revolutionary at Cambridge: the political ideas and schemes of James Bernard, 1834–1839', *Historical Journal*, xxv (1982), 583–603.

147. *Poor Man's Advocate*, 10 March 1832.

148. Sykes, 'Popular politics', 425–70.

149. 'Yorkshire slavery', quoted in C. Driver, *Tory Radical. The Life of Richard Oastler* (New York, 1946), 43.

150. U. Henriques, *Before the Welfare State. Social Administration in early Industrial Britain* (1979), ch. 4.

151. Kirby and Musson, 274–302. Weaver, 81–112.

152. See the extract from *The Law or the Needle* reprinted in P. Hollis (ed.), *Class and Conflict in Nineteenth-Century England 1815–1850* (1973), 203–4.

153. See the extracts of speeches by Stephens in ibid., 208–10, and in Cole and Filson (eds), 334.

154. Sykes, 'Popular politics', 462–4 ably refutes the traditional view of Stephens, as portrayed by J. T. Ward, 'Revolutionary Tory: the life of Joseph Rayner Stephens of Ashton-under-Lyne, 1805–1879', *Transactions of the Lancashire and Cheshire Antiquarian Society*, lxviii (1958), 93–116.

155. *Northern Star*, 23 June 1838, quoted in Epstein, *Lion of Freedom*, 97.

156. Dorothy Thompson, *The Chartists*, 58–9.

157. Carlos Flick, *The Birmingham Political Union and the Movements for Reform in Britain 1830–1839* (Folkestone, 1978), ch. 7.

158. Dorothy Thompson, *The Chartists*, 62–5. See also T. M. Parssinnen, 'Association, convention and anti-parliament in British radical politics, 1771–1848', *English Historical Review*, lxxxviii (1973), 504–33.

159. Epstein, *Lion of Freedom*, 101–08.

160. Dorothy Thompson, *The Chartists*, 60–1.

161. I. Prothero, 'Chartism in London', *Past and Present*, 44 (1967), 100–1.

162. Sykes, 'Early Chartism and trade unionism', 159–62.

163. Dorothy Thompson, *The Chartists*, ch.6.

164. Epstein, *Lion of Freedom*, chs 3 and 4.

165. Sykes, 'Physical force Chartism', 210.

166. B. Harrison and P. Hollis (eds), *Robert Lowery: Radical and Chartist* (1979), 112.

167. T. M. Kemnitz and F. Jacques, 'J. R. Stephens and the Chartist Movement', *IRSH*, xix (1974), 211–27.

168. T. M. Kemnitz, 'Approaches to the Chartist Movement: Feargus O'Connor and Chartist strategy', *Albion*, v (1973), 67–73.

169. T. M. Kemnitz, 'The Chartist convention of 1839', *Albion*, x (1978), 152–70. For an unduly critical assessment, see K. Judge, 'Early Chartist organization and the convention of 1839', *IRSH*, xx (1975), 370–97.

170. J. Bennett, 'The London Democratic Association 1837–41: a study in London radicalism', in Epstein and Thompson (eds), 87–119.

171. Epstein, *Lion of Freedom*, 138–58.

172. Ibid., 164–70. Behagg, 'An alliance with the middle class', 80–1.

173. Kemnitz, 'Approaches to the Chartist Movement'.

174. Epstein, *Lion of Freedom*, 174–81.

175. Sykes, 'Physical force Chartism', 222–36.

176. Dorothy Thompson, *The Chartists*, 78–9. A. J. Peacock, *Bradford Chartism* (York, 1969), 28–34.

177. David Jones, *The Last Rising: The Newport Insurrection of 1839* (Oxford, 1985). Ivor Wilks, *South Wales and the Rising of 1839. Class Struggle as Armed Struggle* (1984).

178. Epstein, *Lion of Freedom*, 203–12. Dorothy Thompson (ed.), *The Early Chartists* (1971), 27. Peacock, 34–53.

179. Yeo, 'Some practices and problems of Chartist democracy'.

180. Gosden, ch. 3.

181. R. A. Leeson, 'Business as usual: craft union developments, 1834–51', *BSSLH*, 49 (1984), 15–18.

182. Gosden, ch. 7.

183. Gilbert, 149–55. Hempton, 12–16, 92–110.

184. Eileen Yeo, 'Christianity in Chartist struggle 1838–1842', *Past and Present*, 91 (1981), 137–9.

185. Quoted in Yeo, 'Some practices and problems of Chartist Democracy', 351.

186. Epstein, *Lion of Freedom*, 236–49.

187. W. Lovett, *Life and Struggles*, ch.13. See also B. Harrison, 'Teetotal Chartism', *History*, lviii (1973), 193–217; and B. Harrison and P. Hollis, 'Chartism, liberalism and the life of Robert Lowery', *English Historical Review*, lxxxii (1967), 503–35.

188. A. Tyrell, *Joseph Sturge and the Moral Radical Party in Early Victorian Britain* (1987), ch.10.

189. Cooper, *Life*, 222.

190. Lucy Brown, 'The Chartists and the Anti-Corn Law League', in Asa Briggs (ed.) *Chartist Studies* (1959), 348.

191. Asa Briggs, 'National bearings', in ibid., 297. See also D. A. Hamer, *The Politics of Electoral Pressure. A Study in the History of Victorian Reform Agitations* (Hassocks, 1977), 62–90.

192. Epstein, *Lion of Freedom*, 273–86.

193. Dorothy Thompson, *The Chartists*, 280.

194. F. C. Mather (ed.), *Chartism and Society: An Anthology of Documents* (1980), 246–51.

195. F. C. Mather, 'The general strike of 1842: a case study of leadership, organization and the threat of revolution during the Plug Plot disturbances', in Stevenson and Quinault (eds).

196. Mick Jenkins, *The General Strike of 1842* (1980), 64–104.

197. Sykes, 'Early Chartism and trade unionism', 174–84.

198. Epstein, *Lion of Freedom*, 295–8.

199. T. D. W. and N. Reid, 'The 1842 "Plug Plot" in Stockport', *IRSH*, xxiv (1979), 55–79.

200. Jenkins, 93–5, 177–87.

201. R. Fyson, 'The crisis of 1842: Chartism, the colliers' strike and the outbreak in the potteries', in Epstein and Thompson (eds), 194–220.
202. Jenkins, ch. 10.
203. R. Challinor and B. Ripley, *The Miners' Association: A Trade Union in the Age of the Chartists* (1968).
204. Colls, *Pitmen*, 248–301.
205. Dorothy Thompson, *The Chartists*, 129–51. For a less critical view, see David Jones, 'Women and Chartism', *History*, lxviii (1983), 1–21.
206. M. I. Thomis and J. Grimmett, *Women in Protest 1800–1850* (1982), 144–6.
207. Dorothy Thompson, *The Chartists*, 299–306.
208. Epstein, *Lion of Freedom*, 249–57. See also Joy MacAskill, 'The Chartist land plan', in Briggs (ed.), 304–41.
209. Yeo, 'Some practices and problems of Chartist democracy', 367–72.
210. Ernest Jones, 'A song for May', *Labourer* (1847), 193. A. M. Hadfield, *The Chartist Land Company* (Newton Abbot, 1970).
211. David Jones, 'Thomas Campbell Foster and the rural labourer: incendiarism in East Anglia in the 1840s', *Social History*, i (1976), 5–43.
212. See the Wells–Charlesworth debate in *Journal of Peasant Studies*: R. Wells, 'The development of the English rural proletariat and social protest, 1700–1850', vi (1979), 115–37; A. Charlesworth, 'The development of the English rural proletariat and social protest, 1700–1850: a comment', viii (1980), 101–11; and R. Wells, 'Social conflict and protest in the English countryside in the early nineteenth century: a rejoinder', viii (1981), 514–30.
213. A. Charlesworth, 'Risings in East Anglia 1816–31: the background to Captain Swing', *BSSLH*, 45 (1982), 5–6.
214. Hobsbawm and Rudé, passim. R. Wells, 'Rural rebels in southern England in the 1830s', in Emsley and Walvin (eds), 131–7.
215. Belchem, *'Orator' Hunt*, 215–6.
216. Rule, *Labouring Classes*, 357–60; Hobsbawm and Rudé, ch. 13.
217. David Jones, 'Thomas Campbell Foster', 12.
218. A. F. J. Brown, *Chartism in Essex and Suffolk* (Chelmsford, 1982), 39, 50, 54–5.
219. Wells, 'Rural Rebels', 143–9.
220. John Saville, *1848. The British state and the Chartist movement* (Cambridge, 1987), 209.
221. Gosden, 46.
222. J. F. C. Harrison, *Second Coming*, 213–5.
223. A. F. J. Brown, 52–4.
224. Hobsbawm, 'Economic fluctuations', 133.
225. John Belchem, '1848: Feargus O'Connor and the collapse of the mass platform', in Epstein and Thompson (eds), 272–5.
226. *Northern Star*, 15 January 1848. For a useful collection of extracts, see John Saville, *Ernest Jones, Chartist. Selections from the writings and speeches of Ernest Jones* (1952).
227. *Northern Star*, 19 February 1848.
228. John Saville, 'Chartism in the vear of revolution, 1848', *Modern Quarterly*, new series, viii (1952–3), 23–33.
229. *Northern Star*, 25 March 1848. Harney to Engels, 30 March 1846 in F. G. and R. M. Black, *The Harney Papers* (Assen, 1969), 239–45. H. Weisser, *British Working-class Movements and Europe 1815–1848* (Manchester, 1975), 163–71.
230. Weisser, 154–63.
231. Quoted in ibid., 153.
232. Saville, *1848*, 73.
233. J. H. Treble, 'O'Connor, O'Connell and the attitudes of the Irish immigrants towards Chartism in the north of England 1838–48', in J. Butt and I. F. Clarke (eds), *The Victorians and Social Protest* (Newton Abbot, 1973).

234. Dorothy Thompson, 'Ireland and the Irish in English radicalism before 1850', in Epstein and Thompson (eds), 134–9.
235. Belchem, 'English Working-Class radicalism and the Irish', 85–6.
236. Dorothy Thompson, 'Ireland and the Irish', 123–5. G. O. Tuathaigh, 'The Irish in nineteenth-century Britain: problems of integration', in Swift and Gilley (eds), 14–19.
237. B. Collins, 'Proto-industrialization and pre-Famine emigration', *Social History*, vii (1982), 127–46.
238. *Trades Free Press*, 29 July–5 August 1827. Belchem, 'English working-class radicalism and the Irish', 87.
239. Ruth-Ann Harris, 'Whatever happened to Irish republicanism? The failure of republicanism among Irish migrants to Britain 1800–1840', paper presented to American Historical Association, San Francisco, 1983.
240. Moore, 169–74.
241. Ibid., 177–80.
242. See, for example, Hunt, *British Labour History*, 168–9.
243. T. Koseki, 'Chartism and Irish nationalism, 1829–1848: Bronterre O'Brien, the London Irish and attempts at a Chartist-Irish alliance', unpublished M.Phil thesis, University of Birmingham, 1987, 94.
244. Saville, *1848*, 33–6. Rudé, 'Protest and punishment in nineteenth-century Britain', *Albion*, v (1973), 1–23.
245. *Northern Star*, 25 March 1848.
246. Belchem, '1848', 278–9.
247. Saville, *1848*, 107–12.
248. Ibid., 96–8. See also 'The emigration from France', *Punch*, xiv (1848), 165.
249. S. Gilley, 'English attitudes to the Irish in England, 1780–1900', in C. Holmes (ed.), *Immigrants and Minorities in British Society* (1978), 81–110. Saville *1848*, 38–9.
250. Foster, ch. 7.
251. Saville, *1848*, 109, 112–16.
252. Belchem, '1848', 277–81. D. Goodway, *London Chartism, 1838–1848* (Cambridge, 1982), 106–25.
253. Ibid., 72–80. Belchem, '1848', 281–3. See also H. Weisser, *April 10. Challenge and Response in England in 1848* (Lanham, 1983), 105–25.
254. Belchem, '1848', 275–6, 283–6.
255. Ibid., 289–91.
256. Belchem, 'English working-class radicalism and the Irish', 90–1.
257. *Punch*, xiv (1848), 240. *Times*, 2 June and 8 July 1848.
258. Goodway, 80–5.
259. Belchem, 'English working-class radicalism and the Irish', 92.
260. Saville, 150–6.
261. Belchem, '1848', 297–8; and 'The spy system in 1848: Chartists and informers – an Australian connection', *Labour History*, 39 (1980), 15–27.
262. Belchem, '1848', 296–7. Goodway, 91–6.
263. Mayor of Manchester, 22 August 1848, HO 45/2410 (1)A.
264. 'L'ami du peuple', *Northern Star*, 23 December 1848.
265. Belchem, 'English working-class radicalism', 93–4.
266. Saville, *1848*, 217–23. Stedman Jones, 'Rethinking Chartism', 174–8.
267. Noel Thompson, 216–18.
268. G. Claeys, *Machinery, Money and the Millennium. From moral economy to socialism* (Cambridge, 1987), 151–6.
269. Dorothy Thompson, *The Chartists*, 333–9.
270. Weaver, ch. 8. Epstein, *Lion of Freedom*, 248–9.
271. A. R. Schoyen, *The Chartist Challenge. A Portrait of George Julian Harney* (1958), ch. 8.

272. John Belchem, 'Chartism and the trades, 1848–1850', *English Historical Review*, xcviii (1983), 578–9, 586.
273. *Northern Star*, 15 March 1851.
274. Saville, *Ernest Jones*, 44–5 and Appendix III, where the programme is reprinted in full.
275. *Friend of the People*, 19 April 1851.
276. Belchem, 'Chartism and the trades', 587.
277. 'Address to the democratic reformers', *Northern Star*, 8 March 1851; 'The People's Charter opposed to communistic Chartism', *Manchester Examiner and Times*, 3 May 1851.
278. Belchem, 'Chartism and the trades', 584–5.
279. *Northern Star*, 10 August 1851.
280. *Notes to the People*, i (1851), 244–6.
281. Ibid., ii (1852), 862.
282. Belchem, 'Chartism and the trades', 587.
283. Saville, *Ernest Jones*, 45–9.
284. S. and B. Webb, *History of Trade Unionism* (1920 edn), 195.
285. *Monthly Report of the NAUT*, 1 March 1848.
286. Belchem, 'Chartism and the trades', 559–70, 574–6.
287. Ibid., 577–81.
288. Ibid., 582–3.
289. Malmgreen, 182.
290. Foster, 106, 121.
291. Moore, 184–5, 403.
292. Stedman Jones, 'Rethinking Chartism, 115–16. J. E. King, 'Perish commerce! Free trade and underconsumptionism in early British radical economics', *Australian Economic Papers*, 20 (1981), 235–57.
293. Weaver, 91–4. See also Paul Richards, 'The state and early industrial capitalism: the case of the handloom weavers', *Past and Present*, 83 (1979), 91–115.
294. Belchem, 'Radical language and ideology', 256–7.

Chapter 7: The working class observed

1. Briggs, 'The language of "class"', 44–61.
2. Ignatieff, 88–9; David Jones, *Crime*, 17; and Emsley, *Crime*, 31, 48–72.
3. Ignatieff, 86–101.
4. M. E. Rose, 34–6. Himmelfarb, 160–76.
5. For a critical assessment of historians' use of this concept, see F. M. L. Thompson, 'Social control in Victorian Britain', *EcHR*, 2nd series, xxxiv (1981), 189–208.
6. Henriques, 200–5; Hempton, 86–92; and T. W. Laquer, *Religion and Respectability. Sunday Schools and Working-Class Culture 1780–1850* (New Haven, 1976), 80 and passim.
7. R. Johnson, 'Educational policy and social control in early Victorian England', *Past and Present*, 49 (1970), 96–119.
8. Gardner, 3–12, and passim.
9. Thompson and Yeo (eds), 58–60.
10. John Seed, 'Unitarianism, political economy and the antinomies of liberal culture in Manchester, 1830–50', *Social History*, vii (1982), 1–25.
11. Himmelfarb, 405.
12. Sheila Smith, *The Other Nation: The Poor in English Novels of the 1840s and 1850s* (Oxford, 1980), 203–64.
13. J. Stevenson, 'Social control and the prevention of riots in England, 1789–1829', in Donajgrodski (ed.), 27–50.
14. Joyce, *Work, Society and Politics*, ch.4.
15. Obelkevich, 60. Wells, 'Rural rebels', 148–9.

16. Perkin, 275–6, 445–6.
17. Thompson and Yeo (eds), 36–7.
18. Anne Humpherys, *Travels into the Poor Man's Country. The Work of Henry Mayhew* (Firle, 1977), 11–30 and passim.
19. Himmelfarb, 362–9. Emsley, *Crime*, 60–7.

PART TWO: 1850–1875

Chapter 8: 'The mid-Victorian boom'

1. Gareth Stedman Jones, 'Class struggle and the industrial revolution', in his *Languages of Class*, 70–1; Saville, *1848*, 58, 206–7; Joyce, *Work, Society and Politics*, xviii, 3, 147; K. Burgess, *The Challenge of Labour* (1980), 12–16; and Eric Hobsbawm, *Industry and Empire* (Penguin edn, 1969), ch.6.
2. R. A. Church, *The Great Victorian Boom* (1975), 78.
3. E. H. Hunt, *Regional Wage Variations in Britain 1850–1914* (Oxford, 1973), 356–7.
4. Joyce, *Work, Society and Politics*, xiii.
5. Berg, 220–33.
6. Gutteridge, ch. 9.
7. Kirk, 39.
8. Joyce, *Work, Society and Politics*, 55–9, 103–26.
9. Kirk, 38.
10. Hobsbawm, 'Custom, wages and work-load', 356–8.
11. Hunt, *British Labour History*, 79–81.
12. Joyce, *Work, Society and Politics*, 148–9.
13. Treble, *Urban Poverty*, 29–30.
14. Bythell, *Sweated Trades*, 69–70.
15. Gareth Stedman Jones, *Outcast London. A study in the relationship between classes in Victorian society* (Penguin edn, 1976), 22–32, 106–8.

Chapter 9: Living standards

1. Church, 71.
2. G. J. Barnsby, 'The standard of living in the Black Country during the nineteenth century', *EcHR*, 2nd series, xxiv (1971), 224–5.
3. Kirk, 96–9.
4. Burgess, 16.
5. Hunt, *British Labour History*, 74.
6. Burnett, *Plenty and Want*, 149–65.
7. Barnsby, 223–4.
8. A. T. McCabe, 'The standard of living on Merseyside, 1850–1875', in S. P. Bell (ed.), *Victorian Lancashire* (Newton Abbot, 1974), 141–2.
9. Treble, *Urban Poverty*, 43–4.
10. Church, ch. 2.
11. Burnett, *Plenty and Want*, 123–38.
12. Burnett, *Social History of Housing*, 149–50.
13. Kirk, 115–25.
14. Stedman Jones, *Outcast London*, 45–51.
15. John Hollingshead, *Ragged London in 1861* (rpt 1986), 121.
16. M. E. Rose, 'Rochdale man and the Stalybridge riot. The relief and control of the unemployed during the Lancashire cotton famine', in Donajgrodski (ed.), 187–91.
17. Ibid., 190–201.

18.   Stedman Jones, *Outcast London*, 102–6.

Chapter 10: Housing

1.   P. J. Waller, *Town, City and Nation. England 1850–1914* (Oxford, 1983), 1–4.
2.   Burnett, *Social History of Housing*, 127–31.
3.   Hunt, *British Labour History*, 98–9.
4.   Burnett, *Social History of Housing*, 157–64.
5.   Daunton, 212–33.
6.   Stedman Jones, *Outcast London*, 159–78.
7.   Ibid., 179–200.
8.   Ibid., 183–8. Burnett, *Social History of Housing*, 177–8.
9.   Stedman Jones, *Outcast London*, 193–6.
10.   Ibid., 207–9.
11.   E. Hopkins, 'Small town aristocrats of labour and their standard of living', *EcHR*, 2nd series, xxviii (1975), 227–8.
12.   G. Crossick, *An Artisan Elite in Victorian Society. Kentish London 1840–1880* (1978), 144–5.
13.   Ibid., 145–9. Robert Gray, *The Aristocracy of Labour in Nineteenth-Century Britain c.1850–1914* (1981), 35–40.
14.   Crossick, 119–20.
15.   Foster, 125–7.
16.   L. H. Lees, *Exiles of Erin. Irish Migrants in Victorian London* (Manchester, 1979), ch.3.
17.   Kirk, 315–18, 324–34.
18.   Ibid., 320–4. Stevenson, *Popular Disturbances*, 276–82.
19.   Moore, 66–73.
20.   Roger Swift, '"Another Stafford Street Row": law, order and the Irish presence in mid-Victorian Wolverhampton', in Swift and Gilley (eds), 179–206.
21.   R. Samuel, 'The Roman Catholic Church and the Irish poor', in ibid., 267–300.
22.   Lees, ch. 8.

Chapter 11: Work

1.   Foster, 212–38.
2.   Stedman Jones, 'Class struggle and the industrial revolution', 64–9.
3.   M. Freifeld, 'Technological change and the "self-acting" mule: a study of skill and the sexual division of labour', *Social History*, xi (1986), 319–43. See also W. Lazonick, 'Industrial relations and technical change: the case of the self-acting mule', *Cambridge Journal of Economics*, iii (1979), 231–62.
4.   Price, *Labour in British Society*, 81–2.
5.   Ibid., 79–81.
6.   Joyce, *Work, Society and Politics*, 90, 179–93. H. I. Dutton and J. E. King, 'The limits of paternalism: the cotton tyrants of North Lancashire, 1836–54', *Social History*, vii (1982), 59–74. Price, *Labour in British Society*, 88–9.
7.   Ibid., 74–5.
8.   E. Higgs, 'Domestic service and household production', in John (ed.), 125–52, and 'Domestic servants and households in Victorian England', *Social History*, viii (1983), 201–10.
9.   Freifeld, 336–9.
10.   J. Liddington and J. Norris, *One Hand Tied Behind Us. The Rise of the Women's Suffrage Movement* (1978), 57–61, 95.
11.   H. I. Dutton and J. E. King, *Ten Per Cent and No Surrender: the Preston Strike, 1853–4* (Cambridge, 1981). Kirk, 247–301.
12.   Hunt, *British Labour History*, 281–6. Price, *Masters, Union and Men*, 118–28.

Chapter 12: Popular culture

1. P. Bailey, 'Custom, capital and culture in the Victorian music hall', in R. D. Storch (ed.), 180–7.
2. Golby and Purdue, 115–16, 135–8.
3. Cunningham, *Leisure*, 172–7.
4. Ibid., 157–63.
5. Ibid., 151–5.
6. Ibid., 120–8.
7. Richard Price, 'The working men's club movement and Victorian social reform ideology', *Victorian Studies*, xv (1971), 117–47.
8. Hugh Cunningham, *The Volunteer Force* (1976).
9. Frank Prochaska, 'Mothers' meetings and women's welfare 1850–1950', paper presented to the Centre for the History of Social Policies, University of Liverpool, 1987.
10. Gray, ch.5.
11. Foster, 220–4.
12. Kirk, ch.5. Crossick, 152–6.
13. Trgyve Tholfsen, *Working Class Radicalism in Mid-Victorian England* (1976), 244–5.
14. John Vincent, *The Formation of the British Liberal Party 1857–68* (Penguin edn, 1972), 32–3 and passim.
15. Kirk, 227–31.
16. Gray, 41.
17. Obelkevich, 36–7.
18. Joyce, *Work, Society and Politics*, 189–91.
19. Ibid., 276–86.

Chapter 13: Reformism and the labour movement

1. Kirk, ch.4. S. Pollard, 'Nineteenth-century co-operation: from community building to shopkeeping', in Briggs and Saville (eds), 74–112.
2. Musson, ch. 6, Hunt, *British Labour History*, 259–64. Kirk, 272–301. Price, *Labour in British Society*, 75, 85–6. Tholfsen, 68–88.
3. Price, *Masters, Union and Men*, 45–54.
4. F. M. Leventhal, *Respectable Radical. George Howell and Victorian Working Class Politics* (1971), 25–6.
5. Royden Harrison, 'Professor Beesly and the working-class movement', in Briggs and Saville (eds), 205–41.
6. H. Collins, 'The English branches of the First International', in ibid., 243.
7. Leventhal, 46.
8. Royden Harrison, *Before the Socialists: Studies in Labour and Politics 1861–1881* (1965), 80–1.
9. Vincent, 223–27.
10. S. Coltham, 'The *Bee-Hive* newspaper: its origins and early struggles', in Briggs and Saville (eds), 174–203.
11. Leventhal, 73.
12. Stevenson, *Popular Disturbances*, 289–91.
13. Royden Harrison, *Before the Socialists*, 82–3.
14. Ibid., 85–101.
15. Leventhal, 93.
16. Royden Harrison, *Before the Socialists*, ch.4. Leventhal, ch.5.
17. Ibid., 127–31.
18. Price, *Labour in British Society*, 87.
19. Musson, 59–63.
20. Royden Harrison, *Before the Socialists*, 285–90.
21. Leventhal, 153.

22. Ibid., 153–79. Royden Harrison, *Before the Socialists*, 290–302. W. H. Fraser, *Trade Unions and Society. The Struggle for Acceptance 1850–1880* (1974), 140–4.
23. Leventhal, 179–89.
24. J. E. Cronin, 'Strikes 1870–1914', in Chris Wrigley (ed.), *A History of British Industrial Relations 1875–1914* (Brighton, 1982), 74–88.
25. Stan Shipley, 'Club life and socialism in mid-Victorian London', *History Workshop Pamphlet*, 5 (1971).
26. Royden Harrison, *Before the Socialists*, 215–26.
27. Ibid., 230–7. Henry Collins, 243, 262–3, 271.
28. James Hinton, *Labour and Socialism. A History of the British Labour Movement 1867–1974* (Brighton, 1983), 17–8. Royden Harrison, *Before the Socialists*, 239–42. Musson, 65.
29. For details of Samuelson and Simpson, see Eric Taplin, *Liverpool Dockers and Seamen 1870–1890* (Hull, 1974).
30. Hinton, 19–20.
31. Ibid., 20–1. Hunt, *British Labour History*, 252–4.
32. Ibid., 256–8.

Chapter 14: The working class observed

1. Emsley, *Crime*, 84–5.
2. R. Sindall, 'The London garotting panics of 1856 and 1862', *Social History*, xii (1987), 351–9.
3. Emsley, *Crime*, 35, 40. Jones, *Crime*, 6.
4. Himmelfarb, 528–9. Treble, *Urban Poverty*, 8–10.
5. E. P. Hennock, 'Poverty and social theory in England: the experience of the eighteen-eighties', *Social History*, i (1976), 67–91.
6. Hollingshead, 122.
7. Stedman Jones, *Outcast London*, ch. 13.
8. Ibid., 258–9.
9. Rose, *Relief of Poverty*, 25–6.
10. Stedman Jones, *Outcast London*, 256–8.
11. Ibid., 264–70.
12. R. Lambert, 'A Victorian national health service: state vaccination 1855–71', *Historical Journal*, v (1962), 1–18. A. Wohl, *Endangered Lives. Public Health in Victorian Britain* (1983), ch. 6.
13. Rose, *Relief of Poverty*, 38–9.
14. Stedman Jones, *Outcast London*, 274.
15. Kirk, 229–31.

PART THREE: 1875–1900

Chapter 15: 'The Great Depression'

1. S. B. Saul, *The Myth of the Great Depression 1873–1896* (1969).
2. Crafts, ch. 8. See also Sidney Pollard's review of R. C. O. Matthews *et al.*, *British Economic Growth 1856–1973* in *Times Higher Education Supplement*, 10 December 1982.
3. Eric Hobsbawm, *Industry and Empire*, 178–81.
4. Saul, 34–6. Mathias, 314–19.
5. Crafts, 158–65. Mathias, 230.
6. D. McCloskey, 'Did Victorian Britain fail?', *EcHR*, 2nd series, xxiii (1970), 446–59.
7. Hobsbawm, *Industry and Empire*, 187–8.

8. Ibid., 188–9.
9. W. Lazonick, 'Stubborn mules: some comments', *EcHR*, 2nd series, xl (1987), 80–5.
10. Mathias, 355–61. McKibbin, 'Why was there no Marxism?', 301–2.
11. M. Wiener, ch.7 and passim.
12. Ibid., 128. Cain and Hopkins, 1–26. Mathias, 299.
13. Sidney Pollard, 'Capital exports, 1870–1914: harmful or beneficial?', *EcHR*, 2nd series, xxxviii (1985), 489–514.
14. See W. P. Kennedy's review of L. E. Davis and R. A. Huttenback, *Mammon and the Pursuit of Empire: the political economy of British Imperialism, 1860–1912*, in *Times Higher Education Supplement*, 21 August 1987.
15. Rubinstein, 62–3, 106–7. Perry Anderson, 28–35; Nicholls, 71–2.
16. Cain and Hopkins, 2–11.
17. Crafts, 163.
18. P. Cain, 'Political economy in Edwardian England: The tariff reform controversy', in A. O'Day (ed.), *The Edwardian Age: Conflict and Stability 1900–1914* (1979), 36–8, 45–8.

Chapter 16: Living standards

1. Saul, 30–4.
2. Mathias, 362. Hunt, *British Labour History*, 73–6, 114–5. Barnsby, 225–7, 232–3.
3. K. McClelland and A. Reid, 'Wood, iron and steel: technology, labour and trade union organization in the shipbuilding industry, 1840–1914', in Harrison and Zeitlin (eds), 156–7. Eric Hobsbawm, 'The labour aristocracy in nineteenth-century Britain', in his *Labouring Men*, 288.
4. Treble, *Urban Poverty*, 21, 73.
5. Paul Johnson, 'Credit and thrift', 152. Stedman Jones, *Outcast London*, 297–8. Treble, *Urban Poverty*, 72–7.
6. Ibid., 36–7, 67.
7. Ibid., 67–9, 77–80.
8. Quoted in P. Keating (ed.), *Into Unknown England 1866–1913. Selections from the social explorers* (1976), 166.
9. Hunt, *British Labour History*, 38–42. Levine, 191–203. Ellen Ross, 'Labour and love: rediscovering London's working-class mothers, 1870–1918', in Lewis (ed.), 75–7.
10. J. S. Hurt, *Elementary Schooling and the Working Classes 1860–1918* (1979), 205–8. Stephen Humphries, *Hooligans or Rebels? An Oral History of Working-Class Childhood and Youth 1889–1939* (Oxford, 1981), 151–73. Elizabeth Roberts, 'The family', in John Benson (ed.), *The Working Classes in England 1875–1914* (1985), 25–6.
11. Humphries, 63–8. Roberts, 'Family', 21.
12. Liddington and Norris, 35–6.
13. Ibid., 58–60. Roberts, *Women's Work*, 48.
14. Quoted in Liddington and Norris, 37.
15. Roberts, *Women's Work*, ch.3 and passim.
16. R. Whipp, 'The stamp of futility: The Staffordshire potters, 1880–1905', in Harrison and Zeitlin (eds), 114–50.
17. Treble, *Urban Poverty*, 100–01.
18. Whipp, 132–3.
19. Treble, *Urban Poverty*, 104. John Benson, 'Work', in Benson (ed.), 70–2. Elizabeth Roberts '"Women's strategies", 1890–1940', in J. Lewis (ed.), 231–5.
20. Johnson, 'Credit and thrift', 151–3.
21. Tebbutt, 49–51. Roberts, *Women's Work*, 50.
22. Tebbutt, 133–4, 187–9.
23. Johnson, 'Credit and thrift', 154–7.

24. Ibid., 163–5. Crossick, ch.9. Gosden, 98–104.
25. Ibid., 97–111.
26. Green, 12–43, 61–82.
27. Ibid., 7–12.
28. Ibid., 42–61, 90–6.
29. Johnson, 'Credit and thrift', 160–3, 166–70. Gosden, 119–32. Crossick, 179.
30. Meacham, 70–2. Burnett, *Plenty and Want*, 128–32.
31. Ibid., 142–3, 200–1. Meacham, 78–82. F. B. Smith, 'Health', in Benson (ed.), 50.
32. Hunt, *British Labour History*, 88. Meacham, 78–9. Burnett, *Plenty and Want*, 135.
33. Ibid., 166–70.
34. Meacham, 81. D. J. Oddy, 'Working class diets in late nineteenth-century Britain', *EcHR*, 2nd series, xxiii (1970), 314–23.
35. F. B. Smith, 50–8.
36. Burnett, *Plenty and Want*, 146–7, 260.
37. Burnett, *Social History of Housing*, 149–52.

Chapter 17: Housing

1. A. Sutcliffe, 'In search of the urban variable: Britain in the later nineteenth century', in Fraser and Sutcliffe (eds), 256–9. Burnett, *Social History of Housing*, 152.
2. Ibid., 164–6. Cannadine, 'Victorian cities', 466–8. Dennis, ch.4.
3. Ibid., 165–6, 184.
4. Ibid., 108–9, 174–6. Burnett, *Social History of Housing*, 171–4.
5. Robert Roberts, *The Classic Slum* (Manchester, 1971).
6. Dennis, 228–30. Waller, 26.
7. Dennis, ch.9. Stedman Jones, 'Working-class culture', 217–20.
8. Sutcliffe, 250–2.
9. Stedman Jones, *Outcast London*, 200, 214.
10. Reprinted in Keating (ed.), 91–111.
11. Stedman Jones, *Outcast London*, ch. 11.
12. Burnett, *Social History of Housing*, 181–6.

Chapter 18: Work

1. M. J. Daunton, 'Down the pit: work in the great northern and south Wales coalfields, 1870–1914', *EcHR*, 2nd series, xxxiv (1981), 578–97.
2. J. Melling, '"Non-commissioned officers": British employers and their supervisory workers, 1880–1920', *Social History*, v (1980), 183–221.
3. Benson, 64–7; Price, *Labour in British Society*, ch.5. For an introduction to the debate over Braverman's *Labor and Monopoly Capital*, see Zeitlin, 'Social theory and the history of work', *Social History*, viii (1983), 365–74; and Knox, 166–69. On skilled status, see More, and R. Penn, *Skilled Workers in the Class Structure* (Cambridge, 1984).
4. Zeitlin, 'Engineers and compositors: a comparison', in Harrison and Zeitlin (eds), 208–15.
5. Knox, 174–9.
6. Zeitlin, 'Engineers and compositors', 223–34.
7. K. D. Brown, *The English Labour Movement 1700–1951* (Dublin, 1982), 195.
8. Burgess, 69, 89–92.
9. Price, *Labour in British Society*, 110–13. Bill Lancaster, *Radicalism, Co-operation and Socialism: Leicester working-class politics, 1860–1906* (Leicester, 1987), ch. 8.
10. Burgess, 92–3.
11. McClelland and Reid, 176–7.

12. David Blankenhorn, '"Our class of workmen": the cabinet-makers revisited', in Harrison and Zeitlin (eds), 42–3.
13. Whipp, 142–4.
14. More, 16, 215–16.
15. Knox, 176–84.
16. K. D. Brown, 174–5. Benson, 76.
17. Hinton, 26.
18. Treble, *Urban Poverty*, 82–3.
19. Jenny Morris, 'The characteristics of sweating: the late nineteenth-century London and Leeds tailoring trade', in John (ed.), 113–19.
20. Osterud, 61–5.
21. G. Anderson, *Victorian Clerks* (Manchester, 1976), 4–7 and passim. G. Crossick, 'The emergence of the lower middle class in Britain: a discussion', in G. Crossick (ed.), *The Lower Middle Class in Britain* (1977), 11–60.
22. Meta Zimmeck, 'Jobs for the girls: the expansion of clerical work for women, 1850–1914', in John (ed.), 153–78.

Chapter 19: Popular culture

1. Golby and Purdue, 157–8, 180–2.
2. Ibid., 164–9. D. Kynaston, *King Labour. The British Working Class 1850–1914* (1976), 98–9, 109–10.
3. Robert Roberts, 117.
4. Cunningham, *Leisure*, 170–2. Bailey, 'Custom, capital and culture', 186–7, 195–7.
5. Ibid., 193–5, 198–9. Stedman Jones, 'Working-class culture', 225–9, 234–5. Martha Vicinus, *The Industrial Muse: a study of nineteenth-century working-class literature* (1974), ch. 6.
6. H. Cunningham, 'The language of patriotism, 1750–1914', *History Workshop Journal*, 12 (1981), 25–6.
7. Stedman Jones, 'Working-class culture', 229–30.
8. Bailey, 'Custom, capital and culture', 199–201. Meacham, 127.
9. P. Bailey, 'Ally Sloper's half-holiday: comic art in the 1880s', *History Workshop Journal*, 16 (1983), 4–31.
10. H. Cunningham, 'Leisure', in Benson (ed.), 143.
11. Golby and Purdue, 178–9. Robert Roberts, 132.
12. R. McKibbin, 'Work and hobbies in Britain, 1880–1950', in Winter (ed.), 127–46.
13. K. D. Brown, 186–7. Cunningham, 'Leisure', 141. Robert Roberts, 132.
14. Ibid., 123–5. Humphries, ch. 7.
15. R. McKibbin, 'Working-class gambling in Britain 1880–1939', *Past and Present*, 82 (1979), 147–78.
16. Cunningham, 'Leisure', 140–1. Meacham, 121–2.
17. E. Royle, *Radicals, Secularists and Republicans: Popular freethought in Britain, 1886–1915* (Manchester, 1980), 136–45, 328–31.
18. Gilbert, 198–203.
19. Meacham, 120. Kynaston, 89.
20. Ibid., 90–1. K. S. Inglis, *Churches and the Working Classes in Victorian England* (1963), 175–92.
21. McLeod, 10–11, 64. Robert Roberts, 138.
22. H. Pelling, *The Origins of the Labour Party 1880–1900* (2nd edn; Oxford, 1965), 132–9.
23. Liddington and Norris, 122–4. McKibbin, 'Why was there no Marxism?', 306–10. David Clark, *Colne Valley: Radicalism to Socialism* (1981), 2, 32–6, 50–2, 125–6.

Chapter 20: Labour's turning-point?

1. Pelling, 13–18. E. P. Thompson, *William Morris: Romantic to Revolutionary* (2nd edn, 1976), 284–92.
2. Ibid., 292–7, 331–65.
3. Ibid., 366–579. Kynaston, 123–6, 129–30.
4. Burgess, 48–9.
5. D. C. Richter, *Riotous Victorians* (Ohio, 1981), ch.8. Stedman Jones, *Outcast London*, 291–4.
6. E. P. Thompson, *William Morris*, 479–81.
7. Ibid., 482–92. Richter, ch.9. Stedman Jones, *Outcast London*, 295–6. Victor Bailey, '"In Darkest England and the Way Out": the Salvation Army, social reform and the labour movement 1885–1910', *IRSH*, xxix (1984), 137.
8. E. P. Thompson, *William Morris*, 493–5.
9. Quoted in Kynaston, 127.
10. S. Pierson, *Marxism and the Origins of British Socialism: the struggle for a new consciousness* (Ithaca, 1973), ch. 5.
11. Pelling, 56–61.
12. F. Reid, 'Keir Hardie's conversion to socialism', in A. Briggs and J. Saville (eds), *Essays in Labour History 1886–1923* (1971), 17–46. Pierson, 185–9. Pelling, 65–9.
13. Ibid., 148–50. Pierson, 177–84.
14. Burgess, 65.
15. Liddington and Norris, 87, 95.
16. J. Lovell, *British Trade Unions 1875–1933* (1977), 15–17.
17. E. P. Thompson, *William Morris*, 527. Eric Hobsbawm, 'British gas-workers, 1873–1914'; 'Trends in the British labour movement since 1850', in his *Labouring Men*, 158–78; and 327.
18. Burgess, 65–8. Stedman Jones, *Outcast London*, ch. 17.
19. Humphries, ch.4.
20. Hinton, 52–3.
21. K. D. Brown, 175.
22. Hinton, 49.
23. Lovell, ch.2 usefully summarizes the main points made by Clegg, Fox and Thompson, in their *History of British Trade Unions since 1889*.
24. Hinton, 50–1.
25. Hunt, *British Labour History*, 299, 308. Eric Hobsbawm, 'General labour unions in Britain, 1889–1914', in his *Labouring Men*, 181–91.
26. Joyce, *Work, Society and Politics*, 63–4.
27. E. P. Thompson, 'Homage to Tom Maguire', in Briggs and Saville (eds), 276–316. Hinton, 56–60. Kynaston, 132.
28. Pelling, ch. 6.
29. Ibid., 115–21.
30. David Howell, *British Workers and the Independent Labour Party 1888–1906* (Manchester, 1983), 10–11. Pierson, ch. 9.
31. Hinton, 62–3. S. Yeo, 'A new life: the religion of socialism in Britain 1883–1896', *History Workshop Journal*, 4 (1977), 42–5.
32. Pelling, 166–8, 192–3.
33. Ibid., ch.10.
34. Ibid., 194–5.
35. Ibid., 198–201.
36. Hinton, 61. Liddington and Norris, 137.
37. Burgess, 93–4. Price, *Labour in British Society*, 146–7.
38. Lancaster, 94.
39. J. Saville, 'Trade unions and free labour: the background to the Taff Vale decision', in Briggs and Saville (eds, 1967), 317–50. H. Pelling, 'Trade unions,

workers and the law', in his *Popular Politics and Society in Late Victorian Britain* (2nd edn, 1979), 76–81.

40. Lovell, 37–40. Hinton, 80–1.
41. H. C. G. Matthew, R. I. McKibbin and J. A. Kay, 'The franchise factor and the rise of the Labour Party', *English Historical Review*, xci (1976), 723–52.
42. Martin Pugh, *The Making of Modern British Politics 1867–1939* (Oxford, 1982), 141–4.
43. Hinton, 78–9.
44. Liddington and Norris, 39–43, 134–42.
45. Martin Pugh, *The Tories and the People 1880–1935* (Oxford, 1985), 2–16 and passim.
46. D. Cannadine, 'The context, performance and meaning of ritual: the British monarchy and the "Invention of Tradition", *c.* 1820–1977', in E. J. Hobsbawm and T. Ranger (eds), *The Invention of Tradition* (Cambridge, 1983), 120–37. D. Cannadine and E. Hammerton, 'Conflict and consensus on a ceremonial occasion: the Diamond Jubilee in Cambridge in 1897', *Historical Journal*, xxiv (1981), 111–46. Pugh, *Tories*, 74–93, 168–71. McKibbin, 'Why was there no Marxism?', 312, 322.
47. Pugh, *Tories*, 87–8.
48. Richard Price, *An Imperial War and the British Working Class: Working-Class Attitudes and Reactions to the Boer War 1899–1902* (1972), 132–78, 233–42. H. Pelling, 'British labour and British imperialism', in his *Popular Politics and Society*, 82–100.

Chapter 21: The working class observed

1. Keating (ed.), 10–32.
2. A. Toynbee, *Lectures on the Industrial Revolution* (1884), 83–4.
3. Cannadine, 'The past and the present', 133–9. M. Wiener, 82–8.
4. Beatrice Webb, *My Apprenticeship* (1926; rpt 1979), 178–83. Stedman Jones, *Outcast London*, 285. See also H. Lynd, *England in the Eighteen-Eighties: Towards a Social Basis for Freedom* (Oxford, 1945), 318–24, 411–30; and Inglis, ch. 4.
5. Hennock, 70–84.
6. See the extracts from *Life and Labour of the People of London* in Keating (ed.), 112–40; and in Webb, 233, 254.
7. Stedman Jones, *Outcast London*, 302–14, 330–6.
8. Emsley, *Crime*, 65–7.
9. Wohl, 331–2.
10. Treble, *Urban Poverty*, 52.
11. Ibid., 110–11. M. E. Rose, *Relief of Poverty*, 28–30.
12. Hinton, 36–8.
13. H. Pelling, 'The working class and the origins of the welfare state', in his *Popular Politics and Society*, 1–18. See also, Pat Thane, 'The Labour Party and state "Welfare"', in K. D. Brown (ed.), *The First Labour Party 1906–1914* (1985), 183–216; and Stephen Yeo, 'Socialism, the state and some oppositional Englishness', in R. Colls and P. Dodd (eds), *Englishness: Politics and Culture 1880–1920* (1986), 335–62.
14. B. B. Gilbert, *The Evolution of National Insurance* (1966). For a useful short introduction, see J. R. Hay, *The Origins of the Liberal Welfare Reforms 1906–1914* (1975).
15. I shall be discussing these matters at greater length in my forthcoming study of *Class, Party and the Political System in England, 1867–1914*.

Index